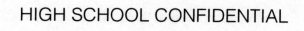

HIGH SCHOOL CONFIDENTIAL

HIGH SCHOOL

CONFIDENTIAL

Secrets of
An Undercover Student

JEREMY IVERSEN

ATRIA BOOKS
New York London Toronto Sydney

ATRIA BOOKS
1230 Avenue of the Americas
New York, NY 10020

For information about special discounts for bulk purchases,
please contact Simon & Schuster Special Sales at
1-800-456-6798 or business@simonandschuster.com.

Library of Congress Cataloging-in-Publication Data

Iversen, Jeremy.
    High school confidential : secrets of an undercover student / Jeremy Iversen.—1st
hardcover ed.
    p. cm.
    1. High school students—United States—Miscellanea. 2. Education, Secondary—
United States—Miscellanea. I. Title.
LB1607.5.I94 2006
373.18—dc22
                                                                                2006047745

ISBN-13: 978-0-7432-8363-2
ISBN-10:   0-7432-8363-5

First Atria Books hardcover edition September 2006

10   9   8   7   6   5   4   3   2   1

ATRIA BOOKS is a trademark of Simon & Schuster, Inc.

Manufactured in the United States of America

I dedicate this book to everyone who dreams of something beyond the track, and to the friends I made at Mirador Senior High School.
This book is yours.

ACKNOWLEDGMENTS

Going back to high school in your midtwenties is so incredibly difficult that it is—for all intents and purposes—impossible. It's the kind of thing that only happens in movies and dreams.

But when faced with the incredible faith, trust, generosity, kindness, help, and goodwill of a number of exceptionally wonderful and courageous people, the laws of probability were confounded, and the dream become real, just once.

Right now I want to thank as many of those people as I possibly can.

First and most important, I would very, very much like to thank the administrators of Mirador who allowed me to become a senior again. Although your names must remain unwritten, without you nothing could have happened. You made a brave and difficult choice, and I know that you have paid a price for your courage. May the world always know that you had the noblest and purest of intentions, and that any fault is mine and mine alone. I am forever grateful to you, and I will forever remember you.

My thanks to my real parents and my grandfather for everything.

My thanks to Christopher Schelling and Peter Borland for liking the idea at the beginning and seeing it through to the end.

To Gregory Newman for showing me it was possible, and Sarah Carpenter for helping make it so.

To Heather R. for a charming evening.

To Dulcie Younger and James from the Valley for being my family.

To Cousin Steph for finding me a home, and Laura for providing it, dinner, and a trip to the post office.

To Andie Lewis, Michele Avignon, and Emily Rawlings, for trying their darnedest.

To Patrick and Jed, for getting the whole thing started.

I also want to thank M.M., G.P., L.P., B.M., the two R.A.s, S.R., S.J., L.M., and J.N. for speaking to the powers that be, Ashley Read for the infamous letter, and Jason Powers for making some phone calls. I gratefully acknowledge MC Lars, and Chris Jay and the Army, for letting me include their words. I appreciate the tireless work of Felice Javit to keep everyone safe and I honor all the wonderful Atrians who place their monumental effort into these pages. Thanks as well to Julie B., Corrie V., Mike T., Haille L., Pamela C., Peter G., Paul S., Ed K., Kyo Y., Maggie R., Josefa Menéndez, and God, because in the end, the whole thing was a total miracle. The fact it actually happened still leaves me blinking.

See you all after last bell.

Jeremy Watt Iversen
Los Angeles, California

CONTENTS

Acknowledgments   *vii*
A Note About This Map   *xi*

PART ONE
   This Night   *3*
   Diving In   *11*
   You Make It Real   *25*

PART TWO
   Popular   *41*
   Collision   *81*
   Give Me a Place to Stand   *115*

PART THREE
   Two Weeks Go Deep   *123*
   Intermezzo in D-Force Minor.   *291*
   O Girls, To War   *309*

PART FOUR
   Accreditation   *365*
   In the Magic Kingdom   *409*
   Graduation   *423*

Notes   *431*

A NOTE ABOUT THIS MAP

High School Confidential is a true story, within limits.

The world is round, and cartographers make sacrifices to draw it on a flat page. The majestic lands of the Earth have qualities like size, shape, and spacing, but when you project a map, some of those sublime traits are going straight into the circular file.

Take your standard Mercator design. Everything has the right spacing and shape, but humble little Greenland looms over the globe like the new breakout geopolitical superpower. Size took a hit. You can only pick a few elements to preserve at the expense of the others.

The world I drew contained hundreds of real people who did and said many things over a span of many months. Most had not turned eighteen. Not only did I want to protect their privacy, but everything had to fit within these pages.

So, as explorers have done ever since ships passed from sight of shores, I chose guide stars.

Almost every word was spoken exactly as you see it. The events you're about to witness actually happened.

I made my compromises with characters and chronology, blurring identifying details and collapsing dispersed events and personalities into composite scenes and people. No specific individual is recognizable in— or should be held responsible for—the thoughts, words, and actions on the following pages. So what a French teacher says or does may well channel an English faculty member, a college counselor, or both plus the vice-principal.

And imagine you see a flashback that happens a month before I am present. You know the events occurred and that the dialogue is copied verbatim. So it's safe to assume I combined words I actually heard people say, together with their quotes from sources like the school newspaper and their online journals, and put them in the mouths of composite characters in composite scenes.

Now that you know all the details, you can safely forget the mechanics of the engine room and prepare to explore.

Like Gerardus Mercator, I drew a map, to the best of my ability.

You can use it reliably to discover another world.

Two days of travel separate this young man (and young he is, with few firm roots in life) from his everyday world. . . . Space, as it rolls and tumbles away between him and his native soil, proves to have powers normally ascribed only to time.
—Thomas Mann,
The Magic Mountain

Our whole lives laid out right in front of us,
Sing like you think no one's listening . . .
—Straylight Run,
"Existentialism on Prom Night"

PART ONE

THIS NIGHT

I had a dream, which was not all a dream.
—Lord Byron, "Darkness"

This night, a silvery, swollen moon floated in a heaven of diamond stars. Beneath the graceful silhouettes of tall palms, water bubbled slowly into a Moorish reflecting pool of rough stone, rocking a bed of fragrant lilies.

A steady beat resonated from the adobe arches and crumbling walls that surrounded a wide square of tables and dripping sprays of red bougainvillea. This court formed the heart of an ancient mission where Father Junípero Serra, driven unstoppably onward by a vision only he understood, had elevated the host and established the future County of Orange. Tomorrow the bells would toll over the chapel as they had for centuries. But here lay no space for yesterday or the morning. Here only the moment unfolded.

This night, my date turned to gaze lovingly into my eyes. Her long blond hair blew in the soft, warm air, danced above her sparkling white gown. I in my tuxedo put an arm around her shoulder as we advanced slowly along the flagstone pathways.

A hundred people stood scattered across the grass, talking and laughing in couples or groups, resplendent in their evening wear. As we passed through them, my date put her hand on mine.

"Nice!" I said, smiling tenderly. "I love it. Nice touch."

"See?" she said. "We're such a happy couple."

We shared another vulnerable grin.

"Jeremy!" Alexis Newton wore a tight pink Dior dress with her hair pulled back into two pigtails. She sipped Diet Coke from a plastic cup through a straw and waved. Her friend Padma hovered nearby, giggling.

"Hey, see, I told you I'd introduce you guys," I said. "This is my girlfriend Heather."

"Hi," said Heather. They shook hands and exchanged warm smiles.

"You've got a good man standing next to you," said Alexis.

"Your boyfriend's really nice," said Padma. Her long black hair was elaborately done up, the silver flower ring in her nose glinted.

"Thanks," said Heather.

"Are you guys going over?" I asked them.

"Yeah, soon," said Alexis. "Our dates have gone missing." She pulled her brows down. "Grrr. I'm about to like hop the fence and go smoke a cigarette."

"Where are our loser dates?" said Padma and started to laugh.

Heather and I continued on. A few dozen paces later, smiling broadly, I said through my teeth, "You've gotta talk to them more. We've gotta get them to like you so we can get invited to the afterparty."

"Oh, my God," said Heather. "Those girls are so catty. I don't even know what to say to these people."

"Well, we've got to come up with something," I said. "That's one of our goals for tonight."

She bit her lip thoughtfully. "I guess I could ask them for a cigarette."

"Smile," I said.

We beamed at each other, exchanged loving gazes.

Other couples passed us, leaving the dancing for the seclusion of the empty archways at the far end of the central courtyard.

Derrick Littlefield stood by a mostly abandoned table. His golden tan and curly blond hair glowed like Renaissance art over a white tuxedo and pink shirt.

He sneezed. Then he sneezed again. "Oh," he moaned. "I'm so sick."

"Dude, I think you're like allergic to prom," I said.

Derrick laughed, displaying brilliant teeth. "No doubt. See, I knew they wouldn't have the dogs and Breathalyzers. They can't afford to bring an officer down."

"I don't think anyone's drinking, though," I said.

He scratched his head. "Yeah, like everybody was saying they wouldn't have a good time if they were sober, but they are anyway."

"This is my girlfriend Heather," I said.

"All the way from Hermosa Beach, huh?" They shook hands. His date Olivia sat alone at the table, adjusting a strap on her tulle dress.

"Are you going to dance?" I asked him.

"I'm coming in a few," said Derrick. "I have to go over for the Prom Court thing."

"Nice to meet you," said Heather.

Amid the flowering boughs and gentle laughter, my eyes met hers in the rapture of young love. "I told him he reminds me of our friend Nick from home," I said. "So remember that if it comes up."

"Nick from home," she repeated to herself. "Nick from home. Do we like Nick?"

"Yeah," I said. "He's one of our best friends. We've known him since junior high."

"Nick is great," said Heather. Then we both laughed, part real, part fake, and part from nerves.

A small stage with speakers rose on the grass. The entire special ed group crowded nearby around their chaperone, a middle-aged woman with a corsage and a worn look on her face. One guy hummed along into a karaoke microphone, holding his wheeled oxygen tank with the other hand. I recognized a senior named Aram who came to the circle sometimes. He danced to the karaoke song, kicking up his legs, whirling around, executing high-energy punches.

Brian Olvera and some baseball players laughed at him as they waited for their turn at the mike. The team had largely gone for striped zoot suits and broad-shouldered pimp outfits, complete with wide-brim hats.

Heather and I clasped hands again, and I looked up at the stars.

"We need pictures of everything," I murmured. "You should take pictures of these people."

Heather pulled the disposable camera from her purse and swung it lightly in her fingertips. Passersby saw her in her shining silver gown snapping away among the weeping trails of flowers. I smiled weakly and looked around when other couples crossed our path, doing my best to seem a little bored, indulgent but embarrassed.

We set off again, nearing the freestanding portico that towered at the far end of the stone courtyard. Its coarse brick and mortar abruptly broke off where the primeval wall had collapsed. A silver and gold banner hung from the arch: MIRADOR HIGH SCHOOL JUNIOR-SENIOR PROM. Lights flashed behind the gateway.

Chubby Evelyn Strout worked at a laptop set up on a slender metal table beside the path. She wore a bright red dress and red plastic glasses.

She had creatively styled her frizzy red hair by sticking in a pair of what looked like chopsticks.

Travis Newton, short and slick, passed her with a smirk and a junior date. He was probably one of five underclass males who had been invited to prom.

"So the sophomores are graduating this year, huh?" he said to Evelyn. "Did you know you put the wrong date on all our class pages?"

Evelyn's head snapped up. Her red face flushed darker. "We spent all year on that. Sorry we spent so long on a yearbook and you're just tearing it apart. All we hear are negative things. That's really rude, I'm serious."

Travis shook his head and saluted me as we passed. I tossed back the lazy gesture.

"Oh, it makes me so mad," said Evelyn, and stabbed the table with a pencil. "Hello, Jeremy. Hello, Jeremy's girlfriend."

"Heather," she said.

We passed the row of steaming buffet trays, strolling the flagstones toward the growing music and lights.

All the spidering pathways converged into one as they prepared to feed through the archway. Here the whitewashed walls of the San Juan Capistrano Chapel itself erupted up from the side of the courtyard to glow in the moonlight. This luminescent ghost was the oldest building in California, one of the string of missions that Father Serra and his disciple had called forth from the wilderness unimaginable ages ago, christening them Santa Barbara, San Diego, San Francisco . . .

Someone grabbed my shoulders, landed with a thud next to me. It was Vic Reyes, wearing a Split T-shirt under his tuxedo jacket, Element wristbands, and a headband around his spiky hair.

"Oh, shit, you scared me, fool," I said.[1]

Vic laughed. We did a handclasp.

"Hey, we don't have dogs sniffing our crotches, bro," he said. "Popper's so full of shit."

Vic's date, sophomore Sara Dunbar, narrowed her lids behind too much eye shadow. "Pooper's a liar," she said.

"Hey, is this your girlfriend?" Vic asked.

"Yeah," I said. "Vic, Heather, Heather, Vic."

"Hi," said Heather, smiling sweetly.

Vic punched me in the arm. "She's too nice for you, bro. Hah, hah, just kidding, fool. No, but seriously, watch out for this guy. Just kidding."

He looked up at the prom banner hanging from the archway. "We're fucking *seniors,* fool. I can't fucking believe this shit."

His date smiled wickedly. "I'd be freaking out," she said. "I have my Peter Pan complex. It means your childhood is over. I'd go catatonic."

"What about college?" I asked.

"College is good, because it's like a buffer," she said. She shuddered and put her arm through Vic's. "Aaah, I don't want to be a junior. I'm not even ready for being a sophomore."

As Heather and I approached the primordial arch, she held me closer. Her sea blue eyes gleamed as she whispered delicate words.

"I should be going somewhere else for college," she said. "USC's boring."

"No, it's too late," I said. "I already said you were."

"The different colleges thing is going to put like a strain on our relationship," she pointed out.

"Yeah, well, the whole moving thing already has," I said. "I already thought you might be cheating on me like a month ago, but we worked it out, and honestly, I didn't even really want to know. But it's had so many ups and downs, and college is going to make it really tough. I think we're gonna break up next fall if I'm still talking to people then."

Heather clung to my arm as we passed through the whispering palms. The strobes before us electrified the sky like lightning. She smiled. "It's your friend."

"Huh?" I asked.

She tilted her head. I followed the angle to see the principal instructor of Mirador Senior High School, Dr. Irma Chao, trotting through the courtyard in a powder blue dress. Behind oval glasses, her eyes flicked across every face. They may have hesitated on us for a split second.

"Avoid, avoid!" I said grimly, turning my face as far as possible the other way, staring up at the mission wall. We quickened the pace.

"I really hope she didn't see us," I muttered under the gathering thunder of music. "I bet she thinks you're someone from Mirador, and you don't know who I really am, and obviously she can't like say anything about it. Oh, God, she must think I'm such a skank."

"I don't think she saw us," Heather said.

"I really hope not. I'm going to have to e-mail her tomorrow and try and explain."

Behind the archway, we've arrived, and we behold the towering sandstone ruins of the Great Stone Church. There a thousand people dance to hip-hop on flooring laid across the dusty ground, their forms dwarfed beside the massive crumbling vaults. The shell is roofless, stars bright above the walls. Lights swirl over the dancers, their movements rebroadcast around them on huge video screens.

"They all dance so well," Heather breathes.

They do. They're incredible. It's effortless, natural, spontaneous for them. I've never seen anything like it. They are sober, they are undrugged. They are just dancing.

"This would never happen at my school," Heather says. "People are so self-conscious. It would be nice if we were like this maybe just once a year, like prom."

A rush of pride swells in me for Mirador, for my school.

We make our way out onto the floor, past couples and groups and circles cheering on people dancing freaky in the middle.

I see some faces I know and we move next to them, staying with the beat. I'm treating Heather like a Fabergé egg made of gossamer, standing inches apart, and I realize our distance would make us a rare sight indeed in a sea of couples holding hips, pressed against each other, sinking down and rising up, running hands along each other's sides.

"Uh," I ask, "is it okay if we like grind? That's what everybody else is doing."

She shoots me an exasperated look. "I *am* eighteen," she says.

"I know," I say. "But I'm twenty-four."

Someone calls out; she sees a shooting star pass by overhead, out there above the broken walls.

This night, we're dancing too, and I glance at my watch and I realize it's going to be over soon. They're going to announce the prom king and queen, and then the night will end. And that will be the end of prom, and you don't get any more of them in this lifetime. And I've worked so, so, so hard to put everything together, summon up all the smoke and mirrors and make everything seem perfect and for a moment I can almost believe it's real, could almost wish it real, but when they call last dance it's going to be over for good, and reality will return and I will go back to my apartment alone and I will graduate in a few weeks, and at the rising of the sun these chapel bells that have chimed through the fall of empires will ring in the collapse of yet another illusion.

Cody Reisling dances next to us, brow furrowed, sweat and intensity gripping his face. He nods at me. "What's up, Hughes." We punch fists.

Freeze-frame.

Heather is not my girlfriend, and Hughes is not my name.

It says Hughes on my ID, but that's fake. It nestles next to a photo of Heather in my wallet, but I never met her before. I'm from three thousand miles away. My senior year of high school came and went the previous decade.

DIVING IN

All your life every man has wanted to be a cowboy. Why play Wall Street and die young when you can play cowboy and never die?
—Will Rogers

FOREVER TOMORROW

Like most monumental undertakings in life, everything started with a total personal crisis. I was on a track, see, this capital-T Track.

Tracks plot our entire lives, nine times out of ten.

They are what we expect of ourselves and the world expects of us. They tell us what to angle for, the right touchstones to hit, how we measure up to our peers.

Some tracks declare you're supposed to have really expensive sneakers and a huge TV. In others, success means publishing a certain number of articles in a handful of botany journals. Of course, it's totally arbitrary; all tracks end at precisely the same spot.

I gave mine the capital *T* just because tens of thousands of people every year not only think that they personally can do no better, but that nothing better exists. The main ethic is to backburner actual happiness and do the most prestigious and lucrative thing possible, as selected from a small list of choices. In exchange, the Track loosely promises that life will be a steady climb upward, and that tomorrows will always be better than yesterdays. All focuses on the day beyond the sunrise.

At first the scheme made sense. I was born in New York City, in midtown Manhattan. I worked hard, and behold, I was rewarded—for high school, I went to what is arguably the nation's premier prep school. The Track doesn't strictly require going to prep school, but it does award the experience some bonus self-denial points.

The boarding school stereotypes were a complete joke. People flaunted wealth, family title, or possessions precisely never. Who cared? We lived in identical dorm rooms and all ate the same cafeteria food. No one was a snob.

They adequately compensated with utter fanaticism and omnidirectional cruelty. It didn't matter the slightest if you emerged from noble patrician lineage or an Appalachian shack, but if you didn't get straight As, weren't tri-varsity, and weren't ripping up every party, then you sucked. Since no one could pull off the impossibility, we all sucked to varying degrees and spent years reminding one another of the fact, often via beatings. We had to wear ties, and we trekked in icy twilight through three feet of snow to Saturday classes, but we gunned for the Ivy League—no, we expected the Ivy League—and we had to make all sacrifices. Joy was a myth, and Harvard was the goal.

And fourteen kids in my class went there, and eighty-four to the Ivys in general, but I headed west to Stanford, only marginally acceptable in the minds of some of my Princetonian dorm mates. ("Duke, shmook," one sneered when I contemplated traveling south.) Still, the Track had delivered the goods—life had become better, life had become more cheerful—and I stood poised for further success.

Stanford was largely a pleasure. I kept repeating in wonder, "People are so nice here." I partied, I went abroad, I did all the right internships, I got the grades. As promised, every year had improved on the one before, brought new skills, new experiences. At last I reached a pinnacle where I was ready to graduate Phi Beta Kappa in the top 15 percent of my class with two majors. I was so excited about the next step up the ladder into yet-unimagined growth and bliss.

At this point, senior year, everything I had ever known and believed in fell apart.

We had this career fair where over two hundred companies set up booths in a campus plaza around a big circular fountain. All my fellow seniors came jostling to meet recruiters, to hand out résumés and try to seem as personable and dynamic as they could. Everybody jealously angled for the really prize jobs, investment banking and management consulting. Aside from further academia, or tech jobs for people with tech majors, those two constituted the next great attainment on the Track.

And there I stood with my stack of résumés, realizing I had no idea why. I knew theoretically those were "good" jobs, but now the reality of the promised future confronted me dead-on. College was obviously better—more fun, more free, more stimulating, more social, more creative—than boarding school. But working eighteen-hour days putting together deal memos with two weeks of vacation a year was in no way better than college.

The progression had stopped making sense. For the first time ever, moving forward meant taking a huge step downward. Had we really worked and waited our entire lives for this?

Doubt about the sanctity of the Track entered my mind for the first time ever.

Among the endless financial, tech, and consulting firms on the fair directory, the name Walt Disney stuck out like a fig tree in the Antarctic ice shelf. Heart racing, I tracked down the Disney booth through the rows. It turned out to be the Disney Strategic Planning & Corporate Treasury Division, Unca Walt's investment banking arm. The RA from my freshman dorm worked the table. He had graduated years earlier and joined up. Deep lines crossed his face and he was balding. I asked him if he liked his job.

"Sort of," he said. He missed college.

At this point, I realized that the Track had lied to us and tricked us. Like almost everyone else, I would miss college, look back on those peak moments as glory days. I could see my whole life spread out in front of me: the years as an analyst, getting the MBA from the right business school, playing all the right games for decades to end up an executive vice-president. Retirement, golf, death. The Track sucked. No day would come when life turned beautiful.

Standing in a daze, I met a girl I knew, and I told her I didn't get it. Together we folded my Phi Beta Kappa–Merrill Lynch–foreign policy developer–neurobiology researcher résumés into little paper boats and sailed them across the great fountain. Recruiters and classmates glanced over in suits, confused. Then I thought "fuck it," and we jumped into the water ourselves, just dove in, and soon we laughed and splashed each other in a sea of little résumé boats under a glistening shower of falling droplets.

At my graduation, our department chair read a brief statement about everyone's future plans as they stood up to claim their diplomas. A formidable recital heavy with approved next steps: Aside from the usual corporate litany, we had dozens moving to top-notch master's programs, Oxford fellowships, Washington think tanks, grants and foundations and research.

The chair got to mine and read, "Jeremy Iversen is going to Hollywood." He chuckled. Then the entire ceremony cracked up, several hundred people, parents and teachers and my fellow graduates all laughing at me. I smiled big as I grabbed my diploma and damped down distant terror of the unknown. I found the laughter awesome and steeling, because I had never been that guy before. Although I was headed to God knew where, I was off the Track, I was doing something new for once in my life.

TEENAGE WASTELAND

The career fair slammed home a lot of harsh realities. When it had seemed like my carefree days of youth were scheduled to end and I had to Get Serious for the rest of my life, I realized I had never had any carefree days of youth.

I had the Track's terminal delay of gratification. I had the surreal experience of growing up amid Manhattan skyscrapers, never having a car or backyard, and half as many young people percentagewise as the rest of America.[1] I had boarding school in Siberian snow with ties and hazing and six hours of homework a night. But possibly worst of all, my teenage life passed over the eight-year span in the nineties when the popular culture largely forgot that teenagers existed. During that dim decade, America completely abandoned the notion that anything meaningful separated us from the jaded ennui of the Generation X set's twentysomething coffeehouse clientele.[2]

Coming of age in a teen wasteland on both the local and national levels, I always dreamed of going to a John Hughes high school.

Anybody born between 1965 and 1986 already knows exactly what I'm talking about. John Hughes created the dynasty of teen movies that helped shape the vibrant youth culture of the 1980s and gave me my vision of paradise ten years later in videocassette version. They featured the polar opposite of my life: typical suburban public high schools at a time when teens mattered.

On a trip to Chicago after my junior year at age seventeen, I actually made a day-long pilgrimage to the school where Hughes had filmed *The*

Breakfast Club in 1985. Thunder rumbled on the horizon as I approached a building that looked exactly as it had on film, almost.

Cracks buckled the parking lot. Window glass was blacked over, the doors sealed. The great gray structure now housed a branch of the Illinois State Department of Agriculture. A crackling intercom told me the famous library had been "torn down and replaced."

A warm summer drizzle fell as I wandered in silence around the drab walls. Behind one streaked basement windowpane I made out some jagged marker left behind on a pillar by some long-departed student. "Metallica '87." I pressed to the dirty glass to see better. That kid's life was unreachable, so close and yet infinitely far. I turned away from the casement into the howling blast of my final stretch of ice and skyscrapers.

After I graduated, I didn't think about high schools again until I dove into that circular fountain senior fall at college and jumped the Track.

I emerged from the water and spent my final months desperately relishing being a sideways-visor-wearing goofball while everyone else compared signing bonuses and grad program acceptances. I felt like the candle not only burned at both ends but also dropped into a blast furnace. Every day was both exhilarating and terrifying at the same time.

Commencement speaker Condoleezza Rice commanded us to pursue our passion, and I moved to Los Angeles with this idea of being in entertainment. And not calculating Excel valuation models in the corporate treasury division, but actually, you know, out there under the bright lights. Total terra incognita for a refugee fresh from the Track.

Here in the land of palms and perpetual sunlight, facing an unknown future when I realized I never had a past, the old John Hughes high school dream came back to me. I saw teens joking around in the Santa Monica mall as an All-American Rejects music video rocked on the televisions outside EB Games, and I smiled sadly to imagine what it must feel like to go to a Southern California public high school as part of this huge new Millennial Generation overflowing with its own music and movies.

I knew, of course, that the idea would forever remain a bittersweet dream, that I could do nothing about it. Not only had time and fate decreed against me, but I had to, I had to . . . Well, I had to do something, right? I always had to do something.

Hang on.

I had spent my entire life unquestioningly fulfilling what other people told me to do, but suddenly nobody was telling me to do anything. I stood under the high glass vault of this mall as a totally free agent.

What if, what if I actually made the dream happen?

It seemed totally and arbitrarily impossible, a quest from a universe completely parallel to the one that everybody I knew inhabited—the Google engineers, the intellectual-property lawyers, the private-equity consultants—where tech start-ups delimited the wildest outer bound of imagination and daring.

If I tried to punch through the encircling shell and achieve the dream, my success or failure could serve as a sort of universal test case. Not just for me and my random Track, but for all people everywhere on whatever prescribed paths their worlds obligated them to follow.

Failure seemed almost certain. I didn't know a single human who had ever achieved anything outside a company office. Hundreds of thousands of global citizens surely realized something I hadn't, and doubtless I had acted immaturely and stupidly in ignoring the Davos consensus on the good life.[3] Humbled and broken, I would have to seriously rethink my choices, fading myself sooner or later into JPMorgan Chase.

But if I could pull this one off, literally *anything* was possible for anybody. What did people dream of? A few million dollars? Their face on a magazine? Their own country? Easy. The world minted yet another round of millionaires, "it" girls, and coups every day. But never in the thirteen-billion-year sweep of universal history had a supposed-to-be-Manhattan-investment-banker in his midtwenties become a Southern California high schooler, ever.

I could shatter the limits for everyone.

Now, at this point in my life cycle, I realized having a real high school experience as a student would mean going undercover. Had it ever happened outside of movies?

My breath caught as I realized the constellations might have aligned above the angled plate-glass dome. Yes, it had. Cinema and any sting ops aside, the last adult who actually went back to high school undercover had been Cameron Crowe. Precisely twenty-five years before, he had pretended to be a transfer senior to create *Fast Times at Ridgemont High*, the book and later the film.

Precisely twenty-five years before. My heart started to pound. His class was the first all-Gen-X class to enter the American school system. He did a great job capturing the state of the kids—but those kids had now reached their forties and sent their own children to Ridgemont. The time had come to find out something about this vast unknown Millennial Generation, yeah?

Okay. I forced my breathing to slow.

Since nobody was telling me what to do, I, I would have to give myself an order for the first time in my life. Just break down the dream into tasks, break the tasks into smaller steps, and, foot in front of foot, walk a new track.

Do it *now*.

Electrified, I turned my head and tried to catch a glimpse of myself by surprise in a mirrored wall, see myself as a stranger would see me. Too tricky. A fair appraisal told me I hadn't gained any wrinkles or lost any hair, necessary but possibly not sufficient conditions.

But I could second-guess how I looked until the day my Medicare card arrived. I needed a serious acid test. I had to find out if I could still pass for seventeen. I needed to go before high schoolers and teachers as a teen, to see if they accepted me or edged away slowly, shooting worried glances.

I would start at my local, neighborhood high school.

Morituri te salutant. I was going in.[4]

INFILTRATION

Back at my apartment, a dictum from the jolly old days of Trackdom leapt to mind: *If you fail to prepare, you prepare to fail.* I couldn't afford to half-ass a single thing. A single slipup at any moment meant no dream and maybe even squad cars.

First, I needed a reason to interact. I could most plausibly deal with administrators, who saw a flood of random students every day. But no kid would wander over to that crotchety woman in the scheduling office just to say "what's up." She knows nobody wants to talk to her. I needed a pretext, but one that wouldn't somehow involve, say, being enrolled as an actual student.

I found the key buried under piles of parent newsletters on my local school's Web site. College application season had arrived, and the Future Center encouraged all interested seniors to come meet with an advisor. I reached back through the mists of memory to dredge up a name I had heard mentioned one very cold winter long before: FAFSA. It was an application form for college financial aid. Yup, they still existed, and they were due soon. I needed one.

I looked up the map of the school and studied it until the block outlines of buildings burned white behind my eyes. It would spell disaster to wander lost, to peer in doors, to make wrong turns.

Since I wanted to maximize face time with the authorities, I decided I'd also take a look at a book in the library. I examined digital photos of the building interior. I couldn't hesitate or act as though I hadn't seen those shelves for years.

I donned jeans, flip-flops, and a hooded sweatshirt. I shouldered my college backpack. It had traveled around the planet with me, from Buenos Aires to Ho Chi Minh City, and now we would go to high school.

Santa Monica H.S. is a humongous, urban, four-block-square monolith with three-thousand-plus students, hundreds of teachers, and eight assistant principals. No one knows anyone, the kids come in every shape and size. If I couldn't make it as a teen there, I couldn't make it anywhere. I might as well just return to the Track and sign myself up as a strategy consultant at McKinsey.

As I turned the corner I saw through the chain-link fence for the first time. Kids wandered out of the gate, and some guys hung around wooden picnic tables and sat on the grass.

Guys dressed just like me, in hoodies and backpacks.

Then it really hit for the first time.

If I could pull off this project, these kids would become my peer group. They didn't just provide background color like festive and identical extras. I had to fit in with them. I had to get them to like me. I had to accept their judgments on me.

In short, I had to take them seriously.

Those figures weren't "kids," they were people.[5]

I had forgotten.

Some waited around the gate for rides home. I made first contact when I walked past a girl writing in her binder. I honestly expected her to gawk and her lack of notice stunned me.

I entered campus past a giant metal sign warning me that TREPASS-ERS WILL BE PROSECUTED. Oh, God, visions of security running up.

"Sir. Sir! Can we help you, sir?" Police tackling me, getting locked in the back of a cruiser. But no Klaxons sounded.

I followed a path between buildings, and people passed me, girls, guys, sitting on low walls watching, groups going by, some talking to teachers.

Slouching a little bit, thumbs tucked behind my backpack straps like I saw other people doing, I stayed riveted on their eyes behind my sunglasses. No one stared at the old guy with a backpack. No double takes or whispering.

I let the strange forms of the buildings collapse into the bright map grid I remembered. I walked into the library and may have hesitated for a split second as I took it all in. The librarian sat at a desk by the door. I glanced over at her and she smiled. Dozens of students filled the room, and I passed through them as I walked to the stacks.

The enormity of my situation sank in as I stood by the books. I had entered deep into the heart of this forbidden place and only the fact that everyone thought I was a high schooler had saved me. I focused on the spine in front of my face: *Honorable Men: My Life in the CIA.* I had ended up in the espionage section. I swallowed, took it down, flipped the pages. I killed another five minutes pretending to search the shelves.

Then I wandered out. I needed to go to the administration building. Could anywhere scarier exist?

I picked a door that looked right. Score. Two secretaries sat behind a big desk, chatting.

My sunglasses dangled from my hand. I had to seem unconfident, seem unpolished. No "excuse me, please."

"Is the Future Center open?" I asked.

One of the secretaries nodded toward a hallway. "You can go check."

"Okay," I said.

I started for the hall and then she said, sharply, "Wait."

Bam, bam, *bam* went my heart. I lost my breath. My hands turned cold.

She pointed to her computer screen. "It closes at four. I think you're a little late. Go check anyway."

"Okay," I managed, and slipped away.

The center contained a bunch of desks and bright college posters, in fact deserted. But I needed a FAFSA form. I needed to interact more.

A side door opened and a woman in her thirties hurried in.

"Can I get a FAFSA form?" I asked her as she passed.

She halted and looked me full in the face at a distance of two feet.

Time stopped. Puffy eyes with crumbly liner raked me over. She saw right through me. To keep pretending would doom me. I wanted to scream. I needed to drop the act, stand up straight, deal with her as an equal, say I was someone's older brother.

Then I broke eye contact, looked down.

"A what?" she snapped. Her lip curled.

"Uh, a FAFSA form," I mumbled, awed before the power of the adult. "It's like for financial aid."

She turned away with a snort. "You come late and you want me to go digging something out for you."

Then she spotted another woman at the end of the hall and called out. "Oh my God, hi!" They walked into an office together, laughing and talking.

I stood alone when a faint smile flicked across my face.

The rudeness. The dismissal. The lack of squad cars.

Victory!

ILLUSIONS SHATTER

I tossed the backpack onto my bed and punched the air. Phase one had met total and wildly improbable success. I had gone to my local high school undercover, blended in, and talked with a few administrators. The stars had begun to glimmer, but I needed a whole lot more evidence before I staked serious time and energy on being seventeen. The hour had come to take everything to the next level.

I dialed a Los Angeles number. My uncle picked up. "Hello, Jeremy."

"You'll never guess who I need to talk to," I said.

He paused to think of the unlikely. "Greg?" he hazarded.

"Wow," I said. "You guessed."

I had two Los Angeles cousins, a younger one and a much younger one. Greg fell into the second category. At family functions, he was always the little seventh-grader running around when I drank beer with the adults.

Currently a high school senior, he had become my peer group.

I threw myself on his mercy. He found the whole project hilarious. He agreed to take me to his private school the next day and introduce me to his friends and teachers as a senior to see if they bought it. We came up with the story that my parents planned to move from New York mid-year, and I had come out with them to look at schools.

In the morning, I put on a different hooded sweatshirt and met him at his house. Adrenaline wired me and I felt ready for anything. I had no fear because I knew I wouldn't get arrested.

"Look at me," I told him. "I totally look like you people, don't I?"

He gave me a critical examination. "You should lose the sunglasses. We don't really wear them."

"I like sunglasses," I protested, taking them off.

"And you're too shiny. People our age don't wear sunscreen."

"You gotta wear *sunscreen*," I mumbled.

Greg shook his head and started the car. It was funny that we were cousins, because we looked nothing alike. He had bright red hair and freckles and had quickly grown to tower over me as a six-foot-five volleyball star. People were far more likely to believe that I was seventeen—or thirty-six, for that matter—than that he and I shared any blood relation.

Like most schools in California, Greg's campus consisted of open buildings spaced around landscaped grounds. Warm November sun rose over the palms.

The gauntlet began the moment I stepped out of the car and didn't end until last bell. I passed guards, signed in at the administration office, went to four classes, got lunch, hung out in the senior lot, met dozens of students and seven teachers.

The day offered nothing if not a sharp awakening. In a handful of hours, two of my most deeply held illusions crumbled.

First, although I had always wanted the John Hughes high school experience, I never truly believed it existed. I thought Crowe had either transferred to the most atypical school in America or had taken severe liberties in the telling. I wanted to believe that things would be fun and ridiculous, but an older and wiser part of me shook its head and told me I was a fool, that high school was high school everywhere. It's lame and then it's over. Even if I could pass and transfer in somewhere, I'd face the reality of six boring and tedious months.

Was I ever *wrong*.

Aside from three definitions the bio teacher read straight out of his textbook, no actual learning took place at my cousin's school. The rest of the time was a total madhouse: *Saved by the Bell* meets the movie *Orange County*—stoners and princesses mingling in front of wacky and largely ornamental teachers. I had stepped straight onto a set.

Second, I had always believed, deep in my heart, that no one would accept me as a teen. They'd gape at me, unable to tear their eyes away, ask my cousin in urgent conference, "How *old* is that guy?" I knew this day would hammer the nail in the coffin, confirm that it was too late, that I had passed the point of no return. I would trudge off with a new and sadder wisdom toward a minivan and a mortgage. The Track knew best. I needed to start interviewing at Lehman Brothers on Monday.

Wrong. I was totally and completely wrong again. Nobody once blinked, much less questioned my story.

The students sympathized with my breaking up my senior year and encouraged me to come to their school. Girls showed special understanding and support.

My cousin watched in a daze. "I've gotta use that moving-to-a-new-city line."

The teachers totally ignored me, except for the head of the upper school. He regretted they didn't accept midyear transfers, but he wished me luck in my search.

By last period, I had stopped feeling like a scared double agent infiltrating a hermit kingdom of robots and had become completely comfortable with acting seventeen.

So wild success, but I still needed to find any chinks in my credibility. That night my cousin took me to a party some teens had at a big gated house up in the hills above Sunset. Facing a moonlit garden, he introduced me to a whole other group from private schools across L.A.

This time, we said I was his friend who went to a public school in Orange County. Not only did I not stand out like a polka-dot cuttlefish, but the most amazing feeling dawned on me: I was subpar for them. I got a few backhanded compliments about my assumed alma mater ("Oh, *I've* heard of Esperanza! Uh, you have a good, uh, soccer team, don't you?"; to which I happily improvised, "Yeah! We've won like CIF six times since ninety-three"), but beyond that the guys patronized me and blew me off, and I struggled to get any acknowledgment from the girls at all.[6] I was clearly just a stupid soccer yahoo from the sticks. Having sixteen-year-olds condescend to me felt both absurdly frustrating and unbelievably perfect at the same time.

As far as my ability to pass was concerned, the night reconfirmed the day. But I needed absolute surety. I needed to probe relentlessly for flaws. People can be polite to your face under a wide variety of circumstances and brutal behind your back. Greg needed to go in the next morning, debrief everyone who had met me, and get their opinion. Did they notice anything, uh, *different* about me?

The next day I watched the clock, waiting for school to get out. I called him three minutes later.

"No," said Greg. "I asked. Nobody said anything."

"Really?" I asked.

"Really," he said.

"Did you really ask everybody?" I said.

"Yeah," he said.

"Both guys and girls?"

"Yeah."

"And they didn't say *anything*?" I pressed.

"No," he said.

"Are you *sure*?" I said.

"Aaah!" said Greg. "Yes, I'm sure. Nobody said anything. Like one girl like said you were cute. They thought you were cool."

Game on.

YOU MAKE IT REAL

They sold it back to us and claimed no correlation: The iMac, iPod,
    iGeneration . . .
Want to be more than info-superhighway traffic,
Want to be more than a walking demographic.
                                            —MC Lars, "iGeneration"

THE DARK NIGHT OF THE SUPERINTENDENTS

Spring semester started in a little over two months.

The time had come to get hard-core.

I needed a statistically average public high school. The Millennials
were the most diverse generation in American history, and I wanted a
location that reflected both their numbers and a typical middle-class
income. I hoped to find something in the suburbs, where the majority
of Americans live.[1] It would do no good to go to a Beverly Hills High
or an inner-city fortress with metal detectors and barred windows.
Those places lay almost as far from the mainstream as, say, New York
City.

To set some realistic boundaries, I picked the five coastal counties of
Southern California. That limit meant a three-hour drive to the farthest
point. The area contained 16.9 million people—and 547 public high
schools.[2]

I looked them all up. The schools, I mean.

Depressingly, almost every site fell into one of two categories: mostly
white, Asian, and affluent, or largely Latino, black, and poor. If statistics
painted joyful and pluralistic harmony, it was because they smashed together two very different types of school. Only a few sites actually had
middle-class diversity, and my list quickly collapsed downward to thirty-
two potential locations. But still—thirty-two possibilities! What an embarrassment of riches.

I figured that selling an administration on the idea could be a little tricky—with maybe a strikeout or two—but certainly not a major issue. After all, hadn't it been easy for Cameron Crowe? Back in 1979, twenty-two-year-old Crowe had simply walked into a typical-looking school near his house, told the principal he knew a popular country musician named Kris Kristofferson, and *pow*—the guy was in. So I imagined my experience would turn out somewhat similar.

As had become a trend, I could not have possibly been more wrong. I started out leaving endless unanswered messages with a string of obstructionist secretaries. Lucky days meant I got shunted to a vice-principal's voice mail. I made follow-up calls every few days, and waited weeks for two-line e-mails. The no's came fast and terse and furious: It would not be appropriate for our high school. We are simply not in a position to accommodate your request. We are not in a position to accept your offer at this time. There is no interest in pursuing this project.

Suddenly, thirty-two schools and two months didn't look so great after all. I operated with tight time constraints and a limited list. Before I knew what had happened, I had slipped to seven weeks and twenty-four schools. I was going nowhere. My chances dropped away. Why was I failing?

I realized I needed a radical change in plans.

Believing they worked as some sort of talisman, I had been repeating the exact words Crowe had used to convince his principal—"The object is to write a book about real, contemporary life in high school"—but nobody bought it.

So I thought of other ways to describe things. I hail from bullet-pointed realms where you Write To Communicate, and the art of prose means crafting everything down with painstaking care to the fewest and smallest words possible. Now I realized I had shot myself in the foot with the clarity, and the time had come to turn one word into eight and dump in the Latinate multisyllabics. An oil tanker spill is also a "logistical petroleum bulk flow discontinuity with scaled impact on terraqueous biomes." And pretending to be a teen to see what's going on in high school is, technically, a "participant observation study." It just sounds better, you know?

I got my degrees in the social sciences and I knew how to give the world a participant observation study, all right, thick reams of paper stuffed with designs and rationales and charts and a brutal castigation of an opposing paradigm for susceptibility "to all the criticisms that Lyotard leveled at metanarratives in general," what with its derivation from "an underlying neo-Hegelian metaphysics of generational change."

Ah, what a difference the thesaurus made. Principals started to speak with me, and the principals showed interest.

The obstructionist secretaries danced offstage, and my new nemesis shimmied on, the magic word *liability*. I quickly realized that sometime over the previous twenty-five years, America had become a land where everybody knew they were victims. Victims who would klutz coffee into their laps and then flail off to sue the human genome for reckless endangerment.

Most principals wouldn't touch the project with one of those long poles the janitor uses to retrieve basketballs from the roof of the math quad. "That's sounds like a very interesting idea, but it's just not going to work at this site," they told me over and over again on the phone. "Because of liability."

On the rare chance I got a face-to-face meeting, they would invariably say: "Well, I must admit I'm excited! Just let me run it by my district first." Then I'd wait a week for the "no." Slightly embarrassed and feeling they owed me insight, the principals would finish by offering their analysis of the situation: "Well, you know, that was twenty-five years ago. The world has changed so much since then. Liability and whatnot."

The meetings themselves shaded toward the bizarre.

One avuncular principal settled back into his chair and steepled his fingers. "Well," he said, after a long time. "I personally don't have a problem with it."

"That's excellent!" I said.

He cleaned a tooth. "It would be very interesting to find out what's going on. I know they have sex in the bathrooms, because we keep catching them at it."

I nodded seriously.

"But what if, say this happens. Say you show up, and some girls decide they like you."

I opened my mouth to launch into my speech about how I was going to have No Intimate Contact. He silenced me with a wave of his hand. "And say the other fellows get jealous, and they think that the new kid is taking all the girls away from them, they decide to beat you up. What happens then? Will you sue me?"

"Oh, no," I said. "No."

He became pensive. "You'd have to sign a piece of paper about that, I believe."

I readied my pen, but he got the "no" from his district, so the point became moot.

I fell to six weeks and twenty schools. I needed to step it up. I began to arrive at my appearances with a dazzling smile, a Ralph Lauren suit, and a leather briefcase. I extracted my formal study proposals from a crimson Stanford folder that I casually left out, offered references and PowerPoint presentations.

Plus I did more research. One source I used to gain information about principals was RateMyTeachers.com, a Web site where students could go and post their opinions of their faculty and score them on a scale of one to five. All eighty students had given one particular principal the lowest rating. Somebody even wrote, pleading: "Look at all the 1s. can't you see everyone hates you. why won't you just go away?" And another, "Usually at least a few asskissers say they like their principal but nobody is stupid enough 2 like you, we all hate you sooooo much demented bitch."

I found a skittish mousey woman with a hunted look in her eye. She kept chewing on her lip.

She glanced at my proposal. "Well, you sold me!" she exclaimed after five seconds, dropping it on the table. "This is more work than my dissertation."

I suppressed my sweeping elation and shared her pleasant laughter.

"You're going to need a new wardrobe," she said, wringing her hands. "Oh, the transformation!"

She rose from her chair. "So who do you want to be? Come on, look out the window."

The lunch bell had rung, and she pointed to the crowds filling her campus. "See? I've got all my groups. I've got my skaters, I've got my jocks, I've got my surfers, I've got my wannabes under that tree."

You know you're doing badly when your principal singles you out as a wannabe under the wannabe tree.

"If you'd like to be a geek," she said, "you could be in the Computer Club!"

"I'd just like to be totally average," I said.

She reflected for an instant. "How good is your English accent? You could be an exchange student."

"I think I should probably be an American," I said.

She went to talk to her district. I followed up several times, but I never heard from her again.

No, no, no. I suddenly looked down and saw that I had five weeks and sixteen schools left. I began to panic, slide into higher gears. Time was draining past, the list was shrinking, the window to make up for the void that had been my youth was closing.

Life became a teenage nightmare of constantly approaching, and being rejected by, a series of high school principals. I spent every waking hour on the phone making calls or planning strategy at the computer. Every week or so, I'd swing a meeting, and then I'd suit up and drive to some random campus around Southern California.

The days on my calendar evaporated and I had gone nowhere. I had to work harder, harder. . . .

One principal wore a Hawaiian shirt (RateMyTeachers.com: "decent guy but condecending"). He had a deep tan and slicked-back blond hair and grinned broadly.

"How are you?" he asked me.

"Great," I said. "How are you?"

"It's a beautiful day in sunny Southern California," he said, "and I'd rather be surfing. So let me get this right. You want me to let you transfer in undercover as a student and take classes?"

"Exactly," I said.

He scrutinized me for a moment. "Well, you look like you're eighteen. Do you want to be a junior or a senior?"

"I'd like to be a senior," I said.

He nodded, and his grin got bigger. "I think rules are there to be bent. Whenever I hear about a rule, I think about a way to bend it."

The vice-principal, who sat quietly in the corner, ventured: "I think rules are there to be followed."

The principal held up a hand. "Don't even get started, Roger. If I get fired, I'm taking you down with me."

Roger must have been very relieved when the district said no.

COUNTDOWN TO NOTHING

I had one month and eleven schools left. I began to go off the deep end.
I couldn't sleep more than three hours a night. I didn't know a single
person in my life who had left the Track and succeeded, I didn't have a
single real-life example that anything else was possible.

Everything fell into a neat pattern. Anytime I couldn't talk to someone face-to-face, they'd reject the idea out of hand. I needed to meet
with both the principal and then the district, but any interested principals insisted on asking their bosses solo first, which meant an inevitable
no. I yearned to grab a principal and scream, "For the love of God, I
must speak with your district in person! This exact same situation has
fallen apart seven times already!"

I had two weeks and four schools left. I hit the wire of desperation.
On the Internet, I saw that the assistant superintendent of a desirable
district would appear on a television panel that evening. The panel
would broadcast live from Carlsbad, a few hours away.

"This is the hardest I've ever seen anyone work for anything in my
life," a friend said carefully.

I barely heard him, because my thoughts had flown to the superintendent. Boy, it would be nice to talk with her and tell her my idea. I
never got to talk to superintendents.

I pounded Eminem's "Lose Yourself" as I tore at ninety-five miles per
hour down the freeway at sunset. "Success is my only motherfucking *option*, failure's *not*," I sang along with Eminem as I adjusted my tie and
met my fixedly bright gaze in the rearview mirror.

I tracked down the building, said the right things to a lot of people,
and got into the broadcast room. I knew I wouldn't be able to catch the
superintendent afterward, so during the commercial break, I climbed
right up to her table onstage.

"Liability, you know? I'm sorry, I don't want to take up any more of
your time."

I had no time left to take. Only a week and a half remained before the
spring semester started. Everyone wrote me off. People kept asking what
I planned to do now that the high school thing hadn't worked out. I just
ratcheted up the intensity of my smile and repeated Eminem at them
until they went away. But I knew the painful truth: My options had basically run out. I had gone through every potential school in Southern
California. I had only two possibilities left.

I looked at the handful of days remaining on my calendar. I had spent months doing literally nothing at all—not even on Sundays, not even at 3:00 A.M.—besides hurling myself at the entire Southern California secondary-school system like a migratory bird at a windowpane. I had already met with the principals of both sites remaining on my list. Mirador Senior High School in Emerald Valley had the better statistics, but the point was theoretical. I had nothing else to do but wait with cheery and fatalistic mania for the "no" from both districts.

I was trying very hard not to think about the future when my cell phone rang.

"This is Irma Chao from Mirador High School," the voice said. It paused briefly. "I've set up a tentative meeting for you with the district tomorrow afternoon. I haven't said anything, because I figured it was probably better to let you tell them what the project's about yourself. Will you be able to make it?"

The next day, my thirty-first school gave me a yes.

TWO COMMANDMENTS

During the district meeting, I established two rules for the new life ahead of me:

1) I would initiate no illegal activity.
2) I would have no intimate contact with any student.

The rest of the technicalities were quite simple:
I would keep the name and location of Mirador secret.
I would play a transfer senior from Hermosa Beach.
I would start school the next week.

HIGH SCHOOL EYE FOR THE OLDER GUY

On my way home from the Emerald Valley Unified School District, I found that despite sitting behind the wheel and pressing pedals, I had no idea what was happening. The waking world had become such a solid wall of bliss that I couldn't drive. I parked on the side of the road and called a few people to share the ocean of universal joy before I felt ready to set off again.

Somewhere on the freeway, I realized I had spent months of anguish wearing suits and trying to impress educational professionals, and now

I had a week to transform myself into a high schooler who lived in Emerald Valley.

I needed an address, a family phone number, identification, teen clothing, and enough youth culture expertise to be a high schooler and not a doof in his midtwenties. Major gear shift.

Emerald Valley? Somewhere in inland Orange County. I had never heard of it before either. I'd been there precisely once in my life when I visited the school.

Did I know anyone at all from Emerald Valley? Not off the top of my head, I sure didn't. And I couldn't even ask around without revealing the school's location. When I got home, I went straight to search my alumni directories.

There I found exactly one possibility. We had gone to boarding school together, but I barely knew her. Another Track refugee, born in Emerald Valley, she had dropped out of one of America's top colleges and moved up to L.A. to front her own rockabilly band under the name Dulcie Younger.

I called her as an act of faith; we had only spoken once before, at an alumni event a few months earlier. At the very least, I believed I could trust her not to tell anyone that I was going to Mirador.

As it turned out, the project charmed Dulcie. The next morning she met me outside her house in full '50s attire, red patent leather Mary Janes and green Capri pants. We set off for Emerald Valley on a mission to find me a phone number and an address.

Attending Mirador meant a captivating bind. I needed Emerald Valley contact information without an actual place to live. Because of the town's small size, I couldn't have an apartment there without fear that someone would find me out, without worrying that I'd go to school with next-door neighbors who knew darn well that I paid the rent. Since I couldn't handle a ninety-minute commute before first period, I planned on moving to a nearby city soon enough. Right now, however, I needed to create the appearance of a house in Emerald Valley without ever having one.

Dulcie first took me on a brief tour of the streets, getting me just barely acquainted enough for a plausible new guy.

We solved the phone number problem easily. I bought the cheapest prepaid cellular plan from a store in a nearby city. It gave me the all-important local area code and a voice-mail box that I could dial in to access from anywhere. I needed nothing else to simulate a family number. Dulcie recorded the "we're not here right now" message in her best middle-aged-mom voice.

The address posed a trickier problem. We talked to a few people that Dulcie knew, but everybody seemed to have children somewhere in the district school system, and we decided not to reveal what we needed in case they couldn't keep a secret.

So we became robust solutions architects. We looked up the locations of all the mailbox rental places in town, and we picked the most obscure and seedy one, located in a mainly residential area. We would get a box in the name of my imaginary parents and high school self. I could just give the rental place as my address, and pretend that the P.O. box was an apartment number. I hid in the car while Dulcie went in to scope out the situation.

Success. The mailbox place was closing, so we took the papers to fill out later. On the freeway back to L.A., our missions accomplished, I turned up the music and hit the accelerator as we cruised opposite the unmoving miles of commuter traffic.

"We should definitely write the alumni magazine about today," I said.

Dulcie laughed.

Next on the list came my X-Treme Teen Makeover. It wasn't the most radical transformation that Hollywood has ever seen. I never felt tempted to roll up in plaid flannel blasting Alice in Chains, expecting nothing to have changed over the previous ten years.

I had always enjoyed new things, and I had stayed focused in the present, instead of throwing up my hands at some point and ignoring new popular culture, which seemed to have slowly happened to even the last of the holdouts around me. I listened to the radio, for example, instead of continually rethumbing a stack of aging Dave Matthews CDs like some other people my age.

So I already had some idea of what went on, but nothing close to enough. The handful of dubious stats and buzzwords gleefully deployed on upward of seventy million individuals when adults tell other adults about "the Millennial Generation" now had to go deep into the paper shredder so I could figure out what life was really like.

I ignored absolutely anything written by anyone over eighteen and went straight to the primary source. I spent countless hours on popular online sites like MySpace, reading thousands of profiles that teenagers had posted about themselves, seeing what kinds of music, movies, clothes they really liked. What they really disliked. What expressions they really used. I poured though incalculable teen postings on message boards and forums, I Xanga'd and LiveJournal'd, opening the virtual online diaries and profiles of hundreds of teens. I learned about video games, TV shows, subcultures, products, slang, self-perceptions, trends. Whatever I hadn't heard of, I looked up. That turned out to be a lot, and I learned embarrassingly vast amounts of information. Eventually I reached a saturation point where everything started making sense, and I suspected I had a decent handle on the actual teen world.

I set up an appointment with my cousin to debrief him on adolescent coolness after his volleyball game. I brought a legal pad to take notes. To start, I asked him to list some bands I should like.

He gave me a name.

"Shyeah, maybe like last summer," I said offhand. "I mean, who's cool right *now?*"

I lifted my pleading eyes to meet his shocked stare. Training day had apparently ended quickly.

A few details remained, of course. Since my home had already been set as Hermosa Beach, I had to customize my identity around the given. I came from a lucky place—far enough away that anything I did out of the norm could be chalked up to the peculiarities of the shore, close enough that I wouldn't have to bring up how warm it was in California every five seconds.

I needed to act like a Hermosa teen, which meant—as in many coastal places in California—an interesting blend of arrogance and mocking self-deprecation. Done. I also had the coastal long hair, versus Emerald Valley's inland short and spiky. Good.

I also had to dress like a beach guy who surfed. I walked into Pacific Sunwear and dropped five hundred dollars on clothes. Now that may not sound like such an impressive sum, and five hundred dollars may net one polo shirt at Comme Des Garçons, but you get a lot of bang for your buck when the fashion staple is a graphic-printed skate T.

I could barely carry the bags stuffed with sneakers, shorts, belts, sweatshirts, T-shirts, jeans, necklaces, long-sleeve Ts, socks, collared knits. As the cashier, himself a high schooler, stammered: "Enjoy your new wardrobe."

Now one day remained before school started. The only piece still missing from the puzzle was a driver license. Every single element in my life required faultless and seamless integration. That's how you make it real. If someone borrowed my cell phone, found my binder, or looked through the glove compartment in my car, nothing could indicate I was anything other than I seemed. Likewise with my driver license—if anyone asked to see it or looked at my wallet, I couldn't mysteriously not have one. The one and only crack in the immaculate armor would be my house, and I needed to save all my secrecy points and awkward evasions for keeping people away from my home sweet mailbox.

I needed an ID. I asked around. I had a friend whose nineteen-year-old coworker planned to get his own card. His name was Paul, and he had exact directions for a place we could go to. There I could get a fake driver license—or, if I preferred, a real driver license. Or green card, birth certificate, Social Security card, or passport.

Ah, this place was not Compton or South Central, with their quaint down-home values. He referred to the Rampart sector of Los Angeles, an urban disaster zone, a vortex that resisted description. The nicest, Chamber of Commerce sort of thing to say was probably that the area was a sea of petty felons and deinstitutionalized insane homeless wandering against the backdrop of a titanic clash of three hostile power blocs struggling for control of the blasted streets.

Paul was an urban tribal kind of guy, with a shaved head, goatee, Chinese character tattoos, and ears gauged by plugs.[3] I guess because I constituted the nominal adult, he still looked to me to lead this venture. Into the wasteland we walked, searching for identification.

We stepped out of the car beside the stagnant lake of a decaying park where dozens of people huddled on the street. One bearded man tried to offer us a lightbulb. "You just turn it on if they come back," he insisted.

A guy across the intersection in a bandana and baggy khakis stopped talking to a fried pupusa vendor and nodded at us.

"That cat's giving us the eye," said Paul. He called everyone "cats."

The light changed, and we crossed toward the bandana man. My secret weapon was that, although I seem like a total gringo, I speak Spanish fluently. The guy wouldn't know that, and I could take decisive action if he started talking about stealing our cash or icing us.

"What you looking for?" he asked us when we arrived. "What you want?"

We had entered MS-13 territory, but he didn't have the right tattoos or colors. I figured he probably claimed a smaller gang, the Crazy Riders, who had bought a Rampart drug and ID franchise from MS-13 in exchange for protection from Eighteenth Street. I had done research for a change.

"Coca? ID?" he suggested.

"ID," I said. (Although part of me wanted to say, "Shoulder-mounted rocket launchers and South African passports." That would have been interesting too.)

"Two ID?" he said.

"Yeah," I said. "But can you do the underage ones? Like with the red stripe and everything?"

My Crazy Rider raised his eyebrows for a second. "You want to be more younger?"

"Yeah, just me," I said. "I need to be seventeen."

He nodded. "Okay," he said. "I can do that."

The pupusa vendor turned to him. "You're charging them fifty?" he asked in Spanish.

"No, seventy each," the guy answered in Spanish.

So I bargained him back down to fifty dollars. Then a burning desire suddenly overcame me to write my ID off on my 1040 Schedule C as a work expense. I wondered if Crazy Riders issued receipts, and was pleased to learn they did.

We followed him a block to a collapsing art deco tower, paint peeling from its carved detailing. We took a cage elevator to a huge office suite, now empty except for a fat woman who waited with a camera amid the flaking columns and paneled ceilings.

The man paced, looking down onto street corners through the grimy windows and speaking nonstop into his cell phone about times and positions. Paul and I proceeded to write down who we would become on small scraps of paper. Our new names, our new hometowns, our new birth dates.

The guy needed some time to get our cards together, and he reappeared across the street forty-five minutes later. We handed off the cash and cards precisely at the moment an LAPD patrol car drifted around the corner.

Paul, the Crazy Rider, and I froze like antelope in the headlights and lived a fight-or-flee nightmare of pounding adrenals. Then the squad car continued onward, and we all shared a hearty laugh before saying good-bye.

Rising up onto the high, arcing freeways that passed over the warren of Rampart, I looked down at the shiny piece of plastic in my hand to confirm who I had become.

I was seventeen. I was from Hermosa Beach. And I had paid tribute to the master whose vision of teenage life had inspired me so many years before.

My name was Jeremy Hughes.

PART TWO

POPULAR

You might take a second look,
It's just a game we play.

—New Found Glory,
"Constant Static"

POSITIVE ATTITUDE

Back in the foundation time, the old monk Serra had trekked across the mighty rivers and burning deserts and frozen mountain ranges of the new world in his simple brown robe. Restlessly driven to seek the spot where all dust ended, he pounded his sturdy walking staff into the rough dirt of the earth and carved out a trail across the trackless wilderness, a royal road that joined all the communities of his embryonic civilization, from his San Diego in the south to his San Francisco in the far north. He walked barefoot.[1]

Now steel, concrete, and the passage of eons had frozen Serra's humble path into California's two main freeways, the 5 and the 101.[2] I sat among the 6:00 A.M. traffic of angry people in SUVs who retraced his ancient pilgrimage for their daily commute. They checked office voice mail on their cell phones, slammed their brakes, gulped Starbucks, and spaced out to the radio.

My first day of class had arrived, and I now lived for everybody who ever dreamed of going back to high school. They would want to be cool. They would want to do and say everything right. I owed it to everyone to make the dream come true. I had resolved to become part of the cool crowd.

Before I even considered becoming a big man on campus, though, I needed to actually get there. The traffic inched past taunting signs proclaiming the speed limit sixty-five.

This commute had to go. Fortunately, the evening before, not only had I found an ad for a perfect apartment in a neighboring city, but I had also traded in my starter mailbox for a major residential upgrade. A friend of my aunt's turned out to live in Emerald Valley, we swore her to secrecy, and I gained an official address with windows and a chimney.

I exited the freeway in Emerald Valley, and turned onto Orchard Road. There the big green-and-gold roadside marquee declared MIRADOR SENIOR HIGH SCHOOL: HOME OF THE MARLINS, next to a graphic of a grinning swordfish in sunglasses. The low set of concrete buildings stretched away among trees and grass. A letter board underneath the marquee added, cryptically, SAVE OUR SCHOOL. $190,000. THANK YOU.

I didn't feel nervous or even energized. I stood so far beyond the normal rules of reality that the scene felt more like a dream than a waking day. Life meant business cards and cubicles and down payments and promotions and everyone going desperately to bars with marriage and babies on the horizon. I wore Dickies shorts and skater shoes. A backpack sat on the seat next to me. I had entered a dreamzone.

A stream of cars lined the road outside Mirador, parents dropping off their sons and daughters. I knew the school had two parking lots, the staff-and-visitor area I had parked in before, and a student lot. A large woman with a walkie-talkie stood by the gate to the faculty spaces, and I felt a pulsing sense of danger surrounding them, an ancient feeling I had forgotten. I realized that if I tried to park there, I would get in *trouble*. Trouble does not come in such a pure form in the adult world.

So I turned with dozens of cars into the student lot. A man with a scar on his forehead scrutinized each of us at the gate, but I just kept my head forward and drove through. I parked, grabbed my backpack, and got out.

One guy leaned from his car window and called to me, "Dude, when does school start today? Is this like a reverse minimum day?"

I shrugged. "Dude, I don't know," I said. "Sorry."

I set off toward the buildings. This guy thought I went to his school. He thought I belonged here. I guess I did go here. I was a Mirador student now. Go, Marlins. Oh, my God. I had entered a dream.

I walked onto the campus, past low cinder block buildings, through quads planted with fan palms, bright-flowered bushes, banana leaves, and tangles of spiky succulents. Hundreds of people talked and laughed in groups, clustered on benches, sat on steps, stood in loose crowds. It felt like virtual reality, a living museum like colonial Williamsburg, as if all the people had shown up just for me. I wanted to stop and stare at everybody and everything, peer into all the classrooms, go up to each group and hear what they were talking about. It required effort to amble along the paths to the administration building, trying to look like everyone else, eyes dully ahead, bored and annoyed to be back for another semester. I was happy to notice that nobody gave me a second glance. I caught sight of the crowds in a big mirrored window and had to hunt to find myself among them, an indistinguishable form, backpack, Volcom T-shirt, shorts.

The receptionist at the desk didn't blink, sent me to a chair in the waiting area until my counselor arrived. I had one fellow spring-semester transfer, a tiny Filipina sophomore. Terror roiled her wide eyes as we sat and watched students and adults rush past, greet one another.

"Where did you go?" I asked her.

"West High School," she said. "In Torrance."

"This sucks, huh?"

"Yeah," she said, with passion and bitterness. "This really sucks."

She didn't seem too up for a chat about the state of her generation, so we sat in silence until a white-haired woman came and claimed her.

A short girl with dark hair, somewhat heavy, hurried past with two sweatshirts tied around her waist, one on the back, one on the front. The receptionist shook her head. "Back again, Sara?"

"He made me cover my legs." The girl laughed, blushing.

A few minutes later, a fat man with glasses and a striped shirt peered around the corner and read off a folder. "Jeremy Hughes?"

Oh, that was me.

"Yeah," I said.

He approached with a big smile and outstretched hand.

"Hi, Jeremy," he said. "I'm Alan Markowitz, I'm going to be your counselor. Could you please come—"

Beeeeeeeep.

At the sound of a tone, he and everyone froze. The room fell deathly silent. All humans swiveled to the corner and lifted their arms. Panic. What was happening?

"Good morning, Mirador Senior High School!" bubbled a staticky beige speaker on the wall. "Please join me in the pledge of allegiance!"

Nobody noticed as I rose and joined in a fraction too late. Neither in New York nor in boarding school had we ever performed this ritual. Curveballs zagged on all sides.

Soon I sat on a chair in Mr. Markowitz's little office as he reviewed my C+/B- records. Of the entire school, only Dr. Chao knew my true identity. None of the staff knew, none of the teachers knew—nobody.

His eyes lit up when he saw my presumed old school. "Oh, my gosh," he said. "My nephew went there! Did you know Ryan Markowitz? He would have been a few years older than you."

"Wow," I said, "that name sounds really familiar."

"I'm going to have to ask him about you," he said happily, as he scanned the pages.

The PA speaker in the background continued listing all sorts of information. I strained to hear, but our conversation and the static made it impossible.

"Hey, it looks like you've done"—my counselor paused—"pretty well. What are you planning on doing next year?"

"I sent in the, uh, applications for UCSC and Cal State Long Beach," I said. "I'm like really hoping for UCSC, but I'm probably going to Long Beach."

"Well," he said, "we've also got a very good school here that you may want to keep an open mind about, which is Emerald Community College." He saw my shocked look and quickly added, "Just in case." He gave me a brochure.

Then he tilted his head. "So how are you holding up with the move?"

"It doesn't even feel real to me," I said, in all truth. "It feels like a dream."

"Well, you seem to have a positive attitude," he enthused, "and that's great!"

An intense guy's voice came on the speaker, loud and sincere. It cut straight through the static. "The Word of the Day," our beige box pronounced, "is *rangiferine*. Adjective. From the Old French *rangier*, a reindeer, possibly from the Old Swedish *ren*, a reindeer, plus the Latin *ferus*, wild, untamed. One. Pertaining to or like caribous. Two. Belonging to the animal genus containing caribous. *Rangiferine*."

Mr. Markowitz watched me for a reaction. "Ah hah hah hah . . . ," he laughed, a little embarrassed.

His laser printer fed out a copy of my new schedule. Algebra 2, Physiology, Third-Year French, American Government, LUNCH, PE, Senior English.

"Let me find an ASB student to take you around and get you set up here, Jeremy," said my counselor, and huffed out of the room. I remembered from my handbook that *ASB* was the Mirador term for student council.

He returned with a guy in a striped polo and khaki cargo shorts. The guy had popped his collar up and radiated haughty disdain.

"What's up," he said. "I'm Ross."

"Hey, what's up," I said. "I'm Jeremy."

Mr. Markowitz beamed and ushered us out. "Feel free to stop by anytime, Jeremy!" he said, and shut the door.

Away we went on our tour of the campus.

In areas of America where the temperature drops below freezing, high school planners favor the construction of a single big building with locker-filled hallways. No such climatic constraints had troubled the architects who sketched the walls of Mirador Senior High School in 1965.

Their creativity found its canvas in a newly incorporated city in the sunny inland basin of Orange County, an hour south of Los Angeles and an hour north of the Mexican border. The population of California's suburban Southland had exploded in the giddy postwar years, which meant a whole lot of teens had either arrived or were scheduled to appear shortly.[3]

Emerald Valley answered their rising challenge with a school that sprawled in the sun like an open-air starfish. Five concrete quads, each one ringed by low classroom buildings, formed the radiant points around a wide central quad.

I have a terrible sense of direction under the best of circumstances, so I tuned out Ross's lengthy explanation of the five-plus-one quad system and concentrated on remaining very calm.

Two months had passed since my day undercover at my cousin's school, and I had spent most of the intervening time interacting with adults. I had to remember: Just act like a normal human being but, uh, on the seventeen-year-old level. Breathe.

Ross saw my eyes glaze over as he explained how I could determine quad based on room number. "You'll get used to it after a while," he said.

Then he ran through a brief overview of the social topography. "Freshmen hang out down there by the parking lot, sophomores in the language arts quad, juniors over there on the steps, and seniors up at that circle."

The circle in question meant a concrete ring of a few benches with a California pepper tree in the middle. How did all five hundred and eleven Mirador seniors pack themselves into that space?

I figured I'd wait and see. Ross looked at my green shirt. "Hey," he said. "You're wearing our senior color."

I smiled. "Nice."

"Red's juniors, blue's sophomores, and yellow is freshmen. You usually want to wear it on rally days and for like special events."

Then we arrived at the ASB office. A digital camera flashed and soon I held my own plastic school ID, which commanded me "You must carry this card with you at all times." I handed over twenty dollars and caught my bundle of gym clothes—mesh shorts and a Mirador T. I preordered my yearbook, got an info packet about class rings, and a sheet with my locker assignment.

The day warmed up, and the electronic beep sounded. We had missed first period, so as students poured from their rooms into the sunshine, Ross brought me to physiology. My first class.

DEMENTED KINDERGARTEN

The Mirador bio lab consisted of two identical rooms, each with rows of black epoxy countertops and a demonstration table in front. A small corridor connected the two rooms. A stream of people flowed in the doors behind me and took seats in either space; the two areas seemed interchangeable and both seemed to contain our physiology class. No one paid me the slightest attention.

The right room seemed pretty full with about thirty people, so I veered left, where I saw only twelve or so. I took an empty seat at a lab table next to a girl with dark black hair streaked through by a single chunk of blond.

She half looked over at me.

"Hey," I said.

"Hey," she said. She wore a vintage Smurfs T.

"I'm new," I said.

"New in this class or new at school?" she asked.

"At school."

"Oh," she said. "I'm so sorry for you. That really sucks. Welcome to an institution founded on popularity, sports, ass kissing, and corruption."

I smiled. "Tight."[4]

"Where are you from?"

"Hermosa Beach," I said.

"Hah. That really sucks. The beach is so much better than here. I like transferred last year from Corona del Mar, and I miss it so much. I still think of it as my school, like all my friends are back there."

Thus bonded, we shook hands. Her name was Thea.

I looked around the room. Posters of the Los Angeles Lakers basketball team covered the walls, along with newspaper clippings that tracked the season so far. Huge purple-and-yellow writing on the whiteboard commanded us to "Think Happy Laker Thoughts Tonight!!!" Stars, confetti, and smiley faces surrounded the words.

"Somebody likes the Lakers, huh?" I said.

Thea shuddered. "Unnnh. That's Ms. Horn. She like grades us down for a week if they lose a game."

"Where is she?" I asked.

"Check the other room. You probably need to tell her you're here."

I pointed to an index card taped to the lab table in front of my seat. It had a number fifteen surrounded by the same magic marker stars and smiles.

Thea rolled her eyes. "Yeah, this class is kinda like demented kindergarten."

I stood. People talked, doodled, or slept. One tall, skinny girl with tons of makeup, an extremely short white skirt, and highlighted hair hid behind a supply cabinet door and yelled into her cell phone. "You're such an asshole! Fuck you, Shawn! I hate you and I'm not fucking talking to you." She hit the hang-up button and clomped to her seat. "Fuck him, Sara, he's an asshole," she said to the same short dark-haired girl I had seen in the office that morning.

I walked into the other room.

Here everybody talked. The teacher sat behind her desk playing computer solitaire.

Oh, my God, I thought.

She was my age. She had short brown hair and three piercings in one ear. If the scene had been Hollywood, I'm sure I would have fallen madly in love with her. But I just didn't feel that special spark. I was too busy wondering how many nanoseconds it would take for her to see straight through me.

Her eyes lit up when I introduced myself. "I have a *new student!*" she squealed, clapping her hands. "Oh, let me see who you have." She looked down at my schedule.

"Okay, okay, oh, Mulligan, I had him when I was here! Okay, ooooh, Lamarque. He screams, and the freshmen can't take it. And Schroeder's okay."

"Thanks for letting me know," I said.

We wandered together into the little corridor. "Where should you sit?" she wondered.

I pointed to the left room. "I had been sitting in there."

"Well, I'll tell you," she said, "that's where I put all the cool people. The annoying people I put in the other room."

"Oh," I said.

She looked me over. "Let's see what the group has to say." We entered the left room.

"Hey, guys," Ms. Horn called over the noise. She picked up a stack of detention forms on the desk. "Guys, I don't want to hand out equalizers." The room fell marginally quieter. She grabbed me by the shoulder and brought me front and center. "This is my new friend Mr. Jeremy Hughes, who's just come to Mirador all the way from Hermosa Beach. Can he stay with us on this side?"

Shrugs. "Okay," some girl said.

Ms. Horn clapped her hands. "We *like* you!" she squeaked. "Let me introduce you to everybody."

She pointed to my seatmate at the front. "This is Theodora, and she's a sophomore. She's a little weird and quiet, but she did a good job with the practice cat."

We moved onward to another lab bench. Ms. Horn pointed to the girl who had been hiding behind the cabinet door. "This is my friend Charity Warner. She's a junior and she has a boyfriend already, but she's a good person to know because she'll invite you to parties."

"Uhh, I am soooo mad at Shawn," said Charity.

"Oh, Ms. Warner, are you having problems with your boyfriend?"

"He's such a liar, I'm so sick of him," said Charity.

"Ohhhh," sympathized Ms. Horn. She pointed to the short, slightly heavy dark-haired girl sitting next to her. "This is Sara, and she's a sophomore. She has a boyfriend who she's too good for and she shouldn't be with. We're hoping they'll break up, so if you're looking for a new girlfriend . . ."

"Heh heh," I laughed. "I actually already have a girlfriend."

"Oh," said Ms. Horn. "Okay." She pointed to a guy with spiky hair, two silver-balled horseshoe earrings, and an eyebrow piercing. "This is my friend Mr. Victor Reyes."

Vic had his face down on the dull black lab table. "I'm so hung over, Ms. Horn," he moaned.

"Me too," said another guy. "Like six of us were drinking last night."

"Right on, bro," said Vic, nodding at him. They punched fists.

"Drinking on Sunday night." Ms. Horn smiled. She sat on the lab bench and shook her head. "Tsk, tsk."

"Take an Advil," said Charity.

"You're a slut," said Vic.

"Viiiiicc!" whined Charity.

"'Viiiiicc!'" mimicked Ms. Horn, making fun of her.

"Ms. Hoooooorn," whined Charity.

"Ohhhhhh," whined the teacher.

Vic put his arms over his head. "Sweet Jesus, which is more terrible? Go ahead, rate them."

"Mr. Reyes," said Ms. Horn, "was that a nice way to speak to a young lady?"

"She's not a lady," said Vic, and he dodged back as Charity swung at him.

"You're such a fag," said Charity.

"Miss Warner," said the teacher, "is that appropriate language for the classroom?"

Meanwhile, of course, everyone else talked or zoned out.

"You're such a homosexual," Charity corrected herself.

"Oh, boy," bubbled Ms. Horn. "I can see what this semester is going to be like. I had this kid last period, this really bad kid. . . . He was giving me such a headache. I sent him straight into the annoying room." Then something occurred to her. "Did anybody watch the Lakers game last night?"

Ms. Jessica Horn actually turned out to be a year older than me, but she could just have easily been undercover as a senior. Even though she dressed far more conservatively than most actual Mirador girls, she wore her faculty ID card around her neck to prevent any embarrassing mistakes. I personally suspected, though, that she loved it when people regularly told her she looked like a student.

After a while she left, and we all stood or sat around in the back.

Sara paced back and forth. "I can't sit still, I'm freaking out about elections tomorrow. I can't sit down."

"Huh?" I said.

"I'm running for spirit officer tomorrow," she said. She climbed up onto one of the stools. "Aaaaah! I'm so nervous."

"You need to do relaxation techniques," said Charity. "You need to close your eyes and breathe."

Sara closed her purple-shadowed eyes. She took a deep breath. "I'm calm, I'm relaxing."

"Just imagine yourself drifting away on a cloud or some shit," said Charity.

Vic slowly began to rotate the top of the stool. Sara still had her eyes shut as she began to spin. "I'm calm," she said. "I'm so calm."

Vic turned her stool faster and faster. She opened her eyes and shrieked before grabbing for Charity, bracelets flailing. Charity yelped and ducked away, and Sara toppled off onto her. The two took a moment to straighten themselves out.

"You're an asshole," Sara told Vic.

He had returned to doing what he was doing before Ms. Horn walked in, which was using a laboratory X-Acto blade to carve several wide pieces of plastic tubing into a bong. He did it in segments to combine later and avoid detection.

He looked at my Adidas. "Those are tight shoes," he said. "I used to have really similar ones."

"Nice," I said.

"What kind of car do you drive, fool?" he asked me.

"Altima GXE," I said. It's just an average car, but I mentioned the GXE part to make it sound cooler.

I could tell he couldn't picture it, but he gave me the benefit of the doubt. "Nice," he said. "Dude, fool, you're at fuckin' Mirador now. This is a fucking crazy school. This is like the number-one drinking school in the country—every day we're gonna be drunk."

"We have so much shit at this school," said Charity. "We have weed, coke . . ."

" 'Roids," said Sara.

"That's weird," I said. "We didn't have 'roids at my old school."

"Yeah, 'roids are big this year," said Charity.

"Everyone gets shitty all the time because there's nothing else to do in Emerald Valley," said Sara. "Bacardi 151 flows like water."

"Well, it's either that or have drama," said Charity. "I swear we have so much drama here, this place is like *90210*."

"There's just so much drama in high school in general," said Sara.

"No, there's so much drama *here*," said Charity. "All the drama is *here*. It really sucks you had to come from the beach to fucking Emerald Valley where there's nothing to do."

"It's actually not that bad," I said. "People are really nice."

"Hah!" said Charity. "People pretend to be nice here and then they talk shit behind your back. All they do is talk shit and cause drama. God, I miss Dove so much, we need him here so badly now."

Vic got up and hid a bong segment in a supply cabinet.

"So what kinda stuff are you into?" asked Sara. "Are you a Christian?"

"Yeah," I said, "but I'm not like hard-core."

She lowered her voice a little. "Do you smoke?" For teens, the obvious referent there is marijuana.

"Yeah," I said. In truth, I had, but I didn't.

Sara mused, turned to the others. "I'm trying to think of who to introduce him to, if he's a Christian, like Derrick and all those people, and if he parties, like Brian and those guys. Vic, you can go take him to meet the whole circle crowd."

"Yeah," said Vic, but it was a put-on-the-spot sort of thing.

"Who's the circle crowd?" I asked.

"It's like all the cool seniors," said Sara. "Who is it? It's like Alexis and Cody, they're supposedly the 'hot couple'—"

Charity stood. Behind her rose a huge pile of cardboard boxes. "Oh my God," she said. "They are *not* the hot couple. Have you ever tried to have a conversation with them? They just stand there next to each other like totally silent. They don't even talk to each other. They're so fucking stupid, they have nothing to say. She's a bitch and he's a fag. Now he lifts and he's a bigger fag. All he can do is talk about the supplements he takes." Charity mimed finding a vein and slamming in a needle. "It's like talking to a rock. This fucking cat has more to say than they do."

She turned around and whammed a cardboard box with her platform sandal. "Stupid cat," she said.

What was the deal with these cats everyone kept talking about? I took a closer look at the cartons. They all had a label on the side: ONE MEDIUM CAT.

"There're cats in there?" I asked.

"Yeah, fool," said Vic. "That's what we do in this class. We dissect cats."

A little while later, I went back to my seat. Thea rummaged around in a little plastic box of cat bones.

She found a triangle-shaped cat jaw and set it upright on the black epoxy countertop. On the top point she placed a set of tiny cat teeth to create the effect of a tiara. She presented her handiwork with a flourish. "It's like an evil bride."

She glided it along the smooth table and hummed "Here Comes the Bride" in an eerie register. "Maaaaarry me," she wailed, "Maaaaaaaarry me!"

"I can't believe we dissect cats," I said.

"Yeah," said Thea. "We skin them in a few weeks. Yes, hah hah, all the jokes."

CLASS COLORS

Eventually Ms. Horn returned and handed out Xeroxed lists of cat anatomy vocabulary words for us to copy down. Most people flipped through them and made the effort to write a few terms while they talked. Then the bell beeped.

"Do you know how to get to your next class?" Thea asked me.

"Yeah, I think so," I said. "I think I'm good. I think I got it figured out."

She found me trapped in a dead end at the side of the shuttered food court windows.

"Uh," I said.

"Come on," she said.

So away we went, past the spiky plants and bright flowers.

Crowds streamed around us. "I'm sure you'll notice how this campus is totally segregated," said Thea. "Everybody has like their own area."

"Like what?" I asked.

"Well, a lot of the Asians all sit together on like this wall by the language quad, and everybody calls it the 'Great Wall of China.' Yeah, I know, it's pretty bad. It's so racist here. Like remember there were a bunch of black people back in the food court by the vending machines?"

I nodded.

"Yeah, that's 'the Projects.' I know, it's so bad. Those are like the ghetto black people. The preppy black people just stand around talking in central quad with the rest of the preps." She nodded to the maybe forty people of all shapes, sizes, and colors gathered around the distant senior circle.

"The guy who showed me around said all the seniors go to that circle," I said.

Thea made the quote marks with her fingers. "No, the 'cool seniors' go there, like all the bitchy people from my class sit together down in the language arts quad."

"Where do you go?" I asked her.

"Like when I first came here, I used to sit in the special ed section with my brother, and then he met some people so he was okay, so now I sit with some of my theater friends behind the library."

I looked at her vintage Smurfs T. "I like your shirt."

"Thanks. I get everything in thrift shops."

"Hey," I said proudly. "You're wearing your class color."

She lowered her head and gave me a two-second are-you-serious look.

"What is it?" she asked.

"Blue."

Thea examined the shirt. "It's periwinkle. Not blue." She cast a sideways glance at the circle. "God, you should be over there with them."

We arrived at my classroom. As the tardy bell rang, and Mr. Mulligan shut the door that sealed me into third-year French, a familiar recurring question popped into my mind: *What the hell was I thinking?*

Usually I ignore that question, but this time it was hard to avoid, with a man pointing to me and speaking in tongues: *"On a un nouvel étudiant en classe ce semestre! Il s'appelle Jeremy Hughes, et c'est un 'senior' de, de quelle ville? Où?"*

I stumbled through Spanish cognates with my best French-sounding accent. I had never taken a day of French in my life. I had picked the subject so I wouldn't have to pretend to cluelessness, plus I figured it'd be a fun challenge.

Now I suddenly realized I had a significant amount of extra homework ahead of me, i.e., learning another language.

BURRITOS IN HELL

With a little bit of confused wandering, I found my American government class. Our teacher Ms. Schroeder, held up a videotape after the bell rang.

"This movie is about the Twenty-Fifth Amendment," she told everyone. "Watch it."

She cut the lights and popped the tape into her VCR. The movie was *Dave.*

The bell for lunch beeped just as presidential-imitator Dave danced with a giant pair of robotic arms and sang "Louie, Louie." I went to put my new stack of books in my locker.

As unreal as everything else had been, the locker was positively ethereal. It glinted in the sun, vivid neon Mirador green, number 6340. I approached it cautiously, hardly daring to think. By the laws of fate and time, I wasn't supposed to have a locker at a Southern California high school. I was supposed to hang my wet tan overcoat by the umbrella stand in a gray stone tower on Wall Street. I knew I had just dozed off at my desk, and this world would roll up and disappear as soon as I touched the too bright metal. I'd wake to cold drizzle on the windowpanes, red lights flashing on the distant bridge spans, and a half-eaten Au Bon Pain wrap next to my ballpoint pen.

I reached out cautiously, brushed the warm aluminum with my fingertips. Then I pressed my whole palm against the locker. I tossed in my books and beat a hasty retreat, should the universe still decide to evaporate.

I now felt like an official high schooler.

Ross and Thea were right about the groups. As I wandered to the food court, I watched with a thrill of sociological wonder as the thousands arranged themselves neatly around campus. I noticed skaters by the arts quad lockers, skinheads on the auditorium steps, druggies against a wall near the parking lot—wow! Devoid of teen issues myself, I fantasized that I would mingle freely among the groups, friends with all the exhibits here in this living museum, learning what made each of them tick.

The food court boasted several lunch options, none especially healthful, except for salads taken by anorexic-looking girls like Charity. Almost everybody got a pan pizza or a burrito, a Pepsi, and some Cheetos.[5]

A massive proctor behind us screamed "One line! One line!" as we queued up for burritos, doled out by a fat old Laotian woman named Crystallina with dyed pink hair.

Apparently the dye job was new. "Crystallina!" people would yell. "I love your hair!"

"Oh, stop!" she'd grin, flitting her eyelashes.

"Save me a bean and cheese," they'd call back. Or they'd cut.

I couldn't bring myself to talk up the incandescent ringlets under her mesh net, so I waited to get my burrito. "Get yo' chips," she demanded, so I snagged a bag of those as well. After wandering joyfully and sociologically among the subcultures for about two minutes, I walked straight into reality and realized I didn't have anyone to sit with.

Everybody had a group. Even the people who didn't have a group had a group, a silent trenchcoatted lineup in one grim brick passageway. I would've been the biggest loser ever to pass 'neath the palm-treed arch of Mirador Senior High School if I just sat by myself somewhere and ate . . . my lunch . . . *alone.* Everyone would stare at me and talk about me and then it would be impossible to break into the social scene. I would be That Guy Who Eats Alone. If I wanted to make the popular crowd, I'd have a horrible and probably unrecoverable start.

I knew my core competency. In my quest for cool I had one great ally: utter and total fearlessness. I was twenty-four years old, and my self-esteem did not depend on what anybody there thought of me, no matter what varsity sports he played or how many fellow students wanted to sleep with her. I could handle all situations and people with the perfect ease of knowing *it didn't really matter.*

But in this case, it didn't help. I couldn't just stride up to some random group with a big smile on my face, stick out my hand, and say, "Hi! I'm new. What are your names?" Only an alien would do that.

I saw the forty people at the senior circle, but I had a deeply tenuous connection there at best. Even finding Thea meant pushing it. I took a shot anyway, but I couldn't deal with the geography well enough to manage "behind the library." I kept ending at walls.

Already I had run out of new places to walk and had begun to circle the same sections. Oh, this lunch had become a disaster. I just needed to clear out until I had some better options in life. I was wandering around too much, passing the same faces again and again, lingering too long with my burrito, loserlike, and people would start to remember me.

I conceived a triumphant face-saving plan: I would go away and call every single person I knew and tell him or her personally that I had begun my first day of high school. Since cell phones weren't allowed on campus under pain of confiscation, and I sure as heck didn't want anybody to hear that conversation anyway, I decided I'd go back to my car and call from there. And, of course, eat my lunch in peace.

I had taken about three steps toward my distant Altima, uh, GXE when the proctor with the scar on his forehead bore down in a golf cart. "Clear the parking lot! No students in the parking lot during lunch," he yelled at me through a megaphone.

"Sorry," I mumbled, and retreated to pace with increasing desperation among the groups, burrito in tow. I circled the campus over and over again, passing the same faces, trying to pull it off like I went somewhere with this burrito and wasn't just a groupless loser wandering aimlessly, killing time until the blissful end of lunch.

I imagined every day like this one, condemned to eternally pass thousands of snickering high school faces, juggling Pepsi, burrito, and Cheetos as punishment for my sin of hubris. I'd be That Guy Who Walks Endlessly at Lunch.

I ate as I circled and pretty soon I had finished the burrito, a minor victory. I ducked into a boys' bathroom to take a break from loserdom, only to realize I had struck the Thug Black Guys Smoking and Gambling with Dice Bathroom. Since about-facing seemed more pathetic than I could bear, I spent the most awkward thirty seconds ever at a urinal as ten of them glared at me, five-dollar bills scattered across the floor. I ditched my Pepsi can by the sink in shock. Then I went back to loop the campus again for another twenty minutes until the ringing of the blessed, blessed bell.

Sartre said that hell is other people. He never spent lunch alone at Mirador High School.

I had two more classes that day. At the final electronic beep of the day, everybody around me whipped out a thousand suddenly licit cell phones. I poured with the newly wired herds to the parking lot.

We all sat sweating under the broiling sun in a miniature traffic jam as we waited to get through the gate. People stood on the backs of cars, blasted stereos, yelled, hanging out, waiting for rides.

I slumped behind the wheel like everyone else, looking spaced out. I really wanted to go somewhere far away and cold and lie down very still for a while.

HANGING CHAD

The next morning in math class, I noticed the labels first.

Almost every object in the room boasted a neat, computerized tag. Very few items had escaped—math posters were MATH POSTERS and textbooks identified themselves as TEXTBOOKS.

At the front of the room, a framed portrait of the district superintendent watched over us all like Vladimir Lenin. Only this room had a picture like that. Our teacher had made it himself on the computer and neatly labeled it OUR SUPERINTENDENT.

If the paramount leader's unblinking gaze became unsettling, and your eyes darted up to the clock to see if you could leave soon, you found the words DON'T WATCH THE CLOCK. TIME WILL PASS; WILL YOU?

You could quickly locate the party responsible for the aggressive taxonomy because he had labeled himself. PERCY M. LAMARQUE read the clean white sticker on his podium. He alone of all teachers at Mirador had a podium.

The man standing behind it had combed his gray hair neatly. Late middle aged, a medium build, with pens lining his pocket.

As my introduction to the class, he presented me with a Xeroxed grid of sixteen sigma signs, Σ, each one initialed by him. The page had a much more direct purpose than management training. Every time we spoke about something besides math, he would take our sheet, rip off a sigma sign, crumple it up, and throw it away. Nobody ever found out what happened when you ran out of sigma signs. It remained forever a great and terrible Mystery of the Unknown.

He sat me next to a junior with a shaved head, black suspenders, and combat boots. The junior wore a "Death to Preppies" T-shirt and had drawn crossed-out swastikas in magic marker all over his canvas backpack.

"You've got Chad's seat," the junior told me quietly.

"Where did Chad go?" I asked.

"Mr. Lamarque killed him," he replied. "Have you ever heard of a 'hanging Chad'? Yeah, he strung him up right here."

I laughed. He kept his voice very low. "Mr. Lamarque is a fascist."

The teacher stared into space by the door while everyone chatted. "Wow," I said. "He seems really calm."

"No. He goes crazy. He flips out."

"I totally want to see him go crazy," I said.

He shook his head firmly. "No, you don't."

The tardy bell sounded its pure electronic note. *Beeeeeeeep.*

Conversation switched off instantly as Lamarque came to life, powering on like a Disneyland animatronic. In the distance, we all saw a guy running breakneck toward our classroom. He reached ten feet away when Lamarque yanked the door shut with a bang. Nobody said a word. The guy trapped outside did not knock on the door or attempt to open it.

Lamarque stood sweating, his chest heaving, his fists clenching.

"I'm pissed off," he shouted.

Thirty-seven pairs of eyes watched him like you'd track a gerbil loose in the NORAD wiring. Mr. Lamarque was as unpredictable as a nonlinear function.

"I'm pissed off, but not at you." He whipped a trembling finger up at the beige speaker box mounted high on one cinder block wall. "I could do the announcements in two minutes, but yet they take seven minutes. They're inefficient and unorganized. The Word of the Day is useless."

Fluorescent light gleamed in his steel-framed glasses as he snaked his hand up and down in a sine wave. "They just go on and on and on like this. When I didn't teach first period, after faculty meeting I would walk or drive as far away from campus as possible so I didn't have to hear them. Then I would return once they were complete, because I find them so deeply offensive."

Mr. Lamarque swore by the binary watchwords *efficiency* and *effectiveness*. Anything that interfered with the mathematically precise and accurate execution of endless drill-and-recall tasks became his scorched-earth nemesis.

He absolutely didn't care what happened before or after Class Time, including students' blatantly copying one another's homework, but Class Time itself embraced a sacrosanct field of totalitarian control.

Because the universe has a sense of humor, Mirador had assigned him to teach first period. During first period, the school passed out surveys, held special assemblies, and blathered the reviled announcements. All of which consumed Class Time.

Beeeeeeeep. Lamarque closed his eyes in a wince and swept his arm to the speaker, palm out, a gray-haired ringmaster presenting the time-wasting circus they called another day at Mirador. Seconds passed, but the PA stayed off.

He beamed at the unexpected rain of manna. He clapped his hands together. He rubbed them with glee. He laughed. "Good! Open to page—"

Beeeeeeeep.

"*Good* morning, Mirador Senior High School!" the perky girl's voice chirped. "Please join me in the pledge of allegiance."

Next she launched into announcements.

"Are you concerned about the *budget cuts?*" she squealed through the static. "Are you wondering if we'll have APs, extracurriculars, sports, and drama for next year? Come to a special Save Our School meeting today at . . ."

Mr. Lamarque stood twitching. I realized that math with him represented the antimatter version of bio with Ms. Horn, giving the impression that if you brought the two classrooms together, the universe would explode.

"Thank you, Mirador, and have a great day!" the voice emoted. A pause before the intense guy cut in: "The Word of the Day is *gloppen*. Verb, transitive and intransitive. From the Old English *glopnen*, to be frightened of, frighten. One. To surprise or astonish. Two. To be startled or astonish. *Gloppen*."

The system clicked off to utter quiet. "I deplore the waste of Class Time," Lamarque whispered. Then his voice grew in strength. "We're behind schedule in our exploration of the logarithm. Open to exercise 17.2 on page—"

Beeeeeeeep.

The PA switched on again. "This is Stanley Popper. First-period teachers, please bring your classes to the auditorium for ASB elections."

Wham. Mr. Lamarque drove all eight hundred and ninety pages of *Algebra and Trigonometry: Structure and Method* down onto his pristine desk.

He gritted his teeth and balled his fists.

"You know," he said tightly, "Mirador High School does a lot of things which may be good but which take up Class Time. With all your reverse minimum days and rallies and assemblies and so on, you spend very little time actually in class. And from a short-term perspective, you like that, because you think, oh, you're spending less time in class, but it hides the reality that the work still needs to get done and so we have to do the next half of the chapter in three days instead of four."

A high, warbling giggle escaped his lips.

"So, come on! I have to take you, I have to lead you by the hand, because we don't treat you like responsible adults. No, you're all little babies with food dribbling down your chins. Mmmmmmm!"

He pantomimed a sloppy baby shoving food into its mouth, making a mess. Then he motioned everyone to stand with an uplifting sweep.

"Quickly, quietly, effectively, and efficiently," he cautioned. "Away we go to Mr. Popper's soup pot."

USE YOUR VOTE

The Mirador auditorium rose at the corner of central quad. It had a very new, very modern design. It sported a weird domed roof that could look like a soup pot, I guess, if you had gone a little schizo.

"Mr. Popper designed it himself like two years ago," my skinhead neighbor told me. "It cost the school exactly a million dollars. All those fascists feel so stupid now with the budget cuts. We can afford a million-dollar theater but we can't afford fucking teachers."

Our Algebra 2 period joined seventy other classes as they swarmed out of their rooms, pouring in toward the center from the five academic quads at the arms of the starfish. Orange-jacketed proctors radioed one another and performed basic crowd control, discouraging a couple of attempted escapes and dealing with the Person Who Threw the Pear.

Soon our math class sat on plush green chairs, lost among the thousands.

The lights dimmed, and a short, fat Latino senior with glasses waddled onto stage. "El Presidente!" a bunch of people screamed. "We love you, El Presidente!"

"I love you all even more deeply," he said into the mike. "I'll keep this quick. Everyone knows this place is going downhill, so this is your chance to use your vote to help make it better. Here's Derrick."

Music began to pound. He hustled out as a handsome guy with curly blond hair and a deep tan charged onto the scene. "Okay!" the blond guy said. "Let's get it started! Our school's had a really strong year so far, and we in your ASB are really proud to have been a part of it. We're not planning on going anywhere until June, but it's already time to decide who you want to see up here when you finally get rid of us."

Hey, I recognized his voice from the Word of the Day. And his face from our student handbook.

"First up, we've got our candidates for next year's spirit officer. LaTyra Wilson!"

The beat became heavy hip-hop. While the crowd yelled, eleven girls, mostly black, ran in with white tank tops and gray track pants.

They started an elaborately choreographed dance under flashing lights. The sheer professionalism of the routine stunned me. A couple of sophomores danced on the sides with huge LaTyra posters.

After a while the song ended, and the girls ran out to applause. "Sara Dunbar!" yelled Derrick.

The music changed. More yelling, more signs. Short, dark-haired Sara from the back of my bio class led in nine girls with identical white T-shirts and tight low-rider jeans. They started their own routine.

I noticed an auditorium door open in the corner of my eye, and glanced over to spot Dr. Chao enter with a group. Yikes. She had never seen me without a suit. I felt like such a kid, felt naked and guilty somehow. I turned back to the stage, one head among thousands.

Sara did a cheer-based routine, a series of complicated group stunts with the other girls. The lights flashed as the girls moved faster, got more complex.

People yelled. A dance-off had emerged between her and LaTyra, who stood on the side of the stage watching with folded arms and legs planted apart.

Sara's team formed a pyramid. Two bases hauled her up onto their hands and tossed her into the air. She sailed up and swung out her arms, eyes on the audience and a big smile on her face.

Then she dropped back, and we watched her plunge right through the arms of the horrified spotter and thump onto the floor. She didn't move.

None of the other girls noticed, and they kept dancing to the pounding music with bright grins, even though the star of their performance lay crumpled in a heap on the ground behind them.

LaTyra looked down at her erstwhile opponent. Derrick stood confused with the mike. Murmurs swept the crowds.

After about fifteen seconds, a man with a red face and a mustache left Dr. Chao's group and stomped up the steps to the stage. He waved his hand and the music stopped.

"Mr. Pooper is a fascist," my neighbor explained.

Apparently Sara had twisted her neck and knocked herself unconscious. We all talked for about five minutes as a proctor arrived with the school nurse.

"Oh, that sucks," people around me were saying. "That's so embarrassing."

"One of the cheerleaders broke her nose doing a stunt in the fall," said my neighbor.

Mr. Popper took the mike out of Derrick's hand and began to make loud shushing noises at all two thousand of us. "I hope you know about The Look. If I give you The Look once, you can figure out what that means. If I have to give you The Look two times, you will be removed by someone or I will remove you." He glared down into the audience at particularly noisy individuals and shook his finger.

Then he and the girls had a quiet conversation on the stage.

We heard an ambulance siren five minutes later. EMTs came out onto the stage with a stretcher, loaded Sara up, and trooped her prostrate body down the aisle on a stretcher. The audience began to applaud and whistle.

"I have just been informed," Mr. Popper said into the mike, "that Sara will be celebrating her birthday in several days. So I think it would be very appropriate for us all to sing 'Happy Birthday' to show her we're thinking about her."

He started off in a flat baritone, and we all joined in. "Happy birthday to you!" we sang to Sara's horizontal form as the EMTs bore her bouncing stretcher down the center of the rows. "Happy birthday, dear Sara . . ."

The skinhead began to chuckle. "Happy birthday," he snorted. "You've knocked yourself unconscious."

The door slammed behind Sara, and Popper gave the mike back to Derrick and marched offstage.

The music started again. "Okay!" said Derrick, attempting to rebuild momentum. "Let's, uh, hope Sara's all right, okay?"

We worked our way through several more candidates and offices. "All right!" said Derrick. "We're moving right along to the vice-presidents. Our first candidate is Travis Newton!" Nothing happened. He gave an exaggerated shrug, looked around. "Where's Travis? Travis?"

The remaining lights cut out. The huge screen behind the stage lit up. Derrick pretended to stagger back in shock. Giant numbers counted down on the screen: 3. . . 2. . . 1 . . .

Here came the roaring soundtrack as an alarm clock beeped on screen. Someone sat up in bed wearing an Armani baseball cap, an Energie T-shirt, and mirrored aviator sunglasses. "It's election day!" the figure said in a faux-deep voice.

It was a tall girl pretending to be a guy, with long blond hair stuffed back under her hat. She ran to the bedroom next door and pounded on the wall. "Drive me to school, Lexi, it's election day," she cried. Then she raced downstairs, where a dad greeted her with breakfast: "Good morning, Travis." She tore past his protests, explaining that it was election day.

We followed her as she jumped into the passenger side of a white Camry. She hopped out in the Mirador parking lot, ran across central quad, leapt a fence next to the auditorium, hurried through the backstage area, and then—

The lights came up. She burst onto the stage to laughter and cheers.

"Hey," she said. "I'm Travis Newton and I'd make a really great vice-president. Well, actually, I'm away for a week kicking a lot of people's sorry behinds in a ninja tournament, so I sent my really cool older sister

Alexis in my place. She's so wonderful, she's the greatest, she's just the best big sister anyone could have." A lot of people laughed.

"Thank you, uh, Travis," said Derrick.

I glanced over at Mr. Lamarque, standing against the wall by our row. He had his hands clasped tightly behind his back and he rocked on his heels like a ticking detonator.

The other vice-presidential and presidential speeches played with different variations on the theme of "vote for me because I alone will save the school from ruin." One presidential candidate spoke with a slight lisp. "That guy's such a faggot," people said to one another. "You're going to hell!" they called, very softly.

THE MIRADOR REICH

When you start out at the absolute bottom of a social structure, you can go nowhere but up.

Thea turned to me in bio class, blond streak brilliant across her dyed black hair. "Wait, who did you sit with at lunch yesterday?" she asked.

"Uh, nobody," I said. "I was like a pathetic loser."

"Oh, that's so sad," she said. "Come sit with me and my friends today."

The hour arrived. I got my burrito and turned to leave, when Crystallina the lunch lady grabbed my shirt and pointed a commanding pink nail at the pile of Cheetos bags. "Get yo' *chips.*" I obeyed her diktat.

Election posters covered central quad. One lucky candidate for ASB secretary had the name Aligra, so she borrowed the "a liger is pretty much my favorite animal" line from the cult classic movie *Napoleon Dynamite* and worked the "Aligra—Pretty Much My Favorite Candidate!" theme about as far as any campaign on any level could possibly take a catchphrase.

"Hey." I turned. Thea waited for me, small and a little out-of-place in the milling crowds. "Come on. We're over here."

On the stage by the administration building, some screamo band called Same Distance Reduced launched into a new set. Smashing drums tore through curtains of distortion. I soon learned that Mirador lunch period often featured a band or a DJ.[6]

Thea stole a look at the stage, where a skinny guy with shaggy black ʼr falling over his right eye slammed on lead guitar and howled into mike. She started breathing fast. "See the guy singing? He's my year.

His name is Wil and he's so hot, like everybody should recognize how hot he is."

I followed her along a route I never would have thought to take, across a grassy lawn speckled with more groups at the front of campus.

"Oh, shit!" some guy screamed. A small pack of freshmen playing Yu-Gi-Oh! scattered on the lawn as a tiny carton whizzed down out of the heavens and exploded, showering them and their deck of monster cards in orange juice and bits of pulp.[7]

"This place is *so* high school," said Thea.

Finally we got to a set of steps by the side of a loading dock. About eight people sat hunched around, a mixed group of plump girls in black gauzy clothes and guys with acne, torn jeans, and Converse shoes.

Thea introduced me around. One girl, Evelyn, wore a blue-and-purple striped scarf and had a butterfly bow in her puff of red hair. The combination produced a hypnotically bizarre effect.

"We call her Yeti because she's so tall and big," said Thea.

"I think you're in my French class," said Yeti/Evelyn. She drank a frothy liquid out of a resealable plastic cup.

"What is that?" I asked.

"It's raw goat's milk," said Evelyn. "It's nature's most digestible food. My family and I only drink raw goat's milk and we only eat yeastless bread. My mother makes it for us specially." She held up a baggie of tan lumps. "It's so much better for you, without all those things that can cause cancer, and all the processing that gets rid of the nutrients."

"Oh," I said.

Another person I saw was the skinhead guy from my math class. He gave me a firm nod of prior acknowledgment.

Everyone seemed reconciled to a new body on the steps. "Talk to people," said Thea, and with that, she left me to fend for myself.

I looked down at the election form we had all been given. "I have no idea who to vote for."

"Just vote for your friends," said Evelyn. "It's what everybody else does."

"I don't have any friends," I said.

They laughed.

"I'm not friends with any of those people either, but I'm voting for Aligra because I like her posters," said one girl.

"You can't vote for people based on a platform of poster creativity," Evelyn snapped.

The girl defended herself. "No, I know it's really lame, and I don't even like *Napoleon Dynamite,* but I've got to vote based on something, right? Otherwise they're like interchangeable. All the ASB people get up there and they're like, 'I'm soooo bouncy, and gosh, I'm not going to do a damn thing to fix this school! Hey, watch me dance!'"

"It's not their fault," said a guy with a spike in his lip. "Some of them try, but they have like absolutely no power. They're just the administration's bitch."

"The administration's fascists," said the skinhead guy. He had a button on his canvas backpack that said NAZIS with a red line through it.

"I feel so bad you had to come to Emerald Valley," said a girl in black.

"It's funny, like everyone keeps saying that," I said.

"It's like this bubble," she said.

Evelyn nodded. "That's what we call it, 'the Emerald Bubble.' It's such a bubble. It's a fake town. They like sweep all the problems away under the carpet and they pretend everything is perfect. It's like Pleasantville."

"Oh, God, yeah," said Thea. "They hide everything bad. They seal away Santa Ana so we don't have anything to do with them, and they almost seal away Fullerton, and everything has to be perfect." She folded her hands primly.

"The school is so scared of looking bad," said the skinhead. "How about the pregnant girl?"

People nodded.

"What happened?" I asked.

"There was like this pregnant senior they kicked out in fall so the school wouldn't look bad."

"There had to have been something else, too, right?" I said.

Heads shook.

"Did you know fast food is illegal here?" Evelyn asked me.

"You've gotta be shitting me," I said.

"No, seriously," said Evelyn. "The city council made like all fast-food places illegal within the town. Look around, you'll see there's absolutely no fast food in Emerald Valley itself."

Thea laughed. "That's why there're all these fast-food places, like KFC and Wendy's, all lined up as soon as you cross the city line. It's like this strip of sin waiting right outside."

"This town is definitely not for kids," said the skinhead. "It's full of old people and they like hate us so much. They're always complaining about us driving too fast on Orchard and they want to raise the driving age to *eighteen*."

I did my best to look as pained as everyone else.

"The Bubble," proclaimed Evelyn triumphantly.

The guy with the spiky lip shook his head. "Everyone just gets messed up all the time. The parents and teachers have no idea what's going on. It's really sad. They like don't want to know."

A more melodic song drifted around the side of the library as the band played some Taking Back Sunday material.

Thea peeked off the edge of the loading dock and then ran back. "Uhh, Wil Kormer is so *hot*!" She preempted the answer. "I know, I sound so preppy and I'm going to stab myself."

"They play all the time now that Rob Doveman isn't DJ'ing," said Evelyn.

Thea looked at the concrete steps. "It's too bad that had to happen. He seemed like such a happy person, you know? Like you couldn't help smiling when you saw him, you know? Nobody else around here is like that at all."

"What happened?" I asked.

Evelyn buried her chin in her scarf. "That was last semester's tragedy." Then she snorted. "That and Sadie's."

Conversations splintered off. Thea, the skinhead, and I found ourselves together.

The skinhead looked down at my Independent skate T, a popular brand. "If you're so independent," he accused me, "why are you wearing the same shirt as everyone else? Are you a fascist?"

Thea tried to save me, but no sooner could she open her mouth than I heard a loud voice behind me: "Did he just call you a fascist? Welcome to my world."

I turned to see a big blond guy wearing cowboy boots and wraparound sunglasses with iridescent lenses.

"You!" bellowed the skinhead, pointing a wrathful finger, totally lost for words. "Fascist!" he managed.

The skinhead called everyone a fascist, but it turned out that the guy in cowboy boots really was a fascist. It almost made for a refreshing surprise. I guess even a broken clock, and all that.

All conversations stopped to watch the encounter.

"You," repeated the skinhead, "you're so racist, you believe the South will rise again. Are you wearing it?"

The blond guy smirked and looked down at his belt buckle. It featured a Confederate flag crossed with a German flag. "You know I'm going to be wearing it," he said.

"You believe the South will rise again, don't you?" pressed the skinhead.

"Yeah," said the blond guy, "it would if it wasn't for all the black people. They were doing great until all the minorities started getting elected, ever since they started running everything, the South is for shit. It's like the same thing here with Mirador. The problem is all the minorities. The school used to be so good until like ten years ago when they started bringing them in from Santa Ana.

"This place is so political. We've got a Chinese principal and a black police chief. They're in charge of all the schools. That's why the standards are for shit."

"You're such white trash," said Evelyn.

"I'm not white trash," he said, "I'm a redneck. There's a difference. Anyway, he should appreciate what I'm saying. He's a skinhead."

"I'm a *skin*," emphasized the other guy. "It's not about being racist. That's not what the movement is about."

"White people need to stick together," said the redneck.

"Fuck that racist shit," said the skin.

"Don't talk to me like that," said the redneck. "I'm gonna shoot you."

"I have a whole nation behind me, my whole skin nation. If you take me out, ten others will stand up to take my place."

"Fuck your skin nation," said the redneck. "I'm in the Assembly of Christ—that's a white, Christian organization."

"What?" said the skin. "The Kristian Kids' Klub? Our nation is going to destroy you."

The redneck laughed and saw the French book in my backpack. "Who's taking French?" he demanded. "French is for pussies."

Before I could figure out what to do about this interesting event, Thea interjected. She didn't know it was my book. "French is so sexy," she said. "It's the second hottest thing next to bondage."

Evelyn turned to her and recited a long phrase in French. Gosh, maybe she could help me with my homework.

Thea moaned. "Stop it," she said, "you're turning me on. Oh, my God, imagine Johnny Depp speaking French." She shivered.

"You just had a mini-orgasm there," Evelyn said.

"Raahhh . . . ," said Thea, "I'm just gonna like slide off the steps."

The redneck seemed sad he had lost the focus of attention. "French is for pussies," he repeated.

"What," said Thea, "we should be taking German?"

"I heard about your drunk ass getting kicked out of German class freshman year," added Evelyn. "You were like sitting cross-legged on the floor in the front."

"Yeah, but that teacher got fired," said the redneck. "Ha. No, the Germans are pussies now, too. I like old-school Germany, the Kaiser and Hitler."

"You like Hitler?" the spiky-lip guy asked him.

"Yeah," said the redneck. "He was a good German."

"He killed six million Jews," said Evelyn.

"So?"

"So you can't just go around killing people for no reason," Evelyn said.

"He was cleansing the Aryan race," said the redneck.

"I guess that makes sense if you're a *Nazi*," said the skin.

The redneck smiled and wandered away.

"Wow," said Thea, after a while. "Everyone's so intense. I don't care about any of that political stuff."

"Me neither," said the fat girl in black. They high-fived. "My world is music, music is my everything. I like metal like HIM, indie stuff like Death Cab, a lot of bands."

"I don't believe in any of it," said Thea, "because I know the government lies all the time and like basically everything they tell us is a lie. I wish I could vote this year to get rid of the Republicans, but I can't, and it's really annoying. But I don't really pay too much attention to politics."

I ate some of my burrito while I tried to process. After a while I picked a question that made my brain scream less.

I turned to the skin. "I'm kinda confused," I said. "What exactly do you believe, like politically?"

"I believe in the workers," said the skin. "America's so stupid because it oppresses the workers. I'm straightedge. I'm a communist. Like the poor get a free ride, the rich pay only a little bit of taxes, and the middle class gets screwed. It's so much better in other countries where the workers are in charge. That's the system that they have in England, Parliament."

The spiky-lip guy turned to him. "Do you like Parliament?"

"Yeah," he said, "I believe in Parliament."

Beeeeeeeep.

Oh my, look at the time. Lunch had ended.

THE WEIRD GIRL

After last bell, I ran into Thea in the parking lot. She waited on the curb with her brother for their ride. He had short dark hair and wore head-phones and nodded along to the music, mouth open and face expressionless.

"What's your name?" I asked him.

He didn't respond. "He gets into his music," said Thea. "His name's Aram. He's your year."

"Hi, Aram," I said.

"Hey," Thea said. "We totally have to hang out. Let me give you my phone number." So we exchanged them.

I got in my car and evasive-maneuvered my way back to the freeway. When I arrived home, I borrowed a friend's SUV and worked until midnight ferrying an apartment's worth of items down to my new home.

The next day at lunch, I found Thea waiting for me in central quad. "Come on," she said, and we began to head toward the lawn.

"I made this T-shirt myself," she told me. It featured a very well-drawn picture of a hand squeezing out a bloody sponge. Lettering underneath read I'M ANTI-SPONGEBOB.

I laughed. "Nice."

"SpongeBob just really, really annoys me," she explained.

"Yo, Jeremy!" I heard behind my back. I turned to see Vic Reyes standing in the middle of the concrete space.

He beckoned to me. "Come over here."

"Hang on a sec," I told Thea.

I walked over to him. "Who are you sitting with?" he asked me.

"Uh, some people I met," I said.

"Are you sitting with the weird girl from bio?" He nodded to Thea.

"Sort of," I said.

He turned around and started to head back to the circle. "Don't sit with them," he said. "Come sit with us, fool."

"Uh," I said.

"I'll like introduce you to people."

"Okay," I said.

"I own this school," he explained to me.

I waved apologetically to Thea's thin form as I followed him and quickly lost sight of her tiny face in the crowds. I mean, I needed a mainstream experience, right?

I know, I felt horrible.

ALL BEST FRIENDS

And so I arrived at the senior circle. Vic walked me around the circumference of the concrete ring and I met everybody, a shower of new names that it took me weeks to get straight.

First he pointed to a group of about four girls. "These are sluts," he said.

The girls burst into laughter. "We're not really sluts," explained Padma, a tall Indian girl with a silver flower ring in her nose.

One blond girl wore camo pants, a Swiss-cross tank top, and amber sunglasses. She looked like she had stepped straight out of the MTV Beach House. I recognized her from the election assembly, when she had pretended to be her brother.

"What's crack-a-lackin'?" she said. "You're in my French class." Her name was Alexis. She ate a sticklike rainbow ice pop, licking up the drips as it melted slowly under the brilliant sun.

"Deep throat it!" laughed a guy in a Mirador baseball jersey and cap. His jersey said OLVERA on the back.

Alexis did, and everyone laughed. "She's not eating the chocolate one today," the baseball guy said. "She usually likes the black one."

"Maybe it's suggestive like unconsciously," laughed Padma.

"Stay over here," said Alexis. "This is the cool side of the senior circle. The other side has all the drama."

"We're all best friends over here," said Padma.

She and Alexis and an energetic girl named Kaylee all hugged. "We're still best friends even though we've hooked up with like five of the same people," said Alexis.

"Is it five?" asked Kaylee. They thought, counting out names on their fingers. They ended triumphantly on number five, "Brian." They said it softly and nodded to baseball-guy Olvera, who was talking to some other baseball people. They grimaced and all started to laugh.

"You came here at such a bad time," said Alexis. "This whole place has been crazy messed-up ever since Dove."

"Who's Dove?" I asked.

"Oh, my God," she said. "Rob Doveman. He was so nice. He always made everyone laugh. He was like my best friend, like you know how close I am with Padma and Kaylee? Like me and Dove were even closer."

"He was such a special person," said Padma. "He was like so unique. He was always smiling, and he could always tell if you were depressed or whatever, and he would try to cheer you up."

"He had no enemies at all," said Kaylee. "He was friends with every-body."

"It's so true," said Vic. "If like nothing had happened, he absolutely would've been the one who won Student Choice Award instead of that fool."

They all turned to look at blond, tan Derrick from the election as-sembly. He sat in the distance, behind a little table in center quad with some sort of sign on it.

"Yeah, it was like such a sad time. But it was really hard on"—Alexis nodded to a big guy in a jersey with the name REISLING on the back—"him."

Vic introduced us. We did the high school handclasp. Cody Reisling looked at me with pale blue eyes.

"Bro," he said, "you should've come here four years ago." He surveyed the people crossing central quad. "This place has fucking degenerated so much since freshman year."

"Really?" I said.

"Yeah," said Cody, "we used to go party every weekend and they'd have a keg and like seven guys."

"Yeah, just guys, fool," Brian interjected with a laugh.

"No, fuck you," said Cody, "they all had girlfriends, and all the senior girls had boyfriends." He pointed around the circle. "They weren't like these girls. These girls are sluts. They'd spread their legs for anyone." He glared at a small pack of freshmen hurrying past. "All the underclassmen are just fucking pathetic, and we've got proctors and drug dogs and a 'campus resource officer.' The administration's cracked down so hard, they're making this place like a prison. Fuck them. Give me that."

Brian passed him a plastic Aquafina water bottle. Cody looked around.

The pentagon of central quad was elevated above the other five quads, with steps descending from its plateau. From the senior circle you could see down across campus to all the distant regions where different groups hung out. And aim.

Cody hauled back and whipped the bottle far into the sky. I watched it vanish, astounded. I had never seen anyone throw something that far and high before in my life. It dropped among people clustered in a quad, scattering their tiny shapes.

He looked back at us as though he had accomplished a solemn and needful duty. Then his eyes fell to the empty box from my pan pizza.

"Why are you just walking around with an empty box?" he asked me.

"The garbage can's right over there," said Brian, pointing to it.

"Yeah, I guess I was like too lazy to go," I said.

Cody took the box from my hands. "Let me show you what we do with these," he said, and tossed it onto the ground. "Fuck this place."

Thea's special ed brother came wandering over with his headphones on and a plastic garbage bag. "Hello," he said to Cody.

"Go away, Aram," said Cody.

"Is that garbage?" he asked, pointing to my pizza box.

"Yeah," said Cody. "Go get it."

Aram picked up the box and put it into his bag. Next he walked over to Alexis, who had her back to him. He poked her shoulder, and she turned around and screamed.

"Do you have garbage?" Aram asked. Someone dropped a cardboard box in his bag.

"Don't touch people," said Brian. "Go away!"

Aram wandered off to the other side of the circle. "Fucking 'tard," Brian called after him.

"Special ed people pick up trash?" I asked Vic.

"Yeah," he said. "It's like a big scandal."

Next he introduced me again to my tour guide from a few days before. Ross nodded and we shook hands, again.

He sat with a few other people, ASB people, I later learned. "So how are you liking Mirador?" he asked me.

"People are really nice," I said.

"Yeah," he said. "It's a cool place."

He opened up the box for his pan pizza, lowered his head and folded his hands for a silent five-second prayer of grace. Then he looked back up at me. "We're in the top twenty percent of all schools in America, according to *Newsweek*," he said. His cell phone beeped, and he pulled it out of his pocket.

"Wow," I said.

Aram came over and hovered, looking at Ross's cell phone. "What's on that?" he asked.

Ross whisked it back. "Go *away*, Aram!" he said. "Uhhnn. You're so annoying."

"Why don't you go somewhere else?" another guy asked Aram. He and Ross turned to each other and started talking.

"Do you have garbage?" Aram asked them.

"No," Ross said. "Go away."

They interrupted their conversation briefly for the other guy to nod grace over his burrito.

Vic finished introducing me to most of the forty people in the circle. Finally, he took me out to the little table in the middle of the quad.

The sign taped to the side read CLUB OLYMPICS. Vic started to present me to ASB public officer Derrick, whose name even I already knew.

"One sec," Derrick said. He dealt with a few people lined up in front of his table.

The first was the skinny musician with black hair falling over his right eye. He wore a T-shirt that said ANTI-SOCIAL CLUB, with the "A" formed out of a hammer and sickle. "Wil Kormer," he said. He pulled the shirt fabric. "I'm a proud member of the Anti-Social Club."

"Okay," said Derrick, noting the name and club on a piece of paper. "You have to create your ultimate In-N-Out burger, like mentally, and then describe it to me, and I'll award you between one and five points."[8]

Wil thought. "Okay. It's got like no burger inside, but instead has like forty Jujubes. Those things are sick. And then it's got like Sour Patch Kids in it, too. And it's the size of my head."[9]

Derrick's brow furrowed. "Okay, um, three points."

Next in line stood a red-haired figure resplendent in a brightly striped scarf and sweatpants. "Evelyn Strout," she said. "Mirador *Mirror*. My ultimate In-N-Out burger is purple and orange, and it has five ostrich patties inside and raspberry sauce and a dozen fried eggs on top."

Derrick concentrated. "Uh, okay, that's three points for the *Mirror*."

Evelyn noticed me standing next to Vic and Derrick and gave me a very strange look, almost a glare. She seemed about to say something, and then she walked away.

"What's your name?" Derrick asked me.

"Jeremy," I said. "You're Derrick, right?"

"How did you know?" he asked.

"Everyone knows you," I said. "You're famous."

And that was the length of my audience. Derrick had to go back to work. "Club reps!" he called through cupped hands. "Club Olympics!"

As lunch ended, I ran into my counselor, Mr. Markowitz, outside the administration office.

"It looks like you've made some friends!" he said happily. "I talked to my nephew who went to your old school, and he said he'd definitely heard your name!"

Classic.

And thus I met the "popular crowd." Despite the sense of monolithic unity their circle gave the rest of campus, I learned very quickly that many of them didn't even like one another all that much. The circle consisted of a bunch of little cliques that interacted to varying degrees, everyone with a preferred spot along the continuum of the concrete ring. They formed a complete and cyclic spectrum, starting at the Christian ASB people, fading through the gossipy girls, to the party people, to the slutty girls, to the So Cali bros, to the athletes who drank and fought, to the athletes who didn't, who in turn faded back into ASB.[10]

Everybody fell under the umbrella of "popular" as far as the wider school was concerned, even though they might barely speak to one another. They just had more in common with the rest of the circle people than with any of the other campus groups.

It probably wasn't surprising, too, that despite their so-called popularity, a broad range of people across the campus didn't like them at all.

The next morning in bio, Ms. Horn assigned us all worksheet groups based on our seats. Mine contained Thea and a couple of other people—a quiet little Korean guy who read car magazines nonstop, and a girl with a tie-dyed shirt and hairy arms.

"Where are you hanging out at lunch today?" Thea asked me. "Are you sitting at the circle again, or are you coming behind the library?"

"Uh, I don't know," I said.

"Jeremy!" I turned to see Vic beckoning to me.

Ms. Horn experimented with new desktop backgrounds on her computer, and everybody talked, so I got up and went to the back.

"Oh, God," said Charity, lip curled, "don't stay up there. Come sit back here with us."

Sara nodded as well as she could with her neck brace on. "Seriously."

Ms. Horn clicked happily away. "Uh, okay," I said. I took an empty seat.

"It sucks you can't be in our group," said Vic. "Those people are gay."

And so life continued for about a week, until it suddenly looked like the whole world had fallen apart and I would have to put on a charcoal gray suit and report to a Manhattan office tower under cold rain.

SURE DO LOVE HEROIN

We all sat around the senior circle at lunch and talked as usual. Most people had stopped by the office to pick up portrait shots from a dance the previous semester.

"Oh, my God, I look so ugly in this picture!" Alexis wailed. She ate a rainbow ice pop and waved her photo. "My arm looks so fat. It's like bigger than my head."

Padma wrestled the picture from her hand. "Oh, shut *up*, you look so skinny. Look at my face in this one! The photographer like hates me so much. It looks like I'm pissed off and I've got a big hickey."

"Whose picture don't I have yet?" Kaylee called.

"Mine," said Alexis. "And let me get yours."

"Do you have this group one?"

Every couple had purchased two big photos of themselves together, and a stack of wallet-sized miniatures. The goal was to collect one small photo of each couple.

"Where's your picture, bro?" Brian asked Cody.

Cody held up a large black folder. "It's fucking ridiculous. Look at this thing. It's huge! It's fucking embarrassing. What am I supposed to do with it, like tuck it under my arm?" He stuffed the folder under his elbow. "Alexis always orders these huge fucking pictures. It's like life-sized."

"What dance was it?" I asked.

Vic laughed. "The administration's worst nightmare."

"Sadie Hawkins," said Padma. "Oh, my God, it was craaaaazy."

Over the course of the first week, I had settled happily into my new high school life. As social psychology teaches us, human beings adapt quickly and thoroughly to just about anything. In Dr. Philip Zimbardo's famous prison experiment in the basement of our Stanford psych building, it took only five days for a group of average college students and professors to truly believe themselves guards, inmates, and wardens when placed into a jail-like environment.[11] I'd had just about the same amount of time, and a backpack and a bell schedule had already become completely normal to me.

If you are fifty-six, and you have worked in a corporate office for the past thirty years—well, those factors simply make no difference. Assuming you could pass appearancewise, if you entered a high school right now in the role of a student, within a month I guarantee you would be acting like a current-day seventeen-year-old. Not yourself at seventeen, but how someone in your role acts at whatever school you ended up attending. None of your clients would matter. Prom would. That's the power of the situation.[12]

So "seventeen" had become my dominant frame of mind when, here at the senior circle, Shawn Ackerman realized he didn't have any cash in his wallet and couldn't buy his pizza for lunch.

"Can anyone lend me money?" he called out to the circle. "I can repay them in drugs and alcohol."

"Really?" I asked.

"Yeah," he said. "My parents run a bed and breakfast, and check this out." He flipped open his camera phone and showed us a few snapshots of cases and cases of beer bottles piled up against a basement wall.

"Whoa," I said. "That's crazy."

"We have so much of this stuff, and it's so easy to get some, it's like all just downstairs. That's just for a wedding this weekend, and they never use it all. Think about all the kids and the women who don't drink, plus you've got all the designated drivers. They always order way too much, and they won't notice anything's missing."

"And the old people don't drink much either," I said.

"No," said Alexis. "Oh, my God, the old people drink a lot. My grandma's a total alcoholic, and she always sends us kids to go get more wine so people don't know it's her. She goes around in a circle and goes through each one of us. She like starts with me, and then she goes to my brother and all my cousins. Then she like goes and takes sleeping pills."

"Wow," I said. "I totally can't imagine your family."

Alexis laughed. "Yeah," she said.

The next day, Saturday, I rode with a few other people in the back of Brian Olvera's Explorer XLT Sport. We headed to get fast-food burgers at Carl's Jr. for lunch.[13]

En route, we picked up a few sophomore girls I didn't know. That night they were going to a party where everyone was going to be on Ecstasy. They needed to meet an older guy at Carl's Jr. to buy their own Ecstasy supply for this party.

One girl turned to me. "I just want to tell you," she said, "there were like these four people talking about drugs, and they heard you might be a narc."

"Me?" I said.

"Yeah," she said. She rolled her eyes. "It's just stupid shit, I'm sure it'll go away."

But it didn't. The next week, a slow transformation came over the circle. People who started out friendly and open suddenly started to act guarded. They suddenly ceased discussing drugs and alcohol around me, and since those two topics formed a good half of every conversation anybody ever had, talk became stilted. When it came time to plan weekends, people walked away and huddled up elsewhere.

In math class, the skin lowered his head, a little accusingly. "I heard a rumor."

"What?" I asked, knowing darn well what it was.

He laughed a little nervously, but didn't say anything.

Oh, God.

When I picked up my burrito from Crystallina, the wall of druggies by the parking lot tracked me as one unit, a dozen eyes fixed on my movements as I passed.

Ms. Horn smiled happily at me when I came into bio class the next day. "I think you should know what the word is," she said. "Like six kids asked me this morning, 'What's the deal with the new kid? He came here at such a weird time after Sadie's. Is he a narc?'"

"Yeah," I sighed. "I know."

"Hee, hee," she laughed. "Like *21 Jump Street!*"

"Yeah," I said.

"You're so not," said my teacher. "I mean, you're just so goofy, and—no offense—you've got oily teenage skin, and you just can't fake that."

"Thanks," I said.

Lunchtime felt very cold and quiet. I heard someone say, "He's right behind you," and turned to see a guilty-looking group.

During passing period, a few people yelled "I love weed" and "I love heroin." On my way to the parking lot, several guys saw me coming and had a loud impromptu conversation based on the theme, "I like to smoke weed!"

That night I talked to an IT consultant friend on the phone. He laughed at my predicament. "Hah," he said. "That sucks. A friend of mine transferred high school senior year, and everybody at his new school thought he was a narc."

"What did he do about it?" I asked.

"Nothing," my buddy said. "He just ended up with no friends. Hah, that sucks so bad for you. Hah."

The next morning, someone walking past me on the path said "narc" under his breath, and I started to lose it. After all this work, an unexpected nightmare had descended out of a clear sky to ruin my life.

As I headed to the library, one guy in a group of three loudly proclaimed, "I sure do love heroin!"

I turned and spotted him. "Heroin is the best, fool!" I said.

He seemed a little taken aback that I had responded. "I'm glad you agree with me," he said.

"Hells yeah!" I said, and did the devil-horns sign with my hand and let my tongue hang out.

"He's so *not*," I heard one guy saying behind me as I walked away.

"Yes, he *is*," insisted the other.

"No, he's not!" I called out.

In bio, Thea loved it and made loud narc jokes. "It takes away your social value." She laughed. "So Alexis Newton and all those people think it?"

"Yup," I said. "I think so."

"You're gonna have to work your way back up again by hanging out with the sophomores and stuff," she said.

A few people passed and heard her narc jokes.

"Wait, he's the narc?" one of them asked.

"No, I'm joking," she said, but they left warily.

"Sorry," she told me.

At the senior circle during lunch, I heard Kaylee tell another girl, "Don't talk to the narc." Vic Reyes avoided me altogether.

Toward the end of the period, I felt a tug at my shirt, and turned to see Aram holding his garbage bag. He pointed at me. "You're an aard-vark," he said proudly.

I looked around and saw Brian Olvera laughing with some other guys. I sighed. "'Narc,'" I told Aram. "The word you're looking for is 'narc.'"

PICKING UP THE PIECES

What had laid the groundwork for mass narc paranoia?

What trauma had struck these people, back when the only face of theirs I knew was a computer screen displaying one statistical profile among twenty-five thousand?[14]

What action had gone down at the Sadie Hawkins dance?

Who was Dove?

Research, research, research. It's the ultimate Track fallback, ingrained to the point right before the heart. You can try to win by charm, clever-ness, courage, or sex appeal, but when the situation goes critical, all Trackstars know you just put your head down and attempt to outwork the universe.

I hunted down old copies of the *Mirror* and the local papers. I talked to people who didn't know one another and cross-checked details. I ex-amined chiaroscuro photos of light and darkness and leafed through es-says on classroom walls that struggled to weld meaning from chaos. I even saw my schoolmates' exact thoughts in their online journals.

I swallowed hard as the two months prior to my arrival unfolded be-fore me.

COLLISION

With your baby's breath, breathe symphonies
Come on, sweet catastrophe.

—Something Corporate,
"Hurricane"

Two Months Earlier

A SON OF THE RIGHTEOUS

The sun blazed in the glory of noon, somewhere beyond a sky of solid clouds that locked Southern California under a smoky gem of horizon-to-horizon gray. The concrete walls of the Calvary African Methodist Episcopal Church lay in a dim and sullen glow, pale light too weak to reveal the colors on the abstract stained-glass mosaics.

A train rumbled past in the cool winter wind, heading westward. It rode the light rail tracks that bisected the City of Emerald Valley like a ruler-straight line drawn by a phantom demographer. Here on the north side of the tracks, Calvary AME rose among low apartment blocks. A distant cry from the orderly ranch homes of the south, and unimaginably removed from the cavernous McMansions that sprang up as the town faded downward into Villa Park. Up here the faces were darker, the accents thicker, the per capita lower.

People from all parts of Emerald Valley had come to fill the walls of Cavalry AME, over seven hundred bodies packed into a space much too small for them. They crammed the pews and stood pressed in dense crowds at the back.

At the lectern, the pastor cried, and droplets fell into his white beard. "The Holy and Almighty One, who is blessed forever, mourns today, because a son of the righteous has departed from this life before his father and mother. . . ."

His voice shook through his tears, and he didn't cry alone. Soft sobbing echoed hollowly on the concrete walls and mixed with the muted whispers of young voices in the clammy air. "I can't believe this is really happening," an empty and dull statement of fact, met the hanging strains of a muffled "Oh, my God, this is a nightmare" that rose into the softer edge of hysteria. The hoarsest voice choked a desperately simple "Why?" answered only by fresh weeping.

Cody Reisling sat in the front pew, his light brown crew cut conspicuous in a row of much darker hues. He was locked between the ocean of tears behind him and the steady gaze of his best friend, Robert Doveman. Dove watched him now from a frame on the altar, half-smiling in his tux on the gauzy royal blue background of his senior photo.

Someone else took the podium, one of Dove's uncles talking about his nephew's love for baseball and getting into mischief. "Lord, did he love those Giants," the uncle said. "He did, I swear his blood ran orange for that team."

Cody's eyes flicked down to the black-and-orange armbands that he and everybody else were wearing. Of course Dove loved the Giants. His family had moved down from Santa Clara years before. But his first love was another team, a smaller team, the Mirador Senior High School Marlins, where he played right field with more enthusiasm than raw talent. The rest of the guys sat a couple of rows back, probably imagining how the upcoming season opener would go down without number seventeen.

"It was just a horrible accident," Dove's uncle said, shaking his head. "He had so much resiliency, so much life, so much love for music. He never cared about what anyone else thought of him."

Cody caught the Dovemans out of the corner of his eye, but he didn't want to turn and see anyone else.

The uncle sat, and a thin woman in her twenties approached the lectern timidly, Dove's manager at Pizza Roma. She had written a eulogy, and stopped reading a few times to blow her nose softly. "If I had a little brother, Rob, I'd wish he were exactly like you, so obstinate and so magnificent. I'm so blessed to have known you."

Dove gazed down at Cody from his picture frame, his half-joking smile oblivious to the tears. Last week they'd put together their yearbook pages, mixing those photos with quotes from Dr. Dre and cryptic shout-outs to friends. To the crew they'd started at the beginning of junior year like a lot of other guys did, PGD. Playas Goin' Drinking. Dove, Cody, a couple other guys. That was who they were. That was what they stood for. The dog tags clinked against his chest. Bros for life.

Cody shifted, the jacket and tie tight and tense around his hulking body. The Dovemans all watched him. The pastor smiled gently.

Cody swallowed and stood.

The community took a collective breath. The friendship between Dove and Cody was legendary, mythologized. Black boy, white boy, joined in love of sports, music, girls, fun. It looked so good, made everyone feel so good about themselves. Their gazes searched over Cody and his pale eyes burned. He held his head up and stared straight ahead as he climbed the steps to the lectern.

He grabbed the cold brass and looked out at the faces. Half of Mirador jammed the room. The seniors from the circle sat together. He made out Alexis Newton red and teary, holding Padma's hand, Brian Olvera biting his lip and looking down, Derrick Littlefield staring right through him in a trance. Around them ranged juniors and underclassmen, teachers. Faculty blew their noses and sniffed. Even Dr. Chao in her black suit looked a little puffy eyed, wearing her armband.

Cody tried to talk, but his voice wouldn't come out right. It cracked like it had years ago in junior high. "Let's . . . ," he blurted, and swallowed. He tried to speak again. "Let's, let's get up and give Dove the standing ovation that he ought to have, okay?"

The plea dissolved. For a long moment no one moved. And then the whole place rose to its feet, students and teachers and friends and the Dovemans, and in the torrent of applause for the glass frame behind him Cody finally let himself cry.

REGRET TO INFORM

In high school all really bad news repeats itself, first as text message, second as a PA announcement.

Most of the circle crowd, those still awake around the cold, silent hours of midnight, had called and texted and IM'ed one another, so all of them had known something.

But the general masses of Mirador Senior High School had to wait until first period, when the ASB junior grabbed her microphone in the administration building and bubbled, "Good morning, Mirador Senior High School!" in her peppiest announcements voice. Beige speakers carried her words echoing off the walls of a hundred rooms.

"Please join me in the pledge of allegiance!"

Every room had a flag, and every single human being at Mirador— from special ed frosh to college guidance counselors—stopped whatever they did to stand, face the banner, and recite along with the piping voice.

"—and liberty and justice for *all!*" the girl concluded triumphantly through waves of static. Two thousand students collapsed back into their seats, a hundred faculty took their hands off their hearts.

The ASB girl picked up her bulletin sheet and read. "Here's today's sports report! Boys varsity basketball versus Edison High at 1:30 P.M., early dismissal. Girls JV soccer wrapping up the fall season at . . ."

By now all two thousand students talked, and the only people in the entire school who listened to the perky announcement girl were ASB Public Officer Derrick Littlefield and the school's principal, Dr. Irma Chao. They stood by her chair in the tiny PA room and had no choice in the matter.

Derrick Littlefield held a dictionary open to a page with his thumb, brow furrowed intently under his blond curls. He had a job to do, the same job he did every morning. Even on a day like today, it was the sacred obligation of the ASB public officer.

"Thank you, Mirador, and have a great day!"

Her six minutes up, the junior girl slipped from her post, giving Derrick free access to the mike. He sat down on the little metal chair and opened the dictionary to the page he had carefully saved ("*wapentake* . . . subdivision of certain counties . . . *wapentake*").

Silence. In the math quad, Mr. Lamarque shook his head slowly and exhaled through his teeth.

Then he clapped his hands together. He picked up chalk and turned to the board. "We have a lot to do today. Open your books to page—"

Beeeeeeeep.

"Good morning, Mirador High School. This is Dr. Chao."

Lamarque's eyes rolled back in his head. He tossed the chalk in the air and began to play an elaborate air violin solo.

"I regret to inform you that one of our seniors, Robert Doveman, was in a severe accident last night."

Lamarque's pantomime came to a quick and guilty end. Bodies froze.

Usually no one cared what the principal announced but now they strained to pick up every word from the static.

"He's in serious but stable condition, and is expected to recover," they made out. "He was airlifted down to the UCI hospital." Then with sudden clarity: "Please keep Robert in your thoughts and prayers."

The PA clicked off, finally, definitely. Confused muttering filled the classroom.

"That's tragic," said Mr. Lamarque grimly.

He shook his head. He had a lesson plan to follow, and the hour had come to draw hyperbolas.

Yes, Robert Doveman—joking, laughing, goofy-smile Dove, never said an unkind word, four-year Mirador senior and friend to all, an athlete with extra doses of heart, singing along to the music playing on his big headphones, adored by every student and teacher—had on a chilly and painfully unremarkable Tuesday night found another vehicle somewhere on the vacant roads of Emerald Valley and crashed. His modified Integra had smashed into a pile of aluminized steel sometime during the ghostly hours after 10:00 P.M. when the streets of the bedroom communities of Orange County emptied as if under curfew, which of course they were for a seventeen-year-old like Dove, except the law granted him a special exception to remain outdoors under the stars because he came back from work. He liked cars and he liked to race them, so this shocking turn of events made tragic sense. You ran a risk racing, you gambled your chances; pushing the limits meant riding a current of danger. When he got back from his hospital stay, he would have some serious badass points attached, and maybe some of the girls he hit on would reciprocate instead of writing him off as silly, clowning-around, just-best-friend-in-the-world Dove. Balloons, cards signed by everyone, and frequent bedside visits were now in order.

Or so it seemed.

Bits of the story filtered out over the hours. So many people had different pieces that they tried to assemble in a vast schoolwide jigsaw of rumor.

During passing period, Alexis Newton hunched on the ground inside the senior circle and cleared her blond hair from her eyes. Padma and

Kaylee stood in front of her as she pressed against the concrete blocks, shielding her forbidden cell phone from the wandering proctors and the imaginary video cameras in the bushes.

Everybody believed with burning faith that the school had trained an array of nonexistent security cameras on the area in central quad where the seniors hung out. Graduating classes handed down the legendary locations as received wisdom to their rising replacements, heads nodding surreptitiously toward shrubs, trees, the tops of buildings. Accepted truth declared that Vice-Principal Popper monitored them all in his office. Even people who visited him repeatedly didn't let the total lack of video screens stand in their way—the phantom cameras still existed and they *watched*.

So Alexis kept her phone well sheltered. "He what?" she whispered into the plastic box. "What happened?"

After a few minutes, she dropped the cell into her bag and tugged frantically on Padma's arm.

Apparently the police had arrived at the scene of the accident immediately. Literally. Dove had crashed into a police car. And Dr. Chao's perky assurances to the contrary, the hospital had kept Dove on the critical list.

Junior Charity Warner snuck off campus during lunch. Makeup caked on her haggard face, she curled her long legs with their ten-inch skirt and five-inch platform sandals into the dizzying trunk of Sara Dunbar's car. Sara had decent attendance and an off-campus pass, so the proctors waved her Impreza out of the gates of Mirador with little hassle. Charity met up with guys she knew from work, did a few shots, and returned to fifth period with news of Dove. "No, it's really bad," she informed her bio class with bleak world-weariness. "He's still unconscious and he has two blood clots in his brain."

After school, students and parents made phone calls. The trauma center at UC Irvine repeated firmly that no one should visit.

Dr. Chao handed down no announcement the next day, but the blob of rumors sliding around school began to form an ominous new shape. Dove was actually not doing very well at all.

Vic Reyes got a text message as he sat in in-school suspension, hiding his phone low behind the desk, cap down sideways over his spiky hair. He looked frantically around the room, but of course he couldn't talk.

Yeah, Dove and a cop had collided. But the cop had crashed into Dove.

After school, Alexis's younger brother Travis sneered at the irony, detached and calm behind his mirrored aviator sunglasses. He forced himself to drink his protein shake as Wil tabbed out chords on a black Jackson guitar.

Robert Doveman hadn't been racing, Travis drawled. He had just been driving home at the speed limit. He was sober. The only way to fault Dove is he wasn't wearing his seat belt. He entered an intersection on a green light.

Then a patrol car going fifty-five miles per hour through the red had blindsided him.

Pretty soon everybody knew what had really happened. The news even filtered down to the steps behind the library at lunch the next day. There Evelyn Strout held forth indignantly over her Tupperware container of home-dried fruit, a lime green striped scarf draped over her Astrocamp T-shirt.

The officer who hit Robert Doveman, she huffed, was on a low-level car chase. He was supposed to exercise due caution, which meant stopping first to make sure the intersection was clear, and then crossing at around fifteen miles per hour. Instead he blitzed the light forty miles per hour too fast without stopping, guilty of reckless driving and excessive speed. He had suffered only minor scrapes and bruises.

"Rob should sue," said sophomore Theodora Danielian uncertainly, a single blond streak in her jet black hair. "He could make so much money."

A pause. "Cities have a lot of money," added Leo, the chubby theater-tech freshman.

The next night, seventy members of SpiriTeen closed their eyes as ASB Public Officer Derrick Littlefield led them in a plea. "Lord, I'd just like to say a prayer for Robert Doveman and for his family for healing. . . ."

The next Wednesday, UCI Center announced that a few friends could visit Dove, a little group of the people who knew him best.

They drove down after school. The blocky white towers of the medical complex loomed over the seven small figures of Charity and a few seniors from the circle. They entered through sliding glass doors and wandered in a maze of twisting and self-similar corridors until they spotted the right number over a featureless door.

Dove lay in bed next to a window that faced high over the endless parking lot, attached to a drip stand. Snow white bandages wrapped his dark head. Casts covered most of his body.

"Do you know who Alexis is?" Brian asked him.

Dove's eyes scanned the faces hesitantly.

"She's always on her cell phone," he said after a while.

Alexis giggled nervously and waved. "That's me!"

"Can you do a thumbs-up?" asked Vic.

Dove's hand slowly came forward in a kind of rock-n-roll, devil-horns point.

Doctors kept the visit short. Charity laughed as she told Sara Dunbar about it, but amusement probably didn't form her dominant emotion.

A few nights later, the news cycle started all over again, information leaking down a number of paths. Somebody's mother worked at the hospital. A close friend of the Dovemans called other parents. Dr. Chao spoke to Mr. Mulligan, who coached baseball, and he called the families of the players. It was late, around midnight. A lot of people slept.

Cody didn't. Everyone else had experienced the weeks through a tangle of rumors and innuendos and text messages, but Dove's best friend lived a simpler story. Dove had called him from work one empty Tuesday night around 9:45. Cody had said, "I'm doing math, bro, I'll talk to you later," and hung up.

The phone rang again, sometime later. Days? Weeks? Coach Mulligan's scratchy voice delivered a very plain message.

MORNING

Alexis Newton woke late. She brushed her blond hair, pulled on a baggy gray Gucci sweater and flip-flops, and drove straight to school. She rushed past people milling around in central quad. She had hurried for nothing because her first-period math class was only half-full.

She sat at her desk, zoned out in the morning chill, when Brian Olvera caught the door frame and ran to her.

"Alexis, Dove died last night," he said as fast as he could.

"What?" she said. "No, he didn't."

"We just had a team meeting," said Brian. "He's dead."

Alexis shivered and looked at her binder. "What are you talking about? That's not funny."

"No," said Brian, "I'm not joking."

She shook her head. "He can't be dead. He's alive."

Brian grabbed her hands and looked her in the eyes. "I wouldn't lie to you," he said. "He's gone. Trust me."

She kept shaking her head. "No," she said. "No. He's not."

Beeeeeeeep.

"This is Dr. Chao," intoned a hundred speakers.

For the first time in Alexis's four years at Mirador, they had skipped the pledge. Her heart started to pound, fast and hard.

The principal's voice barely emerged from the crackles and hisses and pops. "I regret to inform you that Robert Doveman passed away last night from complications relating to his accident. Let us all take a moment of silence in remembrance of him."

Alexis couldn't move and couldn't speak. Brian and the world vanished around her. Then her body weakened and she slipped out of her chair and fell to her knees and started to cry.

"There are counselors available in the library for anyone who . . . ," Dr. Chao said.

But Alexis just knelt on the ground and cried.

CANDLES IN THE DARKNESS

The echoes of Dr. Chao's voice faded across the rings of classrooms. "Anybody who would like to may leave," Vic Reyes heard his teacher saying, but he had already risen, throat tight.

In classrooms across campus, shaken faculty surrendered the discipline of the bells and let their students wander out into the cold morning air. Alexis and Padma and Kaylee found one another desperately among the crowds and hugged tightly.

Over a thousand students emerged from their rooms, silent except for tears. The packs drifted slowly inward from the five arms of the starfish toward the heart of the school, the concrete senior circle in central quad.

Derrick Littlefield stood wordlessly by the low ring of benches, blond curls still plastered limply to his forehead from the shower. As the crowds grew around him, he hugged people mechanically, Ross, Alexis, Padma, Kaylee, even Vic.

He felt a hand on his shoulder and turned to see the red face and thick mustache of Vice-Principal Popper. "How are you doing?" Popper asked, awkwardly.

Derrick looked at girls hugging and drying one another's faces. Guys standing in small circles, speaking softly, water hovering in their eyes. All different class years, groups who never talked. "It's surreal," he mumbled.

"Maybe you could make some posters," said Mr. Popper, "get some photos of Robert or something like that."

Derrick dove into the job, grabbed Ross and Padma and some other ASB people, and went to work in the office under the big banner proclaiming that THE ASSOCIATED STUDENT BODY IS YOUR VOICE! Soon an impromptu shrine rose in the center of the circle. ASB handed black ribbons to the crowds that pressed up to sign poster boards with Dove's name and senior photo.

Charity Warner signed with purple marker, tears streaking her thick layer of makeup. Despite the white-pride manifesto she had composed on the front of her binder, she made case-by-case exceptions. Heck, almost all of Dove's friends were white.

For legal reasons everybody had to stay on campus until last bell, class or no class. Many just sat alone and cried. Counselors waited at the library but the sixty students and teachers that clustered inside sobbed instead of talked.

Some of the underclassmen had a different story. For them Dove had just been a silhouette that laughed in the distance of the senior circle, mock-fighting with Cody or some of the older guys during passing periods.

But when mourning got you a day without class?

"I was really tight with him," sniffed Travis Newton. "You know, he was like a good friend of mine."

His teachers offered sympathy. And with a shrine erected at the senior circle and the library converted into a crisis center, nobody would dare protest.

So Travis and some of his likewise bereaved buddies sat on the sophomore benches in the language arts quad and made the difficult call about which of the freshman girls were the biggest sluts. They ate the free food from the crisis center. As the long hours passed, one sophomore wondered if they could get away with a game of Texas Hold 'Em poker, but nobody wanted to risk it. Eventually, government teacher Ms. Schroeder doubted their grief and sent them to class.

Theodora Danielian watched them with disgust, the blond streak in her black hair flipped over her left eye.

"I mean, I didn't know the guy," she said to Evelyn, "but it's still traumatic. It doesn't matter if you know him or not, if your fellow student is killed, it's still a tragedy and you should at least shed a sincere tear or two. Those idiots don't give a crap about the whole ordeal."

"We're doing a feature spread on him in our next issue," said Evelyn Strout, who edited the spotlight pages of the Mirador *Mirror*.

As the day wore on, Coach Mulligan took Cody, Brian, and the rest of the baseball guys out to the field. They tossed a ball aimlessly and talked about Dove.

Brian remembered a notorious warm spring Friday when Cody and Dove had ditched school junior year. Dove tried to scramble up middle-aged women in downtown Anaheim to pretend to be their mothers and call them in sick to the attendance office. The plan would have met total success, except his "mother," a tourist who hadn't spoken until she held the phone, turned out to have a strong British accent. A tad unusual for a black lady from Emerald Valley. Mr. Popper shook his head all the way to their in-school suspension.

Cody smiled faintly. The day drew to a close.

Usually people ran for their cars the instant that last bell rang at 2:45. Today everyone lingered, not ready to go home and be alone.

Cody needed escape and asked Brian to come with him to the Pizza Roma on Terrace Boulevard where Dove had worked his first and only job. They drove in silence and parked in the strip mall.

He opened the door to Pizza Roma and Dove stared back at him. The restaurant employees had hung a huge picture of their fallen coworker on the wall, stretching a red-checked apron underneath to collect money for his family. THE ROB FUND. "I can't stay here," Cody blurted, and they about-faced to the car again.

Brian remembered how Dove would take out a slice of pizza to a homeless person every day.

Throughout the afternoon phone calls were made. Everyone knew the cause of death now: A weakened vessel in Rob Doveman's head had burst, instantly flooding his brain with blood in a massive hemorrhagic stroke. But nobody wanted to remember him that way, lost in bandages among antiseptic walkways. For them Dove had ended when the medical helicopter lifted him from a shredded wreckage of silver metal and glass into the star-dripping skies for his final flight.

A candlelight vigil was scheduled for sunset at Mirador.

As red fire burned on the western horizon, the first students trickled toward the senior circle. Derrick Littlefield and the other ASB people had worked for hours, and now huge portraits of Dove, signing boards, and flowers filled the concrete ring. Kaylee had painted a symbolic canvas of a dove flying away from a wrecked car amid tears. Beneath it, in the center of the circle, lay the fallen senior's green baseball jersey: DOVEMAN 17.

ASB silently handed out white tapers and black ribbons to the arrivals.

The light faded and the numbers grew. One hundred students, five hundred students, a thousand students. Their parents, Mirador's teachers, recent alumni, Dove's family and coworkers, principals from nearby schools, the school district, community members, the mayor.

They stood in silence and darkness, crying unseen, before the candles began to glow, tiny fragile flames filling central quad with a new constellation of light.

Not every death mattered so much to Mirador. The year before, a transfer senior had killed herself at the end of spring. The PA made an announcement, the *Mirror* printed a one-line item—but no general reaction beyond, "Who was that? That's weird."

And then the music started.

You could run to me when you need me, I'll never leave.
I just needed someone to believe in, as you can see. . . .

2Pac's remix of "Broken Wings" faded up on speakers beyond the perimeter of the candlelight. At the request of the ASB, musician Wil had put together a suitable compilation CD for the occasion.

"I tried to find songs he liked about like loss and healing," Wil explained to Thea's mother.

Thea's eyes met Wil's briefly. "Hey," he said.

"Hey," she said.

Later on she grabbed Evelyn. "I talked to him!" she whispered urgently.

"'I talked to him!' Oh, my God, you sound like such a prep." Evelyn clutched her candle and raised her head righteously.

Vic Reyes stood with his friend Shawn toward the front of the circle, black ribbon pinned on his sideways hat.

"Victor." The familiar voice made him tense on instinct, but Vice-Principal Popper just stood by his side. Together they watched silent tears slide down cheeks. "I think they did a good job with all of this. With the music. I think it's a very appropriate way for people to release their emotions."

"Yeah," said Vic. They stood in silence for a while. "It hits you harder as time goes by. It just hits harder and harder." He stared at the thousands of crying people, the shining flames.

"I've been here for thirty years," said Popper. "I've never seen anything like this, never. There's a lot of compassion here."

He patted Vic on the back and walked away.

Vic shared a shocked look with Shawn. "For once the administration is actually really cool about everything."

Shawn nodded. "They're trying, you know?"

Alexis and Kaylee and Padma stood holding signs in the crowd. WE LOVE YOU, DOVE. WE WILL ALWAYS REMEMBER YOU, ROB.

"I don't know anyone who ever died," said Kaylee.

Alexis saw Charity Warner in the crowd and they nodded to each other briefly before the bodies shifted around them.

Charity sighed. She looked down at her candle flame within the mass of people. "Doesn't it feel like we're actually part of a community?" she said to Sara. "Like everyone's forgotten about all the stupid drama for once, and they're not talking about their homework or the budget cuts."

"Where's Shawn?" asked Sara.

Charity shrugged and kept looking forward. After a while she spoke in a small voice. "I wonder who'll care when I die."

Her hand-printed sign fluttering, Alexis's blond hair blew in a gentle wind that made the constellation of candles twinkle. "This happened for a reason," she told her own group of friends, face red with tears. "Dove died because he wanted us to become close to each other."

Derrick and Ross and twenty of the other SpiriTeen people joined hands and said a prayer for the peaceful repose of Rob's soul.

Afterward Dr. Chao brought Derrick over to speak with the mayor. "The students are just devastated, aren't they, Derrick?" the principal said. "Robert was such a good example for the school."

Derrick swallowed. "He really impacted a lot of people. He was a really genuine person. He didn't care what anybody thought of him."

Among the press of bodies, Shawn came over and put his arm around Charity.

Cody stood at the front of the crowd, next to his dad and mom and the Dovemans. Rob's green jersey lay before them in the circle on its bed of lilies. They hugged one another repeatedly. Above them, hanging from the gracefully dripping branches of the California pepper tree, the paint slowly dried on the huge canvas of the bird in flight.

Hours passed. The night had deepened and chilled before figures began to slowly drift away from the edges of the crowd, their candles extinguished.

WEEKEND PLANS

Most people returned to class the next day at the penetrating beep of the tardy bell. During passing periods between subjects they crossed central quad and saw fresh flowers on the shrine, saw piles of half-burned candles carved with Dove's name.

A few of the seniors who hung out at the circle took another day off from class. They sat near the memorial, mostly in silence. Coach Mulligan talked quietly with some of the baseball guys.

Sophomore Travis Newton hadn't even gone to the rally, and decided not to push his luck in trying to get his teachers to excuse him again.

By the end of the week, everyone had returned to class. The Dovemans scheduled Rob's funeral for Sunday at the Calvary AME Church.

On Friday night, Brian Olvera had a party. Two dozen people, mostly seniors and juniors, came to his grandiose Santa Fe contemporary house, all square adobe walls and red-baked tiles, at the northern edge of the gated communities. Brian's father owned a string of Ford dealerships across inland Orange County.

Alexis lay on the tan leather sofas under the two-story ceiling of the great room with a bottle of Southern Comfort. "I'm all spaced-out," she said. "I'm just all spacey and sad and cried-out."

Music played softly on surround-sound speakers but nobody danced or laughed. It wasn't a fun party, it was a drinking party. Everyone slumped around the immense space with bottles and cases.

Padma looked at the shapes huddled in small groups, some crying. "This is so grim. You sure you don't want a beer?"

Derrick sat alone at a granite counter and shook his head. "I'm good, thanks."

Point lights picked out Kokopelli petroglyphs, silver and turquoise jewelry, geometrical sand paintings.

Charity gulped vodka and Sprite and told Shawn about the time she and Dove ditched class and hung out in the gym talking music. "I feel he's still here. I just can't grasp it. I keep telling myself that he's gone and he's not coming back. I'm not like emotionally stable enough to handle this. I went to work crying today."

She opened her purse and pulled out a carefully folded pencil drawing of a guy and a girl holding hands. "I made this drawing for you today. It's a picture of us together forever."

Shawn took it and looked up at her, awestruck. They hugged.

Brian shot pool in the games room by the wide windows that looked out onto a cactus-bordered rock pool. He showed his Playas Goin' Drinking dog tags to Kaylee. She ran her fingers across the letters on the cold metal. BRIAN OLVERA. ROBERT DOVEMAN. CODY REISLING.

They looked up to see the third namesake yelling at Vic Reyes by the light pool around a black Pueblo bowl. The clock glowed 9:45 and Cody had drunk seven forty-ounce cans of Steel Reserve malt lager since three in the afternoon.

"I'm fucking angry," he said. "I'm sick of all this bullshit. Everyone's like, 'Oh, I'm going to make sure I say all my I-love-you's.' Fuck that bullshit. I just want everyone to go away.

"He was such a real person, you know? They should remember him exactly the way he was, but they're making everything into bullshit.

"There's no point in getting to know anyone ever, right? You don't know if they're going to be there tomorrow. There's no point to anything. I'm angry. I hate reality."

Vic looked down. He and Shawn had smoked weed outside on the patio by the grapevine trellises. "I'm sorry, bro."

Cody had always gone through mood swings, but now they became a lot worse. Everything touched him off, and each conversation with his parents exploded into a fight.

He lived in a cul-de-sac Victorian toward the south of town. His father had worked his way up from nothing to a successful law practice, and took great pride in the two late-model SUVs in his garage. A week after the funeral, Cody's mother knocked on his door while Mr. Reisling, Esq., hovered behind her.

"I think you may need to see a counselor," she told him, her dyed-blond hair sprayed rigid.

"I'm not crazy," said Cody.

"No one's saying you're crazy," she said. "I think you may need help, like some kind of anger management."

"I'm concerned about your drinking," his father said. "I'd like you to go to an AA meeting."

"You keep telling me the same thing over and over again," said Cody, his voice rising. "Every time you talk to me you just tell me what I'm doing wrong. You think everything I do is wrong."

Over his strident protests, they found a therapist and made him go to a few weekly appointments.

For a while he simply didn't speak to them. They ate meals in silence.

Then they got into a terrible fight, worse than all the others. "Fuck you," Cody screamed. He gathered his stuff and moved out to live with his twenty-one-year-old brother in a nearby city.

MAGIC HAPPENS

Time, as it tends to, passed.

With exquisite care, the school took down the portraits and signing boards and the painting and gave them to the Dovemans. Late one afternoon, the janitors cleaned the flowers and candles from the senior circle. People paused the next day at seeing the familiar concrete swept clean, but no tears fell.

They started to smile and laugh again, and the laughter felt great, and they started to play beer pong and dance again. They once more permitted themselves nasty comments about their enemies and certain friends out of earshot. Everything they saw and did no longer reminded them of guilt and the absence of Dove.

At least once a day he'd come up, and occasionally troubled silences descended as a thousand tongues of internal hysteria screamed. But the nightmare slowly subsided as the bell rang relentlessly, always bringing something new to deal with. In a little over two weeks, on the surface at least, it looked like life might have rebounded.

Beeeeeeeep.

"Good *morning,* Mirador Senior High School!" gushed the perky announcements girl. "Please join me in the pledge of allegiance!"

The thousands stood, pledged, sat. They began to talk. With each cheerful exclamation shrouded in static, Lamarque's lip curled further.

At the PA room, ASB Public Officer Derrick Littlefield carefully held his thumb in the dictionary. Vice-Principal Popper stood next to him, red face sweating in the heat of the broadcasting electronics.

The girl finished reading her list of club events and finals-week schedules for the end of fall semester. "Thank you, Mirador, and have a great day!" she concluded, and fled.

Derrick took the metal chair and opened the dictionary. His brow furrowed. "*Chionablepsia,*" he said carefully into the microphone. "Snow blindness. *Chionablepsia.*"

Mr. Popper nodded, and Derrick put the dictionary back and rushed away, through the office of the Associated Student Body. Past the pictures of himself hanging in the lobby of the administration building. Outstanding Scholar-Athlete. Senior Leadership Award Honoree. Student Choice Award. Out the door.

Back at the administration building, Mr. Popper cleared his throat and leaned in toward the mike. "This is Stanley Popper. We have the Sadie Hawkins Rally in the auditorium now, so first-period teachers, please lead your classes over." He pressed the bell button.

Beeeeeeeep.

In the math quad, a wild, looping giggle exploded from Mr. Lamarque's lips.

Derrick Littlefield jogged into the back of the auditorium. Small theater-tech underclassmen bustled by dressed in black, arguing.

ASB Vice-President Padma Kalyani waited for him backstage in a plaid hillbilly shirt and a straw hat. She looked beautiful, tall and thin, long dark legs in white clogs.

She tossed her shiny hair and presented him with a pile of hick clothes. "Somebody's late."

"I had to do the Word of the Day," said Derrick, pulling off his T-shirt.

Padma looked over his tan, his curly blond hair, his green eyes, his arms. "Oh, my God," she said. "Your biceps are so big. Can I feel them?"

Derrick looked down, unbuttoning his plaid shirt. "I was just at the gym. They only look bigger."

Padma clamped her hands around the muscles, drawing her eyes across every available inch of skin. "Oh, look at you! You've got abs. Is that a six-pack?"

"No," said Derrick, blushing. "I'm a mess. I'm fat. I've got a four-pack and this." He pinched the skin on his stomach. "I hurt my ACL and I can't run, so I'm just fat."

He put on the plaid shirt, pulled on overalls over his shorts.

Padma looked at her watch. "Oh, my God, I've gotta find Ross! Ross!" Her clogs clunked on the stage as she raced away.

As she squeezed past the pack of seven girls who formed the Matadora dance team, she smiled at Kaylee.

"I am *so* going to be his first kiss," she said.

Derrick was a senior, and he had never kissed a girl in his life. He had never drunk alcohol. The Bible had proclaimed both activities Wrong.

He was captain of the volleyball team, and class salutatorian, and he had gotten into the University of Virginia early decision. As ASB public officer, he provided the omnipresent face and voice of Mirador High School. If you asked almost any student who came to mind first when thinking of school, you'd hear Derrick Littlefield. Who was the most popularest person of all the popular people? Derrick. The positions of president and vice-president were vaguely merit based, but public officer meant a straight-up popularity contest.

The Matadoras, in hillbilly gear, watched him don his straw hat from the corner of their eyes.

"Derrick just doesn't get it," said Kaylee.

"He doesn't realize how hot he is," said Samantha. "He was at the beach and they were rubbing suntan lotion on his back, and I was just like ohhhh. . . ."

"He has such big muscles, and his back is so hard," added Sara Dunbar.

"You've gotta love him," said Kaylee, "he's such a nice guy."

"I remember last year," said Vic Reyes. Vic wasn't supposed to be backstage, but he was anyway to hit on the Matadoras. "We'd all be like stoned and playing multiplayer Halo on Xbox, and Derrick would be like the only guy who wasn't fucked up. He'd be like, 'Gosh! This is fun!'"

Everyone shared a moment of stunned silence as they contemplated the enigma of Derrick.

At last Kristie spoke. "You gotta respect him. He's just honest like that, you know. He's straight up."

In the back of the auditorium, behind a one-way window, the theater-tech people sat around a dim world of sliding levers and blinking lights.

The door swung open and Leo the little freshman huffed in wearing a Strong Bad T-shirt. "Padma said the slides are in order and not to worry about them."

"Ooooh, 'Padma said,'" repeated Evelyn Strout, waving her fingers in the air.

"What?" asked Leo.

"We don't trust popular people," said Evelyn. She had on her lime green scarf and blue sweatpants.

Thea Danielian pushed back the blond streak in her jet black hair. "Actually, we're using them to play Do, Date, or Dump right now. Evelyn just told us she'd Dump Cody Reisling."

"He's a steroid freak and an asshole," said Evelyn. "He's in my government class and he's always saying like the most infuriating conservative things. We'll be trying to talk about the material, and he'll like start having a political discussion."

"Wait, he's going out with Alexis Newton, right?" asked another theater tech.

"Yeah, they're supposed to be the 'hot couple,'" said Evelyn. "Hah. Hey, how about Alexis Newton? Do, Date, or Dump?"

Thea smiled. "That would be kinda kinky. Oh, yeah, Brian Olvera was going on in geography about how God hates gay marriage, and I was like, 'Excuse me, I'm bi over here.' Possibly Date."

Evelyn looked at the clock and stood.

Moments later, the auditorium lights cut out. Spotlights whirled around the blackness, streaking over two thousand people.

"It's the end of fall semester, Mirador," Derrick's voice boomed out from everywhere in the darkness.

Wild cheers went up across the seats.

"Forget homecoming. Forget prom. It's time for the girls to ask the guys for a change! But if you want to find out just where our Sadie Hawkins dance is going to be, you're gonna have to wait. First, let's give it up for our very own Matadoras!"

"Sadie Hawkins Dance" by pop-punk band Relient K kicked onto the sound system.

The pack of Matadoras charged out and executed a high-energy dance under swiveling colored beams. Lots of air punching, synchronized head-turning, and jumping back and forth.

At last the curtains rose to reveal a bail of hay, and Derrick ambled in, chewing a piece of grass. "We're going to the library."

The music slammed back as beams of light from the control room projected towering images of gardens and fountains across the walls. In the flashing slides, Derrick, Padma, Ross, and the other ASB people wandered the elegant formal grounds of the mystery site dressed like hillbillies.

"Your Associated Student Body," proclaimed Derrick, "has found you an exclusive luxury location right here in Orange County, with a huge dance floor and an outdoor stage."

Above his head a new slide appeared, a tremendous bronze bust looming over the Mirador assembly hall. The gleaming eyeless visage of America's thirty-seventh president gazed down upon them.

Derrick looked right out at the crowd and said into the microphone: "Magic happens at the Richard Nixon Library & Birthplace."

Sophomore Travis Newton snickered and slid down his mirrored aviator sunglasses, but otherwise the auditorium filled with wide eyes, unironic smiles.

DANCING ON NIXON'S GRAVE

Charity Warner stumbled over a black lump of stone in the grass and threw up.

What assholes put a stone on their lawn? She peered at it blearily through smeared eyeliner.

EVEN IF PEOPLE CAN'T SPEAK YOUR LANGUAGE, THEY CAN TELL IF YOU HAVE LOVE IN YOUR HEART.

She wobbled on her heels and lifted her head to see the rest of it. PATRICIA NIXON (1912–1993).

Another black stone lay a few feet away, but it was more important to deal with the four freshman girls who were laughing at her.

"Are you talking shit over there?" she shrieked. "You better watch your back, bitches!"

The girls stepped away a little and giggled as Charity heaved again.

Police sirens wailed across the expanse of night. Sadie Hawkins had gone over the edge.

Now the freshmen girls edged closer to the stumbling Charity. One turned to the others. "I hate that girl," she whispered, nodding at Charity. "She really annoys me. If she was like in our grade or younger I'd say something. Now I'm just like, 'You'll be gone in a year, bitch.'"

Behind them floodlights bathed a prim little cottage surrounded by roses. A baby President Nixon had emerged blinking from his Quaker mother into this clapboard farmhouse back in 1913. Now stately formal gardens surrounded it, bordered on one side by a modern cement convention-center-plus-library erected in homage to Yorba Linda's favorite son.

Out here in the backyard, visitors could experience the awe of, and/or throw up on, Nixon's grave itself. Charity reeled.

"She gave blow jobs to like the entire water polo team," one freshman girl whispered to the others.

A third curled her lip as they crept closer. "She's such a slut."

Charity snarled and swiveled, but policemen arrived before it got too ugly.

The problems with Sadie Hawkins had started in the limos, in the ninety-five-dollars-a-head party buses, when one driver had been doing shots himself and ran a couple of red lights.

Cody hadn't even made it to the cement steps of the Richard Nixon

Library & Birthplace. He had drunk a bunch of Jägermeister and taken four Ecstasy pills and ended up going into spasms in their stretch Hummer limo. His parents were called, his date Alexis sent home, and away he went to the UCI emergency room to get his stomach pumped. He stayed a few floors down from the room where his best friend had died three weeks earlier.

But most people had paced themselves a little better. Knowing they'd get searched at the door, they preloaded at home or in the limos. Now, across the gardens and library, dozens staggered and yelled and groped and hooked up and fought and vomited in their own private worlds of debauchery.

The officers, called in by the hysterical Nixon Library staff, didn't know where to begin. One policeman followed noise and found two drunk sophomores having sex behind a row of neatly clipped shrubs.

Another tried to secure the front parking lot. There a junior screamed, "I'm surfing! Hey, I'm surfing!" as he stood on top of a slow-moving car driven by his buddy.

Kaylee stationed herself in the doorway. "It's so funny to laugh at all the drunk people," she said to Padma. She turned to see that Padma had disappeared.

The junior fell off the top of the car and hit the ground hard, cutting up the side of his face.

Oh, there had been "bad" dances before. Five students had gotten arrested for drinking and fighting at the Homecoming Ball in November. And maybe the behavior this night resulted from a deep collective need to release emotions pent up in the horror of the Dove affair.

But Sadie's promised to set an entirely different standard for "bad."

Derrick Littlefield stood utterly immobile in his farmer's hat at the epicenter of the maelstrom. Within the sweaty ballroom of the Nixon Library itself, he watched the throngs grinding and shoving and stumbling on the dance floor. The air stung with the acidic breath of metabolized alcohol. His date had gone to the bathroom fifteen minutes before and never returned. Even a committed SpiriTeen girl had a hard time enjoying an evening with Derrick; he was about as sexual as a Buzz Lightyear figurine.

He looked down and saw sophomore musician Wil Kormer passed out under a table.

Suddenly something struck Derrick from behind. A wasted Padma threw her arms around him and tried to force his head to her mouth. "I'm going to kiss you!" she hollered. "I'm gonna be your first kiss!"

Derrick struggled to break free, tried to control her flailing arms. Her mouth landed on his neck and she kissed the available skin before he detached her. He leapt back a couple of yards and watched her, wide-eyed.

"What the heck!" he said, face flickering between shock and amusement. "You just tried to rape me!"

Padma laughed like a madwoman and pointed a finger. "Just you wait, Derrick Littlefield! Bwah hah hah!" She laughed wildly and ran off to Kaylee. "I got his neck!" she screamed.

Derrick's date returned. "Hey," he said.

She rolled her eyes. "The bathroom's filled with throw up," she said, "and there's like a policewoman standing inside."

So the two of them just leaned against the wall and watched Mirador proctors and Yorba Linda officers fan out across the dance floor, wading through the masses in search of inebriated students. Amid the flashing strobes and pounding music, men in uniform grabbed the most obviously drunk revelers, shined Maglites into their eyes, and hauled them off for interrogation under the giant bronze Richard Nixon bust in the hallway.

Vic Reyes soon found himself thrust into a row of chairs next to Charity Warner as they awaited the Breathalyzer.

"Where's Saaara?" she moaned. "Where's Shaaaawn?"

Vic shrugged.

Charity looked down the line at the officers. "What the fuck is this bullshit? I'm not even that drunk."

"You fell down the steps coming in," said Vic, trying to stop the room from spinning.

"Everyone was falling down the steps," whined Charity. "Those fucking steps were like extra steeeeep or something."

"God, your voice is so annoying," said Vic.

Charity wrinkled her nose. "I'm not talking to you," she said.

"Why?"

"I'm mad at you. You're an asshole." She stared meaningfully at the far wall, where Vice-Principal Popper and a police sergeant traded frantic gestures.

"You try too hard," said Vic after a little while.

"Huh?" said Charity.

"You try too hard to fit in," he said. "Have you ever seen yourself at a party?"

Charity gave him a death-warmed-over stare. "See, it's because of stuff like that that I'm not talking to you."

Above their heads the metal Richard Nixon beamed.

"Look," said Vic, "I've only got a little while longer and then you'll never see me again."

"Yeah, I will," said Charity.

"No, you won't," he said. "You don't know that."

"No," she moaned. "I wiiiiill."

Vic inhaled sharply. Popper and the sergeant stayed deep in conversation. "Sweet Jesus," he said. "I'm out of here." He stood, unsteadily.

Mr. Popper looked over at him. "Hey!" he called. "Get back in your seat."

Vic panicked. "I'm not sitting for you, Popper," he slurred.

Then a hysterical Dr. Chao popped up right in front of him, eyes bulging. "You sit *now*," she screamed, pointing at the chair.

Vic sat. He spoke to her in a soothing tone for about thirty seconds, darting sidelong glances at the exit. When he decided she was sufficiently duped, he bolted. An officer tackled and handcuffed him.

The grand total of arrests reached fourteen. An additional thirty-six parents, awakened by late-night phone calls from the school, rolled up in jackets and nightgowns to collect crying sons and daughters whose breath reeked of Bacardi 151.

Dr. Chao shook her head in a daze as she spoke with the media.

"I'm embarrassed," she told the local paper. "I've never seen anything like this Sadie's. This is the worst dance I've seen in nine years at Mirador."

ASB representative Ross Hayes snorted, off at the side. "Every dance is like this," he said to Kaylee. "The only difference is more people got caught this time."

THREE STRIKES AND A HOME RUN

Two days later, the sun rose bright and clear over a finals-week Monday.

Charity Warner screeched into the parking lot in her pink Mustang GT. She had tinted the glass the darkest legal shade, and the back window sported a large iron cross decal. It matched the one she had drawn on the front of her binder, surrounded by the manifesto she had composed. ("Why do we have César Chávez Day but no White Pride Week? It's not about being racist. It's just about having pride in who you are.")[1]

Out swung a skinny leg in a platform sandal, followed by an extremely short skirt, followed by a skintight top, followed by Charity's frazzled face. She groaned, hauled herself upright, and began to totter to class.

Mario stopped her.

Mario was an enormous man in his early thirties; a scar streaked his forehead right above his sunglasses. He used to serve in the Mexican marines but had now found his true calling as one of Mirador's proctors, working in the enforcement arm of the administration. He clutched a stack of pink slips in his hand.

"Charity Warner?" he said, looking at a slip.

She nodded weakly.

"Mr. Popper wants to see you in his office."

The vice-principal stared across his desk, face red and mustache twitching.

"What's the first problem?" he asked her when she sat.

"I don't know," she said.

"What are you wearing?"

She looked at her nonexistent clothing, and anguish rent her angular face. "Oh, come on. Pleeease, Mr. Popper?"

"You are hardly within the boundaries of the Mirador dress code." He rummaged in a big cardboard box he kept by his desk as he ticked off items on his hand: "Excessive cleavage, bare midriff, extremely short shirt."

Charity became frantic and untied a black sweatshirt from her purse strap. "Here. I'll wear this."

Mr. Popper glanced at it and shook his head. "What's wrong with that sweatshirt, Charity?"

It had a big white iron cross emblazoned on the back. "The logo?"

"The dress code considers that a racist symbol," said Mr. Popper. "It's on page twenty-three of the handbook."

Charity yanked the sweatshirt inside out, but to her horror the cross showed through the other side as well.

"I can go home," she said quickly. "I live right—"

Popper looked at his watch. "You don't have time. The bell rings in five minutes."

She slumped back in defeat.

With glacial slowness, Popper withdrew Charity's worst nemesis from the crate, unfolding before her doomed eyes an old gray XXL Mirador Marlins sweat suit from the 1993 track season. The process seemed to take ages, like more cloth always remained to pull out of the box.

"Please put it on, and then you can go to three days of in-school suspension for fighting and drunkenness at the Sadie's dance. We'll set your finals up for you in there."

Charity left the office, her little pale face shuffling along grimly on top of a mountain of baggy fabric. Outside, she donned her big white glamour sunglasses so she could preserve some dignity.

The pack of four freshman girls burst into fits of laughter as soon as they saw her.

She walked right up to them. "Because of my circumstances," she said tightly, "I'm not going to touch you at school. But if I see you like at a party, you better watch out because I'm going to get you."

"Okay," snickered one of girls.

Charity sniffed. "Okay. Great. Consider yourself warned."

The girls kept giggling. "We know something really bad," said one of them.

"What?" said Charity.

"It would totally ruin your life," added a second. They all started to laugh.

A horn tooted as a golf cart whined out from behind the administration building. Mario sat behind the wheel, and Mr. Popper roosted on the backseat. "You're going to ISS *now*, Charity," he said. "You're not stopping to talk to people."

She glared at the freshman girls. "This isn't over," she hissed, and waddled off, swathed in the reams of cloth, huge sunglasses perched on her thin nose.

Vic Reyes vroomed into the parking lot blasting a Yellowcard CD on the custom audio system in his Baja Bug. The best way to understand a Baja Bug is to take a VW Beetle, raise it off the ground, stick on huge off-road tires, rip off the back to expose the engine, install big shocks, and fit a steel cage onto the rear. The overall effect resembles the International Space Station latching on to an innocent Bug for docking maneuvers. Drive it like Vic into the desert, take it off road, go anywhere, with full confidence that the Baja Bug can handle it, thanks to the amazing suspension standard in all Beetles.

In California, cars matter.[2]

Vic flipped the CD into his Discman knockoff, pulled on headphones, and stepped out of his car and into Mario.

"Sorry, man," said the proctor, holding a pink slip in one massive hand.

Mr. Popper waited for them on the backseat of his golf cart, parked at the end of the lot. "Get in, Victor," he said.

Vic dropped onto the cushioned plastic. Mario climbed behind the wheel. With a cheerful toot of its horn, the cart took off.

"What's the first problem, Victor?" the vice-principal asked as they bounced along.

"Uhhh. I don't know."

"I don't want to cite you for a dress code violation. Your shorts are far too low, and you're exposing your underwear, which is unacceptable and unsightly." Vic pulled them up.

The cart whizzed past crowds of students hanging outside during the dwindling minutes before finals. Popper sighed. "In the last few years the number of expulsions has been overwhelming," he said. "I haven't looked at the total numbers for your class yet. It's too sad."

Vic sat silently, wind blowing around his spiky hair.

"I'm sure you've seen all the white slips. In the past few weeks a number of people have been ushered to the door."

Vic wouldn't look at him. "Tomás Serna isn't going to be able to graduate."

"Inter-district transfer," said Mr. Popper, "is a wonderful opportunity to come study here in Emerald Valley, but it sets a high bar."

The cart banked around the senior circle. Mr. Popper noticed Vic glancing at the faces of his classmates. "Sadie's was a very serious situation, and we just can't afford to have a repeat of that."

He turned over his clipboard. Vic looked down at the white pages fluttering in the wind, and then up at Popper.

"So here's your notification," said the vice-principal. "You have two more chances to get your act together. The third time we have a problem, it's going to be mandatory expulsion without a hearing. Think of it like a ball game: three strikes, you're out."

"Do I have a choice?" Vic asked over the whine of the cart.

"The alternative is to leave on Friday and finish up this year in Santa Ana."

The golf cart bumped over rough concrete as they approached the modular buildings by the gym. Vic's throat tightened. "You can't expel somebody just because of what happened at the dance."

"This isn't something that we're discussing, Victor. I'm offering you a three-strikes contract. If you don't want to sign it, we can fill out the transfer papers."

Vic exhaled. He took the clipboard from Popper's hand. He steadied it on his leg, and wrote his name with a complex looping swirl.

The cart stopped outside the side modular building, at the door to the in-school suspension room.

"You're here," said Mr. Popper. "Drinking and defiance. You've got five days of ISS."

At the circle during lunch, Brian held aloft a green fruit dripping from Crystallina's ice bin. "I got an apple," he said.

"Gimme that," said Cody, and palmed it behind his back. He looked around. The coast was clear—no proctors. The phantom cameras passed out of mind.

"I'm going for the sophomores," said Cody. The cool tenth-graders talked and laughed in a tight group down on benches in the language arts quad. They had let down their guard, and forgotten that lunchtime meant ballistics from the heavens.

"Hey," said Brian. "Remember before when we threw down the pumpkin on Halloween and it hit the guy in the wheelchair? And he all wanted to fight and shit? He was like, 'I'm gonna fuck you up.' That was hilarium! I was like laughing my ass—"

But Cody had already pulled into the familiar and perfect motion, taking a small step back, pivoting the foot, raising his knee high, body straight, swinging back his arm, and now with fluidity and grace he plunged forward into the stride, brought his elbow up—

A golf cart honked its cheery toot.

"Dude!" yelped Brian.

Cody whipped around, fumbling the apple onto the ground. It rolled under one of the concrete benches of the circle.

If Mario the proctor saw anything, he didn't mention it. "Cody Reisling," he called, holding up the pink slip.

Mr. Popper tapped a pen on his desk as he scrutinized Cody's jeans, T-shirt, Mirador baseball cap. Every member of the team had written the same words in ballpoint ink inside the brim of their caps. "The strength of the School is the Marlin, and the strength of the Marlin is the School."

"Well," said Popper. "You're the first person I've spoken with today who's not violating the dress code."

Cody fixed him with pale blue eyes. "It's all the media's fault," he said. "You know? It's affected our whole generation. Now you see girls walking around wearing barely nothing, and it's all that Britney Spears junk. Girls see it and they want to copy it. Four years ago it wasn't like that, I'm sure. I'm sure you've seen it."

Mr. Popper cleared his throat. "Well," he said. "I'm not allowed to look. I can only look head up. Otherwise it's inappropriate looking. People can get in trouble, and they lose their jobs. That's why I have to look over everyone's heads when I look around a classroom."

"I mean have you seen the freshman girls?" pressed Cody. "It's unbelievable. Like what do their parents say? How can their mothers let them leave the house like that?"

"No, I agree with you," said the vice-principal. "But we need to talk about something else, which is your eligibility."

Cody's eyes fell to the desk, pages heaped loosely around an immaculately clean space.

"Your grades have been off, and now you're getting sent to the hospital. You're an athlete, so you realize a lot of people are watching your behavior, I mean, you're extremely visible to the school and to the community. According to the rule book, your behavior at Sadie's means you should be suspended and disqualified for spring."

Cody's head jerked up and his fists clenched.

"But," said Mr. Popper quickly, "we don't want to lose our pitcher, and you don't want to lose your final season." He turned the pen around on its point.

The senior circle watched Cody storm back a few minutes later.

"They're turning this place into a fucking prison," he yelled, as the band rocked on in the background. He swept his hand around at the trees, the library, the administration building. "They have cameras everywhere, they have cameras in the bushes. They're on top of the buildings over there. You can fucking see them! They're watching the circle, they're watching to see what we're gonna do."

He jumped up to sit on the ring next to Brian. An awkward silence. Then worried conversations started.

"This place is such bullshit," Padma agreed.

Kaylee nodded, anxious. "I went into Pooper's office, and he was like monitoring it all. He had a big screen that was split into the different cameras."

Cody unwrapped his burrito under the bright sun. "Fucking Popper," he told Brian. "I have trash pickup before the scrimmage."

Up on stage, Wil dragged out the last chord. "—*diiiiiiieeeeeeeeeeeee,*" he finished. "Thank you, we're Same Distance Reduced." The dozen people really into the show clapped and hooted, and so did a few others across the quads.

He swung the guitar strap off his shoulder and jumped down onto the ground, where Alexis's younger brother Travis Newton stood in his mirrored aviator sunglasses and an FCUK T-shirt. Together they watched the distant form of Cody hurl something up into the air. Reflected in Travis's lenses, the object vanished against the blue sky, seemed to lose itself in the sun. Then the dark shape plunged back to Earth, rocketing toward the steps of the fine arts quad where the slutty junior girls hung out. A distant yelp.

"He's a good customer," said Travis, "but he's totally losing it. He got into a fight with my sister a few weeks ago and he slashed her tires."

"Well," said Wil, black hair hanging over his eye, "isn't that your fault, kinda, indirectly?"

"No," said Travis. "I told him he should be taking hGH, but he said it was too expensive. See, if you're in the gym subculture, you know the right steroids to take. All the people here are so stupid, they're like him. They're gonna be saggy, bald, and fuck their shit up. I just try to get a hundred and forty-eight grams of protein a day."

He took a swig from a plastic Lexan bottle filled with a chalky white amino acid liquid.

"And," he said, "I'm not actually selling. Other people sell and give me the money. It's a weird feeling not to be actually selling myself, and just do nothing, and the money comes in."

Wil laughed. "Dude, that's indirectly. You sell to them."

"I'm the man behind the curtain," said Travis. "I'm gonna be Big Brother. Thank you, Orwell. Oh, yeah, *Burmese Days* is pretty boring, and I'm like having to make myself finish it, but then I'm finally going to be done. I told myself I'd finish all his books, and I'm going to."

"Let me see," said Wil.

Travis pulled it out of his messenger bag. Wil read the back cover, flipped through the pages.

"I'm thinking about getting into Ecstasy," Travis mused. "They sell it by the boatload. A boat's like this big." He indicated a shoebox-sized space with his hands. "It costs a thousand dollars, and you sell it for a hundred and forty thousand."

Wil clicked his tongue, still looking at the book. "That's like a hundred and forty times profit margin."

"Well, that's drugs." Travis shrugged. "It's really risky, though. I mean, I could do cocaine and stuff, too, but then you have to deal with cocaine dealers. Ecstasy is nice because it's just rich white kids, and no one dies from it." He reflected. "Well, some people die from taking it, but you don't get killed like with coke."

Wil smirked and closed *Burmese Days*. "I don't like this book. It's got too much long description."

"I like description, fool," said Travis.

Wil handed it back. "Next year is going to suck because all the books are going to be like this."

"No," said Travis, "freshman year was good, this year is good, next year will be good, and senior year will be good." He drank more protein. "I don't want to sell to people who know what to pay, and I'm excited about the new eighth-graders, because they don't know what they're doing."

He climbed up onto the now-abandoned stage and surveyed the pentagon of central quad, the thousands of students spread across the campus under the brilliant sun.

"This school has cancer," he announced. "I just walked by the library, and I heard a grip of dorky people talking about how fucked up they were getting. That's all anyone talks about now. I mean, it's okay for people like us, but they're supposed to be the good ones. I only heard one conversation about something else, and that was Magic cards."[3]

A little red-haired freshman came over to the side of the stage. "Hey," he said quietly. "I got forty." He looked around nervously.

Travis knelt. "Don't worry," he said. "People do drug deals all the time under the cameras, and you're just giving me money."

"There's cameras?" squeaked the freshman.

"Yeah," said Travis. "But they don't do anything."

The freshman looked around again and stuffed two twenties into Travis's hand. "Jackie says she already gets it from her brother," he said.

"Find out exactly how much he's paying," said Travis. "I can get a better deal."

"Okay," said the freshman.

"Or I can get him women," said Travis. "Whatever, we'll figure out something." The freshman hurried off.

Travis smiled a dazzling grin at the world. "'I could get him women. I'm selling drugs.' God, I sound like such a fucked-up loser. You'd never know I was taking all these APs."

A horn tooted as a golf cart pulled up to the stage. Mario stepped out and looked up at him.

"Are you, eh, Travis Newton?" asked the proctor. He held up a pink slip.

Mr. Popper pursed his lips beneath his bristly mustache as he tapped a stack of pages on his desk. Mario lurked in the corner, walkie-talkie crackling. Travis had done a very rare thing and taken off his mirrored aviator sunglasses.

"Well . . . ," said the vice-principal.

Travis tried to keep his breathing calm.

"I've gotten a very interesting piece of news here," said Popper.

Travis's hands sweat. Time seemed to slow as the vice-principal checked his pages.

"It seems, uh . . . ," said Popper.

He clicked his tongue and stared straight at Travis with bloodshot eyes. "It seems you've been selected for a Golden State Merit Award." He handed a letter across the desk. "Congratulations."

Travis looked down at the paper in his hand. "Governor Schwarzenegger wishes to recognize . . . you are one of five hundred exceptional scholars in the state of California . . . outstanding achievement . . ."

A long pause. "Great," he said.

Popper looked at him. "You don't seem that excited about it," he said.

Travis shrugged. "I just get these things and I don't think about it," he said. "I just move on. Pilot's certificate, master's dan in Shotokan, governor's award, I just put them in my sack. *Doop.*" Seeing the bizarre look on Popper's face, he quickly added, "I meant that to be humble, I didn't mean it to be obnoxious."

Popper's voice took on the slightly unnerved tone that accompanied most conversations with Travis. "Well, it's quite an honor, especially for a sophomore." He looked down at the papers. "You know, the governor's making the award himself. Him and Gray Davis are going to be here in Emerald Valley next month for some sort of an appearance together, and I guess you'll be a guest of honor."

"Tight," said Travis.

"I know Dr. Chao is going to be very happy to hear about this," said Popper. "We've got the accreditation coming up this spring, and we just can't tolerate the current behavior that's going on."

"Yeah, absolutely," said Travis.

"Sadie's was a disaster for all of us. The situation is so serious that I'm even considering having an undercover officer on campus."

Mario's walkie-talkie squawked and Travis clenched the governor's letter in his hand. "Do you really think that would help?"

"Oh, they can certainly be very effective. A school in the district had one once before, I believe, a number of years ago. Some strapping twenty-year-old Samoan fellow who practiced with the water polo team. Heh, heh. He unraveled it all. I think they ended up with a dozen arrests."

Wil had just dropped the last guitar amp back in the ASB office when Travis wandered toward him. Slender, silent, and cold behind mirrored lenses.

"Dude," he said, "I am so fucked. Popper's going to send in a narc."

STONE CANYONS

I had shown up one week later, and unwittingly stepped right into the me-shaped hole that the past few months had dug.

Simply no point existed to my being in a school where everybody thought I was a narc. I could only look forward to months of "I love heroin!" and people huddling up away from me to lead their real lives. I would hardly have an insider perspective, and I would hardly have a true high school experience.

That night I sat in my apartment and watched thin clouds blow across the moon. The frigid wind bore a damp hint of the stone canyons of the city of my birth. Time and fate had caught up with me. Either I could spend a dwindling handful of months wandering alone and outcast among the concrete quads, or I could just quit and drop out of Mirador.

GIVE ME A PLACE
TO STAND

He changed the whole premise of the story, he packed half a liter of walnut ice cream into his stomach instead, and he ruined the moral of this tale about chocolate bunnies, deducing that all final options are a trap.

—Subcomandante Marcos of
the EZLN, *Tale of the Magic
Chocolate Bunnies*

The next morning, light haze spread a translucent cast across an extremely long day.

Thea waited for me after math with Leo the little freshman and one of the girls in gauzy black.

"Everybody was talking about it in class today," she told me. "Someone was like, 'What do you think about the narc?' and people were like 'Aw, fuck that shit.' You have to watch your back. Cody was talking about approaching you and doing something, and I think him and some people are planning on jumping you, like one of the Mexican dealer guys said he had brass knuckles."

"We're going to walk you to your next class," Leo said.

"God, this must be such like a terrible nightmare for you," said the gauzy girl. "Stay with us."

Thea handed me a note as the two of them took me away. "Hey," it read. "I am really sorry about everything that is going on. I am also sorry about my big mouth. Sometimes it goes with out my brain operating. Once again I am sorry. It wont happen again. Take care, Thea."

So now I could either leave Mirador or get thugged in the parking lot with brass knuckles.

Okay, universe, I got the point already. Clearly the entire cosmologi-cal order had destined this meaningless heap of sensate dust to pass its eyeblink flicker as a hedge fund analyst.

But damned if I wouldn't go down swingin'.

Until the final breakdown point, I would do whatever I needed to make everything okay. I had my two rules, and I would obey them until the bitterest end, but as far as I was concerned, absolutely anything else had become fair game.

Franz Kafka says, "In the fight between you and the world, back the world."

With an attitude like that, Kafka would never make prom king.

Game on.

When the bell rang for lunch, deep driving guitar riffs mounted and heavy drums pounded. Same Distance Reduced had cranked the amps a little louder.

The black crowd who hung out by the food court vending machines sneered at the music. "Dang, what is this shit?" one guy asked.

I grabbed my burrito from Crystallina and bore down on the senior circle.

Based on my core competence of fearlessness, I had only one element of leverage to move a mountain of two thousand people: individual ac-countability. In high school, everyone fears embarrassment or being sin-gled out of the group so mightily that I had a stunning force at hand.

A dozen people stood in front of the stage, jumping around and mosh-ing into one another, but a far bigger group had formed a crescent to laugh at the real attraction, the special ed students. Six of them linked arms and skipped in circles to their own rhythm, switching off partners with big smiles on their faces. Aram and his wild, thrashing dance starred solo.

"That's just sad," said Alexis.

Brian pointed out a girl to Cody. "Yo, that one retard in the wheel-chair keeps staring at me. Maybe she wants a neck."

"That's so wrong, bro," laughed Cody.

I crashed into this pastoral scene and headed straight for Vic Reyes. I went off, very very loudly, so everybody heard. "This narc shit is fucking unbelievable," I yelled. "It's driving me crazy."

Vic looked awkward. "Don't worry about it," he said.

"It's just like a joke," said Alexis.

"No, it's totally not," I said. "The thing is people actually believe it." I pointed to Kaylee. "She honestly believes I'm a narc. Yesterday she was all like 'Don't talk to the narc.'" Kaylee looked flustered.

I pointed to Cody. "He totally believes it too. Everyone's like telling me he's all going to jump me or something. Aren't you gonna shank me?" He looked down, a little clumsily.

Everyone was silent, watching. Vic Reyes was completely on the spot. "Stop trying to sell me drugs," he joked weakly.

"It was so fucking hard to come here in the middle of senior year," I yelled at him, "and now I have to deal with all this and I'm in trouble for a grip of shit you know I never did."

"It wasn't me," mumbled Vic. "Everyone else was saying it."

"Yeah, it sucks here," said Cody.

"It wouldn't suck if people weren't assholes," I snapped. More awkwardness. Hysteria entered my voice. "This whole thing was really hard, and I've been like trying to keep it together really hard, and this is just like, unbelievable to have this happen."

Alexis touched my back. "Relax," she said. "Don't worry."

"You came at the worst time," said Padma, "like right after the dance when they started talking about the whole accreditation thing."

"The thing is everybody hates the administration," said Brian. "If anybody's pissed at you, it's because they're pissed at the administration."

"God, Emerald Valley is so lame," said Cody. "What pussies."

"So you don't have anything to do with it?" Shawn asked me.

I stared at him. "With *what*? With being a narc?"

He squirmed, embarrassed. "Uh, yeah."

"Dude, did you miss the whole point of this?" I said.

A few more moments of painful silence passed.

Cody looked down. "I, I was totally calling you out." Then he swallowed. He looked up at me and took a deep breath. "I'm sorry I called you out, bro."

"No worries," I said.

He put out his hand. We shook, firmly.

"A cop is bad enough," he said. "An undercover cop is so much worse."

He smiled, a little awkwardly. I smiled back.

"Dude," I said. "It's so true." Then we laughed.

"Hey," said Vic, "what are you up to after school? We're gonna be drinking."

So after last bell we all headed to the outdoor pool in a tract-house development, a square blue oasis in a land of gray one-story contemporaries. A few guys brought a cooler full of Keystone Light.

"Do you want a beer?" Brian asked. A dozen people watched me.

"Sure," I said. I fished one out of the ice, opened it, and drank.

I heard sighs of relief. "Let me feel it," said Alexis. She weighed the can in her hand, and her face split into a big smile. "Half-empty! Okay, now we know one hundred percent you're not a narc, because they can't do stuff like drink. They'll like refuse it."

Hey, whatever worked.

"You didn't trust me," I accused.

"I trusted you, fool," said Vic, "we just weren't sure."

Padma twined her fingers through the pool net. "Like Alexis's brother got back and he was all like, 'Don't be stupid. We had Sadie's a week ago, and now in the middle of the year this random guy shows up, and suddenly he's hanging out with everybody and talking about drugs. Don't you think he could be a cop?' and stuff like that."

I shook my head and smiled in disbelief.

Kaylee laughed. "I was like, 'I don't know, maybe. He doesn't have any beard or anything. He could maybe pass, I guess.' Like, you know, anybody could be if you try to imagine it. . . ."

"And everybody was like, 'Oh, my God, getting a narc is so the kind of thing that Mirador would do,'" said Padma.

"Yeah, dude, that's *so* Emerald Valley," said Brian. "This place sucks."

Cody opened a beer. "We're going to do our best to squash it when we hear it. Now if anyone says it, we're gonna be like *'No!'*"

"Thanks," I said. We punched fists.

"What would a new kid be without a scandal?" Padma asked happily.

And over the next week and a half, as quickly as it had appeared, the whole thing rolled up. It was amazing to watch news of my okayness spread—interestingly, the popular people in the different grades accepted it quickly, and then it spilled out from the center to the periphery, trickling down to figures less plugged in to the system.

Finally not even the three hard-core punks with patched leather jackets and their hair up in severe liberty spikes gave me a second glance. Every month or so somebody would say, "Hah, I can't believe people actually thought you were a narc!" and we'd all laugh about it for a minute before conversation moved to something else. I got a lot of narc jokes in my yearbook.

How many miracles had I experienced by now?

PART THREE

PART THREE

TWO WEEKS GO DEEP

Anyone can see my every flaw; it isn't hard.
Anyone can say they're above this all.
—Jimmy Eat World, "Pain"

THEODORA MARGARID DANIELIAN

Thea's round face had paled, and her hazel eyes darted away from my gaze. "Oh, my God, I'm so embarrassed. I can't believe you came this afternoon."

We stood by a bubbling aquarium tank down a side hallway at the Emerald Valley community center. Bright Saturday sun washed in the glass windows and the voices of a hundred parents and friends drifted from the theater lobby.

"Whatever," I said. "Like stuff just happens, you know?"

She shivered. "Everybody was laughing."

"So that's good," I said. "Laughing means they had like a good time."

Thea had manned the light board for a Mirador production of *Hamlet*. Halfway through the show, the lights had gone down for a scene change. The guy playing the tragic prince had positioned himself stage center, assumed a declamatory posture, and spent the next four minutes in total darkness while Thea bumbled furiously at the controls. Everyone had laughed indeed.

"You're so not worried about like anything," she said. "Like when I got here I wasn't so outgoing like you are. I guess I'm really shy, and like I've always had problems trusting people. I guess I've been screwed over by too many people in my life."

I nodded solemnly, sighed inwardly, and hoped sincerely that she avoided all media outlets for the next few years.

"You don't want to be like him," snapped chubby red-haired Evelyn Strout, who loomed nearby. "He's a shallow prep who ditched us to hang out with the quote-unquote cool seniors and now he thinks he's too good for us." She turned to me. "I saw you in the arts quad yesterday and said 'hi,' and you like just kept walking and pretended you didn't see me. So I guess you're ignoring me now, huh?"

I watched tetra fish flit past. "No. I didn't see you."

She snorted and pulled a small green net from her backpack. "Is anyone looking? You have to cover me."

Thea sighed and looked around the hallway corner at the babbling crowd in the lobby. "No, you're good. But do you know what I mean? Like I feel like now I'm just totally out of the loop, and if I don't do something, everyone's just going to think I'm some weird quiet girl forever. Right now nobody knows who I really am, and I don't matter to anybody, you know? This is my chance to matter."

Quick as an osprey, Evelyn scooped the center's rainbow fish from the tank and dropped it into a plastic Baggie filled with water. She shoved the bag into her backpack and zipped it up.

"Hah, hah!" she exulted. "I've wanted that one for weeks. Wait, what were you saying?"

"Nothing," said Thea. "That's a nice fish."

Among her other hobbies, Evelyn liked to steal cold-blooded animals from public places. Her room at home teemed with an enormous menagerie of snakes, turtles, lizards, chameleons, and, of course, fish.

"See you later," she said and left.

I watched bubbles rise in the lighted water. Thea smiled sadly and poked my arm. "Hey," she said. "Don't worry. I understand you have to be with the people you have to be with. Thanks for coming to my show."

Ms. Horn walked into bio on Monday with a #1 TEACHER coffee mug and a big smile on her face. "Good morning, my friends! Did you see the Lakers game last night?"

Thea slid lower in her seat and pushed her bangs over her eyes.

As the class filtered in, the teacher gathered both rooms together for a special presentation before they tore into the cat dissection proper.

"Shhh, guys, shhh," Horn called over the general conversation of forty students. Then she squealed and clapped her hands. "I'm so excited, you guys! We're going to go to the computer lab to take another personality test!"

She went up to the board and wrote "Enneagrams" in purple marker. She carefully surrounded the word with confetti and smiley faces.

"Those of you who had me last semester will remember how we all took personality tests. This time we're going to be taking a different type of test that I heard about called the enneagram test, which is really similar. It should be like really insightful and great for us, and I'm going to assign you to your cat groups based on your type."

Lots and lots of smiley faces on the board. "This is the enneagram flower," said Ms. Horn, sketching a bizarre, nine-pointed star of interlocking triangles. "It comes from ancient wisdom. Everybody has like a point on the enneagram flower, and they're influenced by the different wings around their point. For example, a friend of mine is number seven—the Enthusiast—balanced with a number eight wing. Enthusiasts don't like commitment, so he doesn't want to settle down. He's thirty-five, he's very happy with his studio apartment, and he's in a band. Get it?"

The ten or so people paying attention and not reading or talking or playing with their cell phones or sleeping took on a distressed look as they attempted to fathom the mysteries of the enneagram flower. A few tried to draw it.

Ms. Horn looked down at Thea, who wrote the words "Fuck You" in her binder in heavy ballpoint. Thea noticed class had become quiet, and her hand stopped as she saw Ms. Horn smiling down at her. "Why do you have so much hostility, child? So much rage?"

Thea shrugged, the whole class watching. Her face heated.

"Oh, my goodness," said Ms. Horn, "you must be so *angry* inside. Poor Thea's writing very hostile things in her binder. Do you feel you don't have love, Thea?"

Long, awkward, ringing silence. "I'm okay, thanks," Thea mumbled.

"Come on!" said Ms. Horn, clapping. "Let's go."

So everybody went to the Mirador library to take advantage of several dozen largely unused computers bought by adults eager to throw money at the idea of Technology. Ms. Horn gave out the address of a Web site where one could take the enneagram test online, or alternatively book a private enneagram consultation by phone "with both Don and Russ" for

$275 per fifty-minute hour. A history section explained that a Bolivian man had developed the enneagram from the work of an itinerant Greek-Armenian mystic who had used the nine-pointed flower to choreograph Sufi-inspired dances.

They printed out their enneagram results and rendered the sheets up to an eager Ms. Horn. "Look, Sara!" she exclaimed. "You're a Helper, just like me!"

"Ohhh!" said Sara. "I just want to help people, I guess!"

"Ohhh!" said Ms. Horn. "Just like me!"

"You're so sweet, Ms. Horn," said another girl. "You're such a Helper!"

"Awwww, thank you," said the teacher. "Look, you're a Helper, too!"

Thea stared down at her page and sighed.

A few more people handed theirs in. "Miss Warner, it looks like you are an Investigator. And you are an eight, a Challenger, Mr. Vic Reyes!"

"This is retarded," said Vic.

"Why are you challenging me?" said Ms. Horn. "See, Vic's a Challenger."

The short Korean guy who never spoke handed his sheet over and attempted to flee. "Look," said Ms. Horn, pointing. "Seung is a Peacemaker." Everyone turned to stare at him. "See, he just sits there making peace all the time. He seems so quiet to us, because he's just up there making peace, aren't you, Seung?" He forced a wretched smile.

"Who am I missing?" she demanded.

Thea had no exit. Head down, she gave hers in. "Oh," Horn called. "Look at Thea, everybody! Thea is a four! Fours seem turned in on themselves and it's hard to get a 'rise' out of them, but they're—the *romantic* type!"

"Whoooo!" everyone said. "Romantic! Yeah!"

Thea said nothing, just sat down smoldering as forty people laughed at her.

"See," said Ms. Horn, "see, everybody, we're just not getting a 'rise' out of her."

As the class talked, she scanned through her sheaf of pages. "Okay, shhh, you guys, shhh. See, I'm going over your tests and it's very interesting for me. It's helping me understand the dynamic in my classes a lot better, because a lot of people are getting the sevens and eights, which are the rebellious personality types. So, I'm like, Whew! I'm not a bad teacher, it's the group with which I was given."

During lunch period, Thea sat on the steps with the other behind-the-library people. Same Distance Reduced played a set over in main quad.

"Ah, Wil," she sighed at the music. She bit into the sandwich she brought from home. "I'm so sick of it here. As soon as I turn eighteen, I'm going to get a tattoo, and then I'm going to get on a bus and just go as far away as possible."

"What tattoo do you want to get?" the pierced-lip guy asked.

"I don't know," said Thea. "I'm going to design it, and I'm going to do a really good job. It's going to be really cool."

"You know what I want to do?" said a gauzy girl. "I want to dye my pussy hair green and like get a tattoo over it that says 'Do not step on the grass.' And then I want to tattoo on my butt 'Thank you, cum again.'"

Everybody reflected on the stylishness of the suggestion.

"Hey," Evelyn asked Thea. "Have you thought about what you want for your sixteenth birthday yet?"

"I want Wil," said Thea. "Just kidding. Oh, God, that would be so nice. I want a dildo."

"Any specific kind?" asked Evelyn. "Size? Shape?"

"I don't know," said Thea. "You can surprise me."

Evelyn dunked her tempeh patty in safflower oil. "You could get the weird skinny kind that spins around, that's in like all the porn movies. It's in like ten of them."

"Don't tell me which kind," said Thea. "I want to be surprised. Hey, do you know what I wish I had, but they don't make them? I wish I had a cart with a dildo on it, and I could sit on it and drive along on it over bumps, and I would be like 'oh!' And you could control how fast it went, and you could speed it up or slow it down. Wouldn't that be like such a good idea? I was in my mom's car this morning, and we were going over bumps, and I was thinking, hmmmm. . . ."

The girls nodded appreciatively as they ate their burritos, or—in Evelyn's case—pouch of unprocessed grains.

Thea slumped down in her chair behind the black epoxy lab table in bio class the next day. She read deep into a steamy novel about an immortal

Carpathian magician rock guitarist who needed to seduce his psychic lifemate while battling soulless vampires. "Number Twelve in the Dark Series!" the book proclaimed. The cover featured a pale woman hunched in a graveyard under moonlight.[1]

Voices broke the sinister enchantment. "Ms. Horn!"

"Samantha!" yelped the teacher. "Kayyylee! All my girls!"

Thea looked up to see a group of six Matadoras at the classroom door holding two big Mylar balloons shaped like a bumblebee and a butterfly. Another Matadora lifted up a big wicker basket stuffed full with presents.

"Can we come talk to Sara for a second?" asked Samantha.

"Look, Sara!" said Ms. Horn. "Look what your friends brought you."

"Ohhhh!" said Sara. She had gotten her neck brace off a few days before.

The six girls filed in and trooped to the back where Sara sat. "Happy sweet sixteen, Sara!" Kaylee said. One girl pulled a rhinestone tiara from the basket, and they placed it on Sara's delighted head. "You're the queen for the day!"

"Ohh, that's so sweet," said another girl in bio class. "I wish my friends would do that for me."

"Ohh, thank you, guys," said Sara. "I love you guys *so much*!"

Charity fished around in the basket and pulled out a boxing nun toy. She laughed and used it to punch Vic Reyes.

"Can you take a picture of us, Ms. Horn?" asked Sara, holding out her cell phone.

"I'll pretend I didn't see the forbidden device, Miss Dunbar," said the teacher. "How do I get this to work?"

All the girls huddled and smiled around the tiara-wearing Sara as Ms. Horn snapped the photo.

"Awww," she said, holding out the phone for them to inspect the picture. "Look at you guys!"

"Awww," said Sara. "Ms. Horn, you should be sitting right here, you should be in a seat along with us!"

"Awww," the teacher said, "that's so sweet!"

Thea realized how tightly her fingers had clenched around her pen as she began to write an elaborate new "Fuck You."

*   *   *

Backstage during tech theater, she curled up on a black wooden set piece, reading her Dark Series novel. "This book is so good," she said. "I just want to leave school and keep reading it. Look at some of these parts."

She pointed to a page and handed the book to Evelyn, whose eyes quickly widened. "Whoa," said Evelyn, "this is pretty graphic. 'Licked the cream offering . . . '"

Thea giggled and snatched it back.

"So you're into vampire porn," said Leo the theater-tech freshman.

"It's not vampire porn," said Thea. "They're fighting the vampires. It's more like Carpathian magician porn. But vampires are my weakness, they're so hot. My fantasy is like this guy with black eyeliner grabs a girl and gets really rough with her, and then vampires drag them away." She shivered with pleasure.

"Look, the set piece is dripping underneath you," said Evelyn.

"They need a movie that's one hundred percent hot vampires," said Thea.

"What about *Interview with a Vampire?*" asked another tech.

"No," said Thea. "They tried with the long, blow-dried hair and everything, but it just wasn't right."

Evelyn examined the back cover as Thea read. "Look at the author," she said, bending the thick paper over. A fat middle-aged woman gawked back. "I can't believe she wrote all that stuff about 'cream offerings.' It looks like your mom, Thea." Then she laughed.

The next day during first period, Thea's world geography teacher held a thick stack of Scantron computer answer forms and test booklets in both arms.

"Okay," she said, "I'm sure you remember these, the, uh, California Healthy Kids Survey. That's you. Please pencil in all your spaces heavy and dark on the Scantron. You've got the whole period to finish them, so please take it seriously."

With a thump, a booklet and a Scantron landed on Thea's desk. She began to fill in the boxes.

During the past 12 months, how would you describe the grades you mostly received in school? D. B's and C's

During the past 12 months, about how many times did you skip school or cut classes? A. 0 times

During your life, how many times have you used or tried . . .
Alcohol? A. 0 times
Marijuana? A. 0 times
Other illegal drugs? A. 0 times
A cigarette, even one or two puffs? A. 0 times

Thea looked around the room at all the heads bent down over their surveys. She rested her cheek on her palm.

During the past 12 months, how many times have you been in a physical fight? A. 0 times

During the past 12 months, did your boyfriend or girlfriend ever hit, slap, or physically hurt you on purpose? A. Does not apply, do not have a boy/girlfriend

Thea chewed sadly on her bologna sandwich at lunch. "I want to get drunk," she announced.

Evelyn gave her a watery stare. "God, I wish," she said.

"I mean," said Thea, "I sounded so fucking pathetic on that survey. I hadn't done, like, anything. I mean, I've done bad stuff, but it wasn't on the survey. Like there was no box for something like 'How many times have you peed on a tombstone?' "

"How many times have you peed on a tombstone?" asked the skin.

"Uh, three," said Thea. She sighed. "I almost got to put down the one about ditching school for the time I went to go see *The Lord of the Rings*, but I realized it was more than twelve months ago, and my dad signed me out, so it wasn't really like ditching."

"You know what really annoyed me?" said Evelyn. "Remember how there was like this question about 'does your boyfriend hurt you' like it was oooh, this terrible thing? They didn't have any option for 'E. No, but I wish he would.' "

"What do you mean?" said the skin.

Evelyn tossed her striped scarf. "Alan drives me crazy. He won't hurt me, that's so annoying. I keep like asking him to, but he says he won't because he loves me."

Thea chewed her sandwich. "If he loved you, he'd hurt you, because that's what you want."

Heads nodded. "That's what I keep trying to tell him," Evelyn said. "But the sex is still fun."

"Oh, tell me all about the sex," said Thea. "I'm like living vicariously through you."

"Well, last night, to start off, me and Alan took a shower together."

"I wish I could take a shower together with someone," said Thea.

"Oh, yes," said Evelyn. "We washed the cats and then we took a shower together."

"You and the cats took a shower together?" asked the spiky-lip guy.

"No," said Evelyn. "We washed the cats in a bucket and then we took a shower."

"Oh."

Ms. Horn clapped her hands together brightly in bio the next morning. "Okay, my friends," she said. "Shhh, you guys, shhhh. I've assigned you to your cat dissection groups based on enneagram, which I think is going to be a really positive experience for everybody."

She read off the assignments. "My friends Miss Warner, Miss Dunbar, and Mr. Reyes will be with two other of my friends, which I think will make a great dynamic."

She looked at her paper. "Okay, Thea." She smiled. "I'm sorry, your group is going to be back in the annoying room, so that's where you're going to stay starting tomorrow."

Thea read her vampire book. She took a breath and nodded a little.

After Ms. Horn finished, she hopped up on the side of her desk and swung her legs.

"Shhhh," she said. "Shhhh." The room got a little quieter. "So do you guys want to hear about my horrible date last night?"

"Yeah," called some people over the general background noise.

"Shhhh," she said. "Okay, so I went out with this guy who my friends set me up with, okay? He teaches fourth grade. And like they figured, he's a teacher and she's a teacher, this is going to work or something, right?" She started to laugh. "No!" she said, putting her hands on her head. "It was terrible! Oh, my God!"

"What happened?" Sara Dunbar called out.

"Okay," said Ms. Horn, "so we like went to dinner at Outback Steakhouse, and you know how sometimes there are like awkward silences, right? Well, like the entire meal was like an awkward silence. I'd be like, 'So what kinda stuff are you into?' and he'd be like, 'Oh, a lot of stuff,' and then he wouldn't say anything for like five minutes. I just watched the Lakers game up on TV."

"What a loser," someone called out.

"What a fag," called Vic Reyes.

"What kinda car did he drive?" asked another guy.

"I think it was like a midnineties Focus," said Ms. Horn.

"If he drove a Focus, he's a fag," said Vic.

"Anyway," said Ms. Horn, "so I was like, 'Do you want to go to a club or something?' And then we went, but it was really awkward because it was so late. I really don't like clubs after midnight, you know? Because there's this point when it like stops being fun and you're there for a good time and that happens around midnight. Then everyone is trying to find someone, you know, and it's all icky and creepy."

"Did you guys hook up?" someone asked.

"No," said Ms. Horn. "He just like, went home!"

"What a loser!" yelled somebody.

"What a fag!" said Vic again.

"Mr. Reyes," said Ms. Horn, "is that appropriate language for the classroom?"

Vic laughed.

"Hit him, Charity," said Ms. Horn. Charity Warner slugged him in the arm.

"Ow," he said.

Thea turned the page, slowly.

"I hate Ms. Horn's class so much," she said, backstage in tech theater.

Evelyn cringed. "I've heard scary stories." She sat in half-lotus and colored strands of Thea's blond chunk of hair with a blue marker pen. The result actually looked decent.

"Can you do my hair next?" asked a gauzy girl.

"Sure," said Evelyn. "I used to do this all the time."

"I mean, all she does is gossip with the popular kids," said Thea. "She finds like the queen bee and the cool guys and jokes around with them and ignores everyone else. There's this pack of bitchy girls and she always talks to them. The class drives me crazy."

Evelyn completed a strand and started on another one. "I know this is a shock," she said, "I know this is a newsflash, but"—she mock-gasped for air and looked around, hunted—"Ms. Horn plays favorites!"

"It's so not fair," said Thea.

"Life is suffering," said Evelyn. "That's one of the Four Noble Truths."

"Yeah," said Thea. "And people seem like driven to make it worse for themselves. You know what else is driving me crazy, especially in that class? Everyone's suddenly like, 'What are you giving up for Lent?' 'I'm giving up chocolate! What are *you* giving up for Lent?'" She growled. "Nothing, people. I'm giving *nothing* up for Lent. I'm an atheist. And then they like stare at me like I'm insane. I want to make a shirt that has two pirate swords over each other in the shape of a cross, and put underneath it like in bloody writing, 'Johnny Depp Is My Only Savior.'"

"Alan's an atheist, too," said Evelyn. "But he respects my Buddhism because it doesn't have a personal god."

"You're so lucky you're dating someone who understands you," Thea said.

"We're actually going out now," said Evelyn.

"Wow," said Thea. "That's so great for you guys. I remember when you were just talking."

"Wait," said Leo the techie frosh, "I've never understood how all those levels work in high school, with like talking and stuff."

"It's so easy," said Evelyn. "First you're talking with the other person, then the next level is you're seeing them—which is like nonexclusive— then you're dating, which is exclusive, and then finally you're going out with them."

Thea sighed. "And then you're so lucky," she said.

Evelyn finished coloring and Thea shook her hair out. "Beautiful," she said. "Thank you very much, my dear. Oh my God, I have such lesbian hair."

A girl in a Hawaiian shirt called out, "Who's up for some Boob Wars?"

"I'm in," said Thea. She got off the black set piece and walked to the center of the room.

"I'll judge," said one of the gay theater guys, climbing on top of the set piece.

"What's Boob Wars?" asked Leo.

"You know how like moose butt antlers?" said Evelyn. "Watch and learn."

Thea and the Hawaiian-shirt girl walked to opposite ends of the backstage area. They both stuck out their chests. "One . . ." cried the gay guy, "two . . . *three!*"

With a joyful yell, Thea and the Hawaiian-shirt girl charged forward, giggling as they ran. They tilted their heads to the side and smacked into each other, breast to breast, in the middle of the room. The Hawaiian-shirt girl rebounded back further.

"One point for Thea!" called the judge.

Faces flushed and laughing, the two girls ran into each other's breasts four more times. Thea took the match three-two.

Leo watched, enraptured. "I want to play Boob Wars."

When last bell rang, Thea went by the facilitation quad to pick up her brother Aram. The special ed people were supposed to go on a trip, but it had been cancelled due to the budget cuts.

"Hi, Big A," she said. "How was your day today?"

"My day was fine, Thea," he said, nodding to the music on his headphones.

They had gotten halfway across the quad when Thea saw a few thug-style black guys with sagging jeans and glinting diamond earrings gathered around a blind sophomore with an IQ of sixty. The sophomore was very small because he had been born prematurely, and they laughed and shoved him back and forth, as if they played catch. Dozens of people passed by on their way to the parking lot and nobody said anything.

Thea pulled her backpack straps tight. "Wait," she told her brother, and started to run. She heard and felt nothing besides rage.

"Hey!" she screamed at the pack of guys, who turned in surprise. She was easily half their size but no one even noticed. "What the fuck are you doing? Get the fuck away from him!"

"Aw, what—" started one guy.

"Do you want me to get a proctor over here and get all your asses fucking suspended? What if that was you? How the fuck would you feel if someone did that to you or your brother?"

The guys sneered, and with a final shove, wandered away. Thea closed her eyes for a moment and seemed to shrink back down to her little self again.

"Are you okay?" she asked the blind sophomore.

"Yuh," he said.

She walked back to where Aram waited with his headphones on. The two continued toward the parking lot. "God, it makes me so mad," she said. "People are so stupid."

"No, people aren't stupid, Thea," he protested.

The next day she made an announcement on the steps behind the library during passing period. "I'm going to have a birthday party this year," she said.

Evelyn raised her eyebrows. "You never struck me as a big birthday-party type," she said.

"Yeah," Thea said, "I know, but I used to have one every year back at CdM, and sixteen's like a big birthday, you know?"

Evelyn ate a slice of home-dried kiwi. "Whatever tickles your pickle," she said.

"Who are you inviting?" asked a gauzy girl.

"Like a lot of people, I think," said Thea. "Definitely you guys."

She wrote out invitations as she sat at her new seat in bio, a heavy black lab bench tucked in the back corner of the annoying room. On shelves around her a series of cat embryos at various horrific stages of development floated in glass jars of formalin solution.

She printed fifty invitations, writing each one carefully on its own sheet of notebook paper. The pages said the following:

> Thea Danielian's B-Day Party
> Next Monday @ 3:30
> Bring B-B suit & towel and a happy face.
> My house
> 1016 Los Robles Avenue
> Emerald Valley CA. 92895

One of the lab partners the enneagrams had chosen for her was a junior with a reedy mustache, a limp Caesar cut, and bad breath. "What are you writing out?" he asked her, leaning in.

"I'm having a party for my sixteenth birthday. Do you want to come?" She gave him an invitation.

After class she handed one to almost everybody whose name she knew.

"I'm having kind of a party, if you want to come," she said.

"What is it?" Vic asked.

"For my birthday," she said. "I'm just having like a kickback at my house."

"Oh," he said. "Cool."

As Thea left, she saw Charity look down at her invitation. "I'm sure somebody will be going," Charity said, and laughed. Thea blushed and hurried out the door.

She wrote another forty invites in tech theater. All the techies and everyone behind the library got one, of course. But she went even further during lunch and handed them to the popular sophomores who hung out in the language arts quad. Thea felt like she had missed a beat ever since transferring as a freshman into a class that had grown up together in Emerald Valley. Now the hour had come to stop acting like a shy new kid.

She summoned all her courage to present an invitation to Same Distance Reduced vocalist Wil Kormer in fifth-period Spanish. She justified it to herself because she had already given out eighty or so, and she was just trying to invite her grade.

After class Wil showed the page to Travis Newton. "Oh, yeah, count me in," said Travis. Then he laughed.

At the end of the day, Thea went to the baseball field to take a few pictures of the players' team for the *Mirror*. She had a nice camera, a Nikon D2X. The guys were all upperclassmen, loud and joking around, and she tried to minimize contact as much as possible, just snapped the shots and ran.

The photo editor, a senior, examined her images on the computer. "Hey," he said, "I really like these. A lot of your pictures have been really good."

Thea blushed, hair over her eyes. "Thanks," she said quietly, rocking back and forth.

"Did you hear about this?" he said, handing her a flyer. Apparently the Getty Museum up in L.A. wanted entries from Southern California high schoolers for some sort of visual arts contest in a few months.

"Wow," she said. "This is like a big deal."

"I don't know," he said, "in case you're interested or whatever."

"I'm not gonna win a contest," she said.

He shrugged. Another guy behind her waited with his pictures.

Thea's brother had an afterschool program, so she got on her black Schwinn, a classic 1955-style Cruiser with a basket, and started to bike home on the side of the road.

A few blocks south of Mirador she saw a familiar figure walking down the sidewalk, the tall form, black hair, and tiny T-shirt of none other than Wil. A few other friends surrounded him, including Travis in his mirrored sunglasses.

Thea's heart started to race as her bike closed the gap between them. She sat up as straight as possible and tossed back her hair. She held out her chest. Even though she was small, she was proud of her decent-sized breasts. She raised her chin, trying to slow her breathing as much as possible. She would pass them by like an elegant and otherworldly figure, and Wil would see her and be struck by her beauty and grace, left with a haunting vision of desire imprinted in his mind. When he came to her birthday party on Monday, he would be ready to chase that elusive seductress.

Her bike rolled onward, only a few yards behind. Wil and his friends remained deep in conversation and didn't notice her approach.

Thea turned the pedals slowly, took a final deep breath, and shifted her grip on the handlebars. Bizarrely, it felt like something tugged at her right shoe. She looked down to see the lace from her right sneaker caught in the spokes of the front wheel, slowly winding itself tighter and tighter.

Panic.

She tried to pull on her foot, but the lace dragged it back to the wheel and the bike started to wobble. She watched in horror as the lace ran out just as she reached Wil and his friends and they turned to notice her.

"Ahhh," said Thea, as quietly as possible, and toppled over into the wet gutter with a *sproing* in a sprawl of bike and legs.

The four guys stopped. Thea looked up over the trickle of running water. Travis stared back at her.

"Uh, are you okay?" Wil asked.

"Yeah," said Thea quickly, trying to lever herself up with her palms, foot attached to her bike. "Oh, yeah. I'm fine."

They all watched her flop and flail wretchedly for a little while. "Are you sure?" asked Wil.

"Yeah," said Thea. "Oh, yeah. Yeah, I've done this before."

She hadn't, and she meant it to sound causal, but as soon as the words left her mouth, she realized exactly how pathetic it sounded. She followed it with a nervous wobbly giggle.

"Oh," said Wil. "Okay."

They lingered for another moment to watch her try to pull her left leg over the bike frame before they continued on. "Later," said one guy.

When they were about fifteen paces away, she heard Travis burst into cold laughter. "How do you possibly describe the funniest fucking thing you've ever seen in your life?" she heard him saying, as she lay in the gutter, water soaking her legs.

Thea spent Saturday replaying the scene over and over to herself at least four hundred times. Moment by moment, angle by angle, each word as slow and torturous as the damnation of impure souls seduced into a forbidden web of darkness.

After a while, just for the heck of it, she took her camera outside and shot a few pictures. A white sapote tree against the hot sun. A toddler wearing an Angels of Anaheim hat much too big for him. The east of town where new housing developments abruptly ended beneath empty desert hills and hazy mountains peaked in ice.

On Sunday, she went shoplifting.

A lot of times she'd head to a store and just grab something herself, but now some people from the library steps had organized an expedition. The spiky-lip guy drove them all in his brother's gray Civic.

Evelyn didn't come along because stealing transgressed the Five Precepts and produced karma.[2]

First they pulled up to the swap meet, a huge rusty building that looked like an airport hangar.[3]

The little group squeezed down crowded aisles of plastic-wrapped jeans, sizzling peppers on steel-drum grills, and anime porn videos.

Thea examined occult amulets and charms crammed into one of many stalls hung with herbs and acupuncture meridian charts in Spanish.

She picked up a packet of pennyroyal. "How much is this?" she asked the Korean vendor.

"One dollah," he said.

She leaned in. "How much?"

"One dollah." He held up a finger.

Thea spoke slowly and loudly. "I don't understand. Can you write it?"

While she talked, they grabbed. A few stall blocks away, they all selected their favorite pieces from the haul of funky evil-eye-begone charms.

The spiky-lip guy laughed. "Everything's like a dollar here because everyone's like Mexican."

One of the gauzy girls pointed a plump finger at a wire cage. "Oooh, rabbits! I want to steal a rabbit."

Thea shivered. "I got a rabbit for Easter once, but it like died, and we buried it in the backyard. The dog dug it up and brought part of it in, and my brother just like found half the rabbit lying there."

Next they went to a Chevron the skin knew.

"The clerk here is a *wreck*," he explained. "He's like an idiot and he's tweaked out on meth or something."[4]

"Cover the license plate," said a gauzy girl. They wrapped newspaper around it.

A few customers waited in line when they entered, so everybody just went straight to the back. They took hot dogs from the roller grill, slathered on chili and cheese, and stuffed themselves.

Then the skin approached the clerk, a buck-toothed guy in his mid-twenties with pimples.

"Hey, buddy!" said the clerk, and they shook hands.

"So how's your life been?" the skin asked him.

"Women problems," said the clerk. "The thing is, you need a woman who . . ."

The skin nodded politely while everyone else snatched. The spiky-lip guy went back and grabbed two huge cases of Guinness.

The skin bought a plastic cup of Coke and they had all bid the clerk a happy good-bye when he spotted the beers.

"Hang on . . ." he said.

"Oh, shit!" yelled a gauzy girl, and they shoved out the door.

Everyone laughed as the Civic peeled from the parking lot. "We got like fifteen candy bars and twenty Certs!" giggled Thea.

"Check this out," said the skin. He took the lid off the cup of Coke and drank down the dark liquid to reveal five more candy bars underneath.

A gauzy girl clapped. "Very impressive, my dear."

Finally they went to the mall.

Thea pointed at Hollister Co., Abercrombie's beach-inspired clothing store for teens. "Let's steal preppy shit."

A gauzy girl shook her head. "My sister works at Hollister and the place is filled with secret shoppers who watch you. They watched this one guy who was swapping prices and they had like a ton of people waiting for him when he came back."

"Let's swap prices somewhere else," said the spiky-lip guy, looking at a sporting-goods store. "I want a snowboard."

They walked inside and each one asked a question of a salesperson. Meanwhile, courtesy of the spiky-lip guy, a $549 Burton snowboard exchanged stickers with a $70 discount one.

The group met briefly behind racks of Columbia jackets.

"Seventy dollars," he mumbled. "We need seventy dollars worth of stuff."

Each person went to the changing room at a different time, and each left the store individually. They counted the total clothing tally back at the car.

Thea looked down. "We've got like twelve wristbands, a couple of Von Dutch hats, and a few shirts. Yup, you got your seventy bucks."

"You guys are fucking sick," said the spiky-lip guy. "Thank you all so much. Next week I'm taking this shit back and buying my snowboard with the credit."

Thea had dreaded coming into school and encountering Wil on Monday, but as soon as she saw Death she cheered right up.

Seven feet tall, shrouded in black robes with a skull mask and a scythe, the Grim Reaper burst through the door of her morning geometry class. Two policemen and a student with a video camera trailed the hooded specter.

Mr. Lamarque stopped drawing midcone. Already it was shaping up to be a good birthday.

The younger police officer withdrew a piece of paper. "Roger Adelman," he intoned. "Roger Adelman."

Roger, a small and slightly nerdy boy, stood as the Grim Reaper beckoned him out the classroom door. The other officer followed, and the cameraman tracked their departure.

The young cop began to read his page: "Roger Adelman was a sophomore at Mirador High School, until the tragic evening that he was killed by a drunk driver on the 5 as he was coming back from his job at Quizno's Subs. Roger—"

But a quiet murmuring made him hesitate. Up at the board, Mr. Lamarque had continued with his lesson. "—as I'm sure you see clearly, the base of the cone is just a circle, with an area of pi r-squared, while . . ."

The cop carried on uncertainly, glancing over at the teacher: "Roger took part in a number of activities at Mirador, and he was—"

Mr. Lamarque drew a ruler-straight line. " . . . the height can be measured as a perpendicular extending from the *do you MIND?!*"

He whirled. The officer gasped and backed up, looking very young and scared.

"Holy shit!" whispered someone. "That's George. He graduated last year."

"I'm supposed to read this," George pleaded.

A pause. Mr. Lamarque gave him the bright stare through the steel-rimmed glasses, clutching his ruler. "Can you do it quickly, please?" he said at last in a pleasant voice. "I'm trying to teach my class."

George nodded, swallowed, and raced through the rest of the page. "Every fifteen minutes a teenager is killed by a drunk driver," he concluded. "Make the right choices." He nodded to the room and fled.

"Every Fifteen Minutes Day," said Lamarque. "A biannual treat. I'm sure someone in the administration building considers this valuable."

A few minutes later the door opened and Roger Adelman returned. White greasepaint covered his face, and black zombielike circles ringed his eyes. The guy with the video camera followed him to his seat and took a few establishing shots of the classroom before backing out.

Suddenly Thea understood how the day worked. Her heart pounded.

*   *   *

"The Grim Reaper takes people away . . . and they come back *hot*!"

The gauzy girls who had seen it before nodded. "They get somebody every fifteen minutes," one said.

Thea's mouth formed a little O of wonder. "This is like the best birth-day ever."

Passing period had come and they all sat behind the library. Thea stared in ecstasy at a few zombie people wandering across grass dotted with fake tombstones.

Then Evelyn cleared her throat to make the formal presentation. "Happy sixteenth birthday," she said. "Here's your birthday dildo."

She handed Thea a clear plastic box. It contained a Reflective Gel $8^1/_2$ inches Veined Chubby Dong, made of a translucent purple rubbery jelly-like material.

"Oh, my God, thank you!" said Thea. "I love you so much! This is the best birthday present a girl could get." She giggled and passed the plastic box around so everyone could see and admire it.

"Nice," said a gauzy girl. "This one is tight."

"I guess I'll see you all at my birthday party after school," said Thea.

"How many people did you end up inviting?" asked the skin.

"Like ninety," said Thea.

"Wow," said the spiky-lip guy.

Sixth period got cancelled for the schoolwide assembly on the football field.

Giant video screens had been erected in the center of the grass to play the footage of the Reaper. Dozens of parents of the "dead" zombie students sat in folding chairs, prepared to read fake obituaries they had composed.

In the turmoil as everyone clambered into the bleachers, Cody Reis-ling stood at the front of the risers in his baseball jersey and cap. "Are we paying for this out of our budget cut?" he kept repeating, loudly.

"Oh, God," said Evelyn. "Sit *down*, jackass."

"Fucking popular people can suck my nuts," said the skin.

Thea felt very charitable. "Popular people are people too," she re-minded them.[5]

The program began. A woman from the district attorney's office took the microphone and began to talk about the consequences of driving under the influence.

"Nothing will get you off," she said. "It doesn't matter who you are, how rich you are, anything. There's justice for all, and no special breaks for anyone."

"That's so not true," whispered a girl in the audience. "I bet if you were a celebrity you'd get off."

"Yeah," said another girl.

"Yeah," said a guy. "They can do whatever they want."

"If I was a celebrity," whispered a gauzy girl dreamily, "I would have pearls ground up and put on my eyelids."

That afternoon, the skin pulled up to Thea's house at 1016 Los Robles Avenue. A giant black iron gate with bronze fleur-de-lis pickets and an ornate Empire capital *D* in the center broke a high wall of solid stone.

He pressed the call box through his car window. "Uh, it's Aaron," he said. The gate swung open.

The driveway passed rows of tall white ash trees lined up like an honor guard, and curved around a trilevel fountain. The house itself rose before him, a gargantuan three-story Italian Renaissance palazzo with Palladian windows and a colonnaded portico. Despite the antiqued touches, it looked about two years old, which made sense.

He stood far under a huge wrought-iron lamp and rang the doorbell, which tolled a sonorous note somewhere in the depths of the villa. After a minute, the tremendous portal opened to reveal the tiny shape of Thea.

"Oh, my God!" she said. "I'm so glad that you came! We're out back."

She led him on a several-minute, trek through a vast atrium, with another indoor fountain, out the back of the house. There lay a huge circular pool surrounded by white pillars and Italianate sculptures pouring water from pitchers. A series of pieces rented just for the occasion dotted the garden, including a bouncy castle and a giant trampoline.

Across the sweeping grounds, he saw Evelyn and Leo, the little theater-tech frosh.

"Do you think people just haven't come yet?" Thea asked everyone.

"Maybe," said Evelyn, putting a CD into a little boombox.

Everyone jumped around on the trampoline for a while. Eventually, as the sun started to set, Thea settled grimly onto a white lounge chair by a freestanding bronze brazier. "Am I mean?" she asked the world. "Am I mean? Why didn't anyone come?"

Leo stood over by the barbecue, grilling himself hamburger patties. "It's their loss, Thea," he said. "More food for us."

Evelyn lay on her stomach in a thicket of landscaped bushes. "Leo," she demanded in a harsh whisper. "Give me some more potato chips. There's a turtle here I want to get."

After the three guests had gone that evening, Thea's mom peered at her daughter over wire-framed half-moon granny glasses on a metal chain. Her jolly, fat face did bear a fascinating resemblance to the head shot of the vampire-book author.

"We should go to the mall, Thea," she said. "I need to get new pillowcases."

"I don't want to go to the mall," said Thea.

"I want you to help carry the pillowcases," said her mom.

"No," said Thea. "Please? It's my birthday?"

"Come on," said her mother, slipping on a pair of white orthopedic shoes and pulling a hand-crocheted shawl over her flowered blouse.

So off they drove to an open-air lifestyle plaza a few miles away. They walked by the swaying Canary Island date palms on the way to Linens 'n Things. Dozens of teenagers stood in groups and talked and laughed. Thea trailed about five feet behind her mother.

They passed the Hot Topic outlet. Punk, club, and gothic clothes crowded the windows of the alternative retailer.

Thea's mom looked back and pointed to the wicked red logo. "Don't you like that store?" she asked.

"It's okay," said Thea, dissimulating madly.

"Well, let's go in," said her mom, turning an abrupt ninety degrees and stepping through the doorway.

"Mom," said Thea. She glanced around and ran in behind.

The inside of the store was painted black. Thea's mom lowered her half-moon glasses and began to poke through the racks by the entrance, examining wispy dresses with silver-netted bodices. "Come on, let's go," said Thea.

"No," said her mom. "Why don't we take our time and browse around? You like this store."

Thea quivered momentarily. "Ahh," she mumbled, and slipped away along the side wall, trying to put as much distance between them as possible. She headed into the depths of Hot Topic, displays flashing by under the loud post-hard-core soundtrack.

She reached the shoe area in the rear, and picked up a pair of chunky red Vans as a cover while she examined the situation.

No sooner did she have the shoes in her hand than she heard a familiar voice. "So is it okay if I switch hours with you for Friday?"

She stopped breathing.

She turned, slowly, to see Wil Kormer standing by the counter wearing a Hot Topic employee badge, Wil the love of her life who watched her fall in the gutter and didn't come to her party. He was talking to a salesgirl wearing a black leather choker and severe red lipstick.

"Yeah, that's totally fine," said the girl. She looked maybe a year or two older.

Thea put the shoes down carefully and began to creep backward to the clothing racks.

"Thanks so much," said Wil. "We've got a show at the—" He looked over and saw Thea slinking backward.

She froze.

"Uh, hey," he said.

"Hey," she said. It came out like a squeak. Her face burned and her heart pounded so hard she could barely hear.

"Oh, there you are, Thea!"

She couldn't even move, couldn't even turn her head, as her mother waddled into the scene with her granny shawl, flowered blouse, and a big smile. She turned to Wil and grabbed him by the shoulder. "Excuse me," she said. "Do you work here?"

Thea couldn't blink or feel her heartbeat. She wished for nothing more than instant death.

"Yeah," said Wil. The salesgirl watched the proceedings with interest.

"Wait, I recognize you!" Thea's mom smiled, looked at her daughter, looked at Wil. "You're one of Thea's friends from school, aren't you? Tell me, Mr. Wil—"

She slowly raised up an item of clothing on its plastic hanger. Unwillingly, Thea focused on it.

It was a leather thong with leather straps and a red crotch hole for easy access.

Her mom poked the thong with a pudgy finger. "Tell me," she said. "Do you have these in my size?"

The world blacked out around Thea as her ears rang. She felt as if maybe she weren't there, as if she just lay safe in bed somewhere in a parallel universe.

"Uh," said Wil, "I'm not sure. What size are you?"

Thea's mom patted her hips. "Usually a two or three XL. Do they run snug?"

"Yeah, I guess," said Wil. "I don't think they go to that size."

Thea noticed with surprise that she still seemed to have a pulse, and wished her heart would stop already.

Her mom frowned. Then her eyes lit up. "Or . . . ," she said. "Idea."

She walked over to Thea's petrified frame and held the thong up to her jeans. Its leather straps dangled. The red crotch hole burned like a signal fire. "Don't you think this would look good on my daughter?"

The moment seemed to dilate everlastingly, the tableau of her beaming mother holding the thong against her while Wil stared.

"Uh," he said.

The salesgirl smiled. "Oh, yeah," she said. "It's cute."

They had arrived at Linens 'n Things before Thea could utter a single word.

"What," she attempted to articulate. "What were you doing?"

"Hmm?" said her mother.

"With the thong. What were you thinking?"

"Oh, I thought they were nice. Very modern. Drat, I don't know if this beige would work in the den. We should have brought one of the old covers."

Behind the library at lunch on Friday, the spiky-lip guy turned idly to the group. "Anything happening this weekend?"

The skin sneered. "All the preppy people are going to a party at one of the baseball players' houses after the game."

Evelyn created a new hairstyle for herself with pencils and a big shell clip. "I just talked to my advisor," she said. "I'm going to have like two hundred and twenty-five credits by the end of the year. I could graduate early."

Thea lashed a savage kick at the concrete steps. "Oh, my God," she said, "how many more years do I have before I graduate? You're so lucky if you can escape this hell. I am so ready to grow up. I am so ready to be out of here and finish college and get into the real world and find my dream job that I could scream like the tormented undead and stab myself multiple times in the eye." She took a breath. "Somebody better be having a fucking good time at this place, because it sure the hell isn't me."

CHARITY ELIZABETH SCHULMAN WARNER

Charity grabbed me and shoved me against the tent pole. "Stand right there," she hissed.

I moved only my eyes. "Am I blocking somebody?"

"Yeah," she said, glancing over my shoulder. "Your friend. What are you doing with her?"

The stylized beat of reggaeton music thrummed in the cool night air as coaster wheels clattered under the glimmering orbit of a Ferris wheel. After Thea's play, I had met up with some circle people at the annual fair that spread its canopies across the Emerald Valley campground. Groups became fluid and I started talking to a drunk junior I had met.

"Oh," I said. "That girl. She's in my math class, I don't know, she seemed pretty nice."

Charity shook her head firmly. "I can't stand her. She's so bitchy. I can't stand people like that."

A sophomore guy walked by offering speed, but Charity refused any distraction. "She's a bitch and a psycho. She ate a Twinkie out of a guy's ass cheeks at a concert."

"Really?" I said. "No, she's not psycho."

Charity spoke calmly, with infinite patience. "Do you know that for a fact?"

Clouds of nervous giggles drifted from the concrete women's bathroom by the tent.

"No," I said, "but she doesn't seem like it, and I'm sure it's just like a rumor, you know?"

"No," said Charity. "It's not. And her dad's gay. So's her brother. Her family is all freaks. Her sister is fat and ugly. Don't be associated with her."

I blinked. "Wow," I managed.

Charity smiled tightly. "It's for your own good. I just like want to make sure you don't get a bad reputation. People are assholes here and they'll like talk shit forever about you for anything. I'm trying to take you on so you can be cool like me."

An anguished shriek erupted from the women's bathroom. Silence before the giggling started up again. "What's going on in there?" I asked.

"We're piercing each other's nipples," said Charity. "I'm standing guard."

White glamour sunglasses eclipsing her streaked bangs, Charity stuck her highlighted head out the side door of the administration building. The three-minute bell had rung a couple of minutes before, and only a few stragglers still hurried to class. Hesitating any longer would make her late for bio.

A white platform sandal emerged, followed by a tremendous sail of cloth, followed by the rest of the elephantine gray XXL penance of the 1993 Marlins sweat suit.

Dress-code enforcement at Mirador occurred sporadically at best, so every day before the mirror Charity took a calculated risk. As if under an enchantment, she almost always got to wear her beautiful princess clothes, but once every two weeks she magically had to look like Dumbo.

She had reached the middle of the empty science quad when she spotted the pack of freshman girls marching toward her on the way to their health-skills class. Changing course now would show fear and weakness.

As their two trajectories intersected, Charity preempted the snickers. "If they didn't have the cameras on I'd kick your asses right now. I'll take any of you after school, except you're a bunch of pussy bitches who probably won't fight." Her stride never faltered.

One girl called after her softly. "You're such a joke, you don't even know why your boyfriend broke up with you."

Charity whirled on them. "What? Shawn did not 'break up with me.' You don't know what the fuck you're talking about."

The other girls looked at the one who had spoken. "Whatever," she said quietly. She had braces.

"No, what?" said Charity. "What? Fuck you. I'm going to take you down, you ugly little bitch. You." She pointed to the girl.

The girl's face flushed. A long moment of silence. "Yeah, everybody knows your boyfriend was sleeping with Alexis Newton but you," she said.

Then the other freshman girls turned to her, shocked that she had let the words slip. They hurried away, arms around sides, bumping into one another. Charity caught a few giggles and "I can't believe you—"

In bio she collapsed into her seat with a sick feeling clutching her stomach. The weird girl Thea at the front shot her a nasty look. Ms. Horn sat on the table nearby.

Vic Reyes turned to Charity. "You should keep those sunglasses on your face so no one has to see it."

"Viiiic!" she whined. "I'm not in the mood for it. You always call me fat and ugly."

"No, I don't," he said.

Charity put her head down on the desk and moaned.

"You're a tramp," said Vic.

"You shouldn't call a young lady that," Ms. Horn told him. "I think it's time for you to go to your bench."

"Come *on*," he said.

"I'm sorry, Mr. Reyes," said Ms. Horn. "Please go to your bench."

He pushed down his cap brim and walked out the door. The Vic Reyes Bench lay outside the classroom tucked amid the foliage of the science quad.

Ms. Horn wandered away. Alone with Sara, Charity told her what the freshman girls had said.

Sara looked down. "You know people make up all kinds of rumors."

"You heard it," said Charity.

Sara hesitated. "Well, like a grip of people were talking about it," she said at last, "but I'm sure it's not *true.*"

"Oh, God," said Charity. "And she's not going out with Cody anymore, so it all like makes sense. How long did they say they were hooking up for?"

"Uh," said Sara.

"Oh, my God," said Charity. "What? You've got to tell me."

"Like about a month," said Sara. "But I'm sure it isn't true," she added quickly.

"Oh, God," said Charity, staring at the clock.

Ms. Horn clapped happily. "Come on everybody! We're going over into the annoying room for a special presentation about a really exciting personality test called the enneagram that we're all going to take!"

As soon as the bell rang for passing period. Charity marched to the senior circle.

Even she didn't dare to walk in through the tiny front opening in the concrete ring, not yet, not now. So she approached from the side. She didn't see Shawn anywhere, but she found Alexis's slender back and bright blond hair among the group of senior girls.

"Hey," said Charity, loudly over the song on the speakers. She tapped Alexis on the back.

"Eeep," said Alexis, scrunching up her shoulders. The girls turned around. Alexis laughed and put a hand on her heart.

"Oh, my God, you totally scared me," she said. "I totally thought you were crazy Aram. You can't creep up on people like that." The girls laughed.

"Hey, I didn't know you were a senior," Brian said.

"Did you get lost?" asked someone else. "The steps are over there."

"Hah hah," said Charity. "You're so funny." Alexis started to turn back around again, so Charity let loose with the charge. "People have been telling me a lot of shit about you and Shawn."

"There's a lot of kinds of shit, Charity," said Alexis. "What type of shit are you talking about?"

"That you guys have been hooking up."

Alexis looked her over, her tiny white purse hanging over a gargantuan, gray, sweat-suited arm. The cloth flapped gently in the breeze.

"No," said Alexis, squinting against the sun, "that's definitely the kind of shit that's not true."

Charity glared down at her. "We were going out for a year and a half, so that would be really messed up if you were."

"Hang on," said Brian. "You guys aren't going out now, right?"

"Yeah, so what?"

"So what Shawn does is his own business."

Charity sniffed. "If he was cheating on me with somebody, it's my business, and if he's hooking up with someone else like a week after, it's not respectful to me, and it's my business too." She turned the big white sunglasses back to Alexis. "Just tell me if you are, and I'm not going to be pissed at you."

Alexis shook her head. "Nope," she said. "I'm not. Scout's honors." She smiled.

As Charity walked away, she heard the voices behind her. "Remember in eighth grade when everyone wanted her?" a guy said. "She used to be so pretty."

"Damn, her face just got busted," said someone else.

She caught one last fragment. "—entire water polo team."

At lunch she climbed out of Sara's trunk in the parking lot of the 7-Eleven off Orchard and shed the hated sweat suit with a vengeance.

"This whole thing is really killing me," she said. "I mean I confronted Alexis and I just asked her calmly, and she said no."

"But she might've thought you were going to kick her ass," said Sara.

"If I find out she lied to me then it's all over."

"Yeah," said Sara. "What you need is actual evidence. It's the uncertainty that's killing you."

"I mean," said Charity, "I don't fight anyone. I don't start shit because I respect people, but they need to respect me in return. If someone starts shit with me . . ." She yelped and kicked the trash can with a platform sandal.

"Unnhh, why am I always surrounded by *draaaama* at this fucking school?" she cried. "I think I must not be a girl, because I'm like the only chick at Mirador who's not drama, and everyone around me is always just having it and creating it, and it's really upsetting me."

"Come on," said Sara, "I was supposed to meet Patrick like ten minutes ago."

Charity climbed into the passenger side and away they drove.

"I want to drink," groaned Charity. "Why do I feel so happy when I drink?"

"Well, you should drink, then," said Sara.

"I'm not going to like drink by myself, like me and a bottle of Jack. All three of us should drink. Did you tell your mom about Patrick yet?"

"Yeah," said Sara. "I did yesterday. She like flipped out. She so disapproves, and she doesn't want us to see each other. I mean, whatever. She wouldn't let him stay in the house, which sucked after he flew all the way from Texas just to meet me and see me. Anyway, he's so excited because he just got a place to stay."

"Where's he staying?" asked Charity.

"He's been like staying in a hotel for some days, but now he found like somewhere else so he can be here permanently."

"That sucks he can't stay with you, though," said Charity. The black glass box of Emerald Valley City Hall glided past the window.

"Yeah," said Sara. "I think the whole Internet thing sketched my mom out. She thinks he's all like dangerous or something. I was just like, 'Listen, he's just some random asshole who was like the king of this chat room I went to. And don't worry, he would be like asexual or gay if not for me.' I mean, seriously, he told me he wasn't turned on by things. The guy was like literally always online."

Sara turned into the IHOP parking lot. "I guess the other part is the age thing, which is just so retarded. I told her like, 'Listen, he's not married, and he doesn't have kids,' and I mean, we're not going out or anything, I'm just seeing him. We haven't even done anything beyond kissing, and he's cool with the fact that I'm still a virgin."

"What do you guys talk about?" said Charity. "It was hard enough for me finding things to talk with Shawn about."

Sara turned off the engine. "Yeah," she said, "sometimes it's kinda hard. But sometimes we just totally click, you know? We have so much in common. Like we stayed up really late one night in the chat room talking until like five in the morning, and when I signed off, I was like, 'Wow, this guy is really cool,' and I knew I had found my soul mate. And he's so hot. I have that picture of him with his shirt off and his arms folded, like 'Grrr . . . .' And I'm like, 'Aaaahhhhh . . .'"

"How old is he exactly?"

"He just turned thirty."

Patrick waited for them at a table by the window in IHOP. He bought them lunch. He had pulled his blond hair into a ponytail and seemed like a nice enough guy, maybe a little dorky, but Charity had her mind on other things.

"I want to fight somebody," she said.

"Why?" asked Patrick.

"I just want to fight," she said.

After they ate, she suited up in the gray sweats and climbed into the trunk again. Back on campus, she used the ebbing minutes of lunch period to question everybody she knew about the Shawn and Alexis rumor. It seemed like a lot of people had heard something, but either no one knew for sure or wouldn't say.

"Aghhhh," croaked Charity, curling her toes.

She stopped to talk with a bunch of baseball juniors who lounged around the benches in the fine arts quad. Like the entire team—and the football players in the fall—they wore their Mirador jerseys and caps to school every day of the season.

They seemed evasive.

"I wish someone would just tell me what's going on instead of causing all this drama," she fumed at them. "This is so annoying."

Some of the baseball guys had drunk during lunch. "Just imagine we're like the water polo team," one said, laughing.

Charity rolled her eyes. Meanwhile, another drunk guy had crept behind her. With blitzkrieg speed, he grabbed her baggy gray sweatpants and yanked them down. To his surprise, the tiny skirt caught and went with them too, and Charity stood for a shocked second in the middle of the arts quad with only her skinny legs and a tiny pink thong.

She squawked and yanked her pants back up as all the baseball guys laughed.

Charity's eyes hunted, found on the table a mounting bracket for a car exhaust pipe, probably left by someone after auto shop. It looked like a fist-sized steel ring with two dull prongs.

She picked it up and slipped it over her hand. Turning calmly to the guy who pantsed her, she hauled back and clocked him in the ribs with the pointed end. "Owwww," he said, and clutched his side.

Then she grabbed at his low-rider jeans and yanked them down. The baseball guys all laughed, stunned. Then she decided to go for the glory and pulled down his boxer briefs as well.

"This school is so much fucking *drama*," she said to the world at large
as she clomped off to fifth period behind her big white sunglasses.

Charity had PE during fifth, and the sections combined to play some
sort of mass kickball game. In reality, fifty people just sat on the bleachers by the baseball diamond and talked while fifteen hard-core kickballers screamed at one another on the field.

Charity had brought her binder, and she looked at a homework sheet
where she had to label the insides of a cat by copying the terms off an
identical sheet that was already filled out.

"Ohhhhh," she moaned. "I'm all stresssssed because of today. Everyone at Mirador is a bunch of rich fuckers who have too much time on
their hands and don't have anything better to do than cause other people problems."

She idly traced the outline of her hand on the back of the cat worksheet and began to label her sketch like the cat. "Nails," she added. "Hair,"
with an arrow pointing to the fine follicles on the backs of her fingers.

Then she drew a huge rock on her fourth digit. "This is what I want
for my wedding ring." She added specifications. "5 Carat, princess cut.
Diamonds all around."

Sara sat nearby on the bleachers and talked to mirrored-aviator-
sunglasses Travis.

"It sucks that LaTyra got spirit officer," Travis said. "Even after you
messed up your neck and everything."

"Whatever," said Sara. "I didn't really want to anyway. ASB is going to
be so bad next year, they picked such awful people in the elections." She
paused. "Well, like most of them, except for you."

"No, it was great," said Travis. "The girl I was running against for VP
cried when she found out she lost." He laughed. "I was like, 'Maybe you
lost because everyone hates you, bitch.'"

The sun beat down. Leo the little theater-tech frosh panted past in a
sweatshirt.

Charity gave him a bleary stare. "Why is that fat kid wearing a sweatshirt? I mean, it's like eighty degrees out, and he's fat."

"It's because he's trying to hide his fatness," said Travis. He tracked Leo
steadily with his mirrored lenses. "No, you know what, I'm totally wrong.
You know what it is? He's trying to set up barriers to protect himself from

the world. Like first he tried to do it with food, but he realized that wasn't enough, because his idea of self just grew with him and left him more exposed. So he needed something else, like a physical obstacle that keeps him from feeling vulnerable psychologically. He probably has a really messed-up home life. I'm getting the feeling it's his parents' fault, especially his mom. I bet dad just left, and there might also be a stepdad in this."

Everyone sat in silence for a moment and edited out the worrying feelings that accompanied Travis.

Finally Charity spoke. "I want to driiiink."

Vic Reyes appeared around the corner of the bleachers in his street clothes, pyramid belt around sagging shorts, sideways Skin Industries mesh hat. He walked toward them holding a sixty-four-ounce Double Gulp cup from 7-Eleven.

"Vic!" squeaked Charity. "How did you get here?"

"I'm supposed to be at AVID," he said, "but I ditched." AVID was a study-skills class designed to help underachievers who'd shown college potential.[6]

He sat down. "The PE teachers are so cool about letting me hang out here. You just have to like bribe them with sandwiches. I just say, 'Hey, Mr. Whatever, can I get you a sandwich?' and they say 'Uh, okay.' I get the sandwiches for free at my pool job, and it all like works out, except the guy today told me I was pushing it for just one sandwich."

"It sounds like he's looking for another sandwich," suggested Sara.

Vic banged his 7-Eleven cup down on the aluminum seating and opened it. Pale yellow liquid filled half the container. "Drinking games," he said. "You ready, Charity?"

"Ohhhhh," she moaned, fixing her hair. "I've been so wanting to drink, but I have to work right after sixth."

"So?" asked Vic. "We're playing quarters, okay?"

"Whatever," said Charity.

He produced a coin from his pocket. "You have to bounce the quarter off the bench first, okay?"

"Sure, whatever," said Charity. The kickballers yelled because someone had caught out a runner at third.

Vic spiked the metal disc down at the bleacher. It rebounded and flipped upward, landing in the cup with a soft *ploop* and tossing a few sticky drops.

He presented the cup to Charity. "Drink it."

"Ohhhh!" she whined. "Viiiiiiiic . . ."

"I just won," said Vic. "Now you have to drink it."

"But I have woooork," she pleaded. "I have to work at the ice cream shop."

"So?"

She turned to Travis. "Split it with me."

"What is it?" he asked Vic.

"Vodka and Mountain Dew," Vic said.

Travis shrugged and picked up the cup. It smelled really strong. "Okay," he said, and took a swallow. "That wasn't too bad." He placed the sixty-four-ounce monstrosity back down.

"Okay," said Vic, "he drank half. Now you have to finish it."

"That wasn't half!" said Charity.

Vic winked at Travis and Sara. "That was half, right?"

"Yeah, that was half," said Travis.

"That was half," he repeated.

"Okay," said Charity, and downed the rest of the cup.[7]

Shortly after last bell, she stood by the small mirror in the back room of Emerald Valley's Sweet Mill Creamery. She had already tied the apron, and now she adjusted the little white paper hat on top of her highlighted head as she talked to Sara on her cell phone.

"Oh, my God," she said, trying not to sway. "This shift's gonna be so annoying. I'm drunk as fuck, my manager's in a bitchy mood, and they put me on with the pregnant girl."

"Does she have stretch marks?" asked Sara's voice. "Did you see?"

"I looked and I couldn't find any," said Charity.

"She's *so* skinny," said Sara.

"She's skinny because she's a total spastic cokehead," said Charity. "She's all over the place. She's a crazy fucking girl."

Charity realized she was almost yelling at the top of her lungs and lowered her voice. "She pisses the fuck out of me. She's always talking about her baby, and I'm like, 'Aaah. We know you have a kid, shut up already.'"

The door to the bathroom banged open and the pregnant girl bounded out, rubbing her little turned-up nose. She had given birth about five months before. "Charity!" she sang.

"Bye," said Charity, and hung up the phone. She turned her death stare on the pregnant girl, who spun a little in her field of vision. "What?"

"Hello!" said the girl, and waved. She looked down at Charity's navel. "Oh, you have *such* a cute belly button ring," she said. "I had to take mine out when I got pregnant."

Then she skittered to the front.

Charity glared stilettos at her back. She collected herself. Huge sheets of white butcher paper covered the walls of the back room, scrawled with historical dates, diagrams of triangles, and lists of vocabulary words.

Gripping the metal shelves for support, she tottered slowly into the main room.

Her manager, April, sat at one of the tables in the customer area, writing out physics equations on a roll of butcher paper. She looked up at Charity. "Charity, customers last shift were saying some of the labels were off. Make sure they're right, okay?"

"Okay," said Charity.

She staggered a little as she walked behind the dipping cabinet. The pregnant girl danced to the music on the store system, stomping back and forth in her little Tilt jean skirt, long blond hair swinging.

Charity growled softly and pulled the first tag from its holder. SWEET CREAM. She opened the cabinet and looked down at the tub swirling in vapor. The stuff reflected bright, blinding white, a dazzling, painful glare.

Probably Sweet Cream, right? Or was it French Vanilla Bean or Georgia Peach or White Mint or Tres Leches or Lemon Sorbet or Coconut Delight or Almond Dream or Key Lime or Irish Cream or Gourmet Cheesecake? Suddenly she felt dizzy and weak and grabbed the scoop well for support. Cold water washed her fingers.

The pregnant girl looked over. "Uh, Charity?" she said. "Why don't you just relax?" She laughed and slapped Charity's behind.

"I've asked you to be quiet when we don't have customers," snapped April, smelly black marker pen in hand. "I'm concentrating on my flash pages." She was twenty-one and wore a pink candy-striped shirt.

"Okeydokey!" said the pregnant girl. Charity reached a wobbly hand for a tiny plastic spoon to taste the ice cream.

"You guys are so lucky I'm here," said April. "I have enough talent that I don't have to be here, you know."

Charity groped into the icy abyss of the dipping cabinet. "You're so smart!" the pregnant girl told April. "Just like my little boy. He didn't get it from his father, though."

"Well, I'm not 'smart,'" April corrected. "I'm technically a genius. I've got an IQ of a hundred and eighty."

"Then why the fuck are you taking Geometry I at community college?" Charity mumbled into the vat.

"I mean, I love my kid *so much*," babbled the pregnant girl. "I just wish he had a different father. There's only one thing I hope my boy inherits from him, and that's down there, if you know what I mean." She started to laugh, and indicated a foot or so with her hands.

Charity fished out a little dab of ice cream and popped it into her mouth. It tasted sweet.

"Well, I'm not just smart," said April, "I mean, I'm a model too. I just have so many opportunities in life. I've done so much modeling that I'm like over it now, you know? Like I bet you didn't know I was the FHM Girl Next Door like just last month. I didn't want to tell you guys because Sweet Mill's so conservative, you know?"

"Oh, fucking please," Charity muttered.

The door started to open, and everyone shut up, straightened, and beamed. Maybe the new arrivals wouldn't be able to tell one of their servers was coked up, one drunk, and the third a raging bitch.

When the shift ended, Charity felt nauseous and a headache pounded. She crumpled her paper cap and hurled it into the garbage.

She arrived home a little before six. She lived in a small, low ranch house directly south of the tracks, another tile in a mosaic of almost identical plots. Hers stood out mainly because the shiny vinyl siding was a mint green color instead of peach.

She opened the screen door and stepped into the wood-paneled living room.

"Uhhh, this is such a messed-up day," she announced.

"Hey, keep it down, I'm in history class," said a languid voice. Charity's younger brother sprawled on the couch in a Famous Stars and Straps jersey watching TV.

Charity looked at the screen. It was *Greatest Raids,* something about commandos stopping Hitler from building a nuclear bomb.

"What the fuck," said Charity. "Mom has you watching The History Channel for history class?"

"Yeah," he said. "We kinda stopped using the book, so that's like all I've gotta do now. I missed a few episodes but she passed me anyway. She's so cool."

Charity pulled back his gelled head and looked at his dilated pupils. "You're such a little stoner," she said. "Damn it, I want to be fucking homeschooled."

He pointed to some worksheets on the table. "Look at the math we did today," he said. "Mom's so bad at math, we only do like really basic math." Charity looked at the sheet. $2x + 1 = 11$.

"This is so unfair," she said. "You're supposed to be a sophomore?"

He laughed, pushed back his rubber bracelets. "For PE tomorrow, I have to go snowboarding. Like I *have* to, like it's required."

Charity stomped toward the long hallway. "Mom!"[8]

She found her mother taking clothes from the dryer. Mrs. Warner looked exactly like an older model of her daughter, before they updated the product line with the Millennium Edition: same highlighted hair, same little white skirt, bigger hoop earrings. The doppelgänger effect intensified since Charity appeared more than a little haggard and her mother dressed like a twenty-year-old.

Charity told her about the potential nightmare with Shawn and Alexis. "Don't take shit from them," Mrs. Warner advised. "Show them they have to respect you."

Then she covered her mouth. "Oh, Charity, you won't believe what happened to me today."

"What happened?" asked Charity.

"We had a Mexican bring his dirty ass in here. He came to look at the dishwasher, and he was in the door before I could do anything about it." She shuddered. "First Mexican in my house in five years." She lifted her eyes heavenward. "Thank God, we've never had a black, knock on wood." She thumped the paneling.

That night, Sara came over so they could work on copying the cat worksheet together.

They sat in Charity's little bedroom, Sara on a chair, Charity on her bed under posters of So Cal rap-punk band the Kottonmouth Kings.

A plaintive squeak rose from the corner. "Shut up!" Charity yelled.

She turned back to the cat sheet. "I hate my hamster so much," she said. "I had wanted it so badly, but it's smelly and it's annoying."

"That sucks," said Sara.

"At night when I'm trying to sleep," said Charity, "I hear its water bottle going, and it's so annoying, and I like yell at it, and I go over and I kick its cage and scream, 'I'm trying to sleep,' but like five minutes later I swear it's back at it again."

"Well, you should give it away or something," said Sara.

Charity glared at the cage. "I tried to put it out by the black garbage can, but the man brought it back to the house, and he told my mom like, 'We don't accept live animals,' and she screamed at me. So now I basically don't feed it. I'm just like starving it to death. Shawn was always like, 'If you kill that hamster, I'm breaking up with you,' but I guess that doesn't matter anymore. He liked it. He wanted it."

"So you should've given it to him," said Sara.

"Give him a hamster?" Charity laughed. "I couldn't give my boyfriend a dirtball hamster. That's a bad present. Just say, like, 'Here's a hamster?'"

The wheel squeaked. "You could've left it on his doorstep and ran," said Sara. "I feel so bad for your hamster. You should like give it to someone. Don't starve it."

"I give it water," said Charity. "I'm so mean to it, though. I put it in the corner, and I don't play with it or clean it or feed it." She raised her voice to drop a hint. "If I was a hamster, I would just kill myself."

Charity spent the next few days trying to definitively confirm or deny if Alexis had slept with her boyfriend, but she hit nothing but averted eyes and blank faces, which made her want to hit them for real. Her frustration grew.

On Thursday, Ms. Horn pulled out her two huge boxes of candy. She waved a Mars bar around the front of the bio room.

"Okay, my friends," she said. "I've got milk chocolate, white chocolate, and Rice Krispies chocolate. I've got fruit snacks and Sour Patch Kids and Tootsie Pops and a whole lot more."

"Ohhhh," moaned Charity. "I wish I could so badly, but I gave up chocolate for Lent. It's so hard because I love sweet things so much. I'm like counting the days down."

"Me too," said another girl. "I gave up chocolate too."

"I gave up more than an hour of TV a day," said a guy.

"That's what my mom gave up," said Charity.

"Your mom's great," said Sara. "She's such a MILF. She looks like your sister."[9]

"I love my mom," said Charity. "She's so cute."

"How much are Tootsie Pops?" a guy asked Ms. Horn.

"A dollar," she said.

In order to raise money for otherwise unfunded programs like field trips, a number of Mirador teachers and students sold chocolate bars. Ms. Horn expanded on the concept by offering a wide range of other candies for her own personal profit.

"Hey, Ms. Horn," called a guy named Forrest, "did you get laid—"

She gawked.

"—off?" he concluded happily.

She clutched her chest in mock relief. "No, my friends, I just got tenure this year, so no one can get rid of me. But I'm sure you've seen all the new teachers getting the pink slips, like, uh, Mr. Mannis, Ms. Esquivel, Ms. O'Reilly—"[10]

"I loooove Ms. O'Reilly," whined Charity.

"Yeah," said Ms. Horn, "they make a lot of absurd decisions here about personnel, but they're talking about bringing up the class sizes, and that means losing a bunch of full-time teachers. Fortunately our friend Mr. Mannis found a job at Sacred Heart making like five thousand more."

"What's happening to Mr. Dieeeeetz?" asked Charity.

"Oh, he's gone," said Horn. "They need to cut so much money."

The next morning, the teacher hopped up onto the side of the demonstration desk.

"Shhh, you guys, shhh," she said into the general babble of conversations. "Come on, guys. Shhhhh. Okay, how many equalizers do I need to write?" She picked up the little booklet of yellow detention slips.

"Thank you. I want to give everybody happy grades in this class, but some of you are making it so hard for me. Work with me, please, folks. Okay, we're going to start in with the dissection today, so I'd like every group to stand up and go find themselves a cat from the boxes."

Heads turned. The ONE MEDIUM CAT cartons now lay innocently open. The class approached cautiously. After hovering for a moment, Charity ventured a peek to see what lay in the shadowy depths.

"Oh, they've been shriiiink-wrapped," she moaned.

Indeed, the cats had all been tightly vacuum-sealed into clear plastic envelopes of embalming fluid. They were paralyzed in a comically awful position, with their eyes squinted shut, their paws rigid, and their tongues hanging out sideways amid open mouthfuls of tiny pointy cat teeth.

Everyone paused for a moment. Then Sara spoke. "We're gonna have to get used to these cats sooner or later," she said, and plunged her hands into a box. She began to take out cats and line them up. They had stiffened like boards in their envelopes and they clunked on the counter. "Okay, we need to find one that doesn't remind us of any cats we know."

Her group sorted through the heap of horrors and finally selected a skinny black-and-white one, which Sara named Domino. It had a dozen tiny embalmed fleas in its fur.

Meanwhile, Ms. Horn made an announcement. "The fact that we have cats here at all is thanks to our friend Mr. Kostopoulos who teaches physiology fourth period, and who bought us all these cats out of his own pocket. The school used to pay for them ten years ago when I was a student in this class, but thanks to the budget cuts—no more."

They dropped Domino's bag on their table as Ms. Horn continued. "Unfortunately, we don't have any money for surgical gloves either, so if you want those, you're going to have to go find some yourselves at a medical supply store."

"We don't have *gloves*?" said Charity. Domino gaped back up at her, tongue hanging out.

"Welcome to a free and public education, Miss Warner. Please open your bags, drip your cats dry into the sink, and blot them down with paper towels."

The plastic fell back with the pass of an X-Acto blade, revealing Domino. Evaporating chemicals shimmered in the air above his bag. Suddenly everyone choked, recoiled, and rushed to cover their faces.

"Domino stiiiinks," moaned Charity behind her binder.

They all stared down with a profound appreciation for the terrible powers of their new adversary.

"Somebody's gotta touch it," said Sara.

"Rock, paper, scissors for the honor," said Vic.

The group played a few elimination rounds, and then in a tight battle between Forrest and Charity, she lost.

"Oh, fuck me," she said.

"Touch it!" cackled Sara. "Touch your pussy!"

Charity scrunched up her eyes and her nose. With a little "eep," she daintily grabbed Domino by the two forepaws. He swung back and forth under her long fingernails, dripping formalin. She scooted him to the sink, whimpering.

"Your pussy is wet!" whooped Sara.

Charity's eyes narrowed. "If I'm holding it," she said slowly, "who's gonna blot it dry?"

Everyone examined cell posters on the walls. "Rock, paper, scissors," said Vic at last, putting out his hand.

He lost. He sighed, gathered up some paper towels, and went to work. "That's the closest you're ever going to get to touching pussy," Sara added helpfully.

After Vic gave Domino a brisk towel-off, Charity lowered the cat slowly into a metal pan. As soon as he left her fingertips, she released a muffled cry of horror and began to wash her hands over and over again like Lady Macbeth.

"Okay," said Ms. Horn. "Now, my friends, you will be skinning your cats. There are many ways to skin a cat." She started to giggle. "Sorry," she said, calming down, "that always makes me laugh." She began to chuckle again.

"There are two layers to remove: the skin, and then the fascia right under the skin...." She spent a minute explaining proper cat-skinning technique.

Vic put out his hand. "Rock, paper—"

"It's going to require all the members of your group to hold the cat steady while someone skins," Ms. Horn added.

"*Doh*," said Vic.

With varying degrees of hesitation, everybody grabbed a paw or a side of Domino. He leered up, cold and slippery. Sara attacked with the scalpel.

"Oooh," she said. "The fascias are so fun to cut. It just feels so satisfying. It's like an orgasm." She whisked the blade through one with a snipping sound. "Ooooh!"

Domino's matted fur dropped off in clumps and hairs drifted through the air as Sara cut. "It's important to shave your pussy," she said, having a blast.

After a while, she got tired of skinning and Vic volunteered to take over.

"He's gonna ruuuuin it," moaned Charity.

But Vic worked really carefully. Quiet, a look of total concentration on his face.

Charity began to play with the cat. She stuck a pin through its ear. "I always wanted to pierce my pussy," she said. Then she pushed her blade into its nether regions and giggled.

"Help me cut this thing," said Vic. "It's actually really hard to skin a cat."

"Ewww, no," said Charity.

"How can you think that's gross when you're busy raping its kitty pussy with a scalpel?" asked Sara. "Hey, I guess Domino's a girl. It's still a boy in my mind, though."

Everyone decided to keep thinking of Domino as male.

"I know this guy who had sex with his cat," said Vic as he worked.

The group paused for a moment. "Bleahhh," said Charity. "Who has sex with their cat?"

"He's a weird guy," said Vic. "His name is Chester Koch. He's a freshman. He got really drunk like two weeks ago and he was telling people about it."

Jasmine dropped her paw and backed away, nostrils flared in shock. "Oh, my God," she said. "That's my best friend Chelsea's younger brother. Which cat?"

"I don't know," said Vic.

" 'Cause they have a few," said Jasmine. "They're all female."

"I don't know," said Vic.

"Oh, my God," said Jasmine. She folded her hands quietly in her lap. Domino leered at her. His paw flopped, unheld.

"How the fuck would that even fit?" asked Charity. "He must have like the smallest dick in the world."

"No, he was explaining it all," said Vic. "He said that when cats are in heat, their vagina dilates, and they have loose skin all around it."

Forrest considered. "I guess it's like a big black guy and a small Asian girl. I knew a girl whose pussy was like—" He indicated a quarter-sized shape with his fingers. "It just expands. Whoop."

"Yeah," said Vic, "but when cats go into heat it's like physically painful for them, and they have to like fuck anything to relieve the pressure."

"Dude, it would be so sweet if people went into heat, fool," said Forrest. "Carmen Electra would be like searching out men, like, 'I need any dick! I must have a dick.'"

Eventually the bell rang, signaling a two-day reprieve from Domino. "Label your cats and toss them in the box," called Ms. Horn.

Charity watched as that little weird girl came over from the annoying room to hand people some kind of invitation she had written to a party she was having.

To be polite, nobody said anything until the weird girl was almost out the door. Then Charity glanced down at the torn sheet of notebook paper. "I'm sure somebody will be going." She laughed.

That Friday night, everyone knew one of the junior Matadora girls, Samantha, would be having a real party. Thirty-year-old Patrick had other plans for the evening, so Sara and Charity waited in the parking lot behind In-N-Out with a couple of other girls to meet a senior guy who supposedly had alcohol.

"He's known to be generous," Sara said. And so he was, more or less. He showed up with a handle of vodka as well as an emergency backup supply in a plastic water bottle. Everyone kicked in three bucks to offset the cost.

"I chug vodka," said Charity, "that's what I do. Everybody knows I'm the girl who chugs vodka." She picked up the handle and pounded a few mouthfuls straight, without the Sprite chaser.

A designated-driver Matadora brought them all to Samantha's house. Although virtually any other behavior at any level of parent-gasping magnitude happened at Mirador on a daily basis, the role of the designated driver was inexplicably held somewhat sacrosanct and widely respected. Nobody would pressure a DD to drink, and DDs usually

maintained abstinence for their designated nights with ascetic forbear-
ance and a bare minimum of complaint.[11]

Everything had its limits, of course. "I am going to get so shit-faced
tomorrow night," the designated driver said happily.

Two dozen cars had parked at all available spots in a blockwide radius
among the dark tree-lined streets, but otherwise, the house seemed reasonably quiet from the front.

In the backyard, about forty people stood talking and laughing and
drinking from a keg as music played on big speakers. Inside another
dozen played beer pong and poker and watched TV.[12]

Samantha had trouble standing, but she still had an urgent apostolic
message to impress on each and every guest: "Hey, don't go to the second floor. Hi, don't go to the second floor, okay? Hey, don't go up
to . . ."

"What's on the second floor?" Sara eventually asked her.

"My grandma," said Samantha.

"Your grandma?" repeated Charity. The alcohol had hit her hard.

"Yeah," said Samantha. "This is my grandma's house, and she doesn't
know we're here." Seeing the looks, she continued, "My grandma's kinda
deaf and she sleeps like really heavily."

Sara went off to talk with some Matadoras, and Charity found herself
alone. She wandered and approached a group of senior guys by the
keg.

"Heeey," she said, tiny skirt swaying.

"Go away, Charity," said Brian Olvera. They turned back to their conversation.

She laughed as if it were a joke and stood around for another few seconds. Since nothing else seemed to be happening, she drifted away
through the faces. Someone nearby said, "—such a slut. She mastered
the art of sucking cock, she peaked in eighth grade—" Charity turned,
but all the bodies mixed and blended in the darkness.

She looked in the porch door and saw Alexis Newton sitting at a table
under the glow of the kitchen lights with some of the senior girls, laughing and doing shots.

At last she arrived back at Sara's side and pulled her sleeve. "You know
who's really pissing me off?" she said. "Alexis Newton. She's really getting
on my last nerve. First everyone's been telling me she's probably fucking

my boyfriend, and now I see her laughing her stupid ass off inside. She like planned her entire life from freshman year to be homecoming queen, like her life's mission is to make friends. A few years back no one even knew who she was. I just want to see her flat on her face." Charity gulped her beer down. "Then she can pick herself up or whatever, but I just want to see her fall."

A few cups later, Charity and Sara went into the house. Alexis and five other senior girls split a bag of food from Jack in the Box. Beside the bag sat a three-quarters empty bottle of Absolut Citron vodka.

Alexis looked up from the table, stunning in a simple white T-shirt and blue jeans, blond hair meticulously disheveled. A radiant smile lit her face. "Hey!" she exclaimed, holding out her slender tanned arms in delight. "My favorite girls are in the house! What's crack-a-*lackin'*, Charity? I'm *so* glad you guys stopped by."

"Hey," said Charity, as she and Sara headed to the kitchen.

By the refrigerator, Charity slammed back a few shots of one-hundred-proof Southern Comfort from its special red-label bottle. "I am so disgusted by her," seethed Charity. "She is so annoying. She is such a fake motherfucking bitch. She hates me and she knows I hate her. Oh my God, she is so fake, and she has no respect for me or anybody."

Sara had drunk a lot too, and she got caught up on the wave of emotion. "Yeah. I totally know what you mean. Fuck her."

They heard giggling as Alexis and another senior girl hurried past the kitchen to the hallway. "Bathroom trip," the girl laughed.

Almost automatically, Charity put down the bottle and followed them. Sara trailed behind her as she drifted down the hallway, past framed fading photos of Samantha's parents as teenagers.

A door clunked shut, to the bathroom, Charity realized. She saw blond hair in a darkened doorway across the hall where Alexis stood alone humming in a small guest bedroom, waiting for her turn at the toilet.

Charity shoved her. Alexis stumbled and spun around.

"I think you're a bitch," said Charity. "Everyone knows you're fake."

"What the fuck, whore," said Alexis, and shoved her back.

"Whore?" said Charity. They stood inside the tiny dark guest room. "You fucked my boyfriend. How could you do that? I've never liked you. I'm going to hit you."

She took a swing at Alexis and knocked her in the side of the face.

Alexis grabbed her arms and kicked her in the leg. Charity tried to break free and they scuffled.

"Hey!" said Sara, and barreled forward, shoving Alexis back into the old wooden bed at the center of the room. Alexis fell over the end board squarely into the middle of the dusty patchwork quilt.

With a snap, the bed frame collapsed. The mattress, with Alexis on top, fell to the floor in a cloud of dust. Everyone spent a stunned moment trying to figure out what happened.

Charity ended the silence. "Your fat ass *would* break this bed," she said.

Tears welled up in Alexis's eyes. "Everyone knows you're a slut," she cried. "Everyone hates you. You have no friends."

Sara looked unnerved by the tears. She backed away to the side of the room. "I'm sorry," she said to Alexis. "I don't want to get involved. This is you and Charity's fight."

Charity's mouth dropped open, and she turned to Sara. "What the fuck are you doing? Why are you taking her side?"

Sara didn't say anything. Alexis huddled up, crying hard.

Charity stood motionless for a few moments. "Sorry, Alexis," she said.

On Sunday morning, Charity woke to her brother's electric guitar through the wall.

She jumped out of her bed and stormed next door. He looked up from his punk rawk pose.

"Hey," he said, "either you or me really pissed somebody off, and I know I'm chill with all my bros."

"What?" snapped Charity.

"Did you see outside?" he said.

She stomped down the long hallway. White strips fluttered outside the screen door. She swung it open and pushed through a torn curtain of paper.

"Eh," she said. Her small ranch house, once recognizable by its mint green vinyl siding, was now best identified by its thick mummy-wrapping in dozens of rolls of toilet paper. White streams fluttered from the little tree outside, covered the tiny lawn, her pink Mustang GT, her mom's van with the PROUD PARENT OF A KID WHO SKATEBOARDS sticker. Charity watched the paper blow in the breeze.

She called Sara. "I think maybe I should leave school," she said. "I like really want to go, like everyone else at Mirador is having this great time, but all I ever do is drink and have drama and get into fights. I don't want to be known. I just want to go away and like go somewhere where nobody knows me. I think maybe I should be homeschooled or something."

"Don't worry," said Sara, "there'll be more parties. You can drink your pain away on Friday at Brian's after the game."

VICTOR MARÍA REYES GARCÍA

My cell phone rang on Sunday evening as I sat in my apartment and read a flyer about an upcoming program called Every Fifteen Minutes Day. Caller ID heralded a local number, probably someone from school.

I picked up. "Hey," I said.

"What's up, fool," said the voice. "It's Vic."

"What's up, bro," I said.

"Dude, did you take a look at the bio sheet yet?" We had a cat-parts worksheet due Monday.

"Yeah, dude," I said. "It sucks."

"Dude, I haven't started it yet," said Vic. "Have you?"

"No," I said. "I was just like about to."

"Right on," said Vic. I heard spikes of noise in the background, people yelling. "Dude, my house is driving me fucking crazy. Can I like come over and work on it?"

I didn't even pause. "Sure, totally."

"Tight," said Vic. "Where do you live at?"

"It's off Palmetto," I said. "Listen, dude, we're having like dinner right now, so I'll call you back in like fifteen or twenty, okay?"

"Tight," said Vic. "Later, fool."

"Later," I said, and hung up.

AAAAAAHHHHH!

No, he couldn't come over. Absolutely and categorically not.

I lived in an apartment in another city. It was not a house in Emerald Valley. It lacked bedrooms. It lacked my imaginary sibling. It lacked my imaginary parents. It had a futon and a laptop.

AAAAAAHHHHH!

But I couldn't say no, because that would've seemed not only un-friendly, but possibly suspicious. I had to avoid any suspicion at all costs. So I had to say yes to Vic.

I paced as the clock ticked down.

I sort of had a house, the Emerald Valley residence that I used as my official address on my school documents. It belonged to the daughter of a colleague of my aunt's, so yeah, we were pretty close. But it had a roof and it had multiple rooms and it was occupied by a family. Conceivably *my* family.

I called them. "Hello?" said the woman.

"Hi, Stacy?" I said.

"Sally," she said. "Hi, Jeremy."

"Oh, I'm sorry," I said. "Hi. Listen, I have kinda a funny request. I was wondering if I could use your living room for a couple hours with one of the kids from my school."

No sound.

"Uh, if not, that's okay, too," I said.

A pause. "Oh, Jeremy," said Sally, "listen, uh, we all have strep throat here."

"Really?" I said.

"Yeah," said Sally, "it's pretty bad. Micah came home from school with it yesterday and, uh, we're all on antibiotics. I think I'm taking tomorrow off from work."

"Oh," I said. "Okay. I hope everyone feels better."

I had five minutes left, and really no option. I called Vic back.

"Thank God, bro!" he said. The yelling had swelled in the back-ground. "Sweet Jesus, I need to get out of here. Where do you live at?"

"Off Palmetto," I said. "Listen, bro, though, like my mom's being a bitch. Like my dad's boss is coming over in like fifteen minutes and I told her you were coming and she said she didn't want it to be 'a big produc-tion.' She says she wants you to come over for dinner sometime, though."

A long pause. "Oh," said Vic. "That's cool."

And it was. Whew.

I felt bad, though. I wished I really could've had a house and a family and that Vic could've come over.

*   *   *

Headphones dangling around his neck, Vic dashed across the empty physical and social sciences quad. Shawn Ackerman ran alongside him.

"The administration hates me so much," panted Vic. "They're just looking for me to fuck up so they can expel me. Popper's been trying for four years and he wants an excuse so badly."

"You've got three strikes, fool," said Shawn. "Maybe you should, like, tone it down a bit. We only have one semester."

Vic laughed. "Whatever. I'm so ahead of them."

They burst through the door of Ms. Schroeder's room and Vic dropped into his seat just as the tardy bell beeped. "Made it," he laughed.

Ms. Schroeder's hand drifted from the TARDY to the PRESENT column in her record book. It made no real difference to her what box she checked.

A bony woman in late middle age, Ms. Rebecca Schroeder had a head of graying curls and a wardrobe that cycled through three colors of wrinkled, baggy pantsuit. She had taught American government to seniors at Mirador for twenty-six years.

Now she stood at the front of the room with a stack of computer-graded Scantron test forms in her hand.

"Hi," she said. She sighed. "I'm not going to sugarcoat this. The grades were terrible. I have fourteen failing grades in this class alone."

She flipped through the stack of tests. "I talked to the other teachers, and it's not just our room, either. It's something with your whole grade. What makes this all the more annoying is that the standards for passing this class are as low as they can possibly be."

She dropped the forms into a bin on her desk. "You only need fifty percent to pass this class. That's a D mark. A number of people here are playing the game at around thirty percent."

Dead silence, except for a few soft conversations.

"If you're trying to go to college, this is going to have a major impact on your future. You'll have to get a GED or go to summer school."

She looked around the room to see if her words sank in. Some people had their heads down on their desks, asleep. Most stared off into empty space. A few talked, and the balance had hidden their cell phones behind their textbooks and messaged away.

Ms. Schroeder exhaled a slow breath and picked up a sheet of paper. "Among the more troubling answers you gave on our last unit . . . Okay, in 1920 the right to vote was expanded by the passage of the Nineteenth Amendment. What did the Nineteenth Amendment do in 1920? Brice!"

The guy shrugged. "I don't know."

"Abolish slavery?" tried Cody Reisling.

"No," said Ms. Schroeder calmly. "Wrong century."

"Damn," he said.

"It gave women the right to vote." She looked at her sheet. "Okay, of course, in the Democratic convention of 1960, who was nominated for the presidency of the United States?"

Silence.

"Roosevelt?" Kaylee said.

"No," said Ms. Schroeder. "Hint: he was assassinated."

Silence.

"John F. Kennedy," she said. The utter ringing silence of the void greeted her. The page trembled slightly in her hands. "And I hope the people who said there were fifty-one states weren't serious. What's the fifty-first state?"

"Iraq," joked Shawn Ackerman.

"Yeah," said Vic. "It's the new Glamis."

"Huh?" the teacher said.

"It's out in the desert where you go dirt-biking and get sand in your face," he explained.

"Right," she said. She put the sheet down and rubbed her eyes. "Sometimes I think you don't understand why this material is important. Only by being informed citizens can we keep democracy going. Take a look at the Middle East, if you want to see how many problems you can have from a lack of democracy. Right now, what's the only democracy in the Middle East?"

Silence.

"Spain?" hazarded ASB rep Ross Hayes.

Ms. Schroeder looked out expectantly into the silence for a little while longer. "It's actually Israel," she said at last. She clasped and unclasped her hands. "Well, I hope we all learned something from *Dave*. I think we're going to spend a few days watching another movie next week called *All the President's Men* that's about Watergate."

"What's Watergate?" asked Alexis.

Ms. Schroeder looked out at the room of thirty-five. "Does anybody know?"

Total silence, except for the muted conversations.

"Watergate, *anyone?*" she asked. Finally she turned to Evelyn Strout. "Okay. Go ahead, Evelyn."

Evelyn, as a junior, had received special permission to skip ahead a year into an otherwise all-senior government class. Since she knew the answer to everything, she also had to receive special permission to open her mouth.

"Well," said Ms. Schroeder, after the event had been explained. She looked lost for a moment, wallowing in her baggy cherry red pantsuit. "Well, we have our quiz now. Uh, please clear your desks, take out a pen, and come up here for a quiz sheet. I hope you all studied hard and are prepared to write out the preamble to the Constitution."

People muttered, kicked in their chairs. Vic looked around the room in panic as everyone lined up to get test sheets. Of course he hadn't studied, and neither had half the class. But unlike them he hadn't prepared a way to cheat yet. Since 90 percent of tests at Mirador just involved bubbling multiple-choice Scantron forms or filling in the blanks, cheating couldn't have been easier.[13]

"This is a hoop that every high school student in America must jump through," Schroeder droned.

With his borderline grade, Vic needed this quiz badly to pass government, a required class for graduation.

He took two blank test sheets off the pile, just to keep his options open, and went back to his seat. In front of him, he saw that Shawn had written the preamble on an index card in his lap. Nice. He could just look forward and copy Shawn.

"If I see anyone looking at anyone else's paper," announced Schroeder, "I'm going to take away your test and give you a double zero. I'm watching closely this time."

Shit. Okay, his cell phone. Half the room had them out on their desks. Clearly they had stored this so-called preamble in their cells. He would just text Shawn or someone and get it that way.

"Get your cell phones off your desk," said Ms. Schroeder. "If you have a cell phone on your desk, I'm going to assume you're cheating."

Groans erupted around the room. Obviously people had rested big stock on that strategy. "Ohhhh," said someone. "She knows."

Vic pushed his phone into his pocket and made eye contact with Brice across the aisle from him. He showed Brice the two blank tests, and he slipped one into his desk. Brice nodded and smiled.

"You may begin," said Ms. Schroeder.

Vic and Brice bent down over their test papers like everyone else. Ms. Schroeder stood in the corner and watched the room. Brice pretended to think while Vic wrote out the lyrics to an AFI song and didn't put his name. In about a minute, Evelyn tossed back her horrid stripy scarf du jour, came to the front, and dropped her test in the wire basket on Schroeder's desk.

Vic stood ten seconds afterward, walked up, and placed his paragraph on top of Evelyn's.

No sooner did he drop it on the pile than he rolled his eyes and shook his head as though he had forgotten something. He reached back down for his test and snagged Evelyn's from underneath it. Ms. Schroeder watched him like a closed-circuit camera, but she saw that a page still sat in her basket.

Vic went back to his seat. He studied Evelyn's test until a few more people had turned theirs in and Schroeder had forgotten about him. Then he held the pen inside his desk and copied Evelyn's preamble onto his own blank page, and wrote his name on it. He picked up both pages, stood, and slipped Evelyn's test onto Brice's desk as he headed to the front.

Schroeder, distrustful, headed him off. "Let me see what you have," she demanded. He showed her his test with annoyance, and then dropped it on the pile. She retreated to the corner.

"She suspects the wrong thing," he mumbled to Brice.

A few minutes later, Brice turned in Evelyn's test pressed tightly under his own. We the People of the United States, in Order to form a more perfect Union, do ordain and establish A's for *everyone*.

The next day in bio class, Sara played with her big basket of birthday toys when Vic's cell phone rang, an Usher song barely audible in the general mayhem.

"It's supposed to be worksheet time," said Ms. Horn, reading the newspaper at the front. "Please put the forbidden devices *away*, peoples."

"It's Forrest," called Vic, holding up the phone.

The teacher tilted her head. "Where is he?"

"Let me check," said Vic. He took the call and talked for a little while in the general hubbub. Then he announced, "Forrest's getting bagels. What kind of bagel do you want?"

"Oooooh," squealed Ms. Horn. "I like sun-dried tomato."

"Do you want it toasted?"

She furrowed her brow. "No," she said slowly. "Could they just like . . . warm it? Like not toasted, but just warmed?"

"Done," said Vic, and passed the word along.

He sat down and Charity grabbed his hands. "You need to cut your fingernails," she said. "They're like black and griiiimy."

"Your face is like ugly," he said. "My fingernails get like that from my job."

"How is your job?"

"I don't know," said Vic. "It takes up all my time and I'm really bummed out about it."

She started pulling at his shirt. "I heard you got a tattoo. Let me see your tattooooo."

"Help," he said. "This slut is attacking me."

"Did you get a new tattoo, Mr. Reyes?" asked Ms. Horn.

"Like two weeks ago," he said. "On my back."

"Let's see," said Jasmine.

"Are you going to show us?" asked the teacher.

Vic stood up and pulled off his shirt. The letters R-E-Y-E-S glistened on his back in Gothic lettering, the skin around the print still red.

"Nice," said several people.

Vic had his shirt over his head when he heard Ms. Horn clapping her hands. "Look who's come to visit us today! It's our friend Mary Jane."

He yanked the fabric down and whipped his head around. Outside the window, a policeman walked through the science quad with Mario the proctor. He led a magnificently bright-eyed German shepherd on a yellow leash. Mary Jane.

"That dog gets paid more than some of the teachers," said Ms. Horn. "Including me."

"Really?" said Sara.

Ms. Horn turned a page in her newspaper. "Yup."

"Uh, can I go to the bathroom?" Vic asked.

"Yes, Mr. Reyes," she corrected, "and you also *may* go to the bathroom."

Vic stepped out the door with his pass, and saw the backs of the trio heading up the stairs toward central quad. Once they vanished from sight, he hurried after them.

The Emerald Valley PD had imported Mary Jane from a training compound in Czechia. She had left her native soil and come to the land of opportunity to sniff lockers for weed.

To sniff Vic's locker for weed.

The race had begun between man and beast.

At the corner of the quad near the steps, he hesitated for a moment by the bathroom door. Traveling beyond it meant entering a no-man's-land of trouble if anyone saw him. But not trying meant terrible, terrible trouble for certain, especially for someone with three strikes to expulsion.

He looked around and slipped up the steps.

A tall thicket of banana leaves provided shelter in central quad. He watched as Mario and Mary Jane's handler led their K-9 unit down the stairs to the neighboring language arts quad. Vic's locker was in the math quad, just one over.

He had gotten halfway to its steps when he heard the whine of a golf cart. He turned to see the blue shape zip out behind the assembly building.

Vic lunged and pressed up against a palm tree. He kept the trunk between him and the cart until it vanished down the ramp to the fine arts quad.

Then he moved again, passing benches. He took the steps to the math quad two at a time.

At the bottom he stood between the faculty bathrooms and turned to see a clear path to his locker across the empty quad. Suddenly a toilet flushed in the women's room to his right. He panicked and ran back up the steps, crouching down behind the spiky plants as the big woman proctor slowly climbed the steps from the math quad and walked away.

Vic raced down the steps again and hurried to his metal locker at the far side of the quad. As he passed open classroom doors he hoped no teacher would turn around and no student would say anything.

At last he reached the locker. No sooner did he touch the metal than voices drifted from central quad. He dialed the combination quickly, and slipped up on a number. He had to redial it.

The door clunked, and he yanked it open. He pulled the tiny plastic bag of marijuana out from behind a stack of unread textbooks.

By the top of the steps, Mary Jane padded around the corner on her extendable leash and watched him. Vic froze for a second, and the two looked at each other.

He shut his locker door. He tossed the bag into the corner garbage can. A moment before the policeman and Mario arrived on the top step, he dove into the boys' bathroom.

Everyone crowded at the doors of the nearby classrooms to watch Mary Jane settle onto her haunches before the garbage can. The policeman fished out a mysterious bag with latex gloves, shook his head, and looked at an impassive Mario.

Vic arrived back at Ms. Horn's classroom ten minutes after he had left. He collapsed into his seat, sweating, and put his head on the table.

"Kill me now," he said.

"You must have had quite a time in the bathroom, Mr. Reyes," said the teacher, munching on her bagel—warmed, not toasted.

During lunch, Vic got his burrito from pink-haired Crystallina. As he crossed central quad toward the senior circle, he saw musician Wil Kormer standing by the stage and veered off to talk with him.

"Hey, fool," said Vic, "do you have any weed I could get?"

Wil looked at him through watery, red, baggy eyes. He wore a tan bathrobe and slippers. "What?" he said slowly.

Vic looked at the stage. "Are you guys playing today?"

Wil started to shake his head and then stopped. "No. I ate this flower."

"What?" said Vic.

"I ate this flower, and now I'm way too fucked up," said Wil. He sniffled.

"What flower did you eat?" asked Vic.

Wil tried to clear his throat. "It's called the Devil's Trumpet. It's this little white flower. I ate it yesterday and I'm still fucked up. Last night I thought I was talking to Jimi Hendrix for three hours. Like whatever I wanted to happen would happen, like I was in my own private dream."

"Dude," said Vic, "that sounds fucking tight."

"Dude, it's horrible, fool," said Wil. "It turns out I'm like allergic to the flower and my eyes are running like a bitch." He blew his nose. "And I'm still fucked up, like I don't know if I'm really having this conversation with you. I'm in hell. It's supposed to be like 'shrooms but it's so much more intense."

"Uh," said Vic, "so do you have any weed?"

"I don't," said Wil. "I'll take you to the man to see."

Travis Newton waited out beyond the tennis courts at the metal gate in the galvanized chain-link fence that surrounded Mirador High School. This area formed a miniature Checkpoint Charlie in the border zone between the free and controlled worlds.

"No, it's not a dorm room," he said into his cell phone, "it's a high school. Look, it's right off Orchard. No, I can't come to the road. I just told you why, because it's a high school. Okay."

He hung up the phone and shook his head. Fog covered the sky and a cool wind blew, but he still kept his mirrored aviator sunglasses down.

He looked up as Vic and Wil approached.

Vic wore a pink polo shirt with the collar popped up. So did Travis.

"I started the pink shirt at Mirador," said Travis.

"What the fuck?" said Vic. "I started that trend. I'm thug like that. Now everyone's wearing pink shirts."

"Even Derrick wore them months ago," Travis said.

"But I was doing it *years* ago. I started the pink shirt."

Travis spoke calmly. "The pink shirt started in Milan."

"I buy my clothes on eBay," said Wil. "They cost like a dollar ninety-nine and they come wrapped in plastic. I'm damn proud not to wear the brand names—fuck that poser shit." He sneezed. "Sorry. I'm fucked up. I can't even tell if this is really happening."

An old blue Dodge Spirit rolled up to the gate. Mario the proctor turned a watchful eye at his distant post as Travis met a little bald man at the line where grass hit gravel. The visitor could not enter and Travis could not leave. The bald gentleman produced a bag of take-out food, Travis tendered cash, and they made the exchange.

"*Cám ón*," said Travis as the man waved good-bye, climbed into his car, and drove off.

"What did you say?" Vic asked him.

"That's 'thank you' in Vietnamese," said Travis.

"You know Vietnamese?"

"Only a few words." Travis looked into the bag. "This is so much better. They should have Pan-Pacific fusion here in the food court. Maybe I can make that happen at ASB."

"Hey," said Vic. "Do you have any weed?"

Travis paused. "Yeah. I can hook you up. I just got some cheap from this dealer in Hollywood, it's pretty crazy, he like sells to Cypress Hill too."[14]

"Hey, you're gonna be the new vice-president, huh?" said Vic. "We should smoke sometime, fool."

Travis fired his humorless machine-gun laugh. "I've only smoked out twice in my life. I'm not really a smoking-out kind of person. It doesn't get me where I'm going, you know?"[15]

"Where are you going?" asked Vic.

A moment of silence. "I don't know," Travis said.

The next morning in government class, Vic tried to sleep on his binder under the cover of darkness.

Government only lasted one semester, and Ms. Schroeder had set up the slide projector on the very first day. "I was very lucky," she told the room. "These slides were supposed to go up to the university at Fullerton back in the seventies, but they delivered them here by mistake and I was able to intercept them. I'm sure they're still wondering up at the university where their slides went."

After ten minutes, everyone was sure they weren't.

Class quickly entered a predictable pattern. First the room would chat briefly in a casual and terrifying way about current events. Then she'd cut the lights and—with an admonishment to "take very good notes"—she'd turn on the olive green tape recorder.

The tape would start slowly, the recorded voice beginning deep and sluggish and gradually getting up to normal talking speed. A constant, low, chuck-a-chuck sound like a steam locomotive punctuated the audio as it described the slides, frame by painful frame.

A fuzzy chart of the presidents until Carter, perhaps, would appear on the screen.

"Frame seventy-three," the tape would attempt to say. "The presi-

dents of the United States of America. Beginning with George Washington and vice-president John Adams, from 1789 to 1793 and again
from 1793 to 1797, no political party, and next John Adams with vice-
president Thomas Jefferson, from 1797 to 1801, on the Federalist Party
ticket, and then Thomas Jefferson with Aaron Burr from 1801 to 1805
and then again from 1805 to 1809 with George Clinton in the Democratic-Republican Party, and next James Madison from 1809 to 1813
with George Clinton and then with Elbridge Gerry from 1813 to 1817
as Democratic-Republicans, and then James Monroe with Daniel D.
Tompkins as vice-president from 1817 to 1825, Democratic-Republican
Party, and next John Quincy Adams, nephew of John, 1825 to 1829
with John C. Calhoun on the Democratic-Republican ticket, and
then . . ."

The voice was Ms. Schroeder's. Frequently she would pause or stutter
or correct herself or slur together some words. "When I recorded this
tape," she explained, "it was very dark in the room, so I often had trouble reading correctly."

Occasionally a dog would fall into a frenzy of yapping somewhere
in the background. "Yip!" the dog would bark. "Yip yip yip yip yip
yip."

"That was my Jack Russell," Ms. Schroeder added. "He died in 1983."

The overall effect, assuming the slide held a mess of arrows pointing
around a stylized sketch of Capitol Hill, sounded something like this:
"*Chuck-a-chuck-a-chuck-a-chuck-a* Frame eighty-four. *Chuck-a-chuck-
a-YIP.* The, uh, Constitution in Article I, Section *YIP* Eight grants to
Congress the power to lay and collect taxes, duties, imports, *imposts,*
rather, and *yip* excises, to pay the debts and prob, provide for the *yip YIP*
uh, the common defense and general welfare of the United States; but all
duties, im-imposts and exercises, excises, shall be *chuck-a-chuck-a* uniform *YIP* throughout the United *YIP* States *YIP.*"

Often Ms. Schroeder, busy with papers up at her desk, wouldn't notice when the tape called for a new frame, so everyone spent a good
amount of time listening to her voice describe something completely
different from what they actually saw.

In fact, sometimes she got so distracted that people would just stand
and walk right out the door in a quiet and professional manner. She
wouldn't notice.

So Vic, like many, many others, had just curled up. He lay in the glow of grainy slides and the endless infodump of a droning Max Headroom voice when the sirens went off.

Sleepy heads snapped bolt upright as all the PA speakers started wailing a two-tone cry of alarm. "This is an earthquake drill," Mr. Popper's voice announced over the howling distress signals. "Duck, cover, and hold. Duck, cover, and hold. Duck, cover, and hold. Duck . . ."

Everybody climbed nonchalantly under their desks and gripped the metal legs. Southern California schools had a few earthquake drills every year.

The sirens got louder as bodies huddled under their tables in the darkness. "This is a level two earthquake evacuation!" the PA barked over the gentle susurration of Schroeder's tape. "Proceed to your rendezvous point in an orderly fashion."

Her baggy suit flopping, Ms. Schroeder led the class to the door. Everyone squinted and shaded their eyes when they hit the bright sunlight. Hundreds of Mirador students herded past in different directions with white-gloved proctors directing the traffic. "Leave the school grounds," Mario the proctor screamed through a megaphone. "Go to the parking lot."

Vic followed the rest of Schroeder's class to a triangle-marked lamppost among the cars. He looked around as sirens wailed from the concrete school buildings. Two thousand students clustered under triangles, talking. No Schroeder. No proctors.

Beyond the tennis courts, the gate to freedom lay open and unguarded.

He turned to Shawn. "Hey," he said, "did you park off campus today, fool?"

"Yeah," said Shawn.

"Wanna ditch with me and go drink?"

Vic extracted the weed from the glove compartment of Shawn's massive lifted white F-250 truck as the grinning swordfish billboard receded into the distance. SAVE OUR SCHOOL $270,000. THANK YOU.

As Shawn drove, they rolled the windows up, cut the AC, and smoked, hotboxing the cab. Vic put on a Fall Out Boy CD.

By the time they arrived at Shawn's family's tidy white bed-and-breakfast right on the town border, they couldn't stop laughing. Bright warm sunlight flooded over the golden trumpet trees, miles away from Schroeder's gloomy entrainment chamber.

They parked by the Hyacinth Cottage sign.

"What do you want me to get you?" asked Shawn.

"If you've got it, Bud Light," said Vic. "What are you going to say?"

"Like we got out early or some bullshit."

A few minutes later, Shawn came back with six forty-ounce bottles in his backpack. They drove a block away and parked again, turning up the music and opening the forties.

"This is life," said Vic. "Smoking and getting fucked up with your homies. Next time we'll get some sluts out here too. Charity, bro."

Shawn laughed and punched him. "Shut up, bro," he said. "Don't remind me."

Vic shuddered. "Her whiny voice is just another reason I can't stand Mirador. I can't take it anymore. I'm so fucking sick of school."

"Dude, I feel you on that," said Shawn. "Only a few more months of that shithole."

"You know how all the older people like always come back to games and parties and stuff?" said Vic. "Are they sneerious? I'm not going to anything. I am so done with high school. After June tenth I am so done. You won't see me coming back."

"What are you getting in Schroeder's class?" asked Shawn.

Vic pulled a green slip out of his slim binder and passed it to Shawn. Official Credit Report. He didn't even bother to carry a backpack.

"D," said Shawn.

Vic smiled. "Despicable."

"Yeah, me too," said Shawn. "Schroeder's just a Jew on a power trip." He looked at Vic's form again. "F in ceramics."[16]

"Fs are just As with broken legs," said Vic.

"D in AVID, and D in English."

"I haven't read a single thing in that class, fool," said Vic. "None of the books. I've never read a book cover to cover in my life."

"I read a couple," said Shawn. "I read like the first Harry Potter when I was little."

"It's boring," said Vic. "I don't know, I'm kinda embarrassed about it."

They drank their forties. "Seventy percent of the people here are smarter than me," said Vic, "but I guarantee you I'll be more successful than them. My dad's helping me get my own shop."

"Yeah? That's tight."

"Yeah, I'm gonna like make and install truck customizers. That's such expensive shit, you can make so much money. First I'm just gonna do it in my garage and I'm just going to make the stuff. It's so much easier than installing, because we don't have hydraulics and stuff, all we have is jacks. My dad's so good with metal, he's in the welder's union and he has a license and he does contractor work and everything. I'm lazy about school, but I can really focus when it's real stuff."

Shawn looked at the green slip again. "Yeah, you're getting an A in auto shop. . . . Hey, you're getting an A in physiology too. Wow. That's weird, fool."

"That stuff's easy," said Vic. "It's all about memorizing stuff, and that's easy for me, and you actually like learn new things."

Shawn laughed. "Maybe you should go to med school. Dr. Reyes."

"That's a lot of school," said Vic. "How many years is that, like six, seven?" He chuckled. "*Where's* the money coming from?"

"Dude, it sucks. Cal State's gonna cost like so much more a year with the budget cuts."

Vic turned up the radio. "Fuck school," he said, drinking his forty.

Since Schroeder had already checked them in, they decided to come back at the end of lunch for fifth period. Nobody would know they'd ever been gone.

Shawn parked a block off campus, and they walked past a sluggish stream of student cars heading toward the Mirador gate.

Mario the proctor climbed from his stool as they entered. "Off-campus passes," he said.

Neither of them had the attendance record to get one. "It's in my locker," mumbled Shawn, stumbling slightly.

Mario sniffed. "Have you guys been drinking?"

"No," said Vic. They started to walk past.

"Hey," said Mario, and grabbed Shawn's shirt.

Shawn pulled the fabric back roughly. "Get the hell off me."

"Okay, where were you?" Mario demanded.

"It doesn't matter to you," said Vic. "Why do you always have to give us a fucking hard time about everything?"

"Yeah, fuck you," said Shawn.

"Okay," said Mario. "Now I'm going to report you."

He picked up his walkie-talkie.

Mr. Popper looked at Vic across his desk. "You just couldn't stay out of trouble, could you?"

Vic didn't say anything, stared at the white contract papers in the one clean space in the center of the stacks.

"I'm only giving you one day of ISS," said Popper, "but that's nothing to send up a flag and start marching around about. You're getting a strike. You've only got one get-out-of-jail-free card left before you're out of here for good."

He looked at his computer screen. "Of course, even if you keep your nose clean, your grades may do you in anyway. I challenge you to surprise me with your behavior. I throw down the gauntlet."

"Yeah," said Vic, still drunk and high. He tried to focus on the vice-principal plaque.

Popper's phone buzzed. He spoke for a moment, then turned to Vic. "Your parents are here to pick you up. Tomorrow you go straight to ISS."

A few minutes later, Vic heard yelling outside the door to Popper's office. "Where's the chink principal? I'm gonna talk to the fucking chink principal and tell her what I think." It was his dad's voice. Vic stared at the plaque while Popper sorted through his papers.

"—call the police," Vic heard a voice saying.

His dad again: "Do you think I'm a fucking idiot? Do you?"

More shouting. Eventually Popper's secretary opened the door and Vic saw his mother standing with her hands folded. She was a short, heavy woman with curly auburn hair and a huge purse over her arm. He didn't look her in the eye.

"Come on," she said. "Your father's in the car."

He trailed her as they crossed central quad. The bell had rung the end of fifth period, and they walked right past all the people in the senior circle. Vic avoided their eyes as he followed glumly and drunkenly a good twenty feet behind the stout form.

She looked back once. "Come this way," she said flatly.

*   *   *

Vic didn't even have time to fully sober up. He passed out on his bed for an hour, and then he had to pull on his blue R & M POOL AND SPA shirt and drive to work.

Fortunately it wasn't a construction day, so he didn't have to go out and shovel dirt or bend rebar. His boss gave him a stack of six construction permits to deliver to customers who had ordered pools.

Vic looked at the addresses. "Wow. These are all over the place."

"Yeah," said his boss, stuffing in a mouthful of In-N-Out fries. "Save the gas receipts." He gave Vic thirty-five dollars cash under the table for the day.

Crammed among commuter traffic on the 5, Vic drove the extent of Orange County and back again. He followed the Blessed Serra's ancient pilgrimage from Dana Point in the far south to Brea in the north.

He collapsed into bed at a little after ten o' clock after driving slightly under three hundred miles in seven hours. Who knew if there was homework. He had ISS anyway so it didn't matter.

A stocky attendance counselor from the administration building greeted Vic at the door to the side modular.

"You again," she said, shaking her head. She sent him to sit among the other fifteen people, at the end farthest from Shawn.

"Anyone here who's had me before knows how I am," she told the small chamber.

"You're mean," said Vic.

She paused, and then nodded. "That's right," she said. "I'm mean. My job is to make sure you sit quietly and do your work for the next seven hours. You'll have a fifteen-minute break to get your lunch and bring it back to this room. Any questions?"

"Why can't we get suspended at home?" asked an ISS newbie.

The counselor held up her fingers. "There's two reasons we have in-school suspension. Firstly, it looks bad to say people are getting suspended. The school doesn't want to report the numbers and you don't want to tell your parents why you're at home. Secondly, the school gets money based on how many kids are on campus. If you're at home, we lose the funding for you for the day. Any more questions?"

The bell rang and everyone pledged and Derrick read the Word of the

Day over the speakers *("dwergmal . . . an echo from rocks . . . dwerg-mal").*

Vic pushed up his headphones as slowly as possible.

The attendance counselor looked at him. "Put those headphones away or I'm going to take them away."

The red second hand drifted around the clock dial.

When last bell rang, Vic pulled on his R & M shirt. The boss sent him and a few other guys to help install an outdoor Jacuzzi at one of the big houses down on Los Robles. He got a shovel and worked to clear the dirt away from the excavator. Then they evened and packed the sides of the hole.

The next morning, Vic dropped into his seat in bio class. Charity grabbed his hand. "Let me see," she said. "You cut those nails!"

"What the fuck, bitch," said Vic. "You washed that hair."

Ms. Horn busied herself telling the annoying room to select their cats. Vic seized the moment and shoved Charity's binder off the lab table.

"Viiiic," she said. "Don't be a faaaaag."

"Shut up," he said. "You're having my babies. You know you sleep with me all the time."

He stood up and wandered around. He read some tiny print on a complex laminated poster entitled APPLYING TO THE CAL STATE/UC SYSTEM. "What do you need to have to go to a Cal State?" he asked.

"Like a grip of stuff," said Forrest. "Like three years of math, two years of a foreign language, stuff like that."

Vic smiled softly. "Two years of a foreign language? That's it for me. I'm glad somebody told me that in the middle of fucking senior year."

"You didn't take one?"

"Nope," he said.

"What about Spanish?" asked Sara.

"Dude, my Spanish sucks," he said. "My dad can't even speak it. Yeah, I'm going to dummy college."

"There's no such thing," said Sara.

"Come on, Emerald College is dummy college. But it's so tight, though, people just like walk around the campus smoking blunts. Security drives trucks so you can see them coming."[17]

"Holy shit!" said Forrest. Like the tremendous plurality of seniors, he planned to go there himself.

Ms. Horn jounced into the room and everybody began dissection. Toward the end of class, she clapped her hands over the cat-skinning chaos. "I have a special announcement for everybody! Shhh, you guys, shhhhh."

She smiled happily. "We're going to have a sub next Tuesday. Our friend Mr. Lamarque!"

For probably the first time ever, the room fell completely and utterly silent. Then shocked voices returned, quavering.

"Oh, no," said Charity.

"No," said Forrest.

"What?" said Jasmine. "You can't do that."

"How much do you hate us?" said another guy.

Vic just shut his eyes.

"Awwwwww, I love you guys," said Ms. Horn. "I love all my babies." She pointed to the list of tasks on the board. "It's simple, just Turn In Worksheets/Pick Up Handouts/Cat Dissection."

Vic raised his head slowly. "Can we just have Turn In Worksheets/Pick Up Handouts/Watch Movie so we don't have to deal with him at all?"

Ms. Horn smiled and shook her head.

"Oh, my God," said Sara. "He doesn't like kids. I don't know why he's even here."

At lunch, Vic and Derrick nodded to each other as they headed to their separate parts of the circle. Vic sat with his pan pizza. He seemed distracted, subdued.

"What's crack-a-lackin'?" asked Alexis. "Are you pissed off or something?"

"I'm down to two strikes," he said. "I really don't want to get my ass kicked out of here. I'm just going to go to class and sit quietly in the circle."

Five minutes later he found an apple on the bench.

"Chello," he exclaimed.

"Oh, my God," said Padma. "That's such a Dove word. He like said that all the time."

Everyone nearby got quiet, lost in their thoughts.

Then Vic shivered. "I think too much. That's my problem."

Shawn stood with a group in the center of the circle. He was talking to Kaylee and seemed distracted, so Vic chucked the apple at his back before looking away innocently.

Shawn couldn't find the apple thrower, so he tossed it at Brian Olvera and then turned quickly. Brian saw him and punched him, Vic started to laugh, and then Shawn ran over and grabbed Vic and they started wrestling.

"Street Fighter!" yelled Cody Reisling. "We haven't gotten any Street Fighter going here for a long time."

A crowd formed and a few guys pulled off their shoes and began some low-grade kickboxing.

"So much for your good behavior," Alexis said to Vic, who tried to get a headlock on Shawn in the middle of the pandemonium.

"That lasted like three seconds," said Padma.

"Okay," panted Vic, "I'm just going back to the circle to sit down."

He broke free, calmly returned to the bench, and ate a wedge of pizza.

Mr. Lamarque grabbed Vic as he entered bio on Tuesday. "The class is in two rooms with one teacher?" he asked, steel-framed glasses flashing.

"Yeah," Vic said.

"Of all the ungodly stupid decisions this school makes—" he said. "That's completely inefficient and ineffective. Everybody into the left room!"

The bell beeped, although class didn't start yet for another minute and a half. It had rung on and off sporadically all morning for no apparent reason, which had already driven Lamarque into a preparatory dither during first-period math.

At last he had all thirty-seven students sitting in numbered seats in the left room. The bell rang again. *Beeeeeep.*

"My name," he said, "is Mr. Lamarque." He erased "Think Happy Laker Thoughts" and wrote "Mr. Lamarque" on the whiteboard.

"What's going on with the bell?" asked Sara. "Are we going to be marked tardy?"

Lamarque's eyes bulged and his face contorted. "*No.*" he screamed at the top of his lungs, charging forward. Sleepy heads snapped up. Sara gasped as he bore down on her. "Student thirty-one, if you have a question during Class Time you don't just do that!"

His voice edged into frenzy. "First, you raise your hand and you ask permission to speak, you don't just BLEEAAAAAHHH"—he bellowed, raising shaking hands—"you don't just blurt it out."

"Second, I don't know, I don't know precisely what is going on with the bell but I will find out and I will deal with it at that point in time."

Sara quivered. Spit flew from Mr. Lamarque's mouth. "Third, this is biology, and you either speak about biology or you ask permission, 'Permission to speak about another topic, Mr. Lamarque?'"

He suddenly whirled to fix the whole room with an accusing finger. "This is just incredible rudeness, it's your generation, mine too, it started with—"

Beeeeeep.

The PA turned on. Lamarque fell silent. "We apologize for the confusion," said Mr. Popper's voice. Then the PA switched off again.

During which time Mr. Lamarque had apparently taken a breath.

"—the loss of values and respect in civilized and enlightened speech!" he thundered down at Sara, who shrieked, having now completely forgotten she was being yelled at.

Mr. Lamarque swiveled a precise one-eighty and headed back to the front of the room, his cultured voice quiet and modulated again. "The answer is I don't know. I will find out and take the appropriate action. Irregardless, it's incumbent upon all students to behave in a gentlemanly or ladylike way." He thought for a moment. "Depending upon your particular situation."

Everyone had heard rumors about Lamarque, but anybody who didn't actually have math with him seemed unable to fathom how the familiar chaos of Ms. Horn's class had turned into a day at the Pyongyang Palace of Schoolchildren.

In the dead silence, he wrote "My Rules" on the board. "I have a number of rules. I had to keep the last class I subbed for one and a half minutes over because they didn't know how to follow my rules. I don't want to do that with you.

"Rule one: you stay quiet. Rule two: you remain in your seat. Rule three: the bell doesn't dismiss you, I dismiss you—"

Vic raised his hand.

"Yes, student twenty-eight?"

"State law is the bell dismisses us," said Vic. He paused very briefly. "Mr. Lamarque."

Lamarque peered at Vic over his steel-framed glasses. "Don't even go there," he said quietly. He stared at Vic for ten silent seconds.

He finished reciting his rules and instructed everyone to get their cats. As soon as Vic's group saw Domino squinting up at them through his plastic bag, the grim realization struck that nobody had managed to purchase gloves.

They slid the cat into his metal dissection pan. Strips of skin hung off his muscles. "Oh, my God," said Charity, "Domino is really grossing me out. Look, he like got mysteriously bruised, and he's all warm and slippery."

"Quiet!" commanded Mr. Lamarque. "No talking!"

Vic stood behind Sara's shoulder, looking down at the cat.

Mr. Lamarque snapped his fingers, glasses glinting. "Get in your seat, student twenty-eight."

"Sweet Jesus," muttered Vic. "It's hell. He's the devil."

Mr. Lamarque made several marks on a clipboard. He held the board up for the entire class to see.

"Every time you falter," he said calmly, "every time you're not focused, it goes on my spreadsheet. I am superintelligent. Perhaps too strict, but superintelligent. I am all-knowing."[18]

He giggled without smiling, a manic, high-pitched giggle.

"I see everything that happens in here, I know everything that happens in here. You may not think so, but I do, and I mark it down on this clipboard. When I see the guilty faces, I know. I know."

He brandished the clipboard again.

"Student twenty-eight, I'm taking away three points for talking."

Vic Reyes looked, for once, utterly speechless.

Everybody scalpeled away at their cats in silence for about two minutes. Lamarque paced softly up and down the rows of lab benches.

Then the sound of Usher's "Yeah!" broke the cadaverous stillness.

"Up in the club with my homies, tryna get a lil' V-I, but keep it down on the low key, 'cause you know how it feels. . . ."

All breathing ceased for three seconds. Vic scrambled for his pocket as Lamarque homed in on the offender.

"Put that away," he ordered. "If I see or hear any cellular telephones again, I'm going to give them to the office and your parents can pick them up. I despise them. They continue our society's pandemic of rudeness. Several years ago, I championed the push to have them banned for students in the district. Go back to your work."

Vic muted Usher. Lamarque returned to pacing.

Vic bent over the cat but kept his eyes fixed on the substitute. When Lamarque turned to glare at another whispering lab bench, Vic scribbled something on a piece of notebook paper and passed it along.

For the next two minutes, the paper circulated the room. You could tell who had it because eyes would widen and muted snickers were shushed.

At precisely nine o'clock, all thirty-seven cell phones rang simultaneously.

Beeps and chimes and songs erupted into a total mosaic of glittering tintinnabulation, a spatialized poststructuralist bricolage of electronic, aleatoric, and free-chromatic symphony.

Mr. Lamarque, no arts critic, looked dourly at the clock. "You have exactly thirty seconds of amnesty," he whispered. "Twenty-five . . . twenty . . ."

The concert stopped abruptly. Silence settled again over the room. A few errant giggles ceased when Lamarque produced the clipboard and snagged a few points from the offenders.

Everyone returned to their cats.

About five minutes later, the familiar tinny notes of "Für Elise" pierced the swaddling folds of silence. Horrified, the room went rigid. What suicidal soul had done such a thing? Would Ms. Horn return to class the next day to find them all floating in formalin solution?

They looked around, moving just their eyes, only to see—

—Mr. Lamarque pull a cell phone out of his back pocket. "Hi," he said. "Oh, hi, Charles. No, absolutely, just give me a moment."

He glared at everybody. "Continue to work quietly and efficiently on your cats," he ordered. Then he turned back to the phone as he hurried out the door of the bio room. "How is it? Well, that's certainly an accomplishment, right? No, no, I want to know about it. . . ."

Entranced, the class watched through the windows in silence as he disappeared up the central quad steps, waving his hands as he talked.

Charity broke the spell first. "What the *fuck* was that?"

"That's so classic," said Sara.

Pretty soon everybody spoke again. After five more minutes, Vic dared to sit on the lab bench. Then some of the girls who usually sat in the other room rose hesitantly and went over to talk to one another.

After about seven minutes, Vic dashed across the lab and slammed the front door. It locked.

"Oh, shit!" he whooped, and sprinted back to his seat.

"We'll just say it blew shut," said Sara.

After ten minutes everyone talked and stood up, but they kept shooting terrified looks at the huge windows onto the quad. "I'm tripping, fool!" said Forrest. "What if that freak guy comes back?"

"I think there's like blinds or something," said a girl who usually sat in the other room.

Vic examined the window frames and yanked a fraying cord. Tan polyethylene blackout shades unfurled, isolating bio completely from the outside world. He laughed manically.

Suddenly an enormous pressure lifted. People cheered as they realized what had come to pass: The forces of the cool room and the annoying room had united at last, unsupervised.

Vic grabbed Mr. Lamarque's employee badge off the desk and hung it around his neck. "All right, you fucking maggots," he said. "I'm in charge now! I have the authority."

"Who put *you* in charge?" said Charity.

"Shut up, student sixty-nine," said Vic.

Everybody got up and wandered around. Ms. Horn had a boombox at the front, tuned to Lakers Radio KLAC, and one guy from the other room turned it on. After a brief class discussion, they settled on a Top 40 station during a morning drive-time request block. Vic turned it up.

Sara poked around Horn's desk and brought out a big cardboard box. "Fruit snacks, anybody?"

"Yo, hook me up," said a guy from the other room, and soon Sara tossed colorful foil packets to everybody.

Then Vic winged a little gummy bunch of cherries at Charity.

"You fag!" she shrieked, and threw three fruit snacks back at him. Vic grabbed a metal dissecting pan as a shield and returned fire. Before long a torrent of fruit snacks flew through the air.

"Girls versus guys!" said Sara, and began to whip the little candies with stunning accuracy and stinging power.

She and Charity and Jasmine had backed Vic into a corner when Charity's platform sandals scuffled over a slick puddle on the floor.

"Hey!" she said with delight. "The floor's all slippy over here."

The music played very loudly, and some woman had just called the station to request the OutKast classic "Hey Ya!"

"Shake it, shake it, Sh-shake it. Shake it like a Polaroid picture. . . ."

Charity shook it as she wriggled gracefully across the puddle. "Oh, let me on," said Sara, and pretty soon nine people all tried to slide around and moonwalk on the slippery patch.

"We totally need to make it bigger," said Vic. "Do you think it's this stuff?" He picked up a plastic bottle from one of the lab benches marked LOCKERBIE: THE LOCKER LUBRICANT and dumped the oily liquid all over the ground.

"Ooooh, I think it's helping!" said Sara.

"Dude," Forrest called to the room. "Check it out. Domino is dancing!"

So he was. Forrest had the cat by the paws, and he danced around to OutKast. The tongue flopped up and down and the intestines hung out as the cat grooved.

Some girls from the other room got into it and started their cats dancing, too. *"Shake it like a Polaroid picture!"* Little bits of muscle and organ flew while the cats shook it.

The legs on one cat snapped. "Oops," said the girl who had been its dance partner.

"Hey," said a guy from the other room. "Do you think the cats slide? Wait, move aside."

Everyone dutifully cleared off the patch as he pulled back and bowled the cat skidding across the floor. People laughed, and another cat followed a few moments later.

Then everyone returned to sliding around. "We need to make this slippier," said Jasmine. A yellow mop-wringer trolley filled with water loitered in the corner. She poured its soapy contents over the patch on the tiles, flooding the floor.

"I'm gonna try to skimboard," said Vic. He put Lamarque's badge back on the desk, and then he grabbed a metal dissection pan. He ran toward the patch, tossed down the pan, and leaped on it. He got a little bit of a slide, but not much.

"Try this," said a girl from the other room, tossing him a tube from behind the desk. It was covered in smiley faces and stars and labeled MS. HORN'S HAND CREAM: DON'T TOUCH! Vic squirted it out all over the floor and tried another skim. Forrest grabbed a dissection pan and gave it his own shot.

"We need to slick this up better," Vic decided. He took the mop from the trolley and tried to spread the mixture of liquids evenly across the floor.

Then a key scraped in the lock and before anyone could move, the door swung open and Mr. Lamarque walked in.

He looked at the class. They looked at him.

"What happened here?" he said, simply.

A girl clicked off the radio. Eyes turned to the window as people began to wonder if they could just leap out and flee on foot.

Vic didn't hesitate. "Charity tripped over the big bucket of water," he said, "and I was trying to help clean it up." He showed Lamarque the mop in his hands.

"Why are you all out of your seats?" asked Mr. Lamarque.

"Charity needed a scalpel," said Vic, "and they were all trying to help me clean."

Lamarque pointed to the white cream and the oily yellow Lockerbie. "What's all that stuff on the floor?"

"I don't know," said Vic, "it was here when we got here."

"I slipped on it," said Sara.

"We almost hurt ourselves," said Jasmine. "It's dangerous."

Mr. Lamarque pointed to the fruit snacks scattered across the room. "What are those?"

Vic examined them curiously. "I don't know."

"I saw this weird girl from the other room messing with them," said Charity. "She like left before class started."

Mr. Lamarque threw the empty Lockerbie bottle into the trash. A few moments of silence. "Well," he snapped at last. "How many of you does it take to clean up a floor? Go back to your cats."

The class did, without making a sound. Lamarque watched as Vic shoved the mop around the floor. After about a minute, he exploded.

"I can't stand another second of this!" he screamed. "Don't you know how to mop a floor? Look how ineffective you're being. You're covering the same floor area three or four times over again, and you're just pushing the water around. Give me that."

Wordlessly, Vic passed him the mop.

"When I was your age in high school," said Lamarque, "I had a job mopping in the produce department at Safeway, and I quickly determined how to do my job efficiently and effectively. Here's how to mop. Sheesh."

Vic watched and nodded gratefully as Lamarque worked over a tiny patch of floor. Then he thrust the mop into Vic's hands. "Here."

For about a minute, Vic mopped vigorously with the Lamarque-approved technique.

Then a knock sounded at the open classroom door. The teacher turned in irritation from his position of surveillance.

Into the lab slouched a woman, early middle age, wearing a 1920s-style net hat and smeared lipstick. She leered and swayed like a hooker on heroin.

The expression of annoyance faded from Lamarque's face.

"Oh, my God," he said. He swallowed. "It's been forever."

The woman waggled her fingers. "Hi, Percy."

He turned stiffly to face the benches. "Class, this is the daughter of our mayor, Mr. Weingarten. She's involved in—"

The woman laughed and cut him off. "I don't care."

"Neither do I," he said. He walked over to her and put his arm around her shoulders. They headed for the door. Before walking out, he glared. "Work quietly on the cats."

After a decent pause for this new development to register, everybody turned to look at one another.

"Well, fuck *me*," said Vic.

Sara waved her arms. "Okay, this day is officially bonkers."

Everyone started talking. After six minutes or so, Lamarque still hadn't reappeared. Vic raced over and shut the door. People got up. Sara turned the radio back on.

"*Put you in the SUV, you wanted ice, so I made you freeze, made you hot like the West Indies. . . .*"

"Okay," said Vic, "we're skimboarding for sure this time."

He tilted the mop-wringer trolley and washed another flood of water across the floor. Everyone began to slip around again to the music.

Forrest picked up a couple of big yellow sponges. "Hey," he called, "what if we put sponges on our feet?"

The door opened.

Lamarque surveyed the scene through his steel Himmler glasses, two dozen immobile bodies staring back at him like players in a twisted game of red light–green light. He spoke quietly over the music. "What happened?"

"We were wondering if sponges could help us get it up," Forrest babbled. "We're having problems."

"Yeah," said Vic, "we're having problems."

"The first problem is that there are way too many of you trying to perform a very simple operation," said Lamarque. "Go back to your seats."

He shut off the radio and everyone scattered in silence. He watched as Vic diligently plowed the mop into the sea of water, which had now assumed Adriatic proportions.

"You've accomplished *nothing*," he said. "Absolutely nothing. This is unbearable. Give me that. I'll do it."

He pulled the mop from Vic's hands and scrubbed away for the next fifteen minutes.

"Student twenty-eight," he said eventually. "Pour this into the sink."

The floor gleamed. Vic lifted the trolley and emptied it into the huge metal washbasin.

As he put the heavy plastic cart back down, the wringer's spring-loaded handle popped forward and thumped him in the crotch. "Owwww," he moaned softly.

When he sat back down again, he whispered to the group. "I guess I deserved that."

Mr. Lamarque waggled the clipboard meaningfully—unsolicited speech was not a frivolous crime.

The bell rang shortly thereafter.

Vic popped a couple of Vicodin before auto shop.

Soon he stood with three sophomores underneath a Spanish teacher's jacked-up Taurus, watching idly as they removed the transmission bolts. Sparks flew from a welder two bays down.

"Dude," said one sophomore. "It's so sick. My curfew's like ten, but I like snuck out of my house on Saturday after my mom went to bed."

"Tight," said another sophomore.

They glanced at Vic for approval.

He shook his head slowly, inhaling the sharp sweet smell of oil, rubber, and metal.

"You guys so aren't on my level," he said. "There's no one to talk to here."

The sophomores looked down at the toolbox.

"That's okay," said Vic. "You're younger."

Eventually they removed the transmission and opened it. The sophomores stared at a labyrinth of five hundred metal bits.

"Look," said Vic. "This is so easy, if she's having problems with second. Don't you remember the drawing?" He closed his eyes for a second, and then traced a path over the machinery. "You need a 1.47 ratio, right? The flywheel's turning the small sun gear, the servo locks the ring gear, and that's turning the planet carrier. That's the 2.2 ratio. Then the other band is holding the large sun gear that the planet carrier is turning, which is turning the next ring gear, which is the output. That's the .67 ratio. That's 1.47 when you put it together, fool."

After a while, he snapped the lighter out of his eagle belt buckle and singed some of his arm hair just because. The hideous smell mixed with the chemical fumes. Then he passed around the lighter and the sophomores set their arm hair on fire, too.

One day later, he sat with the rest of government class at the video lab computers.

Like many other faculty members at Mirador, Ms. Schroeder shied away from the essay tests and research papers of a bygone era. Students didn't want to study for exams and found writing assignments painful and arduous. Teachers, meanwhile, didn't relish the chore of reading and grading.[19]

In the place of such old-fashioned and passé activities blossomed not only the multiple-choice Scantron form but also the group video project and final. Everyone loved making or watching a good movie. "MTV is much older than you are, and reality TV started with the *Real World* when you were in kindergarten," Ms. Schroeder told her class. "This just works best for everybody."[20]

Frame by frame, Vic and Shawn tweaked the soundtrack on their community experience project.

"Dude," said Shawn happily, "this is going to be such a bomb movie. This is going to be so tight."[21]

"I need this grade so bad," said Vic. "I need to pass this class."

They had worked on their videos for a month. Now Ms. Schroeder had brought everyone to the lab to survey their handiwork for the first time. She circulated the room in her baggy taupe suit, suggesting final changes before the next week's project deadline.

She stopped at Evelyn's group's computer to preview their film.

"You'll see," mumbled Ross. "She's not going to say anything good about it. She never has anything positive to say about good movies."

"She hates anyone who can make a good movie," said Shawn. "She hates anyone who can make a better movie than she can."

Evelyn's film began with stirring strings and a montage of columns and illuminated portraits. INSIDE THE EMERALD VALLEY CITY COUNCIL. It could easily have appeared on PBS.

Schroeder waved an irritable hand. "Get to the point," she said. The film moved along to a professional-quality interview with the mayor. "You can barely hear him." With council members. "Are those really the best questions?"

"See?" demanded Shawn. "I hate that bitch."

Across the room, Schroeder moved to Cody's group. They had filmed some sort of sock-puppet show in a shoebox about school board meetings.

"Oh!" exclaimed the teacher. "This is so creative."

"That's such crap," muttered Shawn.

Totally absorbed in his editing work, Vic nodded along to the soundtrack on the headphones.

Eventually Schroeder arrived at Vic and Shawn's computer. "Okay," she said tersely. "Let's see it."

Vic rubbed his palm on his shirt and clicked the Play button.

WATER AWARENESS. The movie began with a hard-boiled detective, played by Vic, taking on the case of the mysterious drying up of the water supply in Emerald Valley.

"Stop," said Ms. Schroeder. "Pause the movie. Pause it! What's *that*?"

She pointed to the detective's desk. He had a bottle. A bottle of whiskey. He had poured himself a cup and was about to take a drink.

"It was filled with water," said Vic.

"I don't care what it was filled with!" she said. "I can't believe you two. You can't use shots of alcohol in your video."

"We showed you the script," said Vic. "You said it was okay."

Schroeder laughed scornfully. "No, Vic, no, I did not say that. When you say 'he's at his desk having a drink,' I assume juice, or water."

"Eyes over here," she called to the room. "I can't believe I have to explain this. You can't have anything that depicts minors engaging in illegal activity, which I thought I made very clear, but this group just couldn't manage to figure out." She wrote "Minors & Alcohol" on the whiteboard.

Vic's throat tightened. "What do you want us to do?"

"I don't know what you should do, Vic," said Schroeder. "You're going to have to remove that scene to start with." She shook her head and started to the next computer.

"Do you want to see the rest of it?" asked Shawn.

Schroeder threw up her hands. "Okay."

Vic swallowed and clicked Play.

The next scene had taken them a week and a half to film properly. It featured a car chase between the detective and the criminal mastermind. To get the shots they had to have the camera hanging steady from the back of a third pacer car.

Schroeder gasped. "What? I just don't believe you. Where did you film this?"

"In the parking lot," said Shawn.

"No," said Schroeder. "No." She called to the room. "Eyes over here, everyone." She wrote "Reckless Driving" on the board. "A very familiar group apparently also doesn't understand that we can't have reckless driving. We can't have students screeching and speeding like hooligans around the parking lot. Now they're going to have to remove their footage from the computers."

"We weren't screeching and speeding—" Vic forced out.

"Is this going to be a problem?" said Schroeder. "If it's a problem, we're going to have to turn your footage over to our campus resource officer, and he can issue you citations. You're going to have to delete all of it."

The movie played onward unattended. Now Vic the detective was questioning tourists in Downtown Disney if they knew what had happened to Emerald Valley's water supply.

Ms. Schroeder caught sight of it. "And you're harassing people with the camera!" The board echoed "Harassment." "Eyes, eyes up here. I don't believe this. You can't harass people with the camera. We've talked about this before and it's apparently still a problem for this group. I've seen enough of this. Turn it off. You're getting zeroes on your production and community spirit grades."

She walked away. Vic stood and followed her. The whole class watched.

"I don't see why we get zeroes," was all he could say, because he thought he might cry.

"Go back to your seat," she said.

"No," he said. "We worked really hard on that."

"I told you to go back to your seat," she said.

"No," he said. "It's not bad. It's a good movie." Then he couldn't speak anymore.

"Vic," said Schroeder, "what you don't get is I've had enough of this. You don't get that it's enough. Now you can either go back to your seat the easy way or the hard way."

Vic just stood mute, blinking fast.

"Okay," said Ms. Schroeder, laughing, "the hard way." She walked over to the phone on the wall, picked it up, and dialed a few numbers. "Hi," she said brightly, "this is Becky Schroeder in room three-two-three. Please send a proctor over." She hung up.

About a minute later, Mario the proctor entered the room.

One group had been working on a video titled "A Ride-Along with a Police Officer." With Schroeder's attention fully focused on Vic, they turned up the volume and laughed. It was the *COPS* theme song.

"Bad boys, bad boys, whatcha gonna do, whatcha gonna do when they come for YOU. . . ."

Vic started to cry.

"Please sit down," said Mario.

"I'll sit for you," said Vic. "Not for her." He sat.

"Oh," said Schroeder, "how far do you want to go with this, Vic? The first step is detention."

She wrote him a detention form and handed it to him.

Through his tears, he ripped it up.

"He needs to go to the office now," Schroeder told Mario.

Mr. Popper looked at Vic over the piles of papers.

"It's been—what?" he asked. "Less than a week?"

Vic swallowed.

Popper blew out his cheeks and checked another box on the white contract. "That's your second strike. You've lost your safety net, Vic. Next time we have a problem, it's instant expulsion, no appeals. Do you understand what that means?"

Vic nodded.

"Okay," said Popper. "You've got ISS for the rest of today and tomorrow. I don't think there's anything to discuss."

After last bell, Vic shoveled gravel into the bottom of an Olympic-sized pit until the sun went down.

CODY ADAM REISLING

"—Double-Double, small lemonade, and a 4 x 4, large Coke?"

"Yup," I said, and presented the collection of bills and loose change we had carefully counted.

The In-N-Out cashier passed the bags of food through her sliding window, and Cody took charge of distributing from my front passenger seat. "Two hamburgers and a vanilla shake?"

"Yo," said Brian Olvera, who sat in the back with a guy named Steve that played O-line on football. To avoid the problem of getting picked up at my nonexistent house, I found it a lot easier to clock the miles as the guy behind the wheel.

As we pulled away from the drive-through this Sunday afternoon, Cody opened his burger and threw the lettuce, tomato, and onion out the window. "So much *meat*," he said, and bit into the four beef patties and four slices of cheese.

Then he pointed a rough digit at my lemonade cup. "What's that?" he demanded.

"What?" I said. "Lemonade?"

His finger shook. "What the fuck, bro. That cup is tiny. Did you just buy that?"

"Yeah," I said.

He dropped his burger back onto its wax paper, voice rising. "That's bullshit. How can they sell people a cup that small? You can't let them do that to you."

I shrugged. "Whatever."

He grabbed the cup and thrust it toward Brian and Steve. "Look how fucking small this cup is. Can you believe how small this cup is?" He turned to me. "No. That's not right."

I smiled. "Dude, I like ordered a small."

"That's bullshit, bro." He glowered at In-N-Out through the window and began to breathe heavily. "Go back around."

I laughed and looked for support, but the guys in the back still talked. "Bro," I said, "it's totally okay."

"No," Cody said. "It's not okay, bro. Go back around. I'm serious, go back around."

So we drove through again to the cashier's window. I sat and looked straight ahead as Cody went off. "How can you give people lemonade this small? What are you doing to your customers? Don't you like respect the people who come and buy food from you? What do you have to say to my friend?"

Several minutes worth of accusations and apologies later, the cashier proposed a compromise. "He can upgrade to the extra-large for another fifty cents."

Cody nodded solemnly. He turned to me. "Give her fifty cents."

I looked at the menu, where an extra-large cost fifty cents more, and handed it over. Cody sat back, satisfied that justice had triumphed, while I sucked on a drink way bigger than I wanted.

"You have to like stay on guard, bro," he said, "because the whole world is such unfair crap and it's all falling apart and you can't ever relax for like even *one fucking second*. Otherwise you're gonna be flipping my burgers like that bitch."

I laughed.

He shook his head sadly. "Don't you realize what's going to happen? No one gives a fuck about you once you get out of high school. Your life is over. Instead of being a big fish in a little pond, you're like, no fish in no pond. It doesn't matter how popular you are or anything. You'll see."

*   *   *

Face angled downward, Cody gasped for breath as he finished the final rear-delt flye on Monday morning. He swung the one-hundred-ten-pound dumbbells down to the rubber mat, let the steel touch the floor, releasing it from his quivering fingertips.

He sat up slowly from the incline bench.

"I've gotta represent for him," he said. "I've gotta represent for him here, I've gotta represent for him with H.C."

Brian didn't say anything. With all the weight on the stack of the lat pulldown machine he couldn't speak.

"Do you remember the H.C. game last year? That was straight-up Dove's game. That was like the sickest double play in the seventh, when he caught that asshole's fly and threw it in to third. He won the game right there. Six-five, and Hamilton Cove just basically realized they're a bunch of fags."[22]

Face red, Brian raised the bar as slowly as he could. "He was like so nice about it, though. He didn't have any enemies anywhere, even with those fuckers."

Cody shook his head. "No. He loved everybody, he was cool with them whoever they were."

The giant sunglassed Marlin grinned from a mural on the wall behind him.

"You know what just really tripped me out?" said Brian. "I just realized I didn't think about Dove all day today until just now."

Cody pulled an arm across his chest and tugged, forcing the stretch. "No one's thinking about him. They're all forgetting him, like time's going on and one day everyone's gonna wake up and nobody will think about him at all. That's so dangerous, because it'll be like he totally vanished from reality."

The rattle of plates mixed with Godsmack blaring on the old boombox. Coach Mulligan came by, white hair tousled, kind crinkles around his puzzled eyes.

"Did you finish your sets?" he asked.

"Yeah," said Cody. "We're talking about the H.C. game."

Coach Mulligan looked at the giant swordfish. "Yeah. Right now we're trying to figure out how we're going to get you guys out there."

"What do you mean?" said Cody. The PGD dog tags clinked around his neck.

"Mmmmm," said the coach. "Remember the old days back when we had money, and we could just go visiting schools whenever we felt like it, and the bus was just magically there?"

"We don't have a bus?" said Brian.

"Well," said Mulligan, "not at the moment."

Cody scooped up the dumbbells. He dropped them onto the weight rack with a clang.

He cornered Derrick at the senior circle during passing period. "How can there be no buses?" he demanded. "That's just messed up."

"You're right," said Derrick. "It sucks. That's what happens when they cut one-point-one million dollars. Be happy we're not going to be here next year, 'cause they're supposed to cut over two."

"Well, why are they cutting friggin' baseball transportation? I can think of lots of things that should be dropped if they have to. Like girls' sports. They could save so much if they cut girls' sports. They don't make any money, they lose money. No one goes to their games except their parents. Guys' sports make money, especially football. So does baseball."

"If it makes you feel better," said Derrick, "they're also cutting the transportation for tennis, soccer, us on volley, uh, band, drumline, debate, orchestra, all that stuff."

"Well, you should say something, bro," said Cody. "You should do something about it."

"Yeah," said Derrick. "I wish I could."

Beeeeeeeep.

Cody took his seat the next day at the center of government class. Before Ms. Schroeder cut the lights and clicked on the tape recorder, she liked to start with a free-form discussion of current events.

"Who can tell us what happened today in Iraq?" she asked.

"Four Americans died in Al-Fallujah," said Evelyn Strout.

Evelyn generally stood alone as the one dissenting voice. Schroeder allowed her to speak freely during current-events time in order to have at least some sort of discussion dynamic.

"What about that?" asked Ms. Schroeder.

"Kill them all," said Cody. "If we take them out, then there'd be no more problems."

"That's true," said a girl.

"It *is* true," said Cody.

"You can't just go in and kill everyone," muttered Evelyn.

"Why not?" Brice called out. "Make them extinct!"

"Yeah," said Ross. "They should see they can't do this kind of thing. If we really went in and got them, they couldn't keep messing with us anymore."

" 'Cause they'd all be *dead*," said Evelyn.

"They're just jealous," said Cody, "because America's the best."

Evelyn had one occasional ally, a guy named Doug who had lived in Vancouver until age eleven.

"No," said Doug the Canadian, "they're angry because we invaded their country."

"Yeah, the Canadians are tight," said Shawn. "They sit on their bums and do nothing." He leaned back, smirking. He had written "Fuck Terrorists" on his backpack next to the words "Bud Light" and "I have a boner" and drawings of the Volcom stone.

"That's because nobody's at war with us," said Doug the Canadian. "We don't go around attacking people randomly and sticking our nose into other people's business. That's why nobody hates us."

"Well, I'm sorry if I sound, like, racist," Shawn said.

"No, you're not," said Doug the Canadian.

"Listen, you guys, it's a small planet, and we have to solve our problems without fighting," said Evelyn.

"No," said Cody, "it'll never work that way. You sound like one of those tree-hugger people. You'll never do it. It'll never happen. That's not human nature."

Evelyn's face turned bright red. "You're calling me a tree hugger just because I like yoga? Just because I'm flexible?" She turned back in a huff.

"See, you can't talk about it," said Cody. "There's so much stuff you can't say, you know? If I go over to Garden Grove there's like eight billboards I can't read because I'm the one percent of the population that speaks English, but you can't say you don't like that. It just irritates me so much."

"Yeah," said Ross. "People have to learn to speak English. Like you go into the 7-Eleven and ask for the bathroom and they're just like '*¿Qué?*' "

"You go to a different town and it's like crossing the border," someone said.

"I mean, if you come to America, you should do American things and not worship Buddha or some freak," said Cody.

Evelyn snapped a pencil point on her binder in fury. "Why can't people worship Buddha?"

"I don't like seeing it," said Cody. "Because it's weird."

"That's your opinion," said Doug the Canadian. "We don't think that because we're open-minded people."

"'Open-minded people' are getting killed in Iraq," said Cody. "That's our problem. If we're not going to pull out totally, we need to toughen up. Do you think they'd understand if we bombed *them*? Like their schools?"

"What?" said Doug the Canadian.

"You heard me," said Cody. "I think we should go back tenfold. If they take out a bus, we should bomb . . . a bus station."

"So you're suggesting an eye for an eye, Cody?" asked Ms. Schroeder.

"No," said Cody. "Like an eye for, for an *arm*."

"We should drop crosses everywhere," suggested Vic.

"Would that help?" asked Ms. Schroeder.

Vic thought. "No," he said after a while. "But it'd be funny."

"They should understand we're trying to give them freedom," said Kaylee. "They should be thankful. They have no reason to be blowing us up."

"Or like *beheading* people," shuddered Cody. "Did anyone see that video?"

People shook their heads.

"I saw it on the Internet," he said. "It wasn't, like, quick, they didn't just like behead him. They had a little knife and they kept sawing away at his neck and he was screaming. And then when they cut off his head and held it up, like his mouth was twitching."

Teresa Nogales shuddered. "What's wrong with them? They're sick."

"What's better," asked Cody, "a God who says 'love me' or a God who says 'kill them'? Christianity's always tried to be tolerant."

"Hah!" said Evelyn. "For a thousand years they killed anyone who thought differently, from the Inquisition to the Crusades."

Silence for a moment, until Ross found a way out. "The Iraqis should just like apologize for blowing up our buildings," he declared, "and then we'll leave."

"They didn't blow up our buildings," said Doug the Canadian.

Ross looked at Ms. Schroeder for confirmation. She shook her head "no, no, no."

"Oh," he said. "Whatever." He began to draw triangles.

Evelyn took the opportunity. "We're only there because Bush lied to everyone about the Iraqis having weapons of mass destruction."

"He didn't lie," said Cody.

"Where are the weapons?" asked Evelyn.

"What? No. I'm sure they had 'em," said Shawn. "Like why would Iraq try to start a war against us if they couldn't defend themselves?"

"Uh, I think *we* were the ones who invaded," said Doug the Canadian. Silence.

"Iraq gave terrorists like money, and weapons, and stuff, so they're totally to blame," insisted Cody.

"Not the terrorists who attacked us," said Evelyn. "We gave them more weapons than Iraq ever did. Reagan sold them to them in the eighties, and he also gave Saddam and the Taliban the weapons they used to fight us. Are we to blame? Are we terrorists?"

Pause.

"You're talking about *history,*" some girl accused.

"Shut up, Evelyn," one short guy muttered to himself. "Just stop talking."

"We have to take it to them because they could attack us so easily here," said Cody. "It's so easy to get across the border. Like when you're coming back from T.J., and they ask you if you have anything, and you just say no, and they let you across."[23]

The class had one Middle Easterner, a dark-skinned Persian guy named Darius.

Ms. Schroeder pointed to him. "Well," she said, "could someone like Darius get across easily?"

"No," said Cody.

"Is it overkill or justifiable concern?" she asked.

Dozens of eyes turned to Darius. "Justifiable concern," he said quickly.

"It's not just foreigners," said Vic. "We have our own terrorism. Like gang wars. Like what's the difference between terrorism and gang wars? There is no difference."

"That's not terrorism," said Ross.

"Yeah, it is," said Vic. "They had a shoot-out in the mall down in Santa Ana last weekend, and a bunch of people died."

"No, 'cause terrorists kill innocent people who like aren't involved," said Kaylee.

"Gangs kill innocent people all the time," said Vic. "They call bystanders who get caught in the fire 'mushrooms.' They don't care. They're like, 'oh, we iced a few mushrooms.'"

Silence.

"We should have more security in America," said Alexis.

"That's where we've seen a lot of the new legislation," said Ms. Schroeder, "like creating a cabinet department of Homeland Security and passing the PATRIOT Act."

"What's that?" Cody asked.

"It lets the government tap your phone, read your e-mail, and break into your house without probable cause," said Evelyn. "It also means they can detain you for as long as they want without a lawyer and without trial."

Cody looked up at Ms. Schroeder. She nodded. "Basically."

This girl Nicole who almost never talked in class now spoke. "My grandmother grew up in Nazi Germany. She always used to say 'don't criticize the government.' We were always like, 'whatever,' but now I'm scared that they could use what I say against me. This is how Nazi Germany started."

"Everyone said, 'it can't possibly happen in Germany,'" said Evelyn.

"I usually think things are less bad than Evelyn does," said Errol, a black guy from the north side. "But I really think there's an agenda here. In the future they're going to use this act against us."

"It's an 'act'?" reflected Ross, giving the matter serious consideration.

"That means it's a law," said Ms. Schroeder.

"It's not just about criminal rights," said Alexis. "It's about basic human rights."

"It's all about deception," said Errol. "It's only money that runs the country."

"There's something higher than the two parties," mused Matt. "Some kind of power. . . ."

Uneasy silence.

"It sounds like a lot of people are concerned," said Ms. Schroeder. "So what can you do?"

"Vote," said some guy.

"Or even write your congressperson," the teacher suggested. "Who's your congressperson?"

Silence.

"Does anyone know?" she asked again.

Doug the Canadian gave the name.

"In the end," said Ms. Schroeder, "it's up to the voters to decide. A number of you are eighteen or will soon be turning eighteen, which means this November is the first election you'll be voting in. It's going to be an incredibly important one. I hope you use your new power and use it well, whichever way you may choose to vote."

"Are people getting mad about Iraq?" asked Kaylee.

"Well, are you?" asked the teacher.

Kaylee was trying to send a text message at the same time. "Huh?" she asked.

"You're people," said Ms. Schroeder. "In this room we have lots of different types, a pretty good cross-section of the population. How do you feel about the war?"

Alexis brushed mascara onto her eyelashes. "It doesn't bug me."

"I like Bush's moral values," said Cody. "He has great moral values."

"Unlike the completely amoral Democrats," said Ms. Schroeder.

"Right," said Cody. Then he realized she intended sarcasm. Like almost every teacher at Mirador, she held more liberal views than the majority of her students.[24]

"Well, I live in this country, I guess it bothers me," said a girl.

"I think the government is full of lies," said one guy. "These are just more."

"Anybody that thinks about it realizes it doesn't matter which party's in power," said Errol. "It's gonna be the same. You pay taxes, you have your little house. Some people think everything they hear on the media is true. It's not."

Ms. Schroeder nodded. "That's an important issue in a democracy. Where do you go to get unbiased news?"

"You don't," said Alexis.

"Another country," said Evelyn.

Cody snorted. "Pffff, uh, *no.*"

The room lapsed into silence.

Ms. Schroeder surveyed the class. "Let's see hands. How many of you think we're doing the right thing in Iraq?"

Four hands went up, including Cody's.

"Okay," said Ms. Schroeder, "how many of you think we're doing the wrong thing?"

Three hands went up, including Evelyn's.

The room contained thirty-five people.

"Well," said Ms. Schroeder. "I guess the rest of you don't think." She laughed to herself. "Is it a 'don't care' issue?"

"Yeah," said a girl.

"Yeah," said a guy, snickering.

"I'm glad about all the time I spent marching for the Twenty-Sixth Amendment," said Ms. Schroeder. She saw the blank looks but she didn't bother. She sighed. "Okay. My generation had the country. We screwed it up. Your turn. We left you a mess. You're either going to make it messier or better."

Another long silence. "Does anyone care?" she asked.

Cody strode into the senior circle at lunch, Marlins baseball cap down tight over his eyes like always.

"Did you see the friggin' drug dog here during second?" he demanded. "Freshman year you could just walk off campus, and now look at this place. It's changed so much, it's hard to explain it. Look at those fuckers playing patty-cake! They're happy everything's getting locked down."

He pointed to a little theater-tech freshman pulling his roller bag across the quad and goofing around with a guy in glasses.

"Go say something," laughed Brian Olvera.

"Whatever," said Cody.

"Nerds rock," said Padma. "I love those little guys!"

"Let's deny the existence of Padma," said Brian, "starting *now.*" He snapped his fingers.

"Where's Padma?" said Cody.

"Where's who?" asked Brian.

Padma laughed. "Fuck you guys." She picked up his backpack.

"Oh, my God," said Brian. "My backpack's floating. The laws of physics have gone crazy!"

She held it over the trash can right outside the circle.

"Don't you dare," he said. "I will fucking kill you."

"No!" cried a voice. "Don't kill her. Kill you!" Aram lurched into the scene with his headphones, holding his trash bag.

"Go away," said Brian.

Aram looked at Padma. "You have something in your hair," he told her. He reached out a hand and started to pull through the long shiny strands.

"Aaaaah," she screamed, yanking back.

Kaylee watched, shaking her head. "I used to work with the retards, but I stopped when one threatened to kill me."

Padma pointed at Cody and giggled. "Hey," she told Aram, "he has a secret to tell you."

Aram pulled on Cody's jersey. "What?" he asked. "What? What's the secret? What?"

"Go away, Aram," said Cody. The girls were laughing.

"What's the secret?" wailed Aram.

"Go *away*," said Brian.

Aram started to flail around with the garbage bag and moan. Alexis winced at the noise.

"That sound is so awful," she announced. "I'm getting an ice pop. Does anyone want to come with me?"

"I do," said Kaylee. They linked arms and marched off to the Save Our School one-dollar ice cream stand in the food court.

Everyone else moved away from Aram. Eventually he left.

"God, he's annoying," said Cody.

"What's his syndrome?" asked one baseball guy.

Brian laughed. "I don't know. Dude, you should totally be like, 'Hey, bro, what's your syndrome?'"

After last bell, Cody went out to the field for three hours of practice. He pitched to the batters, repeating the perfect motion over and over again with slight variations. The fog cleared, and the younger guys kept the hopper full in an endless cycle of eight balls per batter under a brilliant sun and cloudless sky.

Already the light had started to fail when Cody arrived at his twenty-one-year-old brother's apartment. They lived in a typical building, a two-story U-shaped cement edifice wrapped around a sparse court-yard.

Cody found his brother in the kitchen, pouring water into the hopper of a big aluminum machine.

He wore khaki pants and a collared shirt. They shared the same pale aqua eyes and short brown hair, but Cody's brother had harder lines in his face and faint five o'clock shadow. He looked up when Cody came in. "You go run afterward to get your hair done? To get a fucking pedicure?"

Cody lingered by the refrigerator. "Practice is going really long for the opener next week."

"You don't know how to play fucking baseball," said his brother. "I'll go out there and school your ass in two minutes. You'll be crying like a little bitch."

Cody's fists clenched and he started breathing harder. "Screw you."

"Oh, you think you're a big man? You're gonna have a big man attitude?" Cody's brother held out his right palm. He was about two inches shorter and sixty pounds of muscle heavier.

"Punch my hand, big guy," he commanded.

Cody hesitated.

"*Punch it,*" repeated his brother.

Cody grit his teeth, pulled back in a fist, and slammed the palm as hard as he could.

His brother smiled as his hand moved about a quarter of an inch. "You're so weak. It's still like when you had braces and I'd kick the shit out of you every day."

Cody turned away, drained. "I've got a lot to deal with, okay."

"Boo hoo, emo boy," said his brother. "You're still in high school. Your life is so easy. You have no idea what it's like to keep an apartment, and have two jobs, and go to college. You can't complain about shit."

Cody's brother worked as a bartender in one of the Anaheim resorts and as an assistant at a CPA firm.

"What's that?" asked Cody, pointing to the aluminum contraption.

"It's a margarita machine I got from work," said his brother. "It makes the slush. We're having a party tonight."

As Cody crossed the living room furnished with Target pieces, he heard his brother shout after him. "Oh, the guy from the Astros called again and I think the guy from the Mariners. It's on the answering machine."

Brian Olvera called his cell while he sat in his bedroom, trying to do reading for English, and Cody yelled through the door to his brother. "Can I bring some girls to the party?"

"Do I have to smack you for asking that?" his brother shouted back. "You know I like the high school girls."

A couple of hours later, Brian and Cody sat around a circular table with the pack of four freshman girls. They had met up at a pizza place in another city because nobody really wanted to go to Pizza Roma and eat under the eyes of Dove.

One girl giggled as she tore open a pack of Equal and poured it onto her tongue. "Oh, my God, you guys, this stuff tastes so good," she said.

"It's better if you snort it," said Brian. "It's like a rush."

"Are you serious?" said the girl.

"Yeah," said Cody. "Snort it. Do a line."

"You'll be cool if you do it." Brian laughed.

"Uh, okay," said the girl. She opened another pack and dumped the white aspartame granules among the crumbs on the table. She formed them into a neat line, took her straw, and Hoovered the Equal.

Everyone laughed as she broke down into a weird sort of gagging cough.

Another girl saw the entertainment section of a newspaper on the window ledge.

"Is this Britney Spears?" she asked, as she reached for it. "If it is, I'm going to rip it up. Ugh, it's Jessica Simpson. Still." She threw the paper on the floor.

One of the other girls looked down. "Oh, they had something about *The OC* in it. I really don't like that show."

"Me neither," said two other girls.

"I do," said the fourth.

"Why?" demanded one of them. "It's so fake. It's about fake wannabe models who are like, 'I have so much money coming out my ass I don't know what to do with it.' It's so not like high school really is."

"Are they supposed to be high school students?" asked another girl. "They look so old, they don't look like high school students at all."

Brian began to try to toss coins into the girls' tops. Cody got a penny right between one of their breasts. The girl squeaked and threw it back at him, but he just made the shot again.

"You know Parker Kilbourne on your team?" said one girl. "Oh my God, his penis is so small."

The other freshman girls started to giggle, one of them showing her braces.

"I'm like, 'Hey, Parker, how's your dick?' and he's all like, 'Huh? Fine.' And I'm like"—she held up a pen—"'About this size, maybe?'"

Her friends all cracked up as she went on. "Oh, my God, it's so tiny, it can't be more than like two inches. I need my guy to have a dick at least as big as, like"—she indicated a good seven or eight inches. "Not like tiny Parker."

Tortured expressions crept across Cody's and Brian's faces.

"This is any guy's worst nightmare, fool," said Brian.

"Yeah," said Cody.

"He's uncircumcised, though, so that kind of makes it different. It's like a little tube."

"Oh," said one of the other girls. "That's like a whole other story. Once I was hooking up with a junior who was uncircumcised and he didn't warn me when he was coming, it was so nasty."

"Oh, my God," said another girl, "once I was jacking off a guy who was uncircumcised and it bled."

Cody and Brian drew in breath through gritted teeth.

"You've gotta use lotion," said Cody. "Girls think guys just like it hard, but it's like rug burn."

"No," said the girl, "I've had guys who said they liked it."

"That's what they *said*," emphasized Cody.

"No," said the girl, "I mean, they came."

"Desperately," said Brian. "In pain."

Cody had been sliding some ice from his Coke on the table, and now he threw it idly at the girls. A brief ice-throwing fight broke out, frosty chips zipping through the air and shattering into crystal shards.

Then one girl rolled up her straw wrapper. "You know who I hate?" she said. "That stupid slut Charity."

"Charity Warner?" said Cody. "Nobody cares about her."

"I wonder what makes her such a slut?" pondered another girl. "Like where she gains her powers of slutness."

"Like what exactly is the definition of a slut, you know?" considered a third.

They thought. "A slut is a girl who sucks a lot of dicks," said one.

"A slut is a girl who does things with guys and doesn't even like expect to be treated with respect," offered another.

"A slut is all those ten-year-old girls who give the middle-school guys blow jobs in the front row of the movie theater at the mall."

The fourth girl laughed. "A slut is Charity Warner. You just know one when you see one."

Around midnight Cody was drunk and so was one of the girls. It didn't even really matter which one. Not the one with braces, though.

Outside his door a bunch of people shouted and played beer pong while Pennywise blasted on the stereo. He had sex with the girl and then started to fall asleep.

"You've gotta take me home," the girl whined. "Someone has to take me home."

"I think you're gonna have to like walk," he said.

"I can't," said the girl. "This is like another city."

He shrugged slightly, eyelids fluttering. The girl wandered around his room. She looked at his shelves of trophies, the little gilt baseball players holding their tiny bats poised, the small dusty football guys frozen midrush. She inspected the clothes in his closet.

After a while she poked at a cardboard box half sticking out from under his bed. She pulled back the flap and saw dozens of envelopes with college postmarks. Arizona State University, The University of Southern California, The University of California at Berkeley, Notre Dame University. . . .

"What are all of these?" she asked.

"Recruiting letters," mumbled Cody.

"You didn't open any of them," she said.

"I can't deal with it," he said.

*   *   *

Cody only got a little bit of sleep before his brother poured a two-liter bottle of orange Fanta over his own head. Then the guests, mostly co-workers, had a huge flour fight in the living room.

His brother eventually woke him, and they spent the next two hours mopping up the cakey mess that covered the apartment.

The next day Ms. Schroeder decided to take a little break from current events. At the beginning of government class everybody drew posters advertising their movie projects.

Cody worked with Steve and another baseball guy.

"Hey, Ms. Schroeder?" Steve asked her as she walked past. "Do you know who Ron Jeremy is?"

She shook her head. "No. Is he an actor?"

"Don't worry about it," said Steve.

And so they used their magic markers on their poster board to make a giant placard for THE SCHOOL BOARD UNCOVERED, starring porn legends Ron Jeremy and Linda Lovelace.

"Oh!" exclaimed Ms. Schroeder, when she saw their handiwork. "This is a really good poster." She elevated it above the entire class. "Eyes, eyes up here. I want you all to see the nice poster some of your classmates made. Sports are good discipline for yourself. That's why a lot of you are strong athletes and strong performers in the classroom." She glared at Vic and Shawn. "And some of you . . ."

She went to her desk to get a roll of masking tape and headed to the door with the poster.

"Uh," said Cody, "where are you going?"

"I'm going to hang your poster up at the front of the quad so everyone can see it," said Ms. Schroeder.

At lunch, Cody checked the stage and the gate area and the language arts benches, but he eventually found the guy he was looking for in the science quad. Travis held a green grade report in his hand as he ducked out the door of the left physics lab.

"What's that for?" Cody asked his reflection. "Are you failing something?"

Travis shook his head. "I get my grades from all my teachers every week so I can track progress for my records, and then I graph them so I can monitor the trends."

In the background, the PA ordered a couple of juniors to the office. "Oh," said Cody. "Uh . . ."

"Do you need more gear?" asked Travis.

"Yeah," said Cody. "I'm in the middle of a cycle."

"Tight," said Travis. "My supplier just got back from a Mexico run. I got your stuff, and I got the tabs for all the people who want to kill their liver."[25]

"That's like half the guys I know," said Cody.

Travis paused. "It's gonna be seventy now."

"What?" said Cody. "Seventy fucking dollars?"

"It's a tricky run. There's a lot of security, and it's these skinheads who—"

Cody's neck tensed and he shoved a finger in Travis's face. "It's so unfair! There's so much competition, there's so much fucking competition now that no one even notices you if you're not taking anything, and it's just getting like worse and worse. Like it's so easy for everybody, no one tests for it and you can just look around this school and see all the people on fucking shit, and you're on the field and the other people come out there fucking huge, and you're just trying to stay even and now you're telling me it's seventy fucking dollars? That's fucking *bullshit*."

His hands drew back into fists. Little Travis stood passively, limply, facing the massive figure before him with the Zen-like inner peace that comes from having a fourth-degree black belt.

"Well, we need you guys to beat H.C., right?" he said.

Something inside Cody seemed to give way. His arms dropped and he spoke quietly. "We don't have a bus. Gray Davis screwed up the economy, and now there's no money to get a friggin' bus. . . ."

Travis watched, face blank. "What are you doing after school today?"

"I got practice 'til like six," said Cody.

"Okay," said Travis. "Come by our house after it's over."

Cody started to walk away.

"Uh," said Travis, "can you like call, and I'll meet you outside? My dad thinks you're crazy."

"What the fuck?" said Cody. "Why?"

"Well, there was that thing with my sister's tires, and then like you sent him a four-page letter about her or something."

Cody looked into the empty classrooms. "Whatever," he said. "I'm so over that."

Travis shrugged. "Yeah, I don't pay attention to her either."

When Cody got back to his brother's apartment that evening he found no one home. He only found a couple of messages on the answering machine, the Astros person again and something from a guy at the Scouting Bureau.

He went to the bathroom and washed his hands.

Then he entered his room and shut the door. He unfolded the plastic bag he had bought with a painful amount of the money his parents sent him every other week.

From the bag he took a wrapped needle and the little glass vial with the slick hologram of Laboratorios Brovel.

He got the rubbing alcohol and cotton swab out of his desk drawer. He wiped down the top of the vial. Then he pulled off his jeans and pressed the cold cloud onto the top of his thigh. The smell of medicines and hospitals, the smell of the UCI Medical Center.

He unwrapped his syringe and removed the plastic cover from the needle. Pulling back the plunger, he sucked air into the barrel. He drove the needle through the rubber stopper of the vial, forced out the air, flipped the container, and drew back. Three cubic centimeters of oily chemical rose into the chamber.

Cody withdrew the syringe, unscrewed the rubber-dulled needle, and attached a new one, dagger sharp. He tapped the side to float the bubbles to the top, and pressed the plunger to expel the air. A tiny glistening trickle of ester spilled down the side of the needle.

He would feel really good, and he would feel powerful and invincible, and he would feel like banging every Matadora ten times over, and he would feel like he could triumph in this falling-apart busless grudge match against the hated enemy that Dove had miraculously won for them last year. And yes, there were problems, he wasn't stupid, and for someone who understood his body as deeply as he did, he realized that all did not really feel okay, a jittery sense of wearing away, of breaking down—but everything always had a price, didn't it? He had to represent now. He had to be strong.

Like a million other high schoolers nationwide, Cody plunged the needle downward into his leg.[26]

That Saturday night everybody went to the beach.

The moon formed a crisp crescent high over the Pacific waters. Fire pits dotted the strip of shoreline, and dozens of bonfires filled the cool air with a flickering glow and a rich smoky scent. Thousands of young people crowded along the sands by their light. Huntington was one of the few Southern California beaches that allowed fires.

Mirador Senior High School had staked out a pit and most of the circle seniors had come, staying close to the blaze, while other students arrayed themselves on blankets farther away. Derrick Littlefield strummed his acoustic on a log by the high flames and a dozen people sat on the sand around him singing "Sweet Home Alabama."

Two-thirds of Mirador had drunk. Some had drunk a lot.

"Jägermeister means 'anger master,' bro," Cody explained to Brian Olvera.

"Really?" said Brian.

Cody shook his head. "No. But doesn't it sound like it could? And it makes you angry to drink it; you know?"

"Oh, nice!" screamed Brian.

They watched the other main event, Alexis and Padma whacking each other with big padded boxing gloves while crowds screamed and cheered them on.

"Cameraman," said Vic Reyes, darting around the action with a white-lit camcorder, "watch out for the cameraman."

Cody addressed the crowds. "I call next. Who wants to box me?"

Everyone nearby carefully looked somewhere else.

"Dude, Brian," said Cody, "you and me, we're up next."

"Uh, maybe later, bro," said Brian.

"Oh, don't be a pussy," said Cody. "Steve, dude, we're boxing."

Steve drank from the Jäger bottle in a bag. He shook his head and passed it to Cody.

"Ahhh," said Cody, "I really want to box someone, but no one wants to fucking fight me." He drank.

"We're not stupid, bro," laughed Steve.

A thunderous wave crashed on the shore behind them, and Cody turned at the sound. The silver PGD tags felt cold on his chest. He took a step back from the firelit circle and watched the dark surf skim against the sand.

After a while he spoke. "Hey, do you know what Dove said after practice on Tuesday? He told me he thought paradise would be an empty beach with just like waves and wind. You know that?" He drank some more.

Silence except for the shouts of the crowd. Cody turned to see that a drunk Brian had stripped down to his boxers and was chasing Padma around in circles.

She shrieked and giggled. "Oh, my God, don't you dare!"

Brian caught her and tossed her down, pinning her to the sand. Vic closed in with the camera and the crowd laughed as Brian began to dry-hump her, doggy style. He grinned up at the world, little boxered behind wiggling as she tried to break free. The whole performance looked ridiculous and he just kept going and smiling for the camera and everyone was laughing.

Cody smiled faintly and watched for a while. Steve came back from the bonfire area and pointed down to the darkness of the water line. "There're people fucking for real down on the sand. You can go down and see them."

Cody walked a little bit toward the waves and saw the forms, having sex all right. He couldn't tell who they were, but Alexis had vanished right after the Padma fight, and he didn't notice Shawn among the crowds. Whatever. She didn't matter anymore.

He turned and trudged away from the water, trekking a diagonal line toward the bathrooms on the boardwalk. He passed new faces, other groups from other cities clustered around the warmth of their dwindling fires.

"Look at you, walking all tough!"

Cody turned to see a few guys sneering near a garbage can, coastal sort of people with long hair. His beating heart eclipsed a distant pulsing in the sky.

He stopped and began to walk toward them. "What did you say?"

"Nothing," said one of the guys.

"Why do you have to be an asshole?" Cody demanded.

The guys looked pretty big. The one who spoke wore a HAMILTON COVE WATER POLO shirt, and Cody got right up in his face. "Your school is getting the *shit* kicked out of it next week."

The pulsing sound resolved itself into the beat of chopper blades. People glanced at their watches. Ten o'clock, time for the beach to clear. They gathered their stuff.

The guy looked at Cody's Marlins cap. He put a hand on Cody's chest. "Take two steps back."

"Get your fucking hand off my chest first."

A moment of tension. The noise of the blades grew. The guy removed his hand. "Look, I don't want any beef, just please take two steps back."

"Whatever," said Cody, and started to leave.

"That's right," the guy said under his breath. "Walk away, Mirador faggot."

The light beam of the helicopter stabbed down from the heavens and began to flash across the beach.

Cody turned, stepped, and decked the guy in the face. The punch flipped him backward over the garbage can.

"Mirador, motherfuckers!" Cody screamed, as the body hit the ground.

Another guy took a swipe at his face before darting away. He wore a class ring but Cody barely felt any impact. The whole beach was emptying fast.

"What the fuck are you running for?" Cody bellowed as they vanished into the draining sea of crowds.

The helicopter churned above, its thirty-million-candlepower Nightsun turning the world into day. He screamed up at it. "Fucking cops! Come down here right now! I'll fucking squash you!"

Brian, now dressed, ran up with a group of the other guys. He grabbed Cody. "Dude, we've got to get out of here *now*. The— Holy shit! What happened to your eye?"

"What?" asked Cody. He touched his face and pulled away a hand covered in blood.

The skin above his eyebrow had ripped open.

They hustled him to the parking lot. Steve drove an old Chevy minivan with a mattress in the back that he had dubbed the "fuck truck." Brian called "shotgun, no challenges," but then he felt bad for Cody. So

Cody sat in the one passenger seat, pressing a Kleenex to his forehead, while the other guys crouched on the mattress in the dark.[27]

Away they drove to Huntington Beach Hospital, where everyone worried about their curfews. They took their cell phones outside and made vague calls to their parents while Cody got five stitches over his eye.

On Monday, everyone waited outside Ms. Schroeder's government room. She hadn't arrived yet, and the door remained locked.

"I'm going to read this in class," said Cody, passing around an e-mail forward that he had printed out. Over the course of a page, an evangelical minister described the time his probing questions into the intrinsically violent nature of Islam had caused a Muslim imam to "hang his head in shame."[28]

"Nice," said a few people.

It was Every Fifteen Minutes Day. A young female teacher crossed the tombstone-dotted quad on her way to the faculty bathroom.

"Hey," said Ross. "She's pregnant."

"She's not married," said Cody.

"Yeah," said Ross, "I know."

Cody stared aghast. "Are you sure?"

"I'm sure," said Ross.

"I heard it too," said a girl, nodding solemnly.

"There're no morals here," said Cody. "Everyone here is so damn liberal. Now she's going to have some baby and get an easy ride sucking off welfare."

"Some people need welfare," said Evelyn. "My sister has a kid, and she can't work because she needs to take care of her kid."

"That's what I'm saying," said Cody. "People don't work, they have kids, they get welfare. The liberals just want to raise taxes to pay for lowlife junkies. Why should I work hard so my taxes can pay for some lowlife junkie to sit around and watch TV all day?"

"Are you saying my sister's a lowlife?" asked Evelyn.

The Grim Reaper stalked across central quad, trailed by the cops and the cameraman. He led the barely clothed form of Charity Warner.

"Take her away," laughed Steve. "No one talks to her anyway."

Cody looked briefly and then focused back on Evelyn, voice getting louder. "No, but you're so narrow-minded. You need to get out of Emerald Valley and see how the world works. My brother knows this woman, Jalissa, in East L.A. who's had four different kids with different men. She says that's what she does."

"Well," sneered Evelyn, "I don't know about *your* friends, but—"

Cody's fists clenched. "They're not my friends!" he yelled. "Aaah, I'm not talking about politics with you. What's wrong with this fucking school?" He looked down wildly at a Styrofoam tombstone by his feet. RIP Chelsea Koch. "She's not fucking dead! What is this bullshit?"

He grabbed the tombstone and drop-kicked it. The Styrofoam exploded into two spinning shards in midair.

Everyone watched him. He looked back at their pale faces, their wide eyes.

A horn tootled brightly, and he turned slowly. Mario the proctor sat in his golf cart in the middle of the quad, beckoning.

Cody took a few deep breaths. He walked out across the concrete plain, past the rich tangles of foliage.

When he arrived at the cart, Mario looked at him for a long time. "Chill," the proctor said at last. "Chill, man, okay?"

Cody nodded. He started to go.

"Hey," said Mario, voice lowered a bit. "Hey, man, that girl?" He nodded to Alexis, who waited with the rest of class outside Schroeder's room. "What's her name?"

"You mean Alexis?" said Cody. "On the right?"

"Yeah, that's it. Alexis," said the proctor. "I like that name, man. How old is she?"

"I think she's eighteen," said Cody. "I don't know, she might be seventeen. No, she's eighteen, I think."

Mario dropped his voice further. "Hey, man." He grinned, bright white teeth. "I think she's pretty hot. Can you set me up? Can you give me an intro?"

On Wednesday morning, Cody woke to find the apartment trashed for a change.

A few of his brother's coworkers had passed out on the Target couches. He stepped over some empty cases of Coors Light on his way to the kitchen.

There the elder Reisling drank coffee, wearing the button-down shirt of CPA-assistanthood. He threw Cody a copy of the *Valley Monitor*. "Hey, slapdick," he said, "look what I can't go to because I work for a living."

Cody glanced down. Together with the local congressman, ex-Governor Gray Davis and Governor Arnold Schwarzenegger would arrive in Emerald Valley at noon.

Like a third of the school, Cody left during lunch period and just ditched his afternoon classes.

The haze had burned off late in the day, and a cold wind blew as he waited with two thousand other people outside the black glass box of Emerald Valley City Hall.

Mirador clustered together in its own section. A few teachers had ditched, too, and they traded conspiratorial smirks with their students across the crowds.

"Oh, my God," said Jasmine, "when has anything like this ever happened in Emerald Valley?"

Padma pushed through the mass of bodies. "I heard Davis is already in the building."

"Screw that guy," said Cody. "I want to see Arnold."

"Yeah," said Sara. "Davis is a pussy."

Nodding everywhere. "I feel that," said Ross.

"I want to see them all," said one girl piously. "I want to hear what they all have to say about whatever this ballot measure is that they're promoting."

The crowds had already waited for two hours. Arnold was apparently running behind schedule.

Someone yelled, and the crowds turned and strained to see a black Yukon SUV cruise into the lot, surrounded by policemen on motorcycles.

The door swung open. Schwarzenegger stepped out, clad in a brown leather jacket. He grinned and gave the masses a big thumbs-up.

The crowds erupted. They roared, jumped up and down. A thousand cameras flashed.

"Ahh-nohld! Ahh-nohld!" chanted Steve and Brian and Shawn and Sara and dozens of other Mirador people in their best Austro-Bavarian accents.

"Republicans!" screamed Cody. "Whooooo!"

At the back of the multitudes, Evelyn and a few other students held protest posters. "Who will pay our budget?" they yelled, tiny voices fading under the cheers. "We want our education back. We don't want an actor. . . ."

After a minute, Davis and the congressman emerged from the building to mostly noblesse oblige applause at a much lower amplitude.

"Look!" said Kaylee. "It's Alexis's brother."

Travis appeared next to the governor, wearing a tie and his mirrored sunglasses. Dr. Chao stood demurely on the sidelines.

Schwarzenegger motioned for quiet. He spoke into a microphone. "I have always said that children are our future, and there is nothing more important than providing the best education possible for every child. California was once known for its outstanding educational system, and it can be once again.

"The feeling of achievement is the springboard to success, and I am so proud to showcase the extraordinary triumphs of our future architects of progress and innovation. It's my distinct honor to bestow on you, Travis Zachary Newton, this Golden State Merit Award."

Travis took the framed certificate. Applause and more photographs as he shook hands with the governor. "It's an honor to represent Mirador High School here today," he said.

"Now we're going inside to do a little press conference about this ballot issue," said Schwarzenegger. The three politicians waved, and a thick pack of TV cameras and reporters followed them through the black glass doors.

The crowds shifted.

"Yo," said Cody, "let's check it out."

He surged for the entrance, winding his way through the bodies. He looked back once and saw that only Padma had kept up with him.

After five minutes of squeezing past the crowds, they found city hall shut tight, shining like a fortress of glossy obsidian in the sun. "The conference is closed to the public," said one of the aides guarding the entrance.

"Oh, come on," said Cody.

"Please?" said Padma.

He examined them closely and shook his head.

Ten minutes later the bystanders seemed to have become distracted, and the aide turned to Padma. "Hey. What's your GPA?"

"Four-point-oh-three," she said quickly.[29]

He slipped her his business card. "Okay," he said. "You guys go in, and tell them you're interns if anyone gives you a problem."

They realized the conference had just ended as soon as they stepped into the diffuse gray light of the high lobby. All the media looked to the left, pointing cameras where—

They turned to see the thin, white-haired form of ex-Governor Gray Davis bearing down on them. He smiled at them and stuck out his hand. The cameras flashed. Padma shook, mute. Cody shook. He thought Davis's hand felt limp.

Schwarzenegger came right behind him. He gripped Cody's hand tightly, and looked him in the eye for a moment. Then the governor interlocked their fingers and switched up into the rough clasp of an arm-wrestling grip.

"Yeah!" laughed Schwarzenegger.

Then the politicians continued out the door and the media drained after them and pretty soon Cody and Padma stood alone in the lobby under the ubiquitous golden bear flag of the California Republic.

"Oh, my God!" she said, leaning against the wall for support. "My heart's like beating so fast. I can't believe I was that close to such a big celebrity." She stared at her hand in awe. "I wonder if we could get him to come talk at graduation."

Cody nodded, trying to downplay how impressed he felt. "He's got a good, firm grip. I love that."

Outside, the engines of the motorcade roared, and the black SUV departed to cheers.

He saw Evelyn muttering as her tiny group lowered their posters among the dispersing crowds. "We were better off with a real politician than an actor," she said. "The recall was such a joke."

The next morning students and teachers began to wish Cody luck against Hamilton Cove. Somewhere over a hundred people, and game day hadn't even come yet.

Coach Mulligan called the team together for a special lunchtime meeting. They arrived jostling and messing around, nervous, excited, and determined.

Brian's huge postgame party ranked highest as a topic of conversation. "It's going to be insane," he said. "It's going to be like so much bigger than the seniors had last year."

The coach had a few items of business. First, he had found a story in *Sports Illustrated* about steroids in high school sports, and he pointed it out as a curiosity. "I don't think we need to address this per se," he said, "because I don't feel it's a problem here."

Guys who used them looked at the walls. The other guys looked at the guys who used them to see if anybody reacted in an awkward way.

Next the coach offered words of encouragement about the hated rival. "A lot of you have been saying, 'Oh, so-and-so says H.C. are league favorites,' or 'Oh, they were CIF finalists last year,' or 'Oh, the paper says they're the best team in the county,' and that's just not the right attitude." People shifted nervously.

Then he recalled something offhand. "Yes, uh, my understanding is that there're going to be scouts at the game tomorrow." Worried eyes met one another.

Finally he spoke of Dove. The time had come for varsity to play their first game ever without his presence. The coach warned that the experience might be an emotional one, both for them and for all the community members who would be coming to take part in the tribute ceremonies.

Now that everyone had lapsed somberly into their own private hells, he shared the good news: The booster club and the Save Our School Foundation had pitched in, and they had a bus!

Only chili pork burritos remained in Crystallina's warming tray by the time the meeting broke, but Cody didn't feel hungry anyway.

People discussed a new development back at the circle. Apparently some sophomores had filled an Evian bottle with urine. The big female proctor caught them snickering, and someone had stashed the plastic container at the circle to escape detection. Nobody knew what to do with it.

Cody slashed right through the Gordian knot. "Give me that," he said, and he hurled the bottle at the sun.

It plummeted from the troposphere and intersected the rotating geomorphic grid directly at the coordinates of the physical and social science quad steps. The pack of freshman girls fled, but one straggler's sheepskin boots bore the brunt of the blast.

"Eeeeew!" she screamed, kicking them off. "My Uggs!"[30]

*   *   *

Cody saw the signs as soon as he jogged out onto the Hamilton Cove di-amond for pregame warm-up on Friday.

The stands were color coded. Toward the far left clustered a small rough patch of H.C. gray mixed with white, brown, anything really. The rest of the arc contained a solid wall of Mirador green.

Had the entire school come? Had the entire town come?

They had crafted giant banners and hung them from the wire fencing. RIP Rob DOVE Doveman. In Loving Memory PGD. RIP Dove. You're with us #17. They had drawn huge baseballs around the number seventeen, enclosed by heart outlines. They had hand signs, drawings on paper plates, a thousand waving permutations of the symbols DOVE, RIP, and 17.

Cody's step faltered before the undulating wall. He had to focus on what was happening right now or he'd never survive.

He moved into the pregame pitcher's routine, did the laps, the stretch-ing, the tosses, the throws from the mound.

Moist ocean air encircled him here, forty minutes southwest of home. Hamilton Cove had a nice diamond, but so did Mirador. Emerald Valley Unified had constructed it right before the budget sublimed like the synthetic snow at Christmastime Disneyland.

Cody looked up again at the green. Somewhere among those bodies his brother had come to watch the first game of his senior season. "I'm gonna come see you fuck up," he had said.

Practice time drained away, and Coach Mulligan called the team into a huddle on home plate. Nobody smiled or laughed or even spoke. The wall of signs rustled in the wind.

"I know this may be hitting us harder than anyone had expected," he said. "But I want you to remember that this is the game Dove loved, and he wouldn't want us to feel sorry for him. I know he's with us today, and the best way to honor him is by playing this game at your very best, with all your ability. That's what Dove would want from each of us, our very best in this game he loved."

People swallowed. Eyes became a little desperate. Some managed a faint nod.

The huddle dissolved, and the H.C. team came onto the field for the special pregame ceremony. They eyed the wall of signs nervously as Coach Mulligan took the microphone.

"As many of you know, our team has recently undergone a very serious tragedy," he began, and he told the story of Dove. Then he went on, "I'd like to ask the family of Robert Doveman to please come down to the field."

His mother, his father, his uncle, and a few others climbed down onto the dusty earth.

"I'd like to present you with this baseball that the whole team has signed for you," Mulligan said. Mrs. Doveman started to tear as he pressed the hard leather into her hands. "And up in the sky, we've had a star named after Rob." He handed her the certificate and then he stopped speaking because he looked like he would cry, too.

In a single surge, the entire stands rose up—both Mirador and Hamilton Cove—and applauded. No shouts, no smiles, just wordless clapping.

Some of the Mirador players started to cry. Cody gritted his teeth, kept swallowing.

"Our team," said the coach, voice hoarse, "has decided to wear black-and-orange armbands to remember Dove for the rest of our opening game."

The team manager, a junior girl, passed them out from a cardboard box. Cody slipped his on, elastic tight against his forearm.

"And a number seventeen by our hearts," continued the coach. They pinned the little felt seventeens to their uniform breasts.

"Dove's road jersey will be with us at every game this season," said the coach.

The manager lifted it carefully from another box. No one on the team could tear his eyes from the shimmering green fabric. They had last seen it at the candlelight vigil, and for the year and a half prior, they had seen it on Dove. She laid the cloth reverently on a folding chair in the dugout.

"We'll be playing this game and the rest of the season in Dove's memory," said the coach. "Thank you."

He walked off the field. The Mirador and H.C. teams tried not to look at each other. Nobody really knew what to do at that point, but it didn't include a strong desire to play baseball.

After an immeasurable silence, the Hamilton Cove band trumpeted out the opening notes of the national anthem, and the players whisked down their caps, and time marched forward again.

H.C. took the field, and Cody screamed at his teammates as they ran for the dugout. "We are going to *win this fucking game*," he roared. "H.C. is Dove's game, and we are winning this game for him."

And they needed exactly that release. Either the seventeens pinned on their hearts would send them careening over the edge or they had to push all the uncertainty and doubt and screaming panic outward, bludgeon down the world with it, drive it into winning this game. Manic energy mounted like a spring tide.

Three minutes into the game Brian slammed a home run. The wall of Mirador green didn't even cheer loudly. Instead they just held their Dove signs and *watched*, solemn and eager, as if the outcome of this particular contest would spell truth about how the universe operated.

When Cody stepped onto the mound he struck out two H.C. batters. Then two of their hitters knocked flies, and pretty soon a Hamilton Pirate drove a runner in with a single to left. The first inning ended one-one.

The field stayed quiet. No chatter, no insults, nothing. The Matadoras jumped and performed their set routines and led the green wall through the cycle of cheers, but the rote sounds only swelled and decayed like the versicles and responses of liturgy.

"Come on, guys," the Hamilton coach said uncertainly to his gray crew. "Come on. You know what you're capable of. You know you're not playing your game."

In the next inning, a walk, a missed grounder, and a double brought a point to the Marlins, and the Hamilton Pirates followed with their own run after a pair of outfield errors. Two-two.

Cody stood on the mound and threw and threw and threw, reflexively obeying the signal of the catcher. Words insisted themselves over his field of vision, lettered on the cap brim that blocked his view of the sky. "The strength of the School is the Marlin, and the strength of the Marlin is the School."

Around him the haunted match continued in dreamlike stasis. Each inning Mirador scored a point, and then H.C. scored a point. At the end of the fourth, the score stood four-four.

The Marlins went back to the dugout and prepared to bat. Dove's jersey sat next to them at the end of their bench.

The silence deepened. As they waited in lineup, everybody remembered, imagined, envisioned. They saw Dove standing at the end of the bench smiling. Cody recalled some of the girls coming over and Dove telling jokes after practice, his mom making them all fried shrimp. . . .

And on the other side, the Hamilton coach couldn't stand another second of the suffocating quiet.

"Hey," he yelled at his gray team, as they prepared to take the field. "You're getting distracted. You're the best team in the CIF, and right now you're going to start your season off as losers. I'm sorry about the emotion of this afternoon, but who wants this game?"

"We do," said H.C.

"Who *wants* this game?" screamed the H.C. coach.

"We do!" yelled his team.

The Dove signs still rippled, but everything else changed. In the fifth the Pirate defense became ruthless, an unyielding wall. Blazing balls whipped back at black-armbanded Mirador runners, out, out, *out.*

With the last batter up, Cody on third and the guy on first met eyes for a desperate act. On the back end of a double steal, Cody charged home, putting the Marlins ahead five-four.

Again, the rush of cold noise, the cheers wrapped around a core of silence. "He did it for Dove," came a voice from the stands. Murmuring everywhere.

Pitching a fastball is one of the most damaging activities a human body can perform, and Coach Mulligan didn't like to keep his starting pitchers in for more than five innings.

Cody leaned against the wall of the dugout, face red, sweating, breathing deeply, eyes closed, one hand over the number seventeen on his heart.

Coach Mulligan walked over. "I'm going to sub—"

Cody opened his eyes, and the coach saw them.

"Huh?" said Cody.

The coach paused for a moment. "Nothing," he said. "You're playing a great game. Good work."

The signs rippled in the cool ocean breeze.

And the Mirador Marlins charged out onto the field, where the Hamilton Cove Pirates proceeded to crush them. On a changeup and a curveball, two batters got home runs off Cody, and then a double and then a single and finally H.C. led six-five.

No Marlin managed a single run in the sixth, but H.C. scored three more, bringing the score to nine-five Hamilton Cove.

In the top of the seventh and final inning, everyone realized the game had moved beyond the reach of miracles and simply become impossible for Mirador to win. The Marlins had only one batter left in the lineup and only one runner on second, Cody.

Then the wall of green opened its great and multiple mouth and began to chant. The sound started off quietly and scattered and quickly rose into a vast and general protest against everything really, a branding remonstration hurled back at everything wrong—from death and loss to the smug coastal gray—a thousand students and parents roaring with eerie precision in one voice.

"We love Dove! We love Dove! We love *Dove!*"

The third baseman caught the batter's suicide bunt, and H.C. didn't even celebrate, just vanished quickly and quietly from the field as the great thundering voice chanted on desperately behind the wall of RIP signs: "We love Dove! We love Dove! We love Dove!"

The manager held up the shimmering jersey in the soft sea breeze and dimming light. She carefully folded it for the next game. The season contained twenty-eight more of them.

"We love Dove! We love Dove! We love Dove!"

Everyone else ran off the field, getting away from this nightmare and to Brian's party as quickly as possible, but Cody didn't move. He faced into the chanting mass, a tiny figure with the seventeen pinned on his heart.

ALEXIS ROMERO NEWTON

Alexis beamed and hugged me tight.

"Jeremiah!" she cried. "What's crack-a-lackin'? Are you going to give blood?"

"Uh," I said. "Maybe."

I had returned to the exact same community center wherein Thea's *Hamlet* had caught the conscience of Mirador the day before. Now Alexis twirled near a desk under the poster-board standard of the Mirador Service Association, while a nurse registered a steady stream of students.[31]

"Come on," said Alexis. "You don't want to write an *essay*."

In our ongoing quest for community-spirit points and her quest not to grade, Ms. Schroeder had given us the option of donating blood instead of composing a few civic-minded paragraphs.

"Yeah," I said, "totally, but—"

I looked around at a dozen of my fellow seniors. They wobbled out to their cars wearing BE NICE TO ME, I GAVE BLOOD TODAY stickers and expressions of profound unease.

"I feel like I'm gonna faint," said Brice.

"I feel like I'm gonna throw up all over," said Teresa Nogales.

I looked down at stacks of forms and flashing ID scanners, and I decided that I really shouldn't convince a network of blood banks and EMTs of the existence of Jeremy Hughes.

"Yeah, maybe later," I said.

Alexis stepped away from the desk and plopped onto a sofa between high windows and a giant fern. "Sit and talk," she said. "I'm supposed to be standing there but like whatever. So how *are* you? How's Heather?"

"My girlfriend Heather?" I said, sitting. "She's fine. Good memory."

She smiled. "I have a good memory for other people's love lives."

In order to explain to my Mirador friends why I didn't hook up, I had created a devoted "girlfriend from home" whom I had dated for almost two years. Tragically, she couldn't drive down from Hermosa on the weekends; she had gone on a term-abroad program in Barcelona.

I named her Heather, because I liked the name.

"Oh, my God," said Alexis. "So I've just been filling out these blood forms about everybody's sexual history. I feel like I'm the doctor, you know, like when she hints around about whether you need like an HIV test. I actually said to her once, 'It's been in the mouth, it has not been in the vagina, so I think we're okay on that score,' but now I'd have to say it's been in like a bunch of places. How old were you when you lost your virginity?"

"*Sensei ni rei!*" a voice bellowed from one of the side activity rooms.

Through a space between the fronds, I saw fifteen adults bow to her little brother Travis before he exited. He didn't take karate, he taught karate. He wandered over to our sofa with his backpack.

"Hey," he said to Alexis. "Do you have somewhere I can leave my clothes?"

"Just like the blood drive table," she said.

He sighed, shook his head, and turned to me. "Hey, can I put my clothes in your car?" I passed him the keys and he mooched away.

Alexis waited for my answer.

"Fifteen," I said.

As if to atone for the fake backstory, I stayed almost confessionally open and honest with my schoolmates about anything I possibly could.

"With Heather?" she asked.

I shook my head. "Uh-uh."

"See," she said, "that's like a normal age. I didn't sleep with a guy until I was a junior. You know who it was, it's so funny."

"Who?" I asked.

She laughed and named a teen actor on a reasonably big series.

"Hah," I said. "How did that happen?"

"Yeah, my family like went on vacation in Hawaii and I met him on the beach. I don't know, he was an asshole. He was like such a cocky asshole. I don't know, I guess I felt I could save him and make him a better person." She looked at the pattern of leaves. "It's funny, I always think like that, that I can save people. Like with Cody too, I guess. Do you know what I mean?"

Behind the frond latticework, shafts of light angled through the high windows as Alexis put her arm on my shoulder. I watched with horrified detachment as she put the other arm on my other shoulder. Then she leaned in toward me.

Oh, dear.

Here lay the difference between people's Hollywood expectations and actually going undercover. Everybody would root for a film love interest. But you don't really want me to make a move on this, do you?

I laughed as if totally oblivious, twisted my head backward, and glanced out the wide glass windows. There I saw a very familiar-looking Altima GXE signal left, pull out of the parking lot, and replace all statutory concerns with one thought.

"Is that my car?"

I bolted through the leaves and outside found my parking space empty and her brother gone.

Travis Newton had stolen my car.

The sliding doors opened to reveal Alexis. "Oh, geez," she said. "He doesn't have his license yet, he's only got like his learner's permit."

So an unlicensed sophomore with, um, little history of prosocial behavior had just vanished in a many-thousand-dollar, two-ton piece of machinery registered to one twentysomething Jeremy Iversen from

Santa Monica. This turn of events promised such raw potential for dread that I actually laughed a little in disbelief before punching a concrete pillar.

"He's been talking a lot about how he wanted to drive," Alexis offered sadly. She lit a cigarette.

I had never slipped up before at Mirador, but this episode sure reset the score. Zero options remained but to wait and hope he drove right back again.

I sat on a sofa for fifteen minutes and wondered if I should try to grab my passport before, or after, calling the Brazilian consulate for asylum, when Travis walked in the door and handed me my car keys. "My stuff's in the trunk," he said.

I stared at him. "What the fuck. You just grand-theft-auto'd my car."

"Sorry," he said. I turned to see Alexis throw her arms around Steve.

"This is my new dance," Alexis said.

She scrunched up her face and swung her arm in a circle, shaking her behind to Hilary Duff's "Come Clean" on the speakers.

Brian watched the baggy outline of Charity retreat from the senior circle. "Wow, that girl really ended up a train wreck, huh?"

"Their entire class sucks," said Padma.

Kaylee frowned. "Didn't you guys used to be friends like a *long* time ago? Like I'm talking like junior high?"

Alexis shrugged and smiled. "This is my happy dance," she said, and she began to sing along with the music.

"*I'm shedding, shedding every color. Trying to find a pigment of truth beneath my skin. . . .*"

She stopped abruptly. "Oh, my God, you guys. I lost my cell phone *again*. Can you believe it?"

"Check the office," said Brian.

"No, I like lost it over the weekend. I'm so pissed off, I've lost six this year. I lost all my numbers. I had everything in there. I'm going to have to buy a new one, and it's like four hundred and fifty dollars."

"How many phones would you say it's been since freshman year?" asked a girl.

Alexis hopped up to sit on the side of the circle. "I don't even want to talk about it."

"You should get insurance," said Kaylee. "Can't you get insurance? It's only like five bucks."

"I did," said Alexis. "They only give you two phones." She looked at her watch. "Shit. Do I have a time to get a cigarette? Anyone want to go smoke with me?"

"Smoke bud, maybe," said Brian. "Cigarettes are so bad for you."

"Thank you, I agree," said Padma. "Old-skool high five." They slapped hands.[32] "The longer you do it, the harder it gets to quit."

"Yeah," said Alexis. "I know it's going to like kill me, but I'm totally addicted. I tried not buying a pack yesterday but then I figured at least it helps me stay skinny, which I'm not even right now. Oh my God, I really need to lose five pounds. Fat people don't exist."

"There," said Brian, pointing to Leo the theater-tech frosh hauling his roller bag through the quad.

"No, I just block them out," said Alexis. "No one likes fat people, and there's no reason for them to be fat. Watch TV or look at any magazine. Oh, my *God,* those people look so good. If you look good enough, you can get whatever you want."

" . . . Hughes? Lundstrom?" Mr. Mulligan called at the start of next-period French. "Merkler? Moreno? *Newton!*"

"Here," called Alexis.

"Olivier? Pavlis? . . ."

Mr. Mulligan's voice during roll always stayed as low and flat as the Aquitaine Basin until he hit the Pyrenees of "Newton!"

"Bon," he said when he finished. *"Aujourd'hui il faut qu'on—"*

People giggled. "It's back," someone said.

He turned to see a two-foot model Apache helicopter perched atop his miniature Eiffel Tower. "Mademoiselle Horn strikes again," he proclaimed, shaking his tangled white head.

For a week, he and science teacher Ms. Horn had reciprocally hidden this one model helicopter in each other's classrooms.

"D'accord. Please take out all the beautiful maps that you have for me."

Mulligan had assigned each four-desk cluster to draw as detailed a map as possible of the regions of France. Everybody started talking as he began to circulate.

"Do you have our map?" one guy asked another.

"Don't even start," his friend answered.

Maps from different class periods covered the walls. When Mulligan seemed involved with a cluster across the room, the guy reached out and snatched one down.

His entire group started to giggle uncontrollably. "Names in pencil!" his friend said. "They made this one just for us." He erased the old names and wrote in theirs.

Meanwhile, Evelyn Strout unrolled her map from a cardboard tube. *"Voilà!"* she announced, beaming a crooked smile.

"Oh, my God," said a girl in her group.

The cartography dazzled. She had even managed to incorporate the primary industrial production of each of the ninety-six departments.

"I've worked on it like nonstop for a week," said Evelyn. "I came in during lunch period twice to check his reference books." Like most group projects in life, the person who cared the most ended up doing almost all the work.

Mulligan came by her cluster eventually to check the map against a list of thirty-seven points. *"Bien,"* he decided. *"Bien, bien, bien . . ."* They got a score of thirty-four, a 92 percent. Evelyn nodded at the bright red A-.

Then he stopped at Alexis's cluster, a group of pretty blond girls. She grinned up at him. "Oh, Mr. Mulligan!"

"How are you young ladies doing?" he said and pulled up a chair next to her. Their map looked passable at best.

"Oh, my God," said Alexis, tossing her hair. "I love this class so much. *Je l'adore tellement.*"

"You're like a really good teacher," nodded another girl. "Like you really are, seriously."

"And you're such a great coach," said Alexis.

He laughed. *"Merci."*

"Oooh," she said, looking at his button-down shirt. "I *love* the outfit today."

Evelyn coughed sarcastically but listened for the verdict.

"Well," said Mr. Mulligan, after checking through his list. "You got twenty-five out of the thirty-seven points right, but they're small things, really. Your work with this map is beyond college level, and I'm giving you ladies one hundred percent."

Evelyn's eyes widened.

"Don't take it so hard," said a guy in her group. "He's sleazy to all the girls. Everybody knows he's got half the brain of a teacher, half the brain of a coach, and half the brain of a pimp."

After Mulligan moved across the room, Alexis laughed lightly. "I usually ignore him, and the day I need him I'm nice to him."

During passing period, she headed to the sciences quad with Padma and a few other girls from the circle.

They crossed paths with a tall gangly senior wearing a blue Yale sweatshirt and white jeans too short for his legs.

Alexis smiled happily at him. "Hi, Ed!"

He grinned back. "Hey, Alexis."

"Oh, my God," she said, ten paces later. "He is such a dork. He wears that thing every day." The branches of the trees cast lace shadows over her face, and she switched position to walk in the brilliant sunshine.

"Why do you talk to him?" asked one girl.

"My AP stats teacher's been out a lot, and he's having that guy grade all our homework," said Alexis.

"He's so fucking smart," said another girl. "He's like smarter than everybody here. I haven't heard from any schools yet at all."

"Me neither," said Alexis. "I just really want Santa Barbara so badly. That's like my dream school."

"Umm-hmmm," Padma nodded. "Oh, yeah. We're so going there. But the whole college thing in general is so scary, I mean, right? I'm like really afraid of getting old."

"It's starting to be a serious problem," said Alexis. "I'm going to look like such a bad old lady, too. I always go out tanning, and I like bake myself in the sun. I live for the moment, you know?"

When last bell rang, she stopped by the ASB office with Olivia, another tall blond girl and president of the Mirador Service Association. They picked up pens and stacks of construction paper.

"We'll have everybody meet at my house," said Alexis. Olivia pulled out her cell phone.

In the parking lot, they saw Mr. Mulligan lashing the model helicopter to the bumper of Ms. Horn's Jetta with yards of nylon twine. He laughed when he noticed Alexis.

"*Vengeance!*" he cried.

Alexis tossed her cigarette out the car window as she pulled up to her family's low-slung, two-story Craftsman bungalow toward the center of town. Olivia followed her across the front porch to the wooden door under the wide, overhanging eaves.

A heavy aroma enveloped them as soon as they stepped into the foyer. "Why does my house smell so, so good?" Alexis called.

She heard voices coming from the kitchen, where she found her brother and his friend Wil standing over a steaming double boiler on the stove.

Alexis peered into the misty depths of the pot. "Is that . . . chocolate?" she asked.

"Uh-huh," said Travis, checking the time on his cell phone as he stirred.

"Oh." Alexis swooned. "This is tempting me so much! Why did I give up chocolate for Lent?"

"I'm so wondering the same thing," said Olivia.

"Because it'll make me fat," said Alexis. She and Olivia dumped their supplies on the round breakfast table. "Why are you melting chocolate?"

Travis answered in his flat voice. "I'm thinking about getting into Ecstasy, and I want to have a unique product, that's like my trademark, you know? Right now I want to coat the pills in chocolate."

"Wonka," said Wil.

"Yeah," said Travis. "I want to go by the name Wonka."

He pulled a small steel disc from his pocket. The silhouette of a stylized top hat shone through it.

"Oh, wow," Olivia burbled, peering closely. "That looks really cool."

"It is really cool," said Travis. "I made it last week at the metal shop. I want to get a chain and wear it around my neck like a pimp."

Wil saw a jar of pickles on the counter. "You know what would be so tight if you were a pimp?" he said. "If you had like a big pickle jar, and every time one of your hos stepped to you, you just threw one at her mouth and said, 'Stick a pickle in it, bitch.'"[33]

Travis nodded solemnly.

"Oh, sophomores." Alexis laughed.

"Wait 'til junior year," said Olivia. "You'll get sick of everything."

"I'm already sick of it," said Wil. He wore his ANTI-SOCIAL CLUB shirt.

"What happened to your arm?" asked Olivia.

He looked down at the white bandages. "Dude! I had like skin cancer, and they took it out over the weekend."

"Aren't you kinda young for skin cancer?" said Alexis.

"They said, 'You're the youngest person we've ever had.' They shot up my arm and like the whole thing went numb, and I had my headphones on and I was rocking out to The Killers, and I didn't even know what was going on. I looked down like once and they had dug in deep"—he demonstrated an inch—"and my arm fat had all popped out, and then they put it back in and stitched it all up."

"Wow," said Olivia.

"Yeah," said Wil. "Now I'm on painkillers and I had an energy drink, and I'm all like 'whoooo!' I got this psychedelic flower and I'm going to celebrate with that tonight."

Travis kept stirring.

Soon Padma and Kaylee showed up, and the girls sat at the table and began to make posters advertising the upcoming food drive for Sudan. HELP STOP THE FAMINE! DONATE!

Padma quickly tired of sprinkling green glitter. She picked up Kaylee's purse. "Let's see what you've got in here," she said, unzipping it. "I'm nosy."

She hunted around and pulled out a round plastic container. "Makeup!" she exclaimed. She opened it. "Ooooh, not makeup. . . ." A bright ring of pink and blue pills stared back at her.

"Yeah," said Kaylee, "my mom just found out I was on the pill. She was like, 'I'm glad you're protecting yourself.'"

"Wow," laughed Alexis. "My dad would've, wow. . . . It would be really, really bad."

"He thinks you're so good," said Padma.

Alexis shuddered. "I can't even think about it. He almost found my vibrator once and it was such trauma. Anyway, I'm scared pills would make me fat."

"It's better than having a baby," said Kaylee. "Oh, my God, I don't want to have a baby like ever. Losing your virginity hurts so much, I can't imagine like this . . . *watermelon* coming out."

"God, I want to get like a C-section or something," said Padma.

Olivia tested a marker. "But they stick a needle in your back."

"If I got pregnant," said Kaylee, "I'd abort so fast."

"Me too," said Padma.

"Me too," said Olivia.

"I'd do adoption," said Alexis, "because I'm Catholic. But I'd take like a morning-after pill or something."

Olivia drew a big spoon. "I don't want to continue the family tradition of not having a life. My sister had a kid when she was seventeen with some guy named Randy who ran away to the East Coast, and now he owes like twenty-five thousand dollars in child support, and the kid is seven and he's a hellion, like he just grabs his mom's breasts and says 'big boobies!' and stuff."

Padma nodded. "It's just like what happened to the pregnant girl."

Alexis squeezed glue on her outline of Sudan. "I'm never getting married and having kids. I hate kids so much." A dog barked outside. "I like dogs better than kids. If I saw a dog and a baby in like quicksand I'd save the dog."

"Derrick's dog really likes itself," said Padma, giggling, "like really likes itself. It ate itself out for like fifteen minutes last time I was there." She passed Kaylee's wallet to Olivia, who flipped through it. "Wait, is this your boyfriend?" Olivia held up a photo.

"Yeah," said Kaylee. "He's a junior at Esperanza."

"Oh, my God," said Olivia, "he looks so much older."

"He's getting bigger, thanks to me," said Kaylee. "I got him to go to the gym. I told him, 'Sweetie, you're gonna have to work out.' And I got him on steroids."

Everyone nodded approvingly.

"He's been on steroids for two weeks and he's already like so much bigger," said Kaylee. She shook her brown Magic Marker, dry from drawing so many crying Sudanese people. "I don't want his dick to shrink, though."

"Your dick doesn't shrink," explained Alexis. "Your balls shrink."

"Well, I don't think they've shrunk yet," said Kaylee. "In fact, you know, like so much *more* comes out now and it like tastes different."

"How much more?" asked Padma.

Kaylee snipped a rough outline of a tin can. "Like triple. I'm really waiting for him to get taller, though. I want him to get taller."

Up at the pot of chocolate, Travis shook his head. "Steroids won't make you taller. They like fuse your growth plates. That's why I recommend the hGH."

"What's that?" asked Kaylee.

"Human growth hormone," said Travis. "It's really popular now, and it's so much better than steroids. It's like the perfect drug. It lets you build muscle mass without your dick falling off."[34]

"Wait," Kaylee said, "can this hGH stuff make him taller?"

"Oh, yeah." He nodded. "It makes everyone taller."

"Does it make your dick bigger?" wondered Padma.

"It makes everything bigger."

Kaylee grimaced. "I hope he doesn't get too much bigger, though. I mean like *ouch*! That would hurt me!"

"Me and my friend went to this Web site with porn star guys on it," said Olivia. "Oh—my God!—they had such huge penises like a horse. I'd be like, 'Ahhhh! Get it away from me!'"

Alexis shaded a drawing of a steak. "Were they white?"

Olivia nodded. "Yeah, they were white."

"Wow," said Alexis.

"I mean, have you ever seen a white guy like that?" asked Olivia.

Alexis shrugged. "All the white guys I've seen have been on steroids."

That night at the dinner table, Mr. Newton carefully cut the grilled chicken he had picked up from the Outback Steakhouse. He managed the Zara fashion retailer at the lifestyle plaza, and he didn't usually take off his tie until bedtime.

He looked at Alexis and Travis, chewed slowly, and swallowed. "I think I'm going to drug test you two sometime in the next few weeks," he said.

"I don't do anything," said Travis. "I'm drug-free since nursery."

"Your sister is the one I'm concerned about," he said. "Did you hear from any schools today?"

Alexis shook her head and looked at the shrimp on her plate.

"You spent three hundred and seventy dollars on your credit card in the past ten days," he said. "Who's paying for that?"[35]

"I don't know," she said.

Travis muttered to her on the stairs, "Hey, just drink a lot of cranberry juice and you'll do fine on the test."[36]

As the earthquake-drill sirens howled on Wednesday, Alexis decided to take advantage of the chaos and smoke.

She knew at least Vic would go with her, but she couldn't find him or Shawn anywhere, so she slipped away from her rendezvous point and moved quickly and easily across the parking lot until she disappeared around the back of the facilitation quad.

There, between the chain-link fence and the brown cinder block wall, she pulled out her Marlboro Kings and lit one. She checked her watch as she smoked, listened for the PA so she could rejoin the crowds.

"Mademoiselle Newton."

She jolted and dropped the cigarette, red ash tumbling on the concrete. Outlined by the bright sun at the end of the alley, the disheveled shadow of Mr. Mulligan beckoned.

"Come over here," he said.

The thirty-second walk passed in the dizzying agony of a pounding heart and a clenched stomach.

She stood with a dry mouth while he just watched her fidget for a moment. At last he spoke. "Smoking on school property means suspension."

"Mr. Mulligan," she said, faster than she wanted to, "I'm waiting to hear from colleges about—"

He shook his head and she trailed off. He gave her a calm look, gentle blue eyes in a craggy face.

"Just do a little presentation for the class about the dangers of smoking or something, *d'accord*?"

She swallowed. "Oh, my God, Mr. Mulligan, thank you so much for—"

He held up a wrinkled hand. Then he winked at her. "I've just been grading the tests, and I'm giving you a hundred," he said. "You're hot."

After last bell released her from AP English, Alexis found a young teacher hard at work. The busy instructor knelt in the parking lot by the back of Mr. Mulligan's green Lincoln, clanging around with machinery far under the chassis.

With a blue bandana and three piercings in one ear, it could be none other than Ms. Horn.

"What are you doing to Mr. Mulligan's car?" Alexis asked.

Ms. Horn looked up with an eager smile on her sweaty face.

"Our friend Mr. Mulligan thought it would be nice to make me a present of a helicopter on my bumper, so I thought it would be nice to give him a free jack that raises his tires half an inch off the ground. He's not going *anywhere* when he tries to start up."

When Alexis got home she looked in the mailbox. She found something new wedged among the satellite bill and the gas bill and the heap of targeted bulk mail from ADVO and the *PennySaver*. The white of an envelope.

On the corner seal, three cardinal torches blazed under the heraldic rays of a setting sun. "University of Southern California."

Her stomach lurched, and her heart accelerated to thudding. She paused for a moment, just staring at the white paper in the hot daylight. She didn't really want to open it. Now anything remained possible, they could have admitted her, they could have rejected her, but once she—

With a primal lunge she ripped the envelope open, snatched out the thick page inside, and began to read:

"Dear Alexis. . . . Our decision is by no means a statement about your ability to succeed in college, nor is it any kind of judgment of you as a person. . . . It may or may not comfort you to know that this has been an extraordinarily difficult year for our staff. None of us enjoys turning away exciting students."

During dinner, her father's voice rose over the clinking silverware. "Have you heard from any schools?"

"Uh-uh," said Alexis.

"Is that a yes or a no?" he asked.

"It's a no," said Alexis.

"I flew to Las Vegas by myself today," said Travis. "They let me take a 172SP."

"Alexis," said Mr. Newton, "I'm worried about where your grades are going to go this semester. I don't want you to think it's not important and slack off. I'm going to make sure I get home straight from work at five every day, and then you're not going to leave this house for the rest of the night. That's going to be our new policy."

"It only took an hour," added Travis. "I had like a thirty-knot tailwind."

"What about the weekend?" Alexis asked.

Mr. Newton drank his lemon seltzer. "We'll see about the weekend."

Before French class started the next morning, everyone went to the lists posted on the wall to check their test scores by student ID number.

Evelyn dropped heavily into her seat. "Sixty-six," she muttered. "I can't believe he gave me a sixty-six." She turned to the guy next to her. "What did you get?"

"Sixty-six," he said.

"Did *everybody* get a sixty-six?" she wondered aloud.

Up at the lists, Alexis laughed. "Oh, my *God*," she told one of the blond girls. "I got a hundred!"

Evelyn heard. Her eyes widened and she slammed her pencil into the desk, snapping yet another tip. "Okay, that's impossible. He hates me. I think he graded my test differently. I want to see the answer key."

The bell rang, and Mr. Mulligan called roll. "Merkler? Moreno? *Newton!* Olivier? Pavlis?"

"*Bon,*" he said when he had finished. "*La petite guerre* with Mademoiselle Horn over in the science department is heating up. Yesterday I spent forty-five minutes attempting to drive my car only to figure out that she had rigged up a device underneath it, which I had to remove. *Mais le jour de gloire est arrivé!*"

He laughed and held up a white padded seat cushion emblazoned with the Lakers logo. "I've stolen her lab chair from her room and dismembered it."

He pointed to a heap of chrome pipes behind a cabinet. "I'm going to return just this seat to her along with a ransom note that you guys are going to write, *en français, naturellement.* So put something together, like a page long."

Mr. Mulligan sat behind his desk, people got up and walked around, and the class dissolved into its standard muddle.

Alexis didn't bother, just sat at her desk drinking a can of cranberry juice.

"You like that stuff?" one girl asked her.

"It's okay," said Alexis.

The tart liquid made her shiver. She took out her makeup kit, opened the mirror, and examined her teeth. For ten minutes she fell into a daze, dreaming of sleep, of the weekend.

"Newton!" She lowered the mirror to see Mr. Mulligan beckoning. "Take a look at this," he called from his desk.

Alexis got to her feet and walked through the crowd of people to stand by her teacher's side. A kaleidoscopic array of thumbnail images of events from the school year fanned across his computer monitor. Most of the photos contained cheerleaders.

"Oh," said Alexis.

"These are some of the pictures we're using for yearbook," Mulligan said. "Here."

He clicked on a thumbnail, and a huge image of a junior girl, Samantha, filled the screen. She wore her green-and-gold Matadora uniform. She stood frozen, midcheer routine, at the homecoming football game, one arm extended, the other on her hip.

"Newton, how do you think she looks?" he asked.

"I think she's really pretty," said Alexis.

Mulligan smiled. "She's not as hot as you," he said. "You have bigger tits."

Alexis turned to Travis and smiled sweetly when the car honked outside on Friday evening. "It's acting time," she said.

She left him watching *Degrassi* alone in the den and ran down the stairs. Her father sat at the coffee table in the living room practicing chess moves against himself.

"Hi, Daddy!" she said.

He looked at his watch. "Remember your curfew."

"Totally." She started for the door.

"What's the rule?" he asked her.

"I know the rule," she said.

"I want to hear you say it."

Alexis closed her eyes for a second. "Don't drink, don't smoke, don't do drugs, don't have sex, don't get into trouble, don't do anything you'd see on *Girls Gone Wild*."

He smiled a rare smile. "You got it," he said.

*   *   *

Padma waited behind the wheel of her silver RAV4, listening to Simple Plan. *"Jump! Don't wanna think about tomorrow. I just don't care tonight. . . ."*

"That was pretty painless," said Alexis when she climbed in. "I definitely need to be back before curfew, though."

Padma pulled away from the curb. "Ohhh, I am so glad this week is *over.*"

"Tell me about it," said Alexis. She turned the air conditioning vents to her face as they drove.

Kaylee stood talking with her stepmom on the damp lawn of their house. A woman of thirty, she leaned into the car as Kaylee climbed into the backseat. "Is that Simple Plan I hear?"[37]

"Yeah," said Padma.

"Oh, I just saw them in concert! I was going to go with Kaylee, but she had to work. They were so great live, it sounded just like the CD. Like, I saw Dashboard live like two weeks ago and they were just terrible, you know?"

"Totally, Mrs. Roper," said Alexis. "I agree."

She waved. "Have fun, girls!"

"What's the plan?" asked Kaylee as they drove.

"We're picking up some more people, and then we're all going to go drink at Nicole's house," said Alexis, "and then we're going to meet up with the guys at the hookah bar. Then we're all going to Samantha's party."

They headed east, and Alexis talked quickly before the car filled up. "Oh, my God, you guys, Mulligan's getting really sketchy with me."

"Huh?" said Padma.

She explained her week.

"He's such a perv!" Padma said when she finished, wavering between amusement and horror. "Like someone saw him coming out of that really skanky Motel 6 by the freeway, and they were like, 'What are you up to, Mr. Mulligan?' And he was like, all angry and stuff, 'What? Are you following me?'"

Kaylee rolled her eyes. "I'm so glad he knows I have a boyfriend and I'm off-limits."

"It's such a crazy situation," said Alexis. "I don't know what I should do."

"Dr. Chao loves him so much," said Kaylee. "He's been at Mirador for like forever, and she invites him over to her Thanksgiving dinners every year."

"Really?" asked Alexis.

"Yeah."

Dim chrome pendant lights, exposed brick walls, and huge flat screens pounding rap and trance videos defined the hookah bar. Loud college students filled the leather couches and stood packed in groups inside.

The guys hadn't arrived yet, and the girls took a huge table on the patio with space for a dozen. A lot of stumbling.

"Who's eighteen?" called Padma.

"Me," said Nicole. "I turned eighteen last week."

"Yay," said another girl. "Congratulations!"

Nicole shrugged. "I was really happy, but then I was like, 'Okay, now it's a year before my boyfriend and me can have sex without me statutorily raping him.'"

"That law's so stupid, like it doesn't make sense," said Padma. "God, I haven't had sex in so long. I'm like a born-again virgin by now."

"You got started in like eighth grade, though," said Alexis. "I didn't even come out of my shell and kiss a guy until tenth. And even then I just mainly hooked up with everyone but wouldn't sleep with them."

Everyone threw down a couple of dollars and Nicole took her ID inside to get a double-apple hookah for the table.[38]

"I need *nicotine*," said Alexis. She ordered a glass of cranberry juice from the waiter.

"That guy's so hot," said Padma, nodding to someone through the window. "How old do you think he is?" The table turned and looked.

"He's a college guy," said Alexis.

One girl scrutinized him. "How do you know?"

"You can tell," said Alexis. "Look at him, they act different."

Kaylee laughed. "He kinda looks like Cody's brother."

"Oh, my God," said another girl, "Cody is exactly like his brother."

"Except his brother is hotter," said Alexis.

Everyone looked around the table and started to laugh.

"Well, he is," she said. "I guess it's Alexis Confession Time."

"Cody was freaking out about the future again today at lunch," said Kaylee.

"Cody's already thirty," said Alexis. "He's going to go through life in a drug-induced haze. Hey, I have a drunk confession for everybody: You know who I'm totally in love with, but it's totally hopeless?"

"Oh, my God, who?" asked Padma.

Alexis just grinned.

"Who is it?" asked another girl.

Alexis drank some cranberry juice. "Derrick Littlefield."

The whole table burst into laughter.

"Oh, my God!" whooped Padma.

"You could go to SpiriTeen and maybe have a chance," said one girl.

"I used to," said Alexis. "I went all the way until junior year and then I said 'fuck that shit,' and stopped going. My God, I'm going to be so embarrassed tomorrow about pouring my heart out to you."

"He'll probably be at the beach tomorrow," said Padma.

"Oh," said Olivia, "I don't want to be with all the drunk people at the bonfire. I want to make s'mores!"

One girl's eyes widened and her face broke out into a blissful grin. "S'mores!"

Nicole returned with the waiter, who set a hookah on the table. Alexis pulled deeply on one of the tubes, and the water in the pipe bubbled. She held the smoke and then exhaled it, watching the ribbons evanesce in the calm night air.

"I'm going to go find out if that guy's in college," said Padma, and she made her wobbly way inside.

The girls watched their conversation under the hyperkinetic flat screens, the guy looking outside, laughing.

Padma came back and sat down.

Alexis tilted her head. "What's the deal-io?"

"He has a girlfriend," said Padma. "He goes to UCLA."

"What," asked Kaylee, "did you just go up and say, 'Hey, I like you, how old are you?'"

Padma shook her head. "No. I told him my friend Kaylee outside liked him and sent me in to ask."

The whole group laughed as Kaylee turned pink and put her head down on the table. Then she looked up. "Oh, you're so cut," she said, and threw a pretzel stick at Padma.

The pretzel sticks flew until they heard a beep outside the patio. The college guy drove past in his Escalade and waved to Kaylee. His girlfriend stuck her head out the window, blew a kiss, and held up a UCLA sweatshirt.

The girls froze in mortification. Kaylee pinched her eyes shut and giggled. "That's like the most embarrassing thing that's ever happened to me," she said. "Ever."

Alexis breathed smoke into the air. "Oh, I can't believe I'm so drunk already. I had said I like never want to drink again. But I'm going to drink so much more."

One girl turned to her. "Hey. What's that whole deal with you and Shawn and that junior Charity or something?"

Alexis sighed. "That's whatever. There's nothing to do in Emerald Valley but hang out and hook up with other people's friends and have drama with each other."

On Saturday night, she and a few other drunk girls drove to Charity's house and covered it in toilet paper.

On Monday morning Mr. Mulligan grabbed the fleshy part of her hip and squeezed it. He leaned on her desk and smiled at her, which meant placing his behind directly in Evelyn's face across the aisle.

Evelyn tried to tilt her head back but had nowhere to flee. The two plastic buttons on his back pockets closed in on her.

She threw up her hands. "It's looking at me!" she cried. "The buttons are eyes! It's saying . . . 'Hellllooo, Evelyn.'"

The guys around her cracked up.

Eventually Mulligan made it to the front of his chattering classroom and called roll. He gestured to Ms. Horn, who stood intently among the pieces of his overhead projector.

"Well," he said, "Mademoiselle Horn and I have concluded a peace treaty, and she has come to demonstrate her *bonne volonté* and knowledge of *la science* by helping me fix my overhead projector."

Ms. Horn beamed at the class. "Good morning, my friends!"

"Just a little preview of what's to come," said Mulligan, looking at his assignment book. "We're going to have our big test next week on chapters five and six, and *rappelez-vous,* these grades will be going home to your parents as part of your midsemester reports. And of course, to the admissions offices *des universités, n'est-ce pas?* Or you could just say 'forget it,' take a trip to Fort Lauderdale next year, and pretend you're college students."

Scattered laughter.

After school, Alexis tossed her cigarette into the storm drain on the curb outside her house. She searched the packed letter box, and her chest tightened when she saw a gleam of white underneath the direct-mail pile of *Local Values* insert coupons.

Postmarked Malibu, an effulgent cross broke the clouds of darkness over waves crashing on the orange-and-blue seal. "Freely Ye Received, Freely Give." Pepperdine University.

Alexis didn't even stop to think, just wrestled out the envelope and tore it open in one swift motion. She brought the letter to her face as quickly as possible.

"Dear Alexis: On behalf of the Admissions Committee, I regret to inform you that we are unable to grant your request for admission. . . . We want to thank you for the time and effort you spent in completing the application. Be assured that your entire file was given every consideration by the members of the Committee. Please be advised that all admission decisions are final and cannot be appealed. . . ."

Her father came home that evening and found her brushing her hair and flipping channels with a copy of *Cosmo* open in her lap. "Anything in the mail today from the schools?"

"Nope," she said. "Oh, my *God,* these girls look so good."

The next morning in French class, Mr. Mulligan's projector appeared to acquire the higher-order functions of perception, reason, and will. He would approach it with a test-review transparency and the power would suddenly cut out. He'd mention its disobedience and it'd humbly turn itself back on, only to snap off again as soon as he touched it. He fiddled with the switch, which sometimes worked and sometimes didn't.

"*C'est possédé!*" he cried. "This has to be the work of Mademoiselle

Horn." He left it alone in the corner where it strobed rhythmically for attention.

Derrick Littlefield stood with the girls in the Mirador video lab during lunch.

"We need you all to do this as badly as possible," he said. Short, fat El Presidente handed them contestant numbers to tape to their tops.

"What's like our worstest song?" Alexis asked Kaylee and Padma.

Up on the small green-screen stage, Vic Reyes pointed into the camera. "Yo," he said, "*I'm* the next Academic Idol. VIP, let's kick it!" Cap turned straight sideways, he flailed into his most ridiculous rendition of Vanilla Ice's "Ice Ice Baby."

Forty assembled ASB people tried to keep their laughter below the mic's threshold level. On the computer screens, a massive "Academic Idol" logo digitally replaced the green behind Vic's head. ASB had gathered well-known people from across campus to make this *American Idol* parody video for one of their never-ending rounds of rallies.[39]

"'Build Me Up Buttercup?'" whispered Kaylee. The girls exchanged glances and nodded.

Meanwhile Derrick took off his shirt and just stood there in his board shorts.

"Hello?" said Padma.

"Oh," said Derrick. "Uh, they want to do shots of me with my shirt off and kind of flash them through the video like the subliminal stuff in *Fight Club*."

"I'm sorry I quit volleyball," Brian muttered to Shawn. "I miss the eye candy."

They all watched Vic drop into some atrocious mid-eighties breakdance moves.

"Hey," Derrick said to Alexis. He brought her over to a corner of the room.

"What's up?" she asked. She had a can of cranberry juice.

"Hey," he said, "I, uh, heard that Mr. Mulligan was doing some kinda weird stuff with you."

Alexis gasped. "Oh, my God! Who told you that? Was it Kaylee? It was Kaylee, wasn't it?"

Derrick ran his naked arm through his hair. "Uh."

"Oh, my God, I'm going to kill her!" cried Alexis, and started to turn.

He grabbed her shoulder. "Don't get mad," he pleaded. "Oh, gosh, I'm messing this all up, I'm totally doing this wrong. I'm supposed to be a go-between with the administration, and I think I should go do something about it, like go talk to them or something."

"No," she said. "Don't. I don't want his ass to get fired and it to be my fault. Oh my God! You can't tell anyone! Double-pinkie swear that you won't tell anyone."

She held out a pinkie. He hesitated, and looked up at her face.

"Um," he said. "Uh, okay." He slowly locked his finger, let go.

"How's your semester otherwise?" he asked.

Alexis laughed. "I'm having so much fun."

"Uh, where did you apply again?"

"USC and Pepperdine rejected me. LMU, Irvine, like the American University of Monaco or something—weird, I know—they were at this college expo my dad took me to in L.A., and my super-dream school, UCSB."

"Hey," he said. "you should come to SpiriTeen this week. It should be pretty tight, we're having like a hypnotist."

Alexis laughed again, took a mouthful of cranberry juice. Vic rapped on in the background.

"Everyone's like, 'What happened to Alexis? She hasn't come in like two years.'"

"No," she said. "I went once like six months ago. I don't know. I liked it. I liked being Christian more than Catholic, I liked the songs and stuff and how it applied to people's lives. In Catholic church, you stand up and sit down and kneel and pray, and they read to you, and then you leave. It's too traditional, you know?"

"You should come," he urged.

"I don't know," she said.

On Wednesday, two district electricians arrived in French class. They examined the projector while everyone talked among themselves.

"It's working fine," one electrician said. He clicked it on and off a few times to demonstrate.

"No," said Mr. Mulligan. "No, it's really not."

They shrugged and proceeded to open the casing.

Alexis laughed and nudged one of the blond girls. "Look at Evelyn," she said.

The girl looked. "What?" she said.

"No," said Alexis. "Just look at her."

All the girls scrutinized plump, frizzy-haired Evelyn and laughed.

"What is all that outfit?" one of them asked.

After a while, Mr. Mulligan came over to Alexis's desk. He slapped her lightly on her face. "You need it," he said.

Then he sat down on her lap, pinning her to the chair. He chuckled and squeezed her side before getting up.

Eventually the bell rang. The electricians reported that they could find nothing wrong with the projector.

Alexis saw the envelope on the doorstep when she got home. For some reason they hadn't put it in the mailbox. The front bore the blue seal of an open book with radiant starlight streaming down over its pages.

Santa Barbara. Her dream school.

In the frenzy of an instant, she tore it open and yanked out the letter. Her eyes darted around the page, trying to pull out as much information as fast as possible.

"Dear Alexis: Thank you for applying to the University of California, Santa Barbara . . . admission was very competitive . . . application was reviewed a minimum of two times by trained admissions staff . . . detailed discussion of our review process . . . University of California remains your goal . . ." —some Web sites— "wish you every success in achieving your educational goals."

She had to force herself to read slowly from the beginning, see the words that spelled it out.

"Thank you for applying to the University of California, Santa Barbara. After careful consideration of your application, I regret we will not be able to offer you admission as a freshman."

She sat on the front steps and lit a cigarette.

"Did you hear from any colleges today?" her father asked her at dinner.

"Nope," she said, "not yet."

"We should soon," he said. "They're starting to mail out all the acceptances now."

"You were supposed to pick me up at karate," Travis told him. "I waited in the parking lot for two hours and fifteen minutes."

Mr. Newton looked at Alexis sharply. "I'm going to be very interested in seeing your midterm grade report."

Padma grabbed Alexis the next morning at the circle.

"Oh, my God," she said. "I left you like ten voice mails yesterday."

"Yeah, I don't have a cell phone anymore," said Alexis.

"Right. Oh, my God, look at this!" Padma pushed a worn letter into her face.

Alexis took it from her trembling hand, held it at a focusable distance, and began to read.

"Dear Padma: Congratulations! On behalf of the Office of Admissions and the campus community of the University of California, Santa Barbara . . ." —with a pulsing heart she picked out the other phrases— "exceptional personal qualities . . . UCSB has much to offer you . . . challenge you to think critically and independently . . . the Pacific Ocean and majestic Santa Ynez Mountains will inspire you with their breathtaking beauty . . . every reason to be proud of your tremendous accomplishments . . ."

And there in laser-printed letters, seven tiny painful words blew open an unbreachable gulf in their lives: "We are pleased to offer you admission."

Alexis looked up at Padma's eager, breathless face, but it felt like she had met her for the first time, like this person had become a stranger.

"Oh, my God," Alexis said weakly. "That's so wonderful for you. I'm so happy."

The haunted projector took over French class.

"It was perfect yesterday," said Mr. Mulligan. "It was perfect, wasn't it? Right?"

Alexis nodded along with everyone else.

He sighed. "If I call the electricians again, they're going to think I'm *fou* in the head."

He watched it. It had remained on for five minutes.

"*Peut-être?*" he breathed. He crept toward it with the transparency.
The bright beam clicked off.

He turned back to the class and shook his head. "I give—"

The beam turned on again. He looked around sharply. The beam snapped off.

"I—" he said. The lamp went on. He closed his eyes.

Right before the bell, the classroom door swung open and banged against the cinder block wall.

Alexis turned to see Ms. Horn standing framed in the light of the language arts quad. She laughed madly.

"For the love of—" said Mr. Mulligan. "How did you . . ."

"Oh, hah hah hah hah hah," she said, pointing at him. "I don't have class this period. I just hid outside the window with my remote." She held up a plastic cartridge.

"But I had the electricians come," he protested.

She cackled. "I called them up first. They were in on it the whole time. I also told the custodians and district ed tech in case you went to one of them."

Mr. Mulligan sat on the edge of his desk and rubbed his face.

"Hah hah hah," laughed Ms. Horn. "Hah hah hah hah hah."

After a little while he looked up with a smile hinting on his face. "Hey, do the electricians know you told me?"

Horn shook her head.

"Heh," said Mulligan. "I'm going to keep pretending I don't know what's wrong and keep calling them over here. That'll show 'em."

"It can be a prank on the electricians now," Horn whooped, waving her remote control.

The two burst into laughter.

Toward the end of lunch period, Cody entered the circle. Alexis prepared herself for a diatribe on how the world had accelerated on its freeway to hell, but instead he just threw a bottle of urine some snickering underclassmen had ditched. Then he wandered away.

About forty seconds later, Ms. Schroeder power walked up the stairs from the sciences quad with her teeth clenched. Thirty-six seniors watched transfixed as she bore down on the circle. Adults rarely if ever approached.

"Who threw that?" she demanded.

People looked at one another and nobody said anything.

"It came right down outside my classroom from up here. Who threw it?"

Nobody said anything.

"I'm asking you a question. Tell me who threw the bottle."

Shawn offered guileless wonder. "I don't know."

"Oh, please," snorted Schroeder. "Is anyone here capable of telling me who's responsible?"

Silence. "Okay," she said. "You've all chosen to do this the hard way."

She waved to Mario as he drove past on his golf cart. "Proctor!" she said. "I need all these people in my classroom."

"What—" said one girl.

On his way back from the administration building, a confused Derrick passed thirty-six seniors force-marching down the steps to the sciences quad.

Soon they stood in Ms. Schroeder's government room, looking down and shifting nervously amid the American flags and the charts of the presidents. "Eyes," she said, "eyes up here."

She wrote "Code of Honor" on the board. Underneath it she scribbled "Honest/Dishonest," "Honor/Dishonor," and "Brave/Cowardly."

"This is appalling," she said. "I am appalled by all of your behavior. No one coming forward and either admitting they threw the bottle, or telling me who did, was a cowardly action, and everyone needs to be aware of it. Now all of you are going to suffer because of your cowardice and dishonesty."

She pulled out a stack of detention forms. "Each one of you is getting detention to begin with. Does anybody have anything to say now?"

Silence. Nobody wanted to look at anyone else.

"Okay." She laughed. "Proctor, please collect their ID cards. Next we're going to give you all—"

"Ms. Schroeder," said Alexis.

"Yes?" said the teacher. "Thank you, finally."

"Ms. Schroeder," Alexis said, "it's really not fair to punish us for not ratting somebody out. That's not honest or honorable or brave at all. It's much more brave for us all not to say anything despite you giving us all these punishments for not betraying somebody. It would be like so much easier for us to sell them out, and then we would be cowards.

"Are you really trying to say to us that we should turn people in to protect ourselves from getting in trouble? If you were standing here with us, would you rat out your best friend just to keep out of trouble? Like think about who your best friend is and imagine turning them in right now because you're scared and just want to protect yourself. Is that a good lesson? I'm sorry, I don't think so. Imagine your best friend, are you turning them in?"

Ms. Schroeder blinked as everyone stared at her.

After a little while, she said "yeah" shakily. Then she fell quiet again and looked at her desk.

"Well," she said at last. "I guess those are somewhat convincing points."

Everyone stood silent. "Okay," she said, "go." She motioned Mario away from the door and the brilliant light shafted in.

Gangly Ed in his Yale sweatshirt grinned at Alexis as she entered AP stats the next period. She smiled back, warm as a summer afternoon.

"He's here today," said Ed.

"Oh, really?" she said.

She took her seat near the front and the bell rang.

The teacher made it through about ten names in roll before he leaned on his desk and gasped a little, breathing heavily. His face reddened.

"The radiation therapy is hard," he said, after a while. "They micro-wave me every day." He laughed a bit. "I've lost twenty-five pounds."

"Wow," said Alexis. "Twenty-five pounds. That's great."

He looked at her. "Believe me," he said slowly. "You don't want to lose weight this way."

"Newton!" Mr. Mulligan called from his doorway as she passed through the language arts quad after last bell.

"Hey," she called back, and waved.

But he didn't just want to say "hi." He beckoned her over. She crossed toward him on a pathway through the tangle of bright flowers and ser-rated padlike leaves.

"Come take a look at this," he said, and she followed him into the cool, musty darkness of his classroom. Up on the board she saw a re-minder about the test.

He sat down at his computer, and she stood by his side. On the screen she saw herself.

He had the photograph of her from homecoming, right after Derrick had crowned her queen in front of the entire school and a good deal of the town. She stood beaming on the senior float at nightfall, wearing her shimmering snowy white dress with her glittering crown on her golden head.

Mr. Mulligan clicked on her breast and began to zoom in. Click by click he closed in on it, step by step it leapt to become larger until it shut out the rest of the image and it alone filled the screen, and then he kept going, until she only saw her nipple pressing against the white fabric.

He grabbed Alexis and pulled her onto his lap.

"Your nipples are so hard," he said, "it's getting my dick hard."[40]

That evening after dinner, she received special permission from her father to go to SpiriTeen and come straight back. Parents liked the idea of Christian youth group; Brian's party the next night would need a much harder sell.

Seventy Mirador people talked on the couches, chairs, and floor of a living room very similar to Alexis's. She perched on a sofa armrest with her can of cranberry juice.

"You came," said Derrick.

She smiled. The room contained a virtual Who's Who of ASB leadership and nervous underclass girls who wanted to hook up, but no black people and just one Asian guy. She smelled weed and alcohol on a lot of people's breath.

Each SpiriTeen program consisted of three main segments: a madcap activity, a lesson, and hanging out at a strip mall. The activities owed much more to MTV Spring Break than to the Path of Christ as understood by, say, Saint Maximus the Confessor.

"Whoooo!" screamed one of the group leaders, a burly college senior in a BIOLA UNIVERSITY sweatshirt. "We've got a hypnotist tonight!"

Music thumped as the hypnotist jogged out, a slick-looking guy in his late thirties. He clapped to the music and everyone clapped along with him.

"Mirador High School SpiriTeen," he yelled. "They tell me you're the party school, let me hear you scream!"

"Yeahyahhh!" screamed Alexis along with everyone.

He pointed to ten empty chairs at the front of the room. "Right now," he said, "I'm looking for people who want to be hypnotized. And since you'll be allowing us to have a good time tonight, I have a gift to thank you. This is the night you can change your life.

"Does anybody want better study habits? Do you want to lose some weight? How many people would like to quit smoking? No matter what you want, I'll give you the power to make whatever one change you'd like in your lifestyle. You may never get another opportunity like this again."

Half the room surged to its feet. Alexis rose with them, leapt up and down waving her arms. He pointed to her and she skipped through the crowds and dropped into the last chair, looked out at sixty watching faces.

"Excellent," he said. The music dropped to low synth strings and pan flute. "Focus and concentrate on the sound of my voice. Up here it becomes like a tunnel. . . ."

Alexis sank downward as the induction pulled her into a peaceful dark cocoon away from the world of light. The room's laughter hovered distantly and unimportantly at the edge of reality as she entered the dreamy ordeal of a hypnosis stage show, freezing and scalding and dancing on command.

Thirty minutes passed on the wall clock before her awareness returned to her chair. The hypnotist's voice boomed from all points in space. "Here is your moment to imagine your change. Whatever you want, it will take complete and total effect from this moment on for the rest of your entire lives. Just see your change, *now*."

The synth strings throbbed and Alexis couldn't move and her mind felt totally clear but very narrow, only big enough to hold one thought that would sink in and transform her existence.

What did she want more than anything else?

"I . . . ," she thought. "I want to lose five pounds."

DERRICK IAN LITTLEFIELD

"Wait," shouted Derrick, "toss it really high."

I sailed the Frisbee a few feet over his head. He leapt into the air, sandwiched it between two palms, and launched it back in a spin move.

"Anyway," he called, "I mean, I want to thank God for keeping me from temptation, like especially with girls. Even though, heh, I haven't been in that many tempting situations. But, you know, for like keeping me from lust."

The disc blazed over his immaculate lawn and I surged to meet it. He lived a few blocks away from Alexis in a nearly identical house. "Yeah," I said, because I didn't know what else to say.

"And I have to like thank him too so much because I've felt okay lately."

"What do you mean 'okay?'" I asked, gliding back the Frisbee.

He rolled his eyes. "Dude, it's a long story. Oh, dude, do you know what you totally have to do? There's like this crazy hill two blocks down the street that you totally have to longboard. We've all done it, it's such a rush, you just like bomb all the curves and you mess yourself up pretty badly. It's like your initiation to Emerald Valley. I think like everybody at Mirador's lost like a knee or something to that hill. Dude, you should totally do—"[41]

He caught the Frisbee and tossed it onto the grass. "Hey, can you do this?" He somersaulted forward onto his arms and walked around on his hands for a good ten seconds.

"Whoa." I laughed. "No, I don't think so."

He flipped back into a standing position and ripped the Frisbee toward me. I barely got it in time.

"Last night it was pretty crazy, like we were all playing laser tag—a fun Saturday night, right? I know, we're lame-o's. But we all went to this tight—hey, it's my mom! It's Mrs. Littlefield!"

A little unsure I had ridden the bullet train all the way to its station, I just followed his eyes. A large-framed blond woman in an I'M A UVA MOM sweatshirt led a leashed black cocker spaniel up the stone path from the curb.

I froze. I hadn't met any parents yet. What if the situation at school had become like the emperor's new clothes? What if this woman from the outside took one look at me with fresh eyes, called a spade a twenty-four-year-old, and brought the entire megalith of cards tumbling down? What if?

Pow went my hypothalamus, *bang* went my anterior pituitary, *boom* echoed my adrenal cortex. The ol' heart raced for speed in an endless pool of stress hormones. The dog flattened its ears and began to growl at me.

"Hey, mom," said Derrick. "Mom, this is Jeremy. He's new, he's one of my friends at school."

Be calm, be calm, be calm, be calm. . . .

"Hi, Jeremy," said Mrs. Littlefield. We shook hands smiling. Whew. All clear!

Four feet below, the dog strained at its leash and bit me in the leg.

"Ahh," I said.

Derrick stared. Mrs. Littlefield's hand flew to her mouth and she fought to rein in her frenzied spaniel. She closed her eyes as the red puncture marks blossomed on my calf. "Oh—oh, Lord, I'm going to get sued. Are you okay?"

"It hurts," I said.

She turned fervent eyes to me as the dog yanked and snapped and blood ran down my ankle. "Oh, please don't sue us. Do you think your family is going to sue us?"

"I don't know," I managed. "They probably won't unless my leg like falls off or something."

Mrs. Littlefield whirled on the scrabbling dog. "No," she screamed. "No, Trixie, *no*! That's it. You're going to doggie jail. You can't go biting Derrick's friends." She turned back to me. "We've had Trixie for three years and she's never bitten anyone, but now I'm getting rid of her tomorrow. A lady I know always comes by and asks me about the dog, and this time I'm going to tell her she can have it and good riddance."

I started to say something, but words failed. She had already flipped open her cell phone. "Hi, Janet, this is Belinda Littlefield from Rotary. Give me a call when you have a chance, because listen, you know Trixie . . ."

Derrick and I listened in silence as she proceeded to give away their family dog.

"Uh," he said at last, "do you want like a Band-Aid?"

Derrick yelled in the center of central quad at lunchtime the next day, a thick stack of pages tucked under one arm.

"Spring sports rally ballots!" he cried. "Vote for your favorite spring athletes!"

He pressed ballots into the hands of passersby. He walked over to large groups and offered ballots. He stood by the stage and waved ballots at people listening to the music. He directed them to deposit their completed ballots with Olivia at a little table in the middle of the quad.

After a while, Cody and Brian and some other baseball people strode up holding their voting sheets.

"This is bullshit, bro!" said Cody. "This is missing like half of the names of spring athletes. Like at least three guys from my team aren't on this list."

"I'm not on it," said one guy.

"What's up with that?" echoed Brian.

Derrick could see that a bunch of them had been drinking. "Look, like the office makes the lists. I don't have anything to do with who's on them."

"Well, it's bullshit!" said Cody. "How can you vote for people when like half the names are missing?"

"The office leaves off all the names of the people they don't like," said Brian. "They left off so many names for homecoming."

"That's so unfair," said Cody. "ASB should do something about it."

"Yeah," said Derrick. "They don't really listen—"

"You should still try," said Cody. "Why don't you try? Everybody knows ASB doesn't do anything. What do you people do anyway?"

"They fuck around during fifth period," said one guy.

"Actually," said Derrick, "we just did the Sadie's dance, and now we've got a rally for—"

"It's just rallies and dances," said Cody. "It's such bullshit. You know you're just doing it for college."

"No," said Derrick, "I'm like trying to represent the students. I want do my job as a voice of the school."

Cody laughed.

The executive council of the Associated Student Body of Mirador Senior High School watched as Derrick carefully printed the words "Academic Idol" on the whiteboard.

"Yeah," he said. "That's a pretty tight idea."

Ross leaned back in his chair. "Hey," he said. "How about *Proctors*? Like it's like *COPS*, but instead of cops, it's about the proctors."

"Huh," said Derrick. He wrote up "Proctors (like COPS)."

Yells drifted through the door from the main room, where the thirty-three rank-and-file members of ASB joked around and ate late lunch.

Derrick walked over to the door. "Come on, guys," he called.

"You know what would be such a funny rally video?" said the clubs officer, a girl named Alikah. "Like imagine ASB is a reality show."

Padma laughed. "Oh, my God, I can so totally see that," she said. "Who would be what, though? Who's the slut?"

"Ahem," said Ross.

"Shut up!" she said. "You're the asshole frat boy."

"I want to add to the minutes that Padma gives the world's best knob," said Ross. She shoved his chair, and he flailed desperately to catch himself.

"Add to the minutes that Ross is a pervert," she said.

"I've never even kissed a girl," he said.

Padma rolled her eyes. "You can still be a pervert."

"Okay," said the spirit officer, a guy named Evan. "Padma's the token slut and Ross is the token asshole. Who's the scheming bitch?"

"That's so Olivia," said Ross.

Her mouth rounded, shocked. "I am so not!"

"Come on," said the clubs officer. "I'm the token black girl. Who's El Presidente?"

Everyone looked at him.

El Presidente peered back at them through his thick glasses. The Mirador student body had elected him ASB president partly out of sympathy, partly as a joke, and partly because he seemed like such a nice guy. Plus, many suspected he might even be competent. His real name was Rodrigo or something.

"Oh," said Olivia. "He's like the old guy! You know, there's always like the one guy who's like twenty years older than everybody else."

El Presidente chuckled.

"Who's Derrick?" asked Danielle the events officer.

Padma started to giggle. "He's the token gay guy."

"Totally!" hooted Olivia.

"Ouch," said the spirit officer.

Derrick laughed a little with everyone.

"Uh," he said after a while. "You know I'm not really gay, right?"

They kept laughing. "You just don't know it yet," said Padma.

*   *   *

On his way to AP physics, Derrick said hi to over a hundred people.

Ms. Horn had an enormous grin plastered across her face. "Good afternoon, Mr. Littlefield," she trilled as he entered class. AP physics, smaller than physiology, only took place in one room.

Derrick took his seat and the bell rang.

"Do you have a story for us, Ms. Horn?" called a girl.

"Yes," she said. "Yes, I do, my friends. I want to share my cheerful news with everybody." She beamed at the room. "Today at lunch, my divorce came through!"

"Yay!" said a few girls.

"It's been three years," she said. "That's what happens when you do drugs and the relationship falls apart."

Derrick looked down at his problem set. He had spent hours on it, even though Horn rarely collected them.

"Where's your husband?" asked a girl.

She shrugged. "I don't know," she said. "Somewhere."

"In jail?" called a guy.

"Probably," she said. "It's quite likely."

She laughed and spun around on her Lakers stool. "No," she said. "I'm not going to tell a lie. He's in jail. That's what happens when you do drugs." She gazed happily into the distance. "Oh, my God, so it gets crazier," she said, suddenly remembering. "So like at lunch when everyone found out my divorce came through, one of my fellow teachers had been drinking and he started to nibble on my ear! And I was like, 'What are you doing?'"

"Oh, my God, who was it?" called one girl.

"I'm *not* going to tell you," she said. "My only hint is that he's not married and he has no kids."

People started to call out names, but she just smiled. "And then, then he like put his *tongue* in my ear! Can you believe that? I was like, 'ewwww,' and then I started to giggle."

A tiny dark shape shot across the classroom floor. "The mouse!" yelled a guy.

"Hello, mouse," said Ms. Horn. "Has our friend Mr. Bojangles come to pay us a visit?"

Derrick flipped through the textbook and tried to think about the things he would need to know as an incoming freshman in the University of Virginia architecture program.

"It was such a freaky lunch," said Ms. Horn. "Like one of the teachers told this joke about a donkey in Tijuana, and I totally didn't get it. And then another one of my colleagues caught one of my little freshman babies pleasuring himself in the bathroom. Apparently he just heard the guy, and there he was, going at it in one of the stalls."

"Oh, dude," said a guy. "That's so embarrassing."

"I felt so bad for him, my poor little freshman baby," said Ms. Horn.

"Ohhhh," said one girl. "You're so cute calling them 'babies.' You should teach kindergarten, Ms. Horn."

"Yeah!" a few people said.

Ms. Horn smiled. "No, they have 'accidents,' and they make messes, and they can't do things. I love you guys."

"Awwww," said a few people.

The quiet Japanese girl next to Derrick worked on her intricate origami chain as he launched into the next day's uncollected homework.

After last bell, he said hi to sixty people on the way to meet up with Ross and a few other SpiriTeen guys by the parking lot.

"Hey," said Ross. "What are you doing now?"

"Dude, I got work," said Derrick.

Ross looked at him. "Hey," he said, "are you—"

Leo the theater-tech frosh heaved his way past them to the student pickup area. The side wheel of his roller bag trundled over Ross's sneaker.

"Little fat kid," snapped Ross. "I hope a Twinkie gets him."

The group of SpiriTeen guys laughed. Ross crossed himself. "God forgive me," he said.

They laughed again.

"Later," said Derrick.

He got into his hunter green 4Runner SUV, put on The Who's *Quadrophenia,* and drove.

He sometimes worked as a caddy at the municipal golf course, but now he went to wait tables at a small Italian restaurant in downtown Emerald Valley. A largely empty shift of late lunches and early dinners.

At sunset he went home. His little sister talked on the phone upstairs. His dad worked late at the office and his mom had her Parent-Faculty Association meeting. His uncle lived with them and he sat drinking a beer at the kitchen table and reading the *Daily Racing Form,* his utility belt on another chair.

"Were you at your religious group today?" his uncle asked. "Were you praying to God?"

"It's not today," said Derrick.

"Let me ask you a question," said his uncle. "God is supposed to be good and take care of everybody, right?"

Derrick hated this conversation but felt he couldn't walk away from it. "Yeah," he said, "God is good."

"So where was God," said his uncle, "when I was four years old, running down the street in flames? Screaming and crying for help. Tell me that."

Derrick didn't say anything.

"Where was God," continued his uncle, "when I spent my whole childhood in surgery? How about when our family was so poor I couldn't get real treatment?"

"Things can be really hard," said Derrick, "but God is still there."

His uncle shook his head. "You don't know what you're saying," he said. "You don't understand. If God is so good, why didn't he care about me? Why do bad things happen to people? Why do a lot of bad things keep happening? Look on the TV, they keep happening."

Derrick stared at the table. "I don't know."

"I'm just telling you," said his uncle, "because I know you're going to hurt yourself. Don't hurt yourself."

He turned the page of his race sheet. Even though he wore a cap, he couldn't hide most of the burns on his face.

The next morning, Derrick sat behind the microphone in the PA office with his big red dictionary.

"The Word of the Day," he said, and his voice filled all the rooms of the school, "is *tombolo.* Noun. From Italian, from the Latin *tumulus,* a mound. A narrow deposition landform that connects an island to another island or the mainland. *Tombolo.*"

He clicked off the microphone. Mr. Popper nodded at him and the announcement girl. They all left the room. The girl hurried off to her first period, and Popper started back to his office.

Derrick caught up with him in the administration lobby, underneath all the pictures of himself and his awards.

"Mr. Popper?" he said.

The vice-principal turned stiffly. "Yes, Derrick?"

"Uh," said Derrick, "some people were upset about not having like all the names on the spring athletes list, and I said I'd come talk to you guys about it."

Mr. Popper watched him closely for a moment. "Well," he said. "This is not exactly the right forum. The ASB constitution outlines specifically an appropriate time for students to present their concerns, and that's during an ASB meeting."

At lunchtime that day, Derrick and some other ASB people worked the student store in the food court. About the size of a very large closet, the store sold a variety of junk food to benefit ASB funds.

Ross helped himself to a bag of Cheetos, and Alikah ate a Popsicle. Evan tried to get a foothold and climb the comer where the cinder block walls met.

Derrick stood at the counter selling.

"New game!" said Alikah behind him. "Let's try to pat our heads and rub our stomachs at the same time."

The three tried.

"Oh, dude," said Evan. "That's so hard!"

Ross laughed. "Wouldn't it suck if a cop did that as like the drunk driving test? Like, 'Okay, step over here and rub your stomach and pat your head? Ah hah!'"

Vic Reyes reached the front of the customer line. "Dude," he said to Derrick. "What's up with the drug dog? Didn't you guys like promise in all those speeches last year that you were going to do something about getting rid of it?"

"Yeah, you did," said a girl behind him. "I remember you did."

"It caught somebody," said another person.

"It totally violates our rights, and it's so unfair," said the girl. "And what about the cop? The administration's making school feel like jail."

Derrick furrowed his brow. "You guys should totally come in and talk about it during an ASB meeting. That's when people are supposed to talk about their concerns."

Vic Reyes laughed. "You're fucking *joking*, right? Okay, I guess I'll just stop by next time I have fifth period free."

ASB met during fifth period. Every student at Mirador other than ASB members had class during fifth, every single day.

"New game!" Derrick heard Alikah saying. "Let's make up tongue twisters."

The next morning, after Derrick read the Word of the Day, he ran after the vice-principal. He caught up in an office corridor beyond the hive of administration cubicles.

"Mr. Popper?"

"Derrick," said Popper curtly. "Yes?"

"Uh," he said. "People were saying that they can't come to present their concerns at an ASB meeting because they have class then, and that it seems like it's unfair."

Popper stared at him. Derrick shifted.

"You're right, it may not be fair," the vice-principal said eventually. "That's just how life works. You're going to see a lot more of it. If anyone has a problem, they can come talk to me."

He turned back to the corridor.

"Well—" said Derrick. "Then it's—"

Mr. Popper looked at his watch. "Don't you have a first period to go to?"

On Thursday, the rank and file had the student store covered. With a sizable chunk of the student body greeting him en route, Derrick brought his pan pizza to the circle.

"Oh, my gosh," said Ross, indicating with his head, "that girl is so dirty."

Derrick saw the skinny shape of Charity Warner stalking through the quad in her tiny skirt.

"She gave blow jobs to like every guy on my team in like this big drunken orgy. There're so many people here who don't know God." He bowed his head in quick grace over his bean-and-cheese burrito and Derrick nodded over his pepperoni.

"So I found out where Mike Barrington is going to school," said Olivia. She mumbled a fast prayer to sanctify her salad wrap, and then bit in.

"Where?" asked Derrick.

"Chico State," she said. "That school sucks so bad. I was like, 'Why would you go there?'"

"He's a loser," said Ross. "He used to play polo with us like freshman year. He was trying, he had no skills at all, and I was like 'Just give up, bro, what the heck are you thinking even trying?'"

"He's like Rudy from that movie." Olivia giggled.

Aram came by the circle with his garbage bag.

"Whoa," said Brian, "go away."

Aram made a shoutlike noise and swung from side to side. One of his arms knocked Brian's leg.

"Dude," said Brian. "He went for my penis! Now we know what he likes."

Derrick chewed as everyone laughed.

"No," said Alexis, "Aram told me he likes the girls with breasts, big boobs and butts."

Everyone snickered. "I told my mom," said Aram.

"What did your mom say?" asked Alexis.

Aram swung his garbage bag. "I told her 'fuck you!'"

Olivia curled her lip and stared at him as if he had just arisen from a radioactive Superfund cesspit.

"Hey," called Ross, "we don't like the four-letter words around here."

In AP government during sixth, Ms. Schroeder closed a folder and placed it on her desk.

"Who can tell me what happened in current events today?" she asked the class.

"There was like a bunch of gay marriages," said a girl.

"What about that?" Ms. Schroeder asked.

"I think it's a good idea," said the girl. "I think they can't help how they are, and that it's just ignorance to stop them from having an equal right with everyone else."

AP classes generally skewed more toward the liberal wing than regular classes.

"I disagree," said Derrick.

Everyone turned to look at him. Nobody liked to argue with the icon-ographic presence of Mirador. It felt as fundamentally wrong as giving the emperor of Japan a wedgie.

"I don't think gay marriage should be allowed," he said. "Marriage is what our society is based on, and if we start like blurring what it means, there's no reason why we won't end up with polygamy and incest and things like that."

"But it's like segregation or discrimination," ventured a guy. "In Amer-ica everyone should have equal rights, like that's what our country's about. It's just like giving equal rights to black people or women."

"No," said Derrick. "Homosexuality is a huge religious issue, and giv-ing equal rights to different races isn't."

"I agree," said a girl quickly.

"But God made everybody the way he wants them," said another girl. "Why would he want society to stop people from being able to love each other?"

"No," said Derrick. "It's against his will, and it's against the Christian faith."

The room stayed silent.

"Well," said Ms. Schroeder, after a while. "I have a video today. It's from the early eighties, I believe, but it still has a lot to teach us. Why don't you all write down twenty things you learn from the video?"

After last bell he walked to the parking lot with Olivia and a few other people. They took the quick route through the facilitation quad.

"See," said Derrick, "like I don't want Christians to have a bad name, but I think it's really important for us to stand up against the whole same-sex thing."

A group of gangsta guys shouted in the middle of the quad, playing some kind of game or maybe fighting.

"Totally," said Olivia.

"Like I really hope society understands that gay marriage should stay illegal, and I hope they make homosexuality ill—"

Derrick saw better now. The guys shoved a tiny blind underclassman back and forth and laughed.

"What?" said Ross.

"Uh," said Derrick. "Uh, I really hope they make homosexuality illegal, too, but I don't want them as a society to see us as Christians as being like in favor of discrimination or—"

He watched the scene out of the corner of his eye as his group passed by.

"—or like, uh, being in favor of segregation, but I think it's really important, uh, for us to—"

"Hey!" yelled a small girl with black nail polish and a blond streak in her hair. "What the fuck are you doing? Get the fuck away from him!"

"—because we're Christians that have, I mean, I'm proud of the values that—"

He watched this small girl scream at these huge guys.

"Do you want me to get a proctor over here and get all your asses fucking suspended?"

The guys wandered away and the girl put her arms on the little blind underclassman's shoulders.

Derrick trailed off. He swallowed.

"Huh?" said Ross.

"Dude," said Derrick, "I totally lost what I was just saying."

That afternoon, he and Ross and some other guys played Halo 2 on Ross's Xbox and shot baskets outside.

As evening closed in, they took a couple of cars and picked up a few more volleyball and ASB people.

One guy jumped into Derrick's SUV with red liquid swirling in his water bottle. "Dude, I just finished my U.S. history test today and I'm *wrecked*! I drank a bunch of my parents' Bacardi and then I found some Courvoisier and put it in here."

A junior lay dazed on the backseat. "I like smoked this joint the size of my pinkie finger," he said. "It was like a waste of weed, though, 'cause I didn't wrap it tight enough."

"I love SpiriTeen," said the Courvoisier guy. "It's so not hard-core. Like afterward some people go off to pray, and some people go to smoke."

The guy on the backseat smiled. "And some people pregame, fool."

This week SpiriTeen met in the living room of a junior girl whose dad hovered around the door. Three alumni of the program, now in college, led the group of seventy.[42]

"Whoooo!" a sophomore girl from Vanguard University screamed at the riotous crowd. "Ethan, Kristie, Derrick, Erica G. *come on down!*"

The chosen few jumped up and headed to the front of the room amid cheers. A table covered in clear plastic tarp awaited them. "Yeah, Derrick," someone yelled.

"All right," said the leader. "Today we've got a SPAM carving contest. Whoooo!"

On the table lay two pink quivering bricks of gelatinous processed meat, each aside a plastic knife.

"I can smell it," said one girl, burying her face in her shirt.

"Whoooo!" yelled the leader. "Our guys are up first. Ethan and Derrick, you have three minutes to carve whatever you want from the SPAM, and the audience will judge you with their applause when I call time. Ready?"

Derrick nodded, brow furrowed.

"Yeah," said Ethan, a sophomore, a pretty typical guy on junior varsity something.

"Get set, *go!* Whoooooooooo!"

Derrick dropped to his knees, grabbed his knife, and focused on the mission. His polymer blade slid and flicked, SPAM yielding before its serrated edge, drawing his vision down into concrete form.

At his side Ethan whittled away his own cube.

The room yelled. He heard a lot of "Derrick"s, but he had a job to do, and he had to do it right, as well as he possibly could. He still had so much work left when the leader blasted her whistle.

"Okay!" she cried, "let's see what we've got. Ethan?"

Ethan looked calmly at the room, his face bright, a transfinite light gleaming in his eyes.

"I made a cross," he said. It sat upright and definitive. Derrick stared at it. "Could there be anything better?"

The leader held her arm over his head, and the room gave him a decent round of applause.

Then all eyes swiveled to Derrick.

"Uh," he said, "I made an E.T. the Extraterrestrial."

So he had. It even looked somewhat realistic. The leader held her arm over his head, and the cheers reached shuttle-into-orbit decibels.

"Derrick!" people yelled. You *had* to cheer for Derrick Littlefield.

"Whooooooo!" screamed the leader. "We have a winner!"

Derrick gave everyone a dazed grin and then took his seat. People started to do the snap with his hand and then remembered it was covered in SPAM and punched fists instead.[43]

The girls competed next, and then the program moved to a "Lean on Me" sing-along headed by Derrick on guitar. The whole room put their arms around their neighbors' shoulders and swayed back and forth.

Then the big burly college senior stood.

"Hey," he said. "Guys. Please. Fifteen minutes."

After a little give-and-take, the room calmed. Now came the Lesson, the spiritual heart of the program.

The leader raised a felt tennis ball shell with the rubber core cut out. "This was my life in high school," he announced. "It just wouldn't bounce."

He chucked the felt shell at the floor. It landed with a dead *thwack*. He picked it up again sadly.

"Of course, I tried to fill my life up with all sorts of things, like schoolwork." He took a sheet of loose-leaf paper out of his cargo-pants pocket and wedged it into the ball.

"And sports." The plastic whistle went into the felt shell.

"And parties." He pulled a Corona bottle from his pocket. Every eye in the room tracked it as he poured some beer into the middle of the ball. He followed the stares to the bottle in his hand, and then he gave it to the college girl. "Uh, hang on to this," he said.

"But anyway, my life still wasn't going anywhere." He dropped the sodden felt onto the floor. The whistle and paper fell out. It lay weakly. He lowered his voice and looked down. "In truth, my world was . . . empty."

"Awwwww," said some girls around the room.

"Yeah," he said, "it's sad, right?" He picked up the floppy shell and shook out some drops of beer.

"Then," he proclaimed, with firm voice and renewed energy, "I found Jesus." He reached into his pocket and withdrew Jesus, a tight rubber sphere. "This was the real core. This was the only thing that could fill up my life."

He slipped Jesus inside the tennis ball and hurled it downward. *Bam!* A great bounce. He had delivered the Message.

Then, per SpiriTeen tradition, everybody went to hang out at the strip mall. Derrick got a chicken quesadilla.

On Friday morning he defined *koftgari* ("inlaying of gold on steel") for the benefit of the thousands.

The announcements girl approached him afterward to ask a few shy questions about the new activities schedule, so Mr. Popper had already settled down behind his office desk by the time Derrick found him.

"Yes?" said Mr. Popper.

"Hi, Mr. Popper," said Derrick. "Uh, can I come in for a second?"

"You're going to be late for first period," said Mr. Popper.

"I just have like one quick thing," said Derrick.

Mr. Popper leaned back on his padded chair. Derrick stepped through the door frame. He heard distant hammers banging.

"Uh," he said, "like I don't think it's really right that the special ed kids pick up trash at lunch. Like, it seems like it's demeaning to them, you know? Like it's treating them like they're our servants, like to have them pick up our garbage, you know? And I think it's wrong and I hope that we could do something about it."

Mr. Popper looked at Derrick and shook his head slowly.

"Uh," said Derrick.

"Something you may not understand," said Mr. Popper patiently, "is that it's not some type of 'exploitation' going on here. They sort through the garbage for recyclables, and they rinse them and bag them. Once they've finished sorting fifty bags or so, we sell the materials to a trash center, and we use the money to help fund their program. So it really benefits them, Derrick, and it allows us to give them the best education possible, and I don't think you want to take that away from them. Do you?"

"Uh," said Derrick.

"I can't believe you're honestly suggesting that," said Mr. Popper, "especially with the budget cuts. You need to be focusing on preparing for our meeting on Sunday, unless you're telling me now you don't think you can be a leader. Can you?"

A moment passed. Derrick swallowed. "Yeah," he said. "I can."

On Saturday evening Derrick's cell phone rang.

"Yeah," he said.

"We're outside, dude," said Ross.

Derrick closed his eyes as he lay on his bed. "I don't feel like going."

"Dude, come on, don't be lame, bro," said Ross. "We're heading in."

Olivia waited in her car while he and a junior girl rang the bell. Derrick's dad had business travel and his mom had Rotarians, so his uncle opened the door.

Ross went upstairs and the girl waited in the living room with Derrick's uncle. He had the TV tuned to *Everybody Loves Raymond* while he cleaned his shotgun from his hunting trip to the Mojave.

"You're here to pick up Derrick?" he asked her.

"Yeah," she said.

He put the shotgun back inside the closet under the stairs. "How old are you?"

"Sixteen," she said.

"Sweet sixteen and never been kissed," he laughed. "Hopefully that'll change tonight. Isn't that strange? The boy's eighteen and he's never kissed a girl."

"Heh heh," she laughed weakly.

A flight up, Ross stood in the doorway to Derrick's room. As Derrick's best friend since junior high, he formed part of the very small group that knew and recognized this side of the image of Mirador.

"Dude, come on," said Ross. "Everyone's like there already."

Derrick sat on the side of his bed and stared at the floor. "I haven't gone to a party in like three or four weeks," he said.

"That's why you should go," said Ross. "It's not even like a party. It's the beach."

Derrick twisted the sheets around his hands. "It's not going to be fun. I don't like to go out."

"Dude, take your guitar," said Ross. "It'll be fun when you're there. Trust me. *Trust* me."

So Derrick sat by the leaping flames of the beach bonfire, singing Green Day's "Time of Your Life" with a dozen people gathered around him on the sand. The brilliant light held back the engulfing darkness. He did, he felt good, he felt good right now, and he gripped that feeling as hard as he could.

After the final chords, he stood and laughed.

"Dude," said Ross. "I brought the boxing gloves again."

"Are you serious?" said Derrick.

"Yeah, I got all the drunk people boxing each other. It's freaking hilarious."

"Hah! I'll box somebody," laughed Derrick. "I'll box a drunk person."

He jogged over to the ring, where Brian had just climbed off the wasted Padma.

"Oh, Derrick," she said, and hugged him, stumbling.

"Oh, Padma," he said, and hugged her back. "Who's got the gloves?" he called. "I'm up."

Steve passed him one of the big cushioned pairs. "Here you go, bro."

He pulled them on and pounded them together. "Who am I boxing?" He looked around to see Vic Reyes turn with the other pair on his hands.

They both paused for a moment with the bonfire crackling between them. Neither had expected the other would be the guy he fought. The best fights, the most fun fights, happened between close friends or worst enemies. Not people from different worlds with no emotions toward each other. The difference between them looked tangible, awkward and embarrassing.

Bright crescent moon in the sky above him, Derrick raised his gloves. Vic dropped back into a wide-legged combat stance.

"Fight!" someone screamed.

Derrick took the initiative, dashed forward, and Vic tossed a quick jab in his face. Derrick threw up his arm and connected from the side with a solid hook. Vic rode it and answered with a left uppercut as the circle widened and grew around them, everyone yelling and cheering.

They really pummeled each other. Vic bobbed down, weaved to the left, hooked into Derrick's temple. Derrick staggered back and then hit with a right overhand cross.

The blows fell heavy and hard and both of them took time to stand swaying as the dizziness and nausea passed, and then they charged back in to slug each other again, dull thuds in the face, ringing pain.

Derrick had the advantage of strength and endurance but Vic really knew how to fight. One in his black-and-white bandana and sideways hat, the other in brightly colored board shorts with his head of blond curls, they darted back and forth across the sand, fire blazing behind them, locked in essential stalemate.

As the minutes passed and the yelling grew louder, the blows weakened and the stumbling increased, until the fight simply ground to a halt with the two of them staring at each other, shaking and gasping for air. A long moment passed, but it had become too hard to raise fists.

"Good fight," Derrick slurred.

"Yeah, bro," Vic got out. "You too."

With the greatest effort, they pounded gloves.

Then the helicopter came.

Mr. Popper flashed Derrick a tense smile the next evening as Derrick entered the packed Chamber of Education of the Emerald Valley City Hall.

Derrick took the seat the vice-principal had saved him at his side. He adjusted the knot in his tie and looked through the crowds at the piece of paper taped to the door. "EVUSD Mirador Budget Hearing."

Mr. Popper forced a smile. "How was your weekend?"

"Fine," said Derrick.

"Tonight we're going to find out the future of our school."

About three hundred people filled the chamber. Five school board trustees sat and faced them behind microphones on a raised platform. The board needed to slash seven hundred thousand dollars worth of programs, the difference between the million dollars Sacramento had taken away and the money parents had raised through their Save Our School Foundation.[44]

The room buzzed with tension, anger, concern, fear.

At seven o'clock precisely, the chairman stood and rapped his gavel.

"I call this special meeting of the Board of Education of the Emerald Valley Unified School District to order. Let the record show that a quorum of trustees is present, that this meeting has been duly called, and that notice of this meeting has been posted in accordance with Section 54956 of the government code of the state of California."

And then the mêlée began. Members of the community took the microphone at the center of the floor to argue and provide testimony before the board approved the final cuts. What should go? What should stay? What mattered?

The room murmured and bickered and Popper supplied the play-by-play. "This isn't as boring as it can usually be," he said softly to Derrick. "It seems like the trustees are falling backward over themselves to explain that this isn't their fault. . . .

"Heh, it looks like they're saving theater and sports. They're backpedaling so fast to explain they won't be touching them, otherwise they'd be out of a job. Of course, in this community, people would have a hernia if they did touch football, baseball, those things. . . .

"Oh, there goes our class sizes . . . there goes all our transportation . . . well, the teacher salaries are going down . . . there goes the assignments for electives . . . I guess we're saying good-bye to the extracurriculars. . . ."

The chairman wiped his forehead and drank some of his bottled water. He had started the meeting smiling. Now his face had yellowed and brittled like old ivory, hollowed from this death struggle with loss and the future.

"All right," he said after two hours. He looked down at the trembling pages in his hand. "The school resource officer and the canine detection program at Mirador High School, which places a uniformed policeman on campus and allows for random passes with a drug-sniffing dog. The cost for these programs comes to one hundred and four thousand dollars a year. This is a significant expenditure. Is this money well spent?"

One trustee's microphone glowed red to indicate she had the floor. "I'm inclined to question it."

"Are there any comments from stakeholders before we decide on this item?" asked the chairman.

A bearded man took the public microphone. "This seems like a prime waste of money," he said. "We're cutting teachers and classes but keeping policemen and police dogs? They should cut this, and they should get rid of all their 'in-school suspension' and their 'Saturday school.' Every day they hire a person to just sit in a room and watch students sit in the room, all for the sake of some statistics. Easily sixty thousand, plus all this."

A woman with horn-rimmed glasses spoke next. "I think this program is very concerning. I think the district really needs to look at an alternative model."

"I agree," said an older man in suspenders.

The muttering in the room seemed to support him. A trustee caught the chairman's shirt. They mumbled, conferred.

"Go," Mr. Popper whispered firmly to Derrick. "Now. This is very important for the school."

Derrick stood up. Early stars gleamed in the deep indigo sky above the high glass ceiling as he walked to the central microphone.

Surprised murmurs from the hundreds. They hadn't seen any young faces before.

The chairman's microphone glowed red. "Please identify yourself for the board," he said.

Derrick spoke clearly, and speakers filled the chamber with his voice. "My name is Derrick Littlefield. I'm a senior at Mirador High School and the public officer of the Associated Student Body."

"I'm very interested to hear what the students think," said the chairman. "Are they in favor of these programs?"

"Absolutely," said Derrick. "The programs benefit both individual students at Mirador as well as the entire Mirador school community. We think of the officer as a teacher, a mediator, and a counselor, and we actively come to seek him out because he's really become an important and critical part of our campus community. Thanks to him and the canine unit, the number of drug offenses we've seen has declined dramatically. I can tell you with great confidence that the overwhelming majority of students feel safer in school thanks to them."

The hint of a smile twitched under Popper's mustache. This was, of course, precisely Derrick's element. Anyone who really paid attention to the guy as a human being and not a symbol realized that he seemed erratic if not awkward with individuals. But he performed fantastically in front of a crowd.

One trustee even laughed, a little swept away. "You make it sound perfect," she said. "I'd like to hear a bit about the downside."

Derrick smiled ruefully, dimples crinkling. "You know," he said, "there's the general fear of policemen, and some students are worried they might get into trouble."

He stepped back as an African-American woman took the microphone. "It seems to me that some tensions on campus will not be improved but rather actually heightened with the presence of a policeman and a drug dog on campus." She looked at Derrick. "I think if you brought up some communities of color you might hear there's a real fear of the police."

"That's a very valid point," said one trustee. "I really think we need to hear both sides in this discussion. I think we need more than one student representative here, and I think we need to hear from a more diverse group in all ways."

Derrick picked up the central microphone. It glowed bright red. He walked as he spoke, addressing the room and making eye contact as if it were a rally. "I hope I can consider myself a diverse person. By election and popular vote, I'm the authorized representative of the student body, and I associate with a number of African-American and Latino students, who are just really great people, even though the administration considers a number of them to be so-called troublemakers."

The flag of the California Republic stood behind him as his voice echoed through the vault of the chamber.

"Sure, there's always going to be a group that doesn't feel comfortable, but I'll tell you *exactly* what happened with the overwhelming majority. When the police officer and the drug dog first came to campus, they were concerned, they were worried, they were conflicted."

Derrick's voice acquired the tremolo of anguish as he looked into the crowds. "But now a real *relationship,* a real strong *bond,* has been forged between them and the officer and the dog, especially in the classrooms and through the course of interactions, and they've realized that these programs are by no means bad for them or the school, and they've *embraced* them."

Inadvertently he caught Cody's pale eyes staring in shock and horror from a folding chair toward the back of the chamber, where he held his government notebook with "School Board Uncovered" scrawled at the top of the page.

The chairman gazed down at Derrick, almost as if pleading for his strength and resoluteness. "So you and the students support these programs?"

"Absolutely," said Derrick, facing him nobly. "I feel very strongly that the canine detection program and the resource officer should remain on our campus because they help to create a better learning environment for all of us, who are your children."

The crowd had fallen silent, breathless. The board voted. Four in favor, one abstaining.

Derrick gave the whole room a dazzling smile, and then returned to become a face in the crowd. He sat down carefully.

"Okay?" he said.

"Excellent," said Mr. Popper. "The school's lucky to have you as a leader."

And that was as far as Derrick could hold it before the emptiness overtook him.

The Monday morning sun that stabbed through the cracks in the blinds struck a Derrick that almost no one in the school saw, no matter how hard they looked.

On the rare occasion people caught a brief glimpse of it, they edited it out. They thought that Derrick was just acting aloof, that he had rejected them, that they didn't exist at his level, that the fault lay with them. Definitely not with him. In high school, you doubt yourself first.

Forty-five minutes later, his mother became hysterical as she stood in the doorway in her I'M A UVA MOM sweatshirt. "Get up," she screamed at him. "Get up! What are you doing? You've got class in fifteen minutes."

Derrick said almost nothing at school and took long routes to avoid everybody he possibly could. He didn't want them to think something was wrong with him.

When people greeted him on the paths he responded with a hollow "hey." At first he tried to smile but then he stopped. Dozens felt chastised about their places in the social structure.

In volleyball he could barely play. Teammates set him up but he missed the spike or sent it flying wildly. All illumination looked strangely muted, as if the constant light had filtered through smoky glass.

In class he couldn't concentrate. The day seemed never-ending, an endless succession of blank hours. He felt tired, so tired, but his heart raced and he jiggled his leg. He wanted to leave but didn't want to go anyplace. He wanted to scream but found no reason to make the effort.

He saw the Grim Reaper everywhere. The hooded, scythed specter took away a girl in his AP English class. It didn't seem funny or even educational, just morbid. No matter what any of them did, drove drunk or drove sober, death would claim them sooner or later.

He bought a pan pizza but it stuck in his throat like greasy foam and he threw it away after two bites. He waited at the circle for a while and then sat alone in the ASB office and then went back to the circle.

In their ASB meeting, he stood at the whiteboard. He looked down at the dry-erase marker that felt like a rod of slippery lead in his hand.

On the board he had tried to list a rally program, but he couldn't remember what the elements consisted of or what exactly the point was.

"Derrick," Padma said, laughing, "you're screwing this all up."

"I know," he said.

"Well, come on," she said, "do it properly."

But he couldn't. The marker screeched on the slick melamine while everyone at the table smiled and laughed over unfunny jokes. They all connected with one another, but to him they felt a million miles away.

Afterward they went to a loud, hectic, awful event to watch the Reaper on a giant screen and listen to fake death notices. He felt grateful he didn't have to say anything.

When last bell rang, he tried to leave.

"Where are you going?" asked Olivia.

"Home," he said. He had called another server during lunch and switched work hours.

She looked at her watch. "You've only got like an hour before rally setup." He paused. She started to grab people and remind them. "Four to ten P.M."

Derrick heard someone behind him saying, "If ASB spent the amount of time on other things that they spend on rallies, it would be pretty impressive. They could really get something done."

He went to his SUV and lay in the back for forty minutes but couldn't sleep. Then he rose and trekked through the door of the assembly hall.

Thirty ASB people created rally decorations on the stage. While everyone laughed and goofed around, he found a quiet niche in a forgotten corner cutting out construction-paper letters sloppily, badly until Mr. Markowitz called his name.

"Hey, Derrick!"

He turned to see the counselor smiling by the front row of seats. "Derrick, the German exchange students are going to hang out here for a while, and I thought you could keep an eye on them."

A long pause. "Uh," said Derrick, "okay."

He saw a few blond shapes poke a papier-mâché marlin under construction on the far end of the stage. Markowitz left, and Derrick put them out of mind as he cut letters for who knew how long.

"*Heil! Heil! Heil* the master race!"

He looked up to see Travis Newton sitting alone in the front row before him, saluting the backs of the distant blonds with a full outstretched arm.

Derrick didn't know what to do.

"Those are Germans, aren't they?" said Travis.

"Yeah," he said. "How do you know?"

Travis whipped his salute down. "They look like assholes. You know, the girl looks pretty and all, but there's just something so unattractive about her, *nicht wahr? Sieg heil, Deutschland!* Did you know I can actually speak German?"

"Hey," Derrick recited, "congratulations on winning vice-president."

Travis looked up at him, and he avoided the twin mirrors. "Thanks. Do you have any like words of wisdom for me?"

"Yeah," said Derrick. He paused. "You'll have no real power. The whole thing's pretty much a joke."

"Do you have any power?" asked Travis. He drank some liquid protein.

"A little. Not much. Only what I get from the administration."

Travis continued in his flat conversational style. "What would you do if someone told you God doesn't exist?"

Derrick turned the scissors point on the stage. "I debate atheists all the time."

"Do you ever wonder if they're right?" asked Travis.

A group burst into laughter at something near the right curtain. "My biggest problem is doubt."

"What do you mean?" asked Travis.

"Sometimes I'm like, 'This is a fairy story written a long time ago by the people who wrote the Bible to get us to do what they want us to do,' but then I just read it over, and I think about it, and I realize that it makes sense, and it's true, and no scientist has ever disproved the Bible."

Travis looked at the Germans. "Galileo. Darwin."

"Darwin retracted everything he said before he died."

"He did?"

"Yeah," said Derrick. "Because it was wrong."[45]

"Oh, I didn't know that," said Travis. "Thanks, Derrick."

He watched the ASB public chair snip in silence until musician Wil entered the side door. "Yo," said Wil. "Check it out, fool. I got the sickest watch in my cereal." He held up his wrist to show off a red-and-puce plastic timepiece of Donkey from *Shrek*.

Travis stood and pointed. "Germans."

Wil laughed. "Hah. I heard about them. I'm going to smoke those motherfuckers out! They're gonna be so high."

"Poor Derrick," said Travis as the two walked out into the brilliant sunshine.

"What?" said Wil.

Travis smirked and ripped an imaginary blade across his arm. "Can't you tell? The guy's ready to slash his wrists."

In AP government the next day, Schroeder began the five minutes of discussion time. "Who can tell me what happened at the school board meeting on Sunday? They made some very big decisions about what?"

"They talked about the budget cuts, right?" a girl chirped on Derrick's left.

"Exactly," said Ms. Schroeder. "We lost a million dollars, and all we've got is Save Our School to keep this place running. Last I heard the SOS fund was three hundred and ten thousand dollars. That's quite a bit of money, more than my salary for the next few weeks. Of course, now we need to figure out what it will go to."

One pimply guy laughed. "Wood-panel Dr. Chao's office!"

Confused faces turned toward him. "Huh?"

Ms. Schroeder sighed. "We were supposed to have a cost-of-living increase every year. It disappeared, and we found out that the principal's office is now being wood paneled."

Derrick's eyes defocused. He had spent the night lying in tangled sheets, desperately unable to sleep.

"Go on strike," a spiky-haired girl called.

"We already did," said Ms. Schroeder. "It didn't help much."

One guy raised his hand. "Isn't it illegal?"

"Maybe it is," said Schroeder. "I don't know."

*   *   *

During lunch on Thursday, he tried to nap in the ASB office but the distant whine of a drill irritated him. He wandered the side passages of the
administration building, avoiding the warren of cubicles where secretaries and counselors ate lunch and gossiped.

The whine grew loudest at the farthest corner, down the corridor to
Dr. Chao's office. Her door lay open at the end, past a pile of long and
skinny boxes.

Derrick approached silently and stopped at the line of sight into the
room. He peeked forward and saw two maintenance workers mounting
wooden battens on the wall.

He left the building through the side door and passed huge proctors
on walkie-talkies leading a crowd of thirty-six anguished seniors down
the steps to the science quad. The circle lay empty.

He stood by the whiteboard at their ASB meeting. He had written up
something about the rally.

"Hey," he said. "If you guys were going to commit suicide, how would
you kill yourselves?"

"I'd so poison myself," said Alikah.

"I'd like jump off a really tall building," said Evan. "It would be cool,
and then you'd like die instantly when you hit, right?"

"No, I'm with poison," said Padma. "That would definitely be the
least painful way, like a lot of Tylenol and vodka. How about you, big
guy?"

Derrick shook his head slowly. "See," he said, "girls don't want to
look ugly. But poison doesn't work a lot of the time, and then you go
to the hospital and get your stomach pumped, you're still alive, and
then you have to go to counseling, and that would just make life even
worse.

"I'd shoot myself. I'd get a shotgun, put it at the bottom of my jaw,
put a ruler through the trigger, and step on it. It'd be over in like an instant, you know?"

El Presidente rubbed his chin and then nodded.

After school Derrick knelt on the stage, pounding boards together to
make a platform for whatever as the other ASB people joked around in

the background. He didn't really know what he was doing, just pounding boards dully, savagely, shoddily.

He cut his finger on a splinter and watched the blood well up. It fell on the wood and left a red spot. He squeezed his finger and watched another drop fall. He dragged his finger across the board and made an irregular trail of blood.

He walked over to the wall behind the curtain, gripped his finger, and milked a bloody line onto the cinder blocks. He added another line and turned it into a cross. Then he added four smaller lines and made a backward swastika.

"Fascist!"

He turned to see the skin holding a stack of tech theater light gels, eyes wide with unbelieving horror.

"Whatever," muttered Derrick.

Like a good third of ASB, he left early for SpiriTeen. He sat quietly while everyone spent half an hour laughing at the hypnotist show.

When the lights came up, the college girl tried to move into the lesson segment.

"Okay, guys," she said. "Just give us fifteen minutes here. Okay? Fifteen minutes."

The burly guy stood. "Come on, guys," he said. "Seriously."

The room eventually quieted, and the girl smiled.

"Anybody who came a few weeks ago remembers how I gave my personal testimony about my life with Christ in high school, and how God like really helped me when I was having all my difficulties and uncertainties with varsity water polo.

"Anyway, we're going to have you guys give the group some of your testimony about God in your lives too, and one of our seniors today is going to be starting us out. Derrick Littlefield!"

"Whoooo!" screamed the burly guy.

The whole room clapped as Derrick stood. He had agreed to talk three weeks earlier. Now, deep in the numbness, he sat in one of the chairs left empty from the hypnotist's act.

Seventy people watched him, a significant slice of the Mirador A-list.

Now, of all times, now he had to speak. Now, of all moments, he had to offer truth to God and the people.

He inhaled, exhaled, began calmly.

"I want to talk a little bit about my experience with God and with SpiriTeen, and the presence of God in my life, and the meaning of that experience for me. . . ."

He gazed at the far wall. "When I was really young, God was my parents. I grew up in a mostly Christian family, and God made the flood and rainbows and mom and dad." People laughed. "I didn't think too much about it beyond that.

"Life was pretty simple and good, and up through fifth grade everybody liked me a lot." People laughed again. A few guys closed their eyes in annoyance.

"Then in sixth grade I dated this girl who this really big guy liked, and he decided to make my life miserable. By 'dated,' you know," he added quickly, "I mean like sixth-grade dated.

"Every day he'd like make fun of me at school, and soon other people were making fun of me too. Then basically everybody was making fun of me."

Derrick looked down. "I lived in dread of school every day. I hated school. I didn't want to go to school."

The room became very silent as everyone tried to imagine a misty past when an outcast Derrick Littlefield did not like school.

He looked up again. "I was really good at sports." The room laughed, relieved. "Except for soccer, for some reason I sucked at soccer. I played a lot of volleyball, though.

"Then they took away volleyball, and it was only soccer, and I sucked at soccer, so I basically sucked. Nobody talked to me except to mess with me. I had one friend, who was Ross." He pointed to his face in the crowd.

"Eighth grade was a little better," he said, "but I was a really big dork and everyone still made fun of me. I had really tight jeans."

"You still have tight jeans," someone called out.

"Yeah, but that's when baggy was cool. Finally I trusted my mom to get me clothes that were sort of fashionable.

"Ninth grade was really hard. A few things happened that challenged my faith. I have an uncle who's very badly disfigured and he moved in with us. He has to like basically paint in his eyebrow and part of his face every morning, but I see it differently, and I think he's a handsome guy.

My Christianity is very hard for him, because he feels it's almost like an offense to him. But the bigger thing in ninth grade, though, was I started to have a problem that year."

Derrick took a deep breath. His job was to give the truth.

"I'm like manic-depressive, like I have a bipolar disorder or something. I get very, very depressed a lot for a long time. I can't have fun, and even if it looks to me like I'm having fun it's like, 'Okay, it's just a distraction, what's really going on, where's the misery?' I feel helpless. I feel like I can't do anything and that nothing I do makes any difference and that everything is terrible and it's never going to get better ever.

"I mean, I don't like high school at all. I can't wait for it to end and be over already. Senior year has been a little less bad, but I still hate it. I really hate it."

No one even breathed. Their worldviews had just exploded in ten seconds. Derrick *was* the school. The entire thing was designed for him. If he couldn't even stand to show up in the morning, who could?

"I have suicidal thoughts," said Derrick Littlefield, voice of Mirador. "If it wasn't for my friends and for God . . ."

He trailed off. Those who could turn their heads stared at one another in horror. The crowd was dead silent.

On Friday afternoon, he drove straight home as soon as last bell rang.

He went to his room and locked the door. Bright sunshine leaked around the blinds, and the air felt heavy and still. He lay on his bed, the tangled sheets pressing against his skin.

After a while his cell rang.

"Dude, are you coming down to H.C.?" Ross asked. Voices talked and laughed in the background.

"Dude," said Derrick, "I don't think I can make it."

The voices grew louder and Ross's words distorted. "You're coming to Brian's party after, right? It's gonna be *sick*."

"I don't think so," said Derrick.

He hung up, and held his thumb on the Power button until the display winked out in a decaying slide of notes. He shifted on his clotted sheets and stared at the stucco ceiling.

INTERMEZZO IN
D-FORCE MINOR

Everybody's going to the party, have a real good time.
Dancing in the desert, blowing up the sunshine.
—System of a Down, "BYOB"

A glossy-nailed finger hit the red Record button on the camcorder.

Sara Dunbar flipped the lens to her face as her heels clicked on the sidewalk. The LCD glowed in the night and framed a nostril, an eye, and some hair.

She beamed at her phantom audience. "Hello, video watchers! This is Sara. Dunbar, that is. And we are about to go on a journey to Brian Olvera's party! There's no parking anywhere, so we left our car like three blocks away." She captured the rows of vehicles, most with Mirador parking passes hanging inside.

"Ooooh, look at all the people! And you can hear the music." Sara caught the streams of groups making their way forward. "I can just feel this is going to be such a crazy party! With us, viewers, is our partner in crime, Miss Charity Warner. Isn't she so flipping cute?"

The camcorder light uncovered Charity's pale face. She gave a sickly grin.

"Sara's so kinky," said Charity. "Look at her handcuffs."

The camera caught the furry purple handcuffs attached to Sara's purse as the two advanced.

"You know it, bitch!" said Sara. "So, viewers, there's been a lot of excitement tonight. My mom has been giving me a lot of shit about Patrick, like because he's older and because of the Internet, and I'm planning to emancipate myself.

"I sat down with her and I explained to her that this isn't working out. 'You're a mess,' I told her. 'It's making me a mess, and it's better for both of us if I leave.' I thought she wouldn't be able to handle it, but I think she agrees with me.

"My dad pays two thousand dollars' child support every month, and all of it goes straight to me if I move out. I want to go live with Patrick and spend the rest of my money on custom-made skirts."

Her cell phone rang, and she held the number to the lens. "It's my mom!" She picked up. "You can start thinking of a realllly good punishment, mom, 'cause I'm not coming home."

Charity laughed. "You are one crazy bitch!"

A few blocks away, Alexis and the senior girls piled out of Padma's SUV. They navigated the twisty streets of the gated community by cell phone, and ran into Vic and Shawn and some other guys on another identical corner.

"You didn't go early?" said Kaylee. "All the baseball people have been there for awhile."

Vic laughed. "Brian's one of those guys you can only stand to hang out with for an hour. He'll keep hitting you, and you'll be like, 'stop,' and he'll be like 'that hurts, huh?' and laugh at you."

"Hey," said Alexis, as the music got louder, "there's gonna be a bunch of the D-Force guys there."

"Oh, yeah," said Shawn. "Adam Hammersmith is my boy."

"I didn't know you knew those guys," said Kaylee.

Shawn gave her a shyeah-of-course look. "Oh, yeah, we're tight. Hammersmith's my boy. I was telling him, 'We gotta keep D-Force alive, we've gotta initiate new people. It was around at Mirador for like twenty years, and we can't just let it die, you know?'"

"It's so not like it used to be," said Padma.

"No," said Shawn. "It was like a *crew* before. Now it's just like a club with like nobody in it. We've gotta bring it back."

"I don't know," said Nicole. "Some of those older guys are scary."

"They're not that scary," said Alexis, "they're white."

"I'm so much more scared of white guys than black guys," said Nicole. "Like an angry black guy would pull out a gun and be like, 'Yo, I'm coming back with my cousins and we're going to fuck you up,' and a white guy would just be like *bang*."

*   *   *

A three-car caravan parked in the available spots down another street. Olivia stepped from the front vehicle. At the rear, Derrick shut the door to his 4Runner. The horn honked and the lights blinked once.

"How did I end up going to this?" he mumbled to Ross. "I really wanted to stay at home and spend some quality time with my guitar." Hip-hop thudded down the dark streets of the gated compound. "I don't like this music. I don't want to like dance. Do you think anybody wants to go bowling?"

"Relax, dude," said Ross, "it's gonna be fun. Everyone's upset because we lost the game, so you're not like alone. You know you're gonna be getting your moves on."

Olivia tossed her hair. "Uhhh, all the older people are going to be there because of the game. I hate it when all those losers who graduated like four years ago come back and just like start fights and prey on all the little sloots in training."[1]

"It's sad they've got nothing better to do than go to our parties," said Ross.

"It's sad because like nobody ever leaves," said Olivia. "They all think there's no world outside Emerald Valley."

"It's probably going to be a lot of those D-Force people," said Derrick.

"What's D-Force?" asked a girl.

"It's really lame," said Olivia. "A lot of the guys used to go here, there's like twenty total, like a couple are in college, and there's only a few current students. It's like any of our random Mirador crews, you know, they all get each other's backs and drink together and stuff. They're supposed to be like the 'tough guys.'"

"It's so high schoo—" started Ross. Then he thought. "Well, I guess we are."

Sara trained the glowing light of her camcorder on a red-faced Brian Olvera as he stood on the dim ochre flagstones outside his massive adobe-style house. Groups of people crowded under the palms, laughing and yelling above the throbbing music.

"Explain the setup here for our viewers," she said.

"Okay," he said. "We've got four kegs. We've got beer bongs, beer pong, and quarters on the first floor, the kegs on the second, and Bud on the third. Hard alcohol and food out by the pool."

Charity saw the pack of freshman girls staring at her and giggling. She snarled back and tugged Sara's shirt.

"Alcohol," she said, "let's get alcohol."

Inside the dark two-story great room, people danced to thudding surround-sound hip-hop amid the point lights and Navajo art. Maybe a hundred and fifty people total filled the grounds, both there and visible in the floodlit green world outside the back glass doors.

Charity pointed to the bright realms beyond. "Alcohol," she urged.

They passed a cavernous open kitchen behind a granite counter lanced by spears of light. Cody stood in the middle of a crowd around two pyramids of red plastic cups. He held a bottle of Captain Morgan in one hand and a Ping-Pong ball in the other, and he yelled at the guys across the table.

"What is this 'consolidating' bullshit? If you're evening out the level of beer in two cups, you're 'straightening' the cups, not 'consolidating' them. What the fuck is 'consolidating'? What are you even talking about?"[2]

The people playing quarters at the other table had a mellower time of it.

Outside another seventy people talked, drank, and smoked by the waterfall cascading down into a swimming pool designed to look like a natural rock watering hole. Bags of chips and bottles of alcohol covered two glass tables.

While Charity pounced on the vodka, Sara closed in on a group of a dozen drunk girls with her camera. "Tits!" she screamed. "Let's see tits!"

The girls looked at one another and started giggling.

"Come on," yelled Sara. "This is *Girls Gone Wild at Mirador*! Show the viewing audience your tits."

One of the girls yanked up her shirt and flashed her breasts at the camera. "Whoooo!" her friends yelled.

"That's what I like to see!" said Sara. She turned the lens around and repeated for the viewer's benefit: "That's what I, Sara Dunbar, like to see. This is more fun than my wet T-shirt contest in central quad."

Then she whipped her camera back. "More! More craziness!" The music thumped and the waterfall roared, and now that one girl had started them out, the rest yanked their shirts up like a collapsing domino chain as Sara made her way around the group.

"Come on," she screamed, "get wild for the camera!"

Other groups joined in. Guys showed their pecs and laughed. One girl pulled down her pants to uncover a tattoo on her behind and slapped it.

Then a junior stuck her face into her friend's bare breasts as the girl shook them all around. Everyone screamed and laughed. "Whoooo!"

When Sara cornered short and built Steve, he pulled up his shirt. He laughed and put one hand on his belt buckle. "You wanna see more?" he asked. "You wanna see more?!"

"Yeah!" screamed Sara.

Steve paused for a second, then waved the camera light away. "Ah, fuck you, you don't deserve more."

"Awwwww . . . ," she said. She had run out of stars for her video, and she joined Charity by the bottles of SKYY. "I really thought I could get him naked," she sighed. "You know, he really is a stripper."

Charity couldn't speak midgulp, but Jasmine from bio stood pouring Jack into a cup. "I'm not surprised. He always has money, he's always throwing bills around, and I'm like, uh, thanks."

Charity recovered and swigged Sprite. "But he's so small! He's like Mighty Mouse. His body is totally disproportioned. Like a normal person's hands come down to their legs, but his stop at his waist."

Jasmine screwed on the cap. "He should take steroids."

Charity shook her head. "If he's a stripper he shouldn't take steroids because his dick will shrink."

"It doesn't matter," said Jasmine. "If he's a stripper, no one's going to see his dick."

"Please," said Charity. "Strippers are dirty. They'll do anything."

A short figure in mirrored sunglasses grabbed a handful of pretzels. "Steroids don't make you taller," he interjected patiently. "I recommend hGH."

Half an hour later, the party had grown louder and drunker. Padma and Alexis stood in the middle of the crowd playing beer pong against Shawn and Brian.

Brian tossed the ball, but it glanced off the top of one of the girls' cups and skittered across the sticky stone counter.

"Hah!" Padma laughed.

"Dude," said Brian, "you put like a Hindu curse on the cups."

Kaylee grabbed her arm and nodded toward a heavy guy standing in the older crowds around the quarters table. "Oh, my God. That's him."

"Oh, my God," said Padma. "You're right."

They both stared while Brian hunted the ball.

"I can't believe I had such a crush on him freshman year," said Kaylee. "What was I thinking?"

"I used to think he was so hot," said Padma. "I am so over that." She shuddered.

"Hey, Shawn," said Kaylee, "your D-Force boy Adam Hammersmith is here."

Shawn looked up sharply.

A huge twenty-year-old guy with a shaved head and more than a passing familiarity with anabolic androgens turned around. "Did I hear my name over here?"

"Yeah," said Kaylee happily. "Look, Shawn's here! He was just telling us about how you guys like know each other so well and need to save D-Force."

"Who?" said Adam Hammersmith.

"Shawn," said Kaylee, and pointed to him.

Adam gave Shawn a blank look. "Who's that guy?"

"I meant like . . . ," said Shawn, then stopped.

Padma started to laugh. "Ohhh! Hah! You were fronting, and you're so busted. The only way to settle this is a rumble!"

"Rumble!" cried Kaylee. Alexis slammed another drink.

"Uh," said Shawn.

An older girl looked over, beer belly squeezing into her low-rider jeans. "What's going on?"

"They're about to rumble," said Kaylee.

"No," said Shawn, "I mean, I'm not starting any shit. No disrespect, I mean, I was saying how much I respect you guys and how I really—"

"Don't be a pussy," said Padma.

"Watch it," said Adam Hammersmith. "Your class is pissing a lot of people off tonight. First you lost the game, and then there've been a lot of incidences of you guys pulling lame shit."

He turned back to quarters. Brian bit his lip and looked down at the plastic cups.

*   *   *

Another thirty minutes elapsed, and Derrick found himself standing in a crowd of volleyball people and girls on the edge of the dance floor. They all talked and laughed, but he just wanted to leave.

He heard voices behind him.

"Oh, my God, I'm totally scared," said a girl.

"Do it now," said a guy. "He's gonna graduate and then you'll never get a chance. Won't you regret it?"

"Oh, my God," said the girl, "he was like leaning over near me in the office and I just wanted to grab his butt. He's so hot."

"If you're too scared . . ."

"Ahhhh, don't you dare—"

Someone tapped Derrick on the shoulder, and an underclassman thrust a little giggling Asian sophomore into him. "Dance with her, Derrick!"

"Uh," said Derrick, "okay."

He gave it a decent thirty seconds on the floor before the girl seemed to teeter on the brink of aneurysm. Then he returned to his group.

"Oh, my God," he heard her saying. "Don't touch me. I'm . . . like . . . covered . . . in essence of Derrick!"

He stepped out the sliding glass doors to get some fresh air. He poured himself a cup of soda and stared at the falling rush of water while couples writhed and hooked up on the soft lounge chairs.

Then a bright light flashed in his face. A short dark-haired Matadora with furry handcuffs held up a camcorder.

"Hello, viewing audience," she said. "We're so drunk we're accosting Derrick Littlefield! What are you drinking there?"

"Uh," said Derrick. "Coke."

"Do your coke limerick for him!" screeched that tall junior Charity.

"Ahem," said the Matadora.

"There lives a young lady named Sara,
It's really hard to compare her.
She does lines of coke, and that ain't no joke;
She smokes pot and drinks beer that impair her!"

She pounded a can of Bud. Charity clapped. "Yay!"
Derrick went back inside again.

*   *   *

Half an hour passed, and the dance floor turned into a freaking mass, a sea of groping and grinding. The crowds around the drinking games got even louder and rowdier.

One girl finished her beer bong. She took the tube from her mouth and gasped for air. "Jesus wanted me to break up with my boyfriend."[3]

Her friend earnestly nodded. "Absolutely."

A large group stood in the pounding darkness and watched Padma and Steve hook up in the floodlit green world behind the glass doors.

"They totally don't know anyone can see them," said Kaylee.

"It's like watching TV," said Alexis. She glanced at the granite counter-top, then she hurried down a side hallway, then she hurried back again.

"Oh, my God, you guys," she said. "I lost my new cell phone."

Brian laughed. "Call it."

Alexis shook her head in shock. "It was off. I don't believe it."

"Awwww," said Shawn. "I'll help you go look for it."

Things declined rapidly after that point.

The central air conditioning could only do so much to cool a room with a mass of people dancing for hours. The heat and tension rose, and sweaty crowds soon began to pack themselves outside by the pool and the tables of hard alcohol, which they drank.

"Here's to us being losers!" One guy toasted the results of the day's game.

Ross fixed himself a banquet of Ruffles and cheesy popcorn under the grapevines.

Padma stumbled around. "Give me my keys," she ordered.

"No," he said.

She grabbed his arm. "Come on, give them to me."

He put his hand in his pocket. "No."

"I'm not going to drive!"

He pulled out the ring and jingled it briefly. "See, they're safe."

"Come on," said Padma, "give them to me."

Olivia wandered down the second-floor hallway with a few other girls, cracking open doors and rolling her eyes. "People are having sex *every-where,*" she pronounced. "There's like condoms all over the place."

She looked into another room. "*Those* people crushed up Brian's mom's dried flowers and they're having sex in a heap of rose petals."

One girl drank some Fanta. "That's almost like romantic."[4]

On the third floor, Vic Reyes laughed and smoked weed and snorted coke in a bedroom with a revolving group. "I heard you take one-half line for every fifty pounds of weight you have. I weigh one fifty but I did four fucking lines!"

"Nice, fool," said Cody. He had drunk nonstop since the game and now inhaled an immeasurable heap of white powder. He ran into the hallway.

"Fuck yeah!" he screamed.

One guy came out of the bathroom with two bottles of Vicodin. "Look what I found in their medicine cabinet." He pocketed them. "I'm gonna be on like so many pills for Saturday school."

A blond girl with a pierced tongue smiled. "I snagged a grip of CDs downstairs." She showed off her selection.

In the wide dark space beyond the pool patio, a galaxy of sprinklers hissed to life.

Padma stood on the wet flagstones and threw up in the brightly flowered bushes while a few dozen people watched.

"You're drunk," said Charity, lip curled.

Padma threw up again and tried to steady herself on the wall.

"Go in the sprinklers and get sober," said Charity. "You're puking all over his house."

Padma wobbled. Charity grabbed her arm and tried to shove her out onto the grass.

"Go in the sprinklers," Charity insisted. They tussled.

"What the fuck are you doing?" a guy called, as Charity yanked at Padma.

"I want her to get sober!" shrieked Charity, clogs skittering across the flagstones as she dragged. "She has to go in the sprinklers and sober up."

"What's wrong with you?" asked one of the few dozen spectators. "You're being a bitch."

"She is a bitch," said someone else.

"I am *not* being a bitch!" Charity called back, shoving the stumbling Padma closer to the intercrossed sprays. "Why are you starting drama? I just want to help her sober up."

Sara ran over and disengaged Charity. "You're being a bitch," she hissed. "She's drunk and she's not going to remember it anyway. I'm going inside to have fun with my camera."

Charity tottered through the staring crowd, flipped off the guy who had called out, and drank more.

The thumping music gave Derrick a headache. He went outside and tried to eat a handful of Doritos, but they made him nauseous.

On his right, the redneck looked at a couple of black people by the pool. "I feel like I'm in Africa," he sneered to a few football players. Some guys smiled.

"I mean, I really don't like black people," he said. "They're like always whining about how we put them where they are."

A black sophomore stood right behind him, putting ice in a cup.

Wild irritation seized Derrick. "Hey," he mouthed to the redneck, "there's a black girl *right there*. Chill out."

"Huh?" said the redneck.

"There's dark folk over yonder," said another football player.

The redneck turned. "I don't care if she hears me," he said. "She shouldn't be listening."

"Let's not be racist," Derrick said out loud.

"I don't care if I'm racist," said the redneck.

Derrick's voice hardened. "Why would you want to be?"

"It's my heritage," said the redneck. "My family is, and it's my background, and I'm proud of it. Damn, you can smell them. Black people smell worse."

Derrick stared at him.

"No," said the redneck, "isn't it a fact that black people smell worse?"

The girl hurried over to the other black students and said something.

"You better apologize to them," said Derrick tightly.

Brian grabbed Cody in the third-floor hallway and brought him around the corner. Six guys from the baseball team stood outside a bedroom door.

"Bro," said Brian, "one of those freshman sluts is *fucked up*, and we're pulling the train on her."[5]

The door opened and the catcher left. "Dude," he said, "that slut puked all over herself, so I just came on her face and dumped her in the bathroom."

"Fuck that," said one of the guys who hadn't had his turn yet. The group broke up, angry, to go drink outside.

Right off the side of the great room, Adam Hammersmith lost at quarters and slammed his fist on the marbleized granite.

"Fuck that," he said. "I want to punch somebody."

"Get a drink," suggested another older person.

Adam and a group of the D-Force guys headed out to the pool area.

Cody stepped from the first-floor bathroom.

Amid the thundering music, he felt an irregular element. Like an annoying chime that didn't fit the rest of the song at all.

Now that he listened, he could swear a distant bell rang frantically.

The front door formed a tiny rectangle beneath a huge illuminated mosaic of Southwestern tapestry. Out of curiosity, Cody crossed the dark great room and pulled it open.

A furious man with a mustache who looked like a short Mr. Popper in uniform shone a Maglite in his face.

"This party is going to have to shut down," he snapped.

"Huh?" said Cody, squinting.

A walkie-talkie squawked. "We've received a number of complaints from neighbors about community violations, lights and sound, parking violations, and this is—"

Cody looked past the beam at the patch on the man's blue shirt. Bona Vista Security.

"So what are you going to do about it?" he asked.

The guard pushed the light closer. "What am I going to *what*?"

"You're going to do what?" said Cody. "You're just a rent-a-cop with your little badge."

The little man paused. "I'm going to arrest you," he snarled.

Cody looked down at him and spread his arms wide. "Okay," he said, "arrest me."

The guard picked up his walkie-talkie. "Center," he said, "center, we have a lack of cooperation at the twelve hundred block of Monarca."

Cody laughed and slammed the door in his face. He went out back to get another drink.

Sara panned her camera across the dance floor. "Freaking action!" she yelled. "Let's see freaking action!" But only a dozen or so people still danced.

She heard a commotion in the background and turned the lens to her face. "What's that?" she asked. "Let's investigate!"

Wham! She whipped the camera around to capture the door to the master bedroom, framed by two angular obsidian totems.

Alexis Newton had kicked it open. She staggered out into the great room.

"Oh. My. God!" she proclaimed to the crowd. "I just had the best. Fucking. Sex."

She spread out her arms. "The dick was like"—she brought her hands down in a pounding motion at her crotch—"BAM! BAM! BAM!"

Shawn walked out behind her. He put his arms around her and kissed the top of her head. She giggled and writhed happily. Then he headed outside.

Alexis staggered over to a grinning Kaylee. She opened her purse and pulled out a piece of paper. "Oh, my God, look what Shawn drew for me. He said, 'This is me and you.' Isn't that like the sweetest thing?"

Sara numbly hit the Zoom button and closed in on the picture. Shawn had colored in the pencil drawing Charity had given him two months before and changed the names.

"Uh," said Kaylee, pointing at the camera, "this is on video."

Alexis pivoted and noticed Sara for the first time. "Oh." Her head bobbed. "Forget whatever I just said."

Sara processed outside holding the camera a delicate distance from her body like an unstable isotope.

Almost everyone stood packed on the patio between the glass doors and the rock pool. The air hummed with the rarefied and singing tension of a tropical atoll before an electrical storm.

Sara drifted between the drunk and strangely subdued bodies, carrying her fissile payload straight to the heart of the neutron generator.

Charity stood by the Stoli, pale face haggard under her mass of highlighted hair.

She turned sadly to Sara. "This guy was just talking about how much he hates Jewish people." She sniffed. "I'm Jewish. I don't want to be. I can't help it. I was born into it."

"I didn't know that," said Sara.

Charity shook her drunk head morosely. "Nobody does."

A more urgent concern overrode this revelation. "Uh," said Sara. "You were wondering about if Shawn and Alexis were like fucking, right?"

She flipped open the viewscreen. The Manhattan Project would have envied the rush to criticality.

Charity slipped through the crowds. She saw Shawn's back and spiky dark hair in a circle.

"—oh, so much better, fool," she heard him say. "I mean, Charity was an okay fuck, but I always had to like deal with the problem that she's a total bitch."

Charity tapped him on the shoulder with one long, quivering fingernail.

He turned. Five guys all stared at her.

She looked down at the heavy silver ring on her finger, and its big turqoise stone.

"Excuse me," she said calmly, "could you say that again?"

Shawn had an audience and had clearly gotten too drunk to handle this situation. "I called you a bitch," he said firmly.

"No," Charity screamed. "You are not going to cheat on me with Alexis Newton and call me a bitch!" She hauled back and drove her fist into his face.

Shawn stumbled into one of the D-Force guys. The guy shoved him hard. "Chill out, bro," he said.

"You chill the fuck out," said Vic Reyes.

"Who the fuck are you?" said the guy, and shoved Vic.

Vic shoved him back harder.

The guy had been talking to Nicole, and now he handed her his beer. "Hold this," he said. "I have to go fight."

He turned around and punched Vic.

"I got you covered, bro," said Shawn, and punched him.

He kicked Shawn and then Brian punched him back and then some of the D-Force and the baseball guys joined in, and this lurching, punching, shoving mess exploded outward.[6]

Nicole wandered around in shock with the older guy's beer. "Does anyone want this alcohol? I don't want this drink anymore. Anybody?" Someone pushed her into the pool and solved the problem laterally.

Seven more people went into the pool. Water splashed over the crowds.

Some black people threw the redneck down on the ground and beat on him. A football player kicked one of them in the forehead and his face began to bleed. Someone punched the football guy.

Cody talked calmly with Jasmine amid the chaotic spiral of screaming violence.

"Yeah," he said, "so I just like got this new CD that sounds just like Thrice. You gotta check it out."

"That's cool," she said, "I went to a concert—"

A swinging fist struck Cody in the back of the head.

"Dude," she said, "someone just punched you in the back of the head."

"I know," he said serenely, "keep talking."

"Okay," said Jasmine. "Uh, I went to a concert they had down in San Diego a few weeks ago and it was pretty cool. They had another opening band that kinda sounded like them, too, so, uh, maybe it's like . . ."

Cody nodded politely as she talked for another few seconds before trailing off, unnerved.

Then he turned calmly. "Who did that?" he asked the nearest bystander.

She pointed to the bald head of Adam Hammersmith. "That guy."

Cody roared so loudly that even fifty brawling people faltered. "*I'm going to fuck him up.*"

And there went the fusion core. Oppenheimer and Kurchatov drop their Geiger counters and wonder at the gigaton yield.

He yanked Hammersmith around in the crowd.

Hammersmith's eyes narrowed. "What have you got?"

Cody ripped off his shirt in one motion, revealing his tremendous physique. "What have *you* got, motherfucker?" he bellowed. "PGD!"

One of Hammersmith's friends punched him in the jaw. Cody didn't even move, just slammed the guy in the face.

Derrick sensed doom and hurried through the brawl, trying to pull apart the punching, kicking, wrestling tangles. "Guys, come on," he said, "come on, guys, seriously, let's break it up. . . ."

He reached into the center, put hands on Cody's and Hammersmith's shoulders. "Come on, guys," he said. "Please, guys. Let's chill out and—"

Cody decked him. "You are so fucking annoying," he spat. "I want to fight."

Hammersmith lunged, and Cody punched him, and the world seemed to freeze.

Cody laughed, grabbed the enormous glass table covered in alcohol and food and flipped it over. The huge pane smashed and the bottles cracked open and a thousand diamond shards erupted everywhere in a storm of ice and knives. He tugged from the ground a hefty log designed to add to the rustic effect.

"Good times!" he hollered. "Good times! I'm going to fucking fight everybody!"

An unearthly gleam lit his pale eyes. Screaming and panic.

Police sirens howled in the distance.

The smarter people fled at this point.

Charity staggered into the colossal Amerindian darkness of the Olve great room.

"Where are you, bitch?" she shrieked. "I'm gonna kill yo tripped and fell, then stumbled forward.

"Eat a dick, bitch!" she yelled. "He was the love of my life an to take him away." She fell down again. "Eat a bowl of sh going to kill you."

She caught a glimpse of Alexis's blond hair on the sta gled to her feet. "You. I'm gonna get you."

"Whatever," Alexis called back. "You sound like a great

Then a dozen people, including Hammersmith pted to room. They slammed and locked the heavy Plex

Outside in the light Cody beat on the windo the door, wrench it off its track. Bodies splashed arour

"No!" voices screamed as he dislodged th and stepped inside.

*　　*

And then it seemed like police were everywhere.

They had brought four squad cars and two big SUV patrol wagons.

"Can we get some light in here?" a voice asked.

Someone opened a cell phone, and then another cell phone lit and then a third, a triad of electronic fireflies. Hands angled the dim phosphorescence to reveal a washer and dryer, and the huddled shapes of six people who had raced down a side hallway and ducked into this door.

Kaylee's phone beeped with a message. OMFG HIDE. COPS R IN HOUSE. RUOK?

"You think," she muttered. She typed YES T2UL.[7]

Ross rubbed his head. "Dude. I was hit by someone I don't know."

Steve tried to whisper, "This guy like punched me in the jaw and it didn't hurt, and I punched him and it went *crunch,* and he was like, 'Sorry,' and I was like, 'Oh, sorry, I didn't mean it.'"

"I have to go to the bathroom," mumbled Olivia.

Footsteps clunked outside the door.

"Shhhh," urged a dripping Nicole. "The cops are right outside."

Everyone sat silent in the blackness listening to noises outside the door.

"I hope they don't find us," whispered Jasmine.

The door slammed open. Two officers stood in the entrance with zing Maglites. "Surprise," one said.

Io one could breathe. Handcuffs clinked and walkie-talkies led.

 don't want to know what this looks like," said the cop. "Leave the Go home."

ade it to the door first but the officer grabbed him. He yelped

st," said the cop. "No minors are going home yet."

 held out a heap of plastic garbage bags.

ouse, fifty people picked up party trash under the vigi-stabulary. One officer lectured Derrick on civics.

yo said, "that your parents are taking liability for all of

rick, lowering his head in chastisement.

"You have to *appreciate*," said the cop, "that this sort of behavior is totally unacceptable. You're lucky we aren't arresting you kids."

Derrick rubbed his aching cheek. "We're really, really sorry," he pleaded.

"I don't think you *understand*," the cop went on, "what it would mean for you and your friends to spend a night in jail. You're about to become adults. . . ."

Word spread quickly among parents, and Alexis's father pulled up in his silver Lexus with a lot of payments left on it.

She didn't say anything, just got into the passenger seat. Travis climbed into the back.

"You drank," he said.

On the verge of tears, she nodded.

He shook his head. "This is so white trash."

They drove off.

Vic ambled down the staircase. As soon as the police had arrived, he had run upstairs and begun an extensive cleanup of the weed-and-coke room. He had flushed bags, straightened pillows, and hidden in the shower.

"You're a funny drunk," said Samantha, who had watched.

"I was like trying to make the place look nice," he said.

They found Cody standing alone in the silent great room, shirtless and laughing.

"Me and my boys just kicked ass!" he called to them across the emptiness. He shook his fingers. "We should just rent hotel rooms and trash them. My hand doesn't work anymore."

Vic reached the bottom step, and Cody held out his fist. Vic slapped it cautiously. "I don't want to like hurt it."

"Punch it!" Cody commanded.

"Turn that thing off," a cop ordered Sara. She sighed and closed the video camera. Her furry handcuffs dangled forlornly from her purse.

"Help me pick up cups," she said.

Charity scuffled along the sidewalk beside her. She pointed a fingernail at some red plastic tucked in Brian's neighbor's bush.

"I'm going to get revenge," she said.

Sara picked up the cup and tossed it in her bag. "How?"

Charity set her skinny jaw. "I don't know." She tugged her skirt and looked down at the video camera.

And where am I during this party?

The same place I've been most of the time: there.

I drove over with Vic, Cody came outside to find me as his beer pong partner, I watched the video with Charity, I stood talking to Kaylee when the table flipped, I hid scared with Ross and the rest in the laundry room, I helped Derrick pick up cups.

"You're one of my best guy friends," Alexis told me.

"I want to thank you for, uh, coming here and really making my senior year better," Derrick told me.

"I've always got your back, homie," Vic told me.

I've been at class and the circle every day, SpiriTeen every week, the beach and the pizza place and people's houses and even city hall.[8] I've removed myself because my story is secondary. We have gathered for lives and voices not known and heard.

But I am there.

High school has become my world and these people have become my friends.

O GIRLS, TO WAR

To stab at the heart means—when fighting and there are obstructions or it is difficult to cut—to thrust at the enemy. You must stab the enemy's breast without letting the point of your long sword waver.

> —Miyamoto Musashi,
> *The Book of Water*

IRIDIUM PHOENIX

Theodora Danielian leaned against the rough bark of the scrub oak and watched raindrops sluice down velvety leaves.

"My life is for shit," she sighed. "I mean, like imagine I entered this art contest. So I take a picture that I think is good and means a lot to me and I mail it in to whoever their like panel of judges is. Nobody's going to understand it, and I still won't matter to anybody, except then it'll be like official. They'll be saying, 'Oh, Thea, you thought you were good at photography? Well, you're not even good at that. Don't even bother.' Then I won't even have any illusions. You know?"

Evelyn threw her into the mud. "Get *down*," she hissed. "You're compromising Operation Iridium Phoenix."

She stared into the foggy distance, automatic rifle on her shoulder, and listened to faraway cries dissolving across the drifting eddies. "Their command bunker has to be in this sector. Give me the GPS."

Thea lifted her head from the squelching mire, rubbed some of the sludge off her hand, and dug around the canvas pack. Just as her fingers closed on the hard box, a storm of tiny plastic pellets tore into the sagebrush.

Evelyn spun and squeezed a few bursts of ammo into the gray miasma. All fell still.

Her nostrils flared. "The insurgency! Move out."

The two of them set off through the rocky foothills.

Most people at Mirador took a hard line on American military power abroad in their classes and then went home to sit on the couch. Evelyn spent class time arguing for peace and tolerance, and then strapped on her mock M4A1 carbine with M203 grenade launcher and charged straight into a camo-covered MilSim to blow the peoples of the Earth to a nitrocarbon mist.[1]

They trudged past spiny bursts of yucca. "You know," said Thea, "I don't really like my name. I think it sounds butch. Kind of like 'Thor.' I don't know, what do you think?"

Evelyn looked at the bleak rolling hills. "Airsoft inspires me," she decided. "I'd like to be a special agent in the FBI or the CIA, like Agent Bristow in *Alias*. I could kill if I had to. I can deceive people if I need to. In fact, I'm too good at it." She swallowed. "But it would be hard leading a double life, like having to always play a role."

They marched onward in silence for a while.

"I've been turned in to the FBI," she confided.

Thea could only see a damp mop of orange hair under a camo hat. "For what?"

Evelyn shook her head solemnly. "I'm not saying. It's bad. I've done more original shit than most high schoolers."

JUNIOR CLASS DOWN AND FORTY

"Set," screamed Cody. "Hike!"

On the wet field behind the boxy elementary school, Kaylee snapped the football back between her legs just as Nicole lunged. Alexis spiraled it downfield to Padma, who got about five yards before Olivia barreled into her.

Padma yelped and fumbled as she crashed to the muddy grass.

Cody blew his whistle. The heaps of muddy girls in green senior-class shirts turned to him.

A long pause. He rubbed his face. "You need 'roids. I'll go to my house and get my shit. Just find a vein."

"We are not bad!" said Alexis. "We're gonna kick ass."

Padma sat up, winced, and rubbed her leg. "Coach Cody, we won last year."

"You tied last year," he said.

"We so won," said Alexis. "It was all senior refs and Kaylee kept getting touchdowns they didn't count. They said it was a tie, but it was so four-three."

Kaylee raised her shirt to show a huge brown-and-yellow patch on her side. "We've been practicing for powder-puff so long, I've got all these bruises."

"We have to defend the honor of the senior class," said Olivia.

"I hate so many of those bitches," said Nicole. "I'm ready to fight."

"Everyone hates them," said Kaylee. "They're really lame and they've got no class unity at all. The entire thing is just going to be a huge junior-senior battle."

Cody smirked and shook his head in the light rain. "After Brian's, like none of the guys want to fight. They know the cops try and stop the game every year because it's so intense, and everybody's eighteen and they're scared they'll get arrested."

"Last year we were like rolling twenty-five deep and no one came," Steve reminded him.

Alexis laughed. "I want to get drunk. I fight better when I'm wasted. I'm like more courageous."

"I'd bet I'd be a good fighter if I knew what I was doing," said Kaylee. She turned to Cody. "Will you teach me to fight?"

He smiled.

"I'm a good fighter," said Nicole. "I'll just be like, 'Bitch!'" She demonstrated a takedown.

THE BAD GUYS

Charity hurled the lump of Orange Dreamsicle at the frosty slab. She sprinkled on gummi bears and pounded them in as if they had mauled her brother on a picnic.

She jammed the ice cream into a medium fancy waffle cone and extended it to her customer with a sullen glare.

He grinned back. He was a black senior at Mirador, one of the thug-type guys with a diamond earring.

"Thank you so much, Charity," he said.

"You're welcome," she replied coldly, and rang him up.

"What time's your shift over at?" he asked.

"I don't know," said Charity. "Late."

"I see you at school tomorrow, Charity." He smiled again as he left in a jolly tinkle of shop bells.

She turned back to the pregnant girl.

"Oh, my God," she gasped. "He's *such* a creepy stalker. He just like sits there in the corner of the store and watches me for twenty minutes, and he's always bragging about how many white girls he's gotten on. It's making this shitty job even shittier."

Raindrops splattered on the huge glass windows of the Creamery. Their manager April had gone to a meeting at the central office, and the mood had relaxed a little.

The pregnant girl nudged Charity with a skinny elbow. "He wants you, sweetie!"

Charity grappled with her tiny paper hat. "Why do I have to be the slut?" she fumed. "Alexis Newton is the fucking slut! She's a total closet freak who'll fuck anybody, but she has to look so good and so perfect all the fucking time. It's like everybody puts her up on this pedestal of perfection and it's all so *fake*."

"You're so right," said the pregnant girl. "I don't like Alexis Newton."

Charity's scoop clunked into the well. "What?"

"I used to like her," said the pregnant girl. "She became so different, she became like an asshole. Like I haven't been at Mirador this year, but she was in my grade, and she started to hang out with us sophomore year because we were like the cool people. Then she started to make everyone hang out with her all the time, like they couldn't hang out with each other independently, like she had to have all friendships route through her. She got really loud and she thinks she's so cool now and she's always talking about how she gets fucked up so much. She used to be so nice and sweet. You didn't know her the way she used to be."

"Yeah," muttered Charity. She slammed the dipping cabinet.

"And she always goes for the 'bad' guys," said the pregnant girl. "Like the moto bros and even like Mexicans and black guys and stuff."

Charity stared into the fluorescent case. "Oh, my God," she gasped. "Cover for me."

She shoved open the tinkling door and charged out into the driving rain.

PANTIES AND NIPPLES

"Alexis." Ms. Schroeder beckoned her over as she walked into the video lab for community-project presentations. "I thought about the question you asked me regarding the thrown bottle. And the answer is yes. My best friend is my husband, and if he didn't turn himself in, I would turn him in."

"Oh," said Alexis.

She took her seat and told Kaylee.

"'Husband,' whatever," said Kaylee. "She's such a lesbian."

Class began.

"All right," said Ms. Schroeder, "you've spent over a month on your video projects, and now it's time for us all to enjoy the fruits of your hard work. I've assigned the groups in random order, so first we have"— her nose wrinkled—"Vic Reyes and Shawn Ackerman, 'Water Awareness.'"

She glared as Vic slipped the DVD into the player.

The massive screen at the front of the room lit up with a completely redone film. The water detective and car chases had vanished, replaced by a bloodthirsty water pirate played by Steve.

"Yo ho ho," he chortled behind his eye patch. "First I'm going to siphon off the California Aqueduct and turn Emerald Valley back into a desert." He notched his voice up to falsetto. "And then I'm going to paint my pirate ship pink!" He grabbed his nipples and did a little maritime jig.

"Stop, you evil bastard," cried a video Shawn with a mustache. "I am William Mulholland, founder of the State Water Project."

Ms. Schroeder popped out of her chair faster than Mulholland could snatch water rights.[2]

"Stop! Stop this immediately. You're both getting zeroes on this project."

Vic opened his mouth, but the baggy figure had already hit the lights and taken her position at the whiteboard.

"Eyes, eyes, up here. I want *all eyes* in the room up here. *Now.*" Every head lifted. "This is the final time I'm going over this. One group has repeatedly participated in lewd and inappropriate conduct, like twisting nipples—"

The room snickered but Schroeder scowled.

"We never asked him to twist his nipples," Vic protested. "He just did it."

"—and using crude language *and* repeatedly making derogatory references to homosexuals. All of which falls under the unacceptable heading of"—she scribbled on the board as she said the words "Lewd and Inappropriate Conduct."

"Okay? Now I—"

And then before thirty-five pairs of startled eyes, her voluminous pants fell down.

Utter silence.

She looked out at the ranks of twisted faces, swallowed, and casually pulled them up again. "Let's go back to watching our videos."

As the bell rang and everyone left class, whispered fragments tried to frame an unparseable shared reality.

"The granny panties . . . ," began someone.

"The varicose veins on her legs . . . ," tried another.

"It looked like a map of the California highway system," said a third.

Alexis grabbed Shawn. "Hey," she said, "do you want to get a cigarette?"

"I can't," he said, "I have to go talk to her about our grade."

Alexis looked around very carefully before slipping behind the cinder block wall of the facilitation quad.

She shielded her lighter and flicked a spark. She had a couple of fellow smokers.

One black guy with a diamond earring smiled at her. "Hey," he said.

"Hey," she said.

"Damn," he said. "We have some fine-ass girls at this school."

She smiled.

"You smoke bud?" he asked her.

"I do now," she said. "I just finished a drug test."

"Me and my boys just got some phat purple shit," he said. "You got big plans for after school?"

PLAYTIME

Charity's platform clogs clunked on the rubber mats as she clambered up the brightly colored spiral platforms of the play structure tower.

"I'm going to destroy her," she cackled. "The whole world is going to know for real what a slut she is."

Sara followed one platform behind with the video camera.

"I don't think you're going to get a good angle," she said.

Five little eight-year-olds followed Sara. "This is so entertaining," one of them said.

"Okay, that's enough," Charity snapped at them. "Go away."

One grinned. "No. It's our playground." They watched her from a safe distance.

She growled.

"I miss elementary school," said Sara. She smiled at the little pack. "Eight is like the perfect age. That's the only time I can ever remember that nothing went wrong."

One pretended to shoot her.

Charity reached the top of the tower by the slide. She surveyed the houses down the street. "Give me the camera." She snapped open the view screen and angled the lens. "Annnnngh. It's like three feet too low. Whyyyyy does life have to be so much fucking drama?"

A thick tree branch overhung the tower. "There." Looping the camera around her neck, Charity scrabbled up onto the narrow guard wall, unfolded her legs, and stood. She teetered like a deranged stork.

"Uh," said Sara. "That camera cost three thousand dollars."

The eight-year-olds giggled. "We can see your underwear," one said.

"Your mom has underwear just like this," Charity hissed. "Do you want to touch it?"

The third-grade pack screamed and stumbled over one another to flee. Charity jammed the camera into a fork in the branch and worked to position it.

Alexis's bedroom window came into perfect focus on the LCD. Charity zoomed tighter until the bed filled the screen.

"Hah!" she crowed. "Wasn't this like a genius revenge plan? Soon we're going to have a black-guys-with-Alexis-Newton orgy video on the Internet."

"Everybody's making them now," said Sara, "like all those freshman slut girls. This is going to be like the tenth sex video of the year."

Charity slowly climbed down from the ledge.

"Hey," said Sara, "that's Chelsea Koch's house at the end of the block."

"Yeah," said Charity. "Her family's so weird. They're like atheists."

Sara pulled her head back in disgust. "Really?"

"Yeah," said Charity. "I went over there once, and I didn't really know how to argue back, you know? It was so weird. I didn't know how to convince them, like 'there is God.' It's hard."

EVEN BETTER THAN THE REAL THING

A few days later, Thea sat on one of the black set pieces backstage during tech theater.

"Okay," she said, "so how is this for a new concept: finger sex?"

"I think it's a decent idea," said Evelyn.

"What's finger sex?" asked a gay theater guy.

"Okay," said Thea. "It's like sex, but you use your pointer and middle fingers as the legs. See, you can have a girl"—she walked her fingers around the table as sexily as possible—"or a guy, like with a finger penis." She stuck a finger from her other hand out between the imaginary legs.

"Oh, that's cute!" said the gay theater guy.

"See," said Thea, "and you could videotape it, and have like bondage finger porn, and domination finger porn, and like vampire finger porn, like if you attached a couple of little cat fangs."

She made a finger guy and walked it over to start penetrating the gay guy's hand. "Ohhhh . . . ," he moaned.

"Ohhhh . . . ," she said. "See, it's like sexual, and it's totally legal. And for girl fingers, you could like trim the nails to be like heels, you know? You could even get creative." She pushed her thumb out between her fingers and held her other index finger diagonally alongside. "See, that's Harry Potter with his broom and a big schlong."

She marched Harry Potter with his broom and a big schlong across the set piece and finger-sex-raped Evelyn's elbow.

"That's annoying," said Evelyn.

Suddenly Leo the little freshman pushed through the curtains. "Guess what we're watching in the AV booth?" he panted.

The skin stopped sanding a board. "What?"

"Somebody got this tape of Alexis Newton having sex with three black guys!"

Backstage emptied.

Thea looked down at her fingers. "I wish I could have real sex with someone," she mumbled.

YOU'RE PARIS HILTON

Alexis sat in her bedroom that evening, brushing her long blond hair while the popular teen drama *One Tree Hill* played on TV.[3]

Ever since Brian's party, having to be home after five largely meant confinement to her room. Plus she had told her dad about the college rejections. UC Irvine had just posted the denial online, leaving Loyola and that Monaco thing as the only places that hadn't eliminated her yet.

She rubbed a side that ached from constant powder-puff practice and heard her dad talking to Travis through the wall.

"So, you're sixteen," he said, "and that's a time when a lot of, uh, males are probably starting to deal with things we've never really talked about, if you know what I mean."

She heard Travis's level voice. "I'm really like flattered that you're taking an interest in my life, but I promise you that I know more about stuff like safe sex and protection than you do."

Their father chuckled. "Well . . . ," he said.

"Do you know what the difference is between gonorrhea and non-specific urethritis?" Travis asked.

Silence. Alexis turned a page in *Teen People*.

"Not exactly," their father said after awhile.

"Both have like symptoms that look the same," hinted Travis, "but the treatment's a little bit different?"

More silence. "Uh, Travis, I . . . ,"

"It's tetracycline instead of penicillin," her brother said. "But they're still totally different than something viral like hep B, where you need an interferon treatment."

"What's that?" their father asked.

"Do you have time?" said Travis. "Why don't you like sit down?"

Alexis watched TV for another forty-five minutes while her brother explained the chemistry of RU-486 pills and the fail rate of the intra-uterine device.

After awhile, she heard a knock on her door. She expected her dad but it turned out to be Travis.

"Uh, there's something you should probably know if you don't know it already," he said.

"What?" she said.

"You're Paris Hilton," said Travis. "You're a sex video."

"I'm what?"

ANGUISHED FACES

Charity wailed as she collapsed into her seat in Ms. Horn's bio class the next day. "My videooooooo," she moaned. "I lost my stupid Alexis video. I was like showing it to people at passing period and I don't what happened to it. Someone said they thought that weird freshman Chester Koch had it but he doesn't. I can't belieeeeeve I fucking lost it."

Ms. Horn entered beaming with her #1 TEACHER coffee mug. "Good *morning,* my friends! Very fun night last night. I was at this crazy club in Huntington and *I* rode the mechanical bull. Now can we all please come into the other room with a pencil for a special announcement?"

Everyone rose, and soon Horn faced thirty-seven students packed at lab benches.

"Okay," she said, "I just want to clear up this rumor. Oh, my God, y'all think Mr. Kostopoulos and me are dating. We're not! He's engaged, you guys. Apparently people called my name near him to see if he'd turn around, and he did, but it's not because we're like *together*. And he's not the guy who put his tongue in my ear either, okay?"

The news sank in. Sara twirled her pencil. "Was that the announcement, Ms. Horn?"

"No, sweetie," said Ms. Horn. She sighed. "I hate to tell you this."

She began to draw big frowny faces on the whiteboard, crying fat tears with gloomy, burnt-out squiggles over their heads.

"So we had a department meeting, and instead of a normal day with the cats, they decided we needed to administer and grade you on something called the California Science Rubrics Assessment." She wrote it up amid the anguished faces.

"The department was really concerned about student cheating on assignments and copying each other's work, and so they wanted to do a graded skills exam in all our physiology classes, and get a real sample of student work to compare with demonstrated knowledge. They also wanted to create 'anchor profiles,' and standardize what sort of work is A work, B work, and so on.

"It's a fairly extensive exam that'll take us the whole period and that's going to be the most significant part of your semester grade."

Silence.

"Whaaaaaat?" shrieked Charity.

"You've just gone from 'cool' to 'not cool' in like five seconds," said Forrest.

"You're joking," said Vic hollowly.

Ms. Horn grimaced. "I'm really sorry about this, my friends. There's nothing I could do. Please just try your best on the test, because it is going to be the majority of your semester grade."

She began to pass out complex sheets marked "California Science Rubrics Assessment—Physiology." Vic looked down at a question:

27. The phylum Ctenophora does NOT contain which of the following: a) Cydippida, b) Lobata, c) Beroida, d) Nuculoida, e) Platyctenida.

"Please begin," she said. She plopped onto her Lakers stool and hummed tunelessly.

One girl started to cry. People tapped their pencils and bit their lips.

Vic got out of his seat and walked to the front.

"Yes, my friend Mr. Reyes," she said.

"Ms. Horn," he said softly, voice hoarse, "this is the only class I'm even like passing, and I've got an A. But after this I'm going to have like a D. I can't think of the answers to any of these questions."

"They're for both AP and your class," she said.

He swallowed. "I can remember like anything," he said, "if you just show me this stuff and give me like thirty seconds to look at it, I promise I could do this test. Please, Ms. Horn."

She smiled and shook her head. "I'm sorry, my friend. Please go back to your seat."

He sat. A skinny girl choked back her sobs.

About six minutes later, Ms. Horn suddenly spoke.

"What day is today?" she asked.

One guy checked his watch. "The first," he muttered.

Ms. Horn leaned back in whooping gales of laughter. "Ah hah hah

hah hah!" She kicked her feet and spun on her stool. "April Fool's! You all fell for it! Hah hah hah hah hah!"

Charity's pale face snapped up from her exam. "Whaaaaat?"

"I made it all up," hooted Ms. Horn. "The exam, the anchor profiles, the department meeting, everything. We don't even have department meetings. Actually, we don't have departments anymore even, because they can't afford to pay the department chairs."

Vic put his head on the table. "I can't stand school," he said.

Weak laughter and stunned silence mixed through the room.

"So what are we doing today?" Sara asked.

Horn shrugged. "The cats, I guess."

Charity saw a DVD of the George Clooney movie *O Brother, Where Art Thou?* on a lab bench. She held it up. "Oh, can we watch this? It's such a good movie."

"Yeah," voices begged. "Please?"

"Okay," said Ms. Horn. "Go ahead and pop it in."

After class, Charity moped around the outskirts of the arts quad steps, telling anyone who would listen about the unjust tragedy of her missing videotape.

A few girls passed by wearing green senior T-shirts.

"Oh, my God," said Jasmine. "Their class has so much spirit. We have like none."

"It's because our class sucks," said another girl.

Samantha looked around at the group. "Is anyone even playing powder-puff?"

"Hells fucking no," said one girl. "Like I really want to run around in the sun and get hit. The seniors can play with themselves."

"They do," somebody said, laughing.

ALONE

At lunchtime, Thea sat alone before a bright computer screen in the video lab. Pressure behind her eyes erupted slowly into the pangs of a headache. Her hand had cramped from clutching the mouse on detail work.

The screen held the photo she had taken of the toddler drowning under the giant Angels of Anaheim baseball hat. His two parents held his hands, and at first glance everything looked as cheerful and idyllic as a Rockwell painting. Upon close examination, though, you could see they pulled his arms hard in different directions, as if they were tearing him apart. The child had a distressed plea on his face—a very mature look of pain that no one would expect from a child. Of course, people rarely paid real attention to children.

Thea hunched close to the screen, looking at pixels as she nudged the contrast on the hat brim.

She turned her head as the pack of freshman girls wandered into the room and giggled.

"You're always at that computer," one girl said. "This period, other period, after school. Do you do anything besides Photoshop?"

"She sits behind the library," said another girl.

They all laughed. Thea forced a little smile. The girls watched her tap the arrow keys for a moment.

"Oh, yeah, you're cool," said a girl, "you have a lot of friends. Who are your friends?"

"Evelyn Strout," said another girl.

The first laughed. "Oh, she's cool."

And then Thea sat alone again.

GAME OVER

"What are you doing with your life?" a deep voice intoned across central quad at lunchtime.

Bass beats swelled, turbofan engines roared, and a strike fighter jet blazed into a hazy sunset.

The back page of the *Mirror* carried an urgent ad screaming in bold: "MIRADOR SENIORS BEWARE!!!! DANGER!!!! SENIORS BEWARE!!!! Military Recruiters will soon be on YOUR high school campus trying to persuade you to enlist. . . ." It ran through a series of stats on Iraq deaths and homeless vets.

But the giant Air Force screen still presided over the most popular booth at the career fair, even though little ninth-graders formed the bulk of prospective airmen. Some girls wandered past the culinary institute and environmental coalition. Everyone avoided the Emerald Valley PD stall as if they sprayed interested seniors with hantavirus.

At the circle, Alexis leaned against the concrete ring with her arms tightly folded.

"If she has a problem, why doesn't she say it to my face? Who the fuck does she think she is with this shit?"

The other girls didn't say anything, hovering on the fence as they tried to assess how seriously the videotape had damaged Alexis's social status. Everybody slept with everybody, but a little compromising footage just might prove the perfect excuse for a leadership change.

She tried another tactic. "I just can't wait for powder-puff. The junior girls are just so weak."

"Yeah," said Kaylee distantly. "Totally."

Brian smirked.

And then the universe saved Alexis. As the heroic trumpets of *"Fanfare for the Common Man"* rang across the courtyard, Padma hurried into the circle.

"Oh, my God," she announced to everyone. "I heard the juniors don't want to play powder-puff."

"What?" said Vic. "They don't?"

Ross adjusted his collar. "I heard something like that too."

Cody spiked his Pepsi into the garbage can. "That is such *bullshit*. Oh, I'm pissed."

"And here we all are practicing nonstop and I've got all these bruises," said Kaylee. "What the fuck?"

Alexis seized the moment. "That's right!" she called above the roaring fighter jets. "The junior girls are a bunch of drunk sluts with no class pride. They're too weak to even play powder-puff and they're going to call themselves seniors. Like are they going to get our section at assembly? Are they going to wear our senior color? Are they going to sit all over our circle next year?"

"Fuck no," Nicole sneered. "They don't deserve our shit."

"Powder-puff is *tradition*," intoned Cody.

"We'll like destroy the circle," said one girl. "We'll level it."

Padma kicked the concrete. "We'll blow it up!"

"Yeah," a few people shouted.

Alexis looked around the circle and pounded her fist in her palm. "If the junior girls can't even play powder-puff, we're going to pass out shit straight down to the sophomores. The juniors can just stay on the slut steps where they belong for another year."

"They don't deserve any respect," said another girl.

"If they don't play they're going to get their asses kicked," said Kaylee.

"We're going to have water balloons," said Vic. "And eggs."

Brian snorted. "The junior guys are fags too."

Alexis drove it home. "Charity Warner was like talking the worst trash about everyone. She was talking so much shit about the senior class."

"We've gotta make a plan and get her," said Kaylee.

The trumpets crescendoed. "We're going to have to call them *all* out," said Alexis.

The entire circle buzzed with angry voices.

A few minutes later, Derrick arrived from the administration building.

"Hey," he said. "I just want to remind everybody that we need like a senior class performance for spring rally next week. Do we have any ideas?"

The bells rang on and off, sporadically and uncontrollably, on Friday morning.

Mr. Popper's voice stammered in bursts, attempting to explain the difference between printed and announced spring rally schedules.

In his neatly labeled room, math teacher Mr. Lamarque slid a pen into his pocket. "This school is so unorganized it's shameful. Of all the monstrosities and abominations Mirador makes me perform, I am now obligated to take you all to yet another rally. Stand quickly, quietly, and efficiently."

The auditorium stood divided by quadrants. The junior and senior sections faced each other at the front across the central aisle.

All the classes screamed ferociously.

The administration clearly smelled blood, because two police officers and all five proctors stood at attention around the perimeter. They had searched everyone and confiscated bags at the door.

"Soph-mores," chanted a blue bloc.

"Cock-whores," chanted the yellow freshmen.

Musician Wil stood among the sophomores. "I'm so drunk and I'm on Valium," he said. "I don't even know what our color is, fool."

"Look at everybody, fool," said Travis. "It's blue. You're wearing it."

"Noooooo," groaned Wil. "Am I at the right school? We could have just showed up at a random rally, like, 'What up, Esperanza High.'"

"You're at the right school," said Travis.

"Shit," said Wil.

Only a few dabs of red spotted the junior section. Several junior girls even wore green armbands and sweatshirts to show their denial of juniorhood.

Evelyn talked to the skin. "Why do we even have rallies when it costs us so much money, for what? What do we possibly gain from this? It makes me want to like grab Dr. Chao and beg, 'Don't blow money on another rally, *please*?'"

Charity stood toward the front by the low stage. She chewed gum and glared at the seniors.

They faced the juniors and waved paper plates with the word "Seniors" in green. "Pow-der-puff," they howled, "pow-der-*puff*!" Some junior guys got into smack-talking matches, and proctors came to stand between the two sections.

Then the lights went down.

"Welcome," thundered Derrick Littlefield's voice, "to your spring rally."

An event of epic and magisterial proportions unfolded. All the forces of Mirador contributed—ASB, Matadoras, band, sports teams, teachers, even custodians. Videos, smoke, lights, and sounds complemented precise choreography around a giant set with motorized platforms. Minus the incessant taunts and chanting, it could have appeared on network television.

"All right!" said Derrick. "The time has come to wrap up with our grand finale. All the lovely ladies from each of our four Mirador classes will be dancing their hearts out for you up here on this stage, so show some class pride and cheer for your grade! Yeah! Fresh*men*!"

The pack of freshman girls ran onstage with five others in tiny skirts. They all did a chest-rubbing, backside-grabbing dance.

The sophomores had LaTyra and a fast-paced performance of heavy urban attitude.

As soon as the junior girls stepped onstage, everything fell apart.

Forbidden newspapers appeared across the senior section, and everyone pretended to read. "We don't respect you enough to watch," someone yelled.

Mr. Popper appeared next to the senior section. "Hand all those news-papers forward," he commanded. Only a few people did. "Proctors," he ordered, "collect the newspapers."

Huge proctors began to shove their way down the senior aisles, grab-bing newspapers.

The seniors turned their backs to the stage. They held the plates above their heads and chanted, "Pow-der-puff. Pow-der-*puff*!"

"Proctors," barked Mr. Popper, "collect the plates."

As one, everyone threw their plates at the stage, a whirling storm of hundreds of paper discs.

Popper didn't know what to do about that. The junior girls finished their dance and dashed from the stage. The seniors roared their con-demnation.

The policemen looked at each other and shifted.

"It's time for our seniors!" yelled Derrick.

Charity stood by the stage, chewing her gum, arms folded. She inten-sified the skeptical lip-curl on her eternal mask of blasé disgust.

Lil' Flip's taunting, driving anthem "Game Over" filled the huge audi-torium.

"Game over. Game over. Game over . . ."

Four senior girls danced onto the stage with sweet smiles and two giant POWDER-PUFF signs. They positioned themselves on the wings.

Cody, Brian, and all the big senior guys moved out and stood in the aisle with their arms folded like a green-shirted DMZ. They stared down the junior class section.

"Proctors," ordered Popper, "get them back in their seats."

"Game over. Game over. Game over . . ."

Up onstage, slender, graceful Alexis Newton, beaming, led ten senior girls in green shirts out from the left. Kaylee brought in ten more from the right.

They all faced straight toward the audience, hands behind their backs, and fanned into a rectangle. They danced.

Cody argued with the proctors.

Charity glared at Alexis's bright smile.

"Game over. Game over. Game over . . ."

Keeping the beat, the senior girls brought their hands around from behind their backs. Each girl held a water polo ball.

Charity's puzzled sneer suddenly collapsed. Her eyes widened and her mouth fell open.

"Flip, Flip, Flip, Flip, Flip, Flip . . ."

The senior girls dancing around Alexis in the front flipped over their water polo balls. The backs contained letters.

The line of balls spelled out WHO'S A HO?

All twenty girls looked straight down at Charity and smiled. They pushed the water polo balls toward her. Keeping their eyes locked on her burning face, they danced in front of all of Mirador for the next two minutes.

YOU'RE PLAYING

The proctors and police cleared everyone from the auditorium without incident.

Charity descended upon the junior-girl steps like an Olympian Fury.

"We are playing powder-puff football!" she screeched.

She grabbed Jasmine. "You. You're gonna play, right?"

Jasmine cringed. "I'm gonna get killed."

"Yes," hissed Charity, "you're playing." She corralled Samantha. "You're playing."

Samantha shuddered. "I so can't fight. Like when a girl is yelling at me I start shaking and I want to cry."

"It doesn't matter," said Charity. "You're playing."

Her eyes lit on a junior girl wearing a green senior armband. "Take that off," she shrieked, clawing at it. "Poser! Where's your class pride?"

She glared at everyone. "We are all playing powder-puff," she stated.

Eyes looked down. Finally Jasmine sighed. "If it's the same people as last year, okay, I guess. . . ."

Charity nodded solemnly at their defeat. "That's right. We're all playing."

"I remember in PE," said Samantha, "we have this girl in our grade who's huge, like she was just running along and Kristie and me jumped on her back and she just kept running."

Charity saw Evelyn Strout's bright orange hair towering over the crowds outside the library.

"Hey," said Charity. "You're a junior, right?"

It took Evelyn a few moments to realize Charity had addressed her. "Yeah, why?"

"We really need you to play powder-puff with us next week," Charity said.

Evelyn smirked. "That's for people who are all *'whoooo!'* about school."

"I'm not *'whoooo!'* about school," said Charity, "but I'm playing so I can turn around and punch Alexis Newton at the kickoff."

Evelyn looked at her binder. "Heh," she said, "it might be fun."

Charity smiled. "Yup! It will be."

When Charity arrived at the senior circle, she took a quick breath before marching straight through the opening in the front of the ring.

She didn't glance at Alexis or any girl, just advanced on Brian. He drew back as if confronted by a tiny but rabid flatworm.

"We're playing," she told him.

HATE SO MUCH

On Thursday evening the next week, Alexis's father knocked on her door. She muted the TV as he entered.

"You have an appointment with Dr. Wallach for a retainer checkup tomorrow after school," he said. "So you're going to have to head over there straight after class."

Alexis put down her phone, leaving Padma's text unanswered. "Oh, my God, Daddy, I can't go."

"Why is that?" he asked.

She tried to keep her voice casual and matter-of-fact. "I have powder-puff."

His eyes widened. "Oh, no, Lexi. You're not playing that."

She swallowed. "Yeah."

"No," he said. "Absolutely not. It's way too dangerous. It's been going on forever and there's always problems. We always end up hearing about those games in the police blotter."

"Uh," she said, "I'm kinda like the team captain."

Ten frantic minutes later, he delivered his ultimatum: "If you're playing that game, I'm going to be there to make sure you're safe."

"Uh," said Alexis, "parents don't really go."

"I'll keep my distance," he said.

*   *   *

Last bell rang on Friday and Charity and the junior girls came to the circle. Murderous glowers blistered the air as they faced Alexis and the seniors.

"All right," said Cody.

"Drumroll," said Steve. He pounded his hands on his backpack.

"This year's secret location," said Cody, "is the highest field at Cielo Vista Park. Everybody be there in one hour."

The park lay in a neighboring town only fifteen minutes away, which gave every girl three-quarters of an hour to drink fast and hard.

Alexis rode wasted in the front seat of Padma's RAV4.

"It's soooo embarrassing that my dad is coming," she said.

Kaylee knocked back a mouthful of vodka. "Isn't he like going to know you're drunk?"

"No, 'cause he promised he'd stay away and we wouldn't like interact at all."

Padma saw Kaylee pounding the vodka in her rearview mirror. "Save some for me, slut."

"Lick me, slut," said Kaylee. Alexis got the bottle and drank more.

"Oh, my God," said Padma. "This powder-puff is going to be as bad as ninety-seven–ninety-eight. Everyone hates each other so much."

Kaylee stretched her arm. "Remember two years ago when that Mexican guy pulled out a gun?"

"This game is *craziness*," laughed Alexis.

Padma signaled for the exit lane. "Like what's the deal with you and Charity anyway?"

Alexis kept silent for a moment. "Oh, it's like a long story."

"I want to hear," said Kaylee.

"Yeah, tell us," said Padma.

Alexis rubbed her face. "Fuck me, I am *wasted*. Hah. I can't believe I'm telling you this. Okay.

"She was a year younger than me, but we were like best friends all through like our elementary and junior high. And you know, we were kind of like random people, I guess, you know? We weren't like super-outgoing or anything.

"Anyway, at the end of eighth grade she began like avoiding me, and it was really strange, and so finally I went up to her and asked her what the deal was.

"And she turned to me and said, 'Alexis, when I get to high school, I don't think we should be associated. I don't want to be a weirdo anymore.' I mean, isn't that just the meanest thing you could ever say to someone? Like to your best friend for like ten years?"

Alexis swallowed. Her jaw muscle clenched. "So she's like my worst enemy now. I hate her. Gaaaah, I hate her so much. And like sophomore year I saw her sitting alone at a table at lunch and I was with twenty of my friends, and I was like, 'Hah. *Hah*, Charity.'

"I hate her so much."

PLAYING TO KILL

Among the junior girls, Charity staggered up the wide wooden steps to the highest field. Cars filled the gravel parking lot below.

"The seniors have all the big girls," said Jasmine. "We don't."

"We've got her," said Samantha, and pointed to Evelyn, one of three sober people. "We can definitely win."

"They're not playing to win," said Jasmine. "They're playing to kill."

"I'll kill *them*," said one junior. "They're a bunch of stuck-up bitches."

"Oh, my God," said Jasmine, "the cops like kept trying to follow people on the way here. They're going to know something's up when they see all the cars."

Charity trudged along the steps. "I just want to beat the shit out of Alexis Newton."

The red brigade reached the highest field, and three hundred students and young alums turned to watch them. Voices rose, cheering and taunting. Powder-puff was tradition.

Some guys in their early twenties passed with a cooler of beer. "I love to see all the chicks that hate each other scrap it out," one said.

Under the blazing sun, Charity's group walked into the center of the field. The spectators on the left sidelines, mainly juniors, yelled. Alexis's group stood waiting on the other side of a fifty-yard line marked by cones.

Charity cracked her knuckles and stared at Alexis's neck. The senior girls glared and shuffled. The crowd of three hundred fell silent as Cody and the redneck walked out to referee.

"All right," said Cody. "Coin toss for the kickoff."

Charity and Alexis stepped forward. The silver disc flipped and glinted burning light, and the juniors won. Charity growled. Alexis glowered. Sweat trickled and they shifted dirt under their feet.

"We want blood!" someone hollered.

"Yeah!" screamed a few other guys.

Cody looked down at the girls, a little nervously.

"Okay," he said. "Who has the football?"

Alexis turned to her pack. "We don't."

Charity gave him the curled lip. "Huh?"

"Wait," said Cody. "Neither of you brought a football?"

He glanced at the two teams. Heads shook. "Uh-uh."

"Hah!" laughed the redneck. "These girls were so busy getting plastered, they didn't bring a fucking football."

Cody yelled at the crowds through cupped hands. "Does *anybody* here have a football?"

Alums and students looked around. Out of an audience of three hundred, nobody had a football.

"I love Mirador," one alum whooped. "Everything this school does is so fugged up!"

"Okay," said Cody. "Somebody's going to have to drive back home."

Steve volunteered, Cody tossed him keys, and he jogged away.

For the next twenty-five minutes, everybody sat on the grass in the baking sun and sweated. "Ohhhhh," moaned Charity to the juniors. "I just want to kiiiiiiiiill."

Then several things happened.

Groaning and fanning her face with her hand, Charity noticed a man in a blazer standing at the far end of the field, watching them through binoculars. "Mr. Newton," she gasped. "Alexis brought her fucking *father* to the game."

Then five squad cars pulled onto the other end of the field. The engines stopped, and ten policemen just sat surveying everybody behind tinted windows, with no intention of going anywhere until the game ended.

The crowds grumbled at the sudden loss of blood, but Charity keened. "Whaaaaaat the fuck? This is so unfaaaaair. How can I beat the shit out of her with her dad and the police standing there? Fuck this. I don't want to play reeeeal football."

She stood to leave. A sunburned, sweat-drenched Samantha stopped her. "Oh, no," she said. "This was *your* idea."

A squad of angry juniors glared at her.

Steve dashed up the stairs with a football. He held it aloft and the crowds cheered.

And so the game began. Mirador girls played their powder-puff as full-contact tackle football without the pads.

The contest stood as follows: a team that had practiced for weeks versus Evelyn and Charity. Every single junior offensive play consisted of getting the ball quickly to Evelyn and letting her charge. She lumbered downfield and made a few spectacular touchdowns.

Every single junior defensive play consisted of Charity. She would crouch on the line across from an unfortunate guard, hold up her fake fingernails, and hiss, "I'm going to slit your *throat*, bitch." Then she'd rattle her tongue like Hannibal Lecter and add, "I'm a lesbian, and I . . . want . . . your . . . body." When the girl lost her nerve, Charity would fling herself shrieking on the quarterback.

The juniors struggled valiantly, but the game ended five-three seniors.

The whole senior class flooded the field, chanting. Charity watched through an aching, dirt-streaked face as the green-shirted squad leaped with joy.

"The junior girls are losers," someone yelled.

Kaylee launched into her notorious *vata* impression. "*Oye*," she said. "You all better listen me real good. We kick they dirty junior ass, hokay, *ese*?"[4]

Nicole laughed and showed off her bruises. "Look at my war wounds!"

And in the middle of it all, a beaming Alexis screamed. "Seniors! Whooooo! Whoooooooooo!"

Charity ground her teeth and ripped up a clod of grass. "—the *entire* water polo team," she heard someone say behind her.

DEADLINE

Thea spent the next week adjusting her photo. Every time she looked at it she found something wrong, something she could fix. She touched up millimeter details and then changed them back again. She pored through photography books and decided that all the images expressed a higher level of vision and technique than she could ever hope to attain.

Contest entries required a Friday postmark. At lunch she printed the image on nice high-glossy paper she had bought herself, and brought it to her art teacher.

"Hey," she said. "What do you think about this one?"

He glanced at it. "It's nice."

And that was it.

She dropped it in the garbage can and then took it out again. She had spent a month on it.

At home she had already filled out the Getty papers but now sat in her room with the photo. She started to bike to the post office and then stopped midway.

She fought back feelings of doom, kept going, and mailed her entry with an hour to spare.

FUCKIN' BEAUTIFUL

Prom conquered central quad on Monday during passing periods and lunch. A fleet of Expedition limos and party buses with neon tubes and wall-size screens parked across the courtyard.

Scores of juniors and seniors checked out plush interiors and two-thousand-dollar price tags.

"Are you serious?" Cody demanded of a tiny Persian man. "You're serious? Okay, that's it. That's it. We're driving. I'm not spending a hundred and sixty bucks for a twenty-minute ride. Screw this rip-off."

His date Nicole turned in horror. "Uh . . ."

Mr. Popper saw Vic examining corsages and decided to engage in some information warfare.

"Getting excited about the big night?" Popper asked.

"Oh, yeah," said Vic.

"Well," said Mr. Popper, "don't get too excited. We're taking measures to avoid a repeat of Sadie's."

Vic put down the glossy catalog. "Is Mary Jane coming?"

"Of course," Popper lied cheerfully. "We're actually going to have *two* dogs. And we're frisking and Breathalyzing everyone at the door. We're going to have officers, Breathalyzers, and dogs all over this prom all night long."

Vic's eyes widened.

An elevated modeling catwalk stretched under a huge banner that read DONATELLO'S TUXEDO, surrounded by racks of suits.

Donatello, a short Italian man in a silk shirt, grooved around the racks to Al Green's "Let's Stay Together."

"*Whatever you want to do, it's all right with meeee . . .*"

He rolled his shoulders and sang. "Ooooh. I love it. 'The Don's . . . got the best tuxes, tuxes. . . .'"

He grabbed El Presidente browsing the suits. "How much you wanna spend?"

El Presidente pushed up his glasses. "Not much. Little."

"Two hundred dollars, yeah?" said Donatello.

El Presidente shook his head desperately. "Less," he said. "Like you advertised that fifty-dollar special?"

"Hah!" Donatello laughed to his two assistants. "Three hundred fuckin' guys come over already. There's no more special left. But don't worry, the Don is gonna set you up."

He clapped his hands and called out numbers. "Gold shirt, gold hat!"

The assistants rushed over and plomped them on El Presidente.

"It's fucking beautiful!" said Donatello. "I fuckin' set you up. We've fucking got it. Ninety-nine bucks, bambino, don't fucking tell nobody. The Don does it again!"

"Uh," said El Presidente.

Donatello danced away while the assistants closed in with payment slips.

"*Whether times are good or bad, happy or sad . . .*"

Padma and Kaylee flipped through huge volumes of Loralie and Jessica McClintock prom dresses.

"Oh, my God," said Padma. "These are so *ugly.*"

"Look at that one!" gasped Kaylee, pointing to a terrifying rainbow hoop skirt.

The girls cracked up. "Or what about that one?" said Padma, finger on a clinging zebra-striped dress with a slit up the thigh.

Brian wandered dazed from the tuxedo racks wearing a zoot suit. "Hey?" he said, holding out his arms.

"Oh, my God," said Padma, "you are *not* wearing that. It would look so weird with my outfit. We wouldn't like coordinate at all."

"Uh," he said, "I just got it."

Padma stamped her foot. "You've ruined *everything!*"

"And I want to spend my life with youuuuu. . . ."

Alexis and Shawn stood behind the curtain to the catwalk. She wore her tight pink Dior dress and he sported one of Donatello's finest white tuxes.

"He's giving me such a big discount for modeling this thing," said Shawn.

Alexis leaned against some boxes and adjusted her heel. "What happened to his pinkie? He's missing like the tip of his finger."

Shawn laughed. "He got it caught in a fucking fan belt. He'd probably say it was from being in the Mob."

Alexis smiled. They stood for a while under the hot sun as hundreds of voices rang outside the curtain. "I heard from Loyola," she said.

He looked over. "What did they say?"

"I'm a reject."

"Oh," he said, "damn. That sucks. I'm sorry." He put his arms around her. "So, uh, like what are you doing next year?"

She shrugged. "I'll probably be at Emerald College, like try and transfer somewhere."

"Hey," he said, "so's like everybody. You should come to Cal State Fullerton with me in spring. Everybody gets in if you have your recs."

"Yeah," she said.

Donatello shepherded a group of other couples into the area behind the curtain. "Okay, bambini," he said, "you're all fuckin' beautiful. Let's do this."

He turned up the music, grabbed his wireless mike, and headed out.

And soon they stepped through the curtain and took the catwalk, smiling under the bright sun before the eyes of hundreds of students. "Alexis Newton is wearing her own spring Dior, and she's escorted by Shawn Ackerman in Donatello's incredible two-hundred-fifty-dollar Geoffrey Beene special. . . . God bless America!"

THE RETARD BUS

Charity saw them grinning on the catwalk and threw up in a garbage can.

She dropped into her seat in Ms. Horn's bio room and groaned. Horn watered the Swedish ivy. "Awwwwww, sweetie, are you feeling okay?"

"Nooooo," moaned Charity. "I threw up three times, and I went to the nurse, and she just gave me a weird look and like this one little peppermint to eat."

Vic laughed. "That's because I told her you were pregnant last week."

Charity slapped his arm. "Viiiiiiiic," she wailed.

"Mr. Reyes," said the teacher, "that's not a nice thing to say about a young lady." She put down her bottle. "So *how* exciting is prom, you guys! Who here is going?"

A thicket of hands sprang up around Charity.

Ms. Horn sat on a lab bench. "Oh, my God. Your prom is *so* nice. I wish I were in high school so I could take a date to it."

"You should go anyway," said Jasmine.

Ms. Horn shrugged. "Well, my little friend in the other period asked me to go with him."

Charity looked up with bloodshot eyes. "*You* got asked to prom."

Ms. Horn laughed. "Yeah. This junior came up to me, and he was like, 'I think you'd be a lot of fun at prom. Would you want to go to prom . . . with me?' And I said, 'No, sweetie, I don't party with my students.' Isn't that the funniest thing?"

"Oh, my God," said Jasmine. "Who was it?"

"I can't tell you that," said Ms. Horn, "but his last name rhymes with 'Medina.'"

"Oh, my God," said Jasmine. "Eric Medina? He's so cute."

Ms. Horn smiled. Charity let her head fall onto the epoxy table.

"They have some tight stuff out there in the quad," said Forrest. "It was really funny to see all those limos next to the retard bus."

"You mean the party bus?" asked Vic.

"No," said Forrest. "There was like literally a retard bus there too with actual retards inside."

Vic turned to the highlighted head moaning on the table. "You were on it, right, Charity?"

Her frazzled face popped up. "Huh? What bus? What are you talking about?"

Laughter filled the cool room. Charity whirled on the sniggering Vic. "I don't like you. You're a jerk!"

Ms. Horn pounded the desk as she gasped for air between howling gales of laughter. Charity glared at her. "I don't like you, either. You're a jerk, too."

"Charity, sweetie," whooped the teacher, "no one thinks you're actually a retard."

THE PAIN THAT MAKES US PURE

Thea sat on the steps behind the library at lunch. She ate her pastrami sandwich and turned to the skin.

"I really want to go to prom," she said, "but I don't know any upperclassmen, you know?" She watched him carefully. "It sucks not knowing any upperclassmen."

"Huh," he said, staring at a paperclip in his hand. He unbent the silver wire and pressed the tip to his earlobe.

"This is for the nation," he said, and slowly shoved the metal into his flesh. His face sweated and he clenched his teeth as the wire ripped open his skin and tore through his cartilage.

It poked out the other side of his lobe and blood trickled down the side of his neck. Thea gasped. He withdrew the paperclip and threw it on the ground.

"Are you piercing your ear again?" asked Evelyn.

He nodded solemnly. "Whenever it heals, I like pierce it again in memory of the struggle."

One of the gauzy girls watched the stream of blood flow down his neck. "You should just go to the swap meet. Piercing's cheap there."

"Hah," laughed Evelyn. "If you want hepatitis B, go to the swap meet. I have a piercing gun and I'll pierce whoever needs it."

The skin shook his head. "It's the pain that makes us pure."

After a while Thea ventured again. "Hey," she asked him casually, "so what are you doing for prom?"

He dragged his finger through the blood and watched it shine in the sun. "I'm going with this girl I know from Riverside."

Thea finished her food quickly. She left the steps alone and early, well before the ringing of the bell.

A VOYAGE INTO GLASS

That afternoon Alexis tossed her cigarette into the storm drain and walked toward the mailbox. Maybe the new *Cosmo* had come.

Inside she found a light blue sheaf of Valpak coupons, past-due credit card bills, and a white envelope from the American University of Monaco.

She slid her thumb numbly along the flap. The paper tore open.

"Congratulations."

She stood there on the sidewalk, beneath the sun hanging above the palms, listening to the elementary schoolers shout in the park across the street. Wheels clattered on concrete as a guy with spiky blond hair skateboarded past. She turned and looked at the row of houses all designed like hers, and then up at the home she had lived in for her entire life, the house her mother had died in three years before.

In the living room by the old piano she turned on the computer and typed "Monaco" into Google. She looked at a little dot on the other side of the planet, pressed between the coastline of France and Italy.

She clicked aimlessly through the university's page. Do I NEED A VISA? How/WHERE DO I CHANGE MONEY? "Our student body is exceptionally diverse: 24 percent from Asia, 18 percent from Africa, 19 percent from South America . . ." A profile of an MBA from Poland.

She gently rubbed the bruise on her shin from their powder-puff win.

Travis walked in the door smirking forty minutes later, talking on his cell phone. "Listen, it's a good investment. Look at the guy, he used to be my size, and now his arms are as thick as my neck. . . ."

He saw Alexis and the phone immediately dangled forgotten by his side. "What? What happened? What?"

On Friday evening, she and her father drove north, far north, to where the endless grid of Southern California lights coalesces upward into tall glass columns. They went to separate meeting rooms in a reflective tower at the Los Angeles Convention Center.

"Me too," said Sara.

"I'll be in the shade," said Charity. "Have fun."

She spent the twenty minutes getting annoyed under the awning of the beer garden, watching hundreds of drunk people buy and spill clear plastic cups. A few bulky men stepped on her toes.

She thought of a number of different ways to communicate her anger and displeasure, and when she saw the tall and thin silhouette of Wil emerging from the blazing incandescence next to Sara's short and curvy one, she pulled herself up rigidly and prepared her best frosty tone.

She opened her mouth at the same time Sara jumped up and down and grabbed her arms and screamed, "Oh, my fucking God!"

Charity lost the initiative. "What?"

"Water," gasped Wil, leaning on a tent pole. "I need water."

"Oh, my God," Sara said to Charity. "Okay, so we pushed our way to the front of the crowd, and we got up to the gate for backstage, and the guy was like a total asshole and wouldn't let us through because we didn't have the right wristband."

"Hah!" said Charity. "See, I—"

"So," said Sara, "we went *under* the stage."

Charity paused. "You did what?"

"We like slipped underneath the stage," said Sara, "and we came out in the back in this like VIP area. Oh, my God, Charity, everybody was back there. Wil met the lead singer of Something Corporate."[5]

"Yuh," said Wil.

"You're fucking shitting me," said Charity flatly.

"No," said Sara. "And then we met the Kottonmouth Kings."

Charity, who slept under a poster of them, could only manage the word "no."

"And we hung out with them," said Sara. "We all like chilled."

Charity shook her head.

"I showed them the pictures of all of us I had in my wallet," said Sara. "They saw one of the pictures of you, and one of the guys was like, 'How old is she?'

"And I was like, 'Uh, she's nineteen.'

"And he like smiled and was like, 'She should come chill with us next time.'"

It took a few moments for Charity to find speech.

"Oh, my God," she whimpered, "I would just have sex with them any-where. Right now. It's not slutty if you fuck a rock star." She whipped off her sunglasses. "Oh, my God, what if I could get him to go to the prom with me? It's only like a couple hours. How would fucking Alexis New-ton feel then? She'd feel like a piece of shit. Oh, my God, we're going back *right now*."

She lunged from the shade and plowed out onto the field, platform sandals clomping on the grass. "Come on," she screamed. "Run! How did you get back there?"

Sara plodded along. "Wil figured it out."

Charity shaded her eyes and spun wildly. "Where's Wil?"

In the distance, he stumbled slowly toward them across the grass.

Charity grabbed him and propelled him forward. "Come on!" she shrieked. "We've gotta get back there."

They plunged into the back of the crowd by the outdoor theater, an oceanic horde of ten to twenty thousand people. Death Cab for Cutie played on the stage. Charity gripped Sara's arm and pushed Wil along in front of her, driving him like a plow through the flailing bodies.

"Go," she urged. "Go."

In the center of the multitudes, and a few yards from the stage, concert-goers passed along a huge bottle of water. Wil stretched out his fingers to try and grasp it, but she shoved him forward and it drifted out of reach. A camera flashed from high scaffolding, preserving the moment forever.

Several steps later, Charity's dreams crumpled with Wil as he pitched forward, unconscious.

OPENING GRANDMA

On Monday, Thea sat in the back corner of the annoying room. In front of her on the lab table lay their cat, flayed open into a terrifying and col-orful mass of lungs and intestines.

The junior with smelly breath hung over her shoulder as she worked. He ate Chinese food out of a little oily take-out container. "I'm trying to stay back because I like don't want to get my teriyaki chicken on the cat," he said.

Ms. Horn entered through the little hallway. "Hello, my friends," she told everybody. "I have a video that I think will be very educa-tional for us."

She pushed the tape into her player.

On the huge screen appeared a naked, wrinkled, shiny old woman with a head of frizzy white hair. Gloved hands hovered above her with a scalpel.

"This is an exhibition dissection we did at the school a number of years ago," said Ms. Horn cheerfully. "We don't do them anymore because it takes seven gallons of embalming fluid, and we can't afford it. It's someone's grandma, hopefully none of you guys'."

The room, normally a din of random conversations, fell utterly silent except for the steady slurping of teriyaki.

"Up at the university they had someone's aunt, and it was just a bad scene. Mr. Kostopoulos used to dissect the bodies in this room very late at night, like 11:00 P.M., and the janitor wouldn't come into the sciences quad because he thought it was haunted. Well, I hope you all learn something."

She walked back into the cool room.

The image shuddered. "First let's move her arm out of the way here," rumbled a man's voice. He wrenched it sideways and it clunked on the metal table.

"Now," said the man, "watch how we open her skin."

He dug in with the scalpel, and began peeling back layers. They crinkled like paper.

Some people in the room put their faces down on the lab benches. Thea couldn't turn her head.

The hands produced a circular blade. "This is a bone saw." They fired it up and drove it into grandma's exposed ribs with a screeching whine.

Thea's lab partner sucked up some slippery chicken. "I would dissect my mother," he said. "I love my mother dearly, but I'm a scientist and I love to take things apart and see how they work, and the only way to do that is to dissect something."

Thea swallowed. "Hey," she said after a while. "The guys in your grade are pussies. You guys aren't asking any girls to prom this year."

He shrugged and glanced at a table across the room.

"Why do you keep looking over there?" said Thea. "You can go hang out with your other friends if you want."

He looked at her. "Are you sure?"

"Yeah," she said. "I've got the cat covered."

"Thanks," he said, and moved seats. The bone saw whined.

MISSING

On Thursday, a piece of paper appeared on the California pepper tree at the center of the senior circle. Everyone gathered around to read it.

> The Robert Doveman Memorial Award
> A monetary award will be made
> to honor an extraordinary student
> who best exemplifies the Spirit of Dove
> through his or her achievements
> as Scholar, Athlete, and Leader.

Alexis covered her mouth. "Oh, my God."

Derrick stepped back and stared at leaves on the ground. "It's probably his college fund."

Cody didn't say anything or even go to look. He just sat alone on the ring in his baseball jersey and cap.

After a while everyone returned to their sections of the circle and quieter conversations.

Kaylee had a copy of the *Los Angeles Times*. Alexis put her finger on the front page of the Calendar section, a color crowd shot of a concert. "See that guy reaching for the water? That's like my brother's friend. He's the guy whose band always plays at lunch."

"Huh," said Kaylee. "Weird."

The Dove sign flapped in the breeze.

"Hey," said Kaylee, "you're not really going to Europe or whatever, are you?"

Alexis ate her ice pop. "I don't know."

"But everybody's like here," said Kaylee. "You wouldn't know anybody. What if you didn't like it and you got stuck there? It would be so horrible."

"Yeah," said Alexis. "Everybody's telling me to stay. I don't know what to do. I mean, this is my home, I love it here."

"All of us girls have to stick together," said Padma. "I'm gonna be lonely. Come visit me on the weekends, bitch."

Alexis smiled softly. "Yeah, bitch."

"Like the whole process is so random," said Padma. "If you did well next year at Emerald College I promise you you could transfer in. I mean, you have a friggin' three-point-eight."

Ross wore a wristband from Biola University on his forearm. "Yeah," he said. "You gotta stay in So Cal. At least they would give you like vacations, right?"

Alexis shook her head. "Only Christmas. And the woman said most people stay in Europe over the summer too." She sighed. "I'm so confused."

She walked over to the trash can and dumped her Popsicle stick. On the way back she stopped near Cody. He still sat alone, chin on his hand.

"Hey," she said.

His pale blue eyes turned to her face. "It's like he was my brother. It's like I'm missing a part of myself."

She didn't say anything. He looked at the tree. "We were going on a cruise after graduation. We were going to Cabo. Afterward we thought we'd go to the same college."

"Where are you going next year?" Alexis asked softly.

"I don't know. I think I'm going to try to get in on the players draft."

"Do you think you can?"

"I don't know."

A loud pack of sophomores passed behind the circle. "Well, definitely," said Alexis. "Like good luck with all of that, okay?"

He stayed silent and she turned to go.

"Hey," he said. "You know what?"

She stopped and looked back. "What?"

"Last summer," he said, "like me and Dove spent two weeks playing 007 with his cousin and his sister. Dove and me were the best and we won like every time. And that's like basically all we did for two solid weeks, we just played 007. And we ate Starburst ice cream, bowls and bowls of Starburst ice cream." He smiled. "Those were the greatest weeks ever."

THE DREAMERY

That Saturday at work, so many of Charity's fantasies came true that she probably wondered if she had sold her soul by mistake.

Their manager April—she of the genius IQ and model looks, who had daily condescended to grace the Creamery with her presence—dropped her collection of smelly markers into an old SYSCO napkin box.

"I mean, it's fine by me," she said. "It's not *my* problem. It's good for *me*. If Creamery corporate doesn't realize who they had working for them, I clearly need to be somewhere else. I've got a lot of options in life."

She carried a roll of butcher paper out to her car past the blinking eyes of Charity and the pregnant girl.

"Uh," said Charity, "what are we supposed to do?"

"Hah!" April barked at the acoustic tiling. "It doesn't matter to me. I don't care what you do. *I* don't work here anymore. I'm taking my final week as sick days, starting at the end of this shift."

Her two employees stared at each other. "Ding-dong, the witch is dead," whispered Charity. They started to giggle.

The door tinkled merrily, and a tall buff guy walked in hauling a rolling cooler full of Monster energy drinks and a box of Monster condoms.

"Uh, hi," said Charity.

"Hey," said the guy. He gave her a brilliant smile. He had spiky hair and tattoos on his arms. "Like we're doing this promotion for Monster with the local Creameries, and I wondered if it would be cool if I set up here for an hour?"

"Uh," said Charity. "Sure."

The pregnant girl scooped him ice. "He's *hot*," she whispered.

Charity nodded. "He's so fucking hot."

Customers came in and he gave them free energy drinks and condoms. Soon Charity struck up a conversation. "Hey," she said. "Do you ride?"

"Yeah," he said. "I've got two bikes. I actually just got back from the des out at Glamis."[6]

They talked moto for a while. His name was Caleb and he was twenty-five.

"You remind me of my old boyfriend," said Charity. "He looked a lot older too and he had muscles like you."

She went to the back bathroom to fix her hair, and April snapped at her. "Why don't you just get his number while you're at it?"

"Go for it," hissed the pregnant girl, "go for it!"

Over the next thirty minutes, Charity floated ever-so-gently the concept of an upcoming dance in a week, a prom even, and how alas she had become dateless at this late date. And Caleb remembered his days at the prom and what fun it had been. And Charity wondered if perhaps he might wish to recapture those days.

And Caleb laughed and thought it sounded tight.

When his hour ended, he gave her a Monster condom with his number written on the back.

"We'll make this happen," he said, and rolled out with cans in tow.

Charity showed the condom to April on her final exit. Their ex-manager growled and slammed the tinkly door, clearing herself from the Creamery forever.

"Whooohooo!" screamed Charity.

She hugged the pregnant girl and turned up the music on the store system.

"Life is so fucking perfect!" she yelled. "I can't wait to see Alexis Newton at prom and say"—she flung her arms wide—"'Look who I'm dancing with! Look whose penis I'm holding!' She can have Shawn. Oh, my God, she's just going to like fuck off and do a fucking mercy killing and shoot herself."

She raced into the back room where April's giant scrolls of community college teachings hung from the walls, and she spat on them. She and the pregnant girl took turns hocking saliva to see who could hit them the farthest.

Then Charity laughed wildly. "Why didn't we do this earlier?" she shrieked, and began to rip them down. The pregnant girl dove into action alongside her, and the wall of paper collapsed in shreds.

SILENCE

Rays of daylight from high windows lanced through the dusty air backstage on Monday.

Thea walked through the patches of sun and shade until she reached the set piece where Evelyn sat with her legs in lotus.

"Hey," said Thea. She sat on a windowsill and looked down at the scuffed gray floor. "I've been having the weirdest feeling. Do you ever have this like really intense sensation that there's someone out there who might really care about you or whatever, like really care, but they don't even know you exist? Maybe it's all wishful.

"It's like I have a good personality, but that doesn't get you anywhere at this school. It sure doesn't get you friends and popularity. Nobody even knows about it. It's like I'm totally invisible and it's really frustrating. I like so look forward to theater every day. It's the one time I can talk to people. I feel like I'm going crazy without anyone to talk to, I don't know. I write in my online journal and no one even comments on it, like no one reads it and no one cares."

Evelyn sat silent.

"Do you know what I mean?" asked Thea.

Evelyn put her right hand into her pocket, briefly destroying the mudra of union and returning her to duality. She produced a business card and held it out to Thea.

Thea took it and read:

This is the National Day of Silence.
I am being silent today to protest the treatment of gay, lesbian,
bisexual, and transgender youth.
Think about what the silence means.

"Oh," said Thea, and handed it back. After a while she walked away across the creaky floor.

CONFITEOR

After school, Shawn pulled off Alexis's shirt and pushed her down on her Nautica bedspread. Matching curtains hung over the window.

He kissed her. "Stay with us," he said, and kissed her again. "Don't go."

She turned her head and closed her eyes. "I don't know," she said. "I was like about to fill out the papers for Emerald College last night but then I didn't. Everyone's telling me to go there except for one person."

"Who?" he asked.

Her head moved slightly. "I want to do international business, and Monaco has one of the top programs in Europe. That's why I even applied, you know? But I want to stay with my friends too. I like can't sleep, it's not knowing what I should do."

He stood and walked to the glossy folder lying on her desk. He flipped through pictures of women in head scarves and white ships on the Mediterranean. He shook his head and dropped it back on the table.

"When do you have to tell them by?"

"Friday," she said. "Like the day before prom." She curled up in a ball and pulled her pillow under her head. "Oh, my God, Shawn, that Dove thing on the tree is so sad."

He sat in her rolling chair. "Yeah," he said.

For a while only the air conditioning made a sound. "Are you falling asleep?" he asked her.

She shook her head. "He wanted me to ask him to Sadie's."

"Who did?" asked Shawn.

"Dove," said Alexis. "Cody and I had broken up, and Dove told me he liked me and wanted me to ask him to Sadie's. I thought it was pretty funny. You know, he was kind of a dork, he was goofy, and I told him no. And then the whole thing happened two days later, and I just went as friends with Cody."

Shawn looked down. He looked at the simple geometric pattern on a rug that matched the bed and the curtains.

"I was going to fight him," he said.

Alexis opened her eyes. "Who?"

Shawn chewed his fingernail. "Like Dove. He was talking a bunch of shit that really pissed me off, and I was going to fight him, like right before it happened. Cody was caught, like he was stuck in a tough spot, because he agreed with me. Like he took my side and got my back even though Dove was his boy, and then it happened right after. I think that really messed Cody up."

Alexis sat up in bed and pulled her knees to her chest. "I didn't know that." She swallowed. "I didn't even know that. I guess there's a lot of stuff we don't talk about in Emerald Valley."

A high-pitched beeping split the air. Shawn grimaced. "What's that?"

"Don't even ask," she said. "I dropped my old cell phone in the sink and now I've got like this temporary one." She leaned over and pulled it from her backpack. "Hi, Daddy," she said. The clock read three-fifteen, and he returned from work at five.

"Hi," he said. "Have you gotten home yet?"

"Yeah," she said.

His voice cut in and out. "Is anybody there?"

"No," she said, "just me."

"You're home alone?" he said.

"Yeah."

He paused. "Whose truck is parked outside?"

She inhaled sharply.

An instant later, she screamed as the door to her room banged open. Her father looked at the two of them shirtless.

"Get dressed," he said. He pointed at Shawn. "Go home."

Ten minutes later Alexis cried in the driveway as her father yanked open the hood to her Camry.

"I obviously can't trust you at all," he said. He wrenched on gloves and dug into the machinery. "Since I can't trust you, you're not leaving this house after five, you're not leaving this house on the weekend, and you've lost your car privileges."

Something clunked under the hood. "Oh, shit!" he screamed. "Okay, your car's not disabled, it's broken." He threw a metal tube on the ground at her feet.

"I'm ashamed of you," he yelled. "You think you're mature enough to go off across the world, but you're obviously still a child."

He slammed the front door to the house as she sobbed.

DYNAMITE AND NEW DRESSES

A few days later everybody at school heard about a bomb threat at the upscale Westside Pavilion shopping complex in Los Angeles. High-intensity explosives, a credible tip informed the authorities, would detonate and scythe the consumerist ziggurat and nearby federal building from the empire of the infidel. Panic and police had converged, and the media had taken the story national. The mayor weighed in, aides briefed Governor Schwarzenegger. Could any American rest safe?

Charity decided to go shopping. "When like those threats go up," she told Sara, "and we're scared, then we're doing what the terrorists want. And they have the kind of prom dresses I want to show up Alexis Newton and I don't have much time left."

She had talked to twenty-five-year-old Caleb a few times and he definitely seemed serious and on for the prom. So Charity grabbed Sara and drove up to the very same Westside Pavilion on the very same day after school in her pink Mustang GT with the tinted windows.

She marched right past the police into an expensive-looking and very deserted store. "I need the perfect prom dress," she told the saleslady.

The saleslady tilted her head. "What's your price range?"

"It doesn't really matter," said Charity. "I have to show someone up."

Nothing looked right off the rack, so they discussed the option of having a dress custom-made. The saleslady gravitated to the number five hundred and seventy-five in dollars American.

"All right," said Charity.

Sara pulled her behind a gilt mirror for an urgent conference. "That's *expensive*," she hissed. "You're only wearing this dress one night. That's like two months of work for you at the Creamery."

"It's worth it to get a dress that no one else has," said Charity. "Money's like only good if you do something with it. And I have to show up that stupid slut Alexis Newton and her stupid Dior. Oh, my God, I want to kill her."

She slapped down her credit card.

NEWS FROM THE HOME FRONT

Evening fell, and Thea squished open the high hydraulic doors to her villa and stepped into the atrium. According to the photo contest information, winners would receive notice that day. She checked the mahogany reception table by the indoor fountain but didn't find anything, of course. She had gotten beyond the stage of believing she had anything to offer the world.

Her parents sat watching TV in the side octagonal room, mainly news footage from the Westside Pavilion.

"Thea," her father said, "your mother and I have something that we'd like you to take a look at."

Her eyes widened. Her heart thudded. Oh, my God, could it possibly be . . .

He rose, shuffled over to her in his slippers, and handed her several sheets of paper. She glanced down at them:

12. More courteous to her parents and respectful of their wishes, not consistently arguing and talking back.
13. Does not create extra work for the housekeeper by leaving her clothing around the laundry room.
14. Makes a noticeable effort to correct her posture and not slump.

15. Does not continually place her own desires before the needs
of others. . . .

Thea looked up at him. "What is this?"

Her father tapped the pages. "It's a list of things we think you should
work on improving."

Thea's mouth fell slack. "You made a list of ways I'm not a good
daughter."

"It's not just about being a good daughter," he said, "it's everything.
You'll never get a boyfriend keeping on the way you are. Oh, I wanted to
put down about how you make weird sounds with your mouth, which
you do. A little *crkk-crkk* noise." He took a heavy silver pen from a side
table.

Thea started to cry and flung the packet. It fluttered to the floor and
she ran upstairs.

CHANGING THE CURVE

Alexis sat quietly in Ms. Schroeder's class on Friday, waiting for the first
bell. Vic leaned back from his desk.

"Hey," he said, "what's up?"

She looked at her pencil. "Everything," she said. "I like don't know
what I'm doing with my life and I have to figure it out today, and I'm like
basically my dad's prisoner until graduation, and Schroeder gave us a D
on the video project, which means they're probably going to take away
my college offer anyway."

Vic looked around the room. "Hey," he said, "me and Shawn got a zero
even though we like worked really hard and had all the material in it."

She sighed. "Yeah. I know. This class is so unfair."

"I think everybody in this class needs As and Bs on their video projects," said Vic.

Alexis smiled a little.

"See," said Vic. "That cheered you up." He looked around. "I'm going
to do it."

"What?" said Alexis. "Oh, my God, don't, Vic. You've got those
strikes. . . ."

He shrugged. "Go distract her, like get her out of here. That bitch is
such a machine she won't even notice."

He stood. Alexis clutched her head briefly and then breathed and stood. She walked to the desk. "Hey, Ms. Schroeder."

Schroeder poked through a drawer selecting the day's lecture tape. "Yes?"

"Did you hang up our movie poster outside?" Alexis asked.

"No," said Ms. Schroeder. "Why?"

"Because I totally saw our poster on the gate," she said. "Look at this."

She beckoned frantically. Schroeder frowned and waded out the door after her.

Vic dove for the teacher's chair. The whole room stared at him. "I'm changing her grades," he announced. Faces lit up like the power grid after a rolling blackout. He turned to the computer and double-clicked on her electronic grade book.

PASSWORD:

"What's her password?" he called to the class. People yelled out suggestions.

"I'm going to try 'dyke,'" said Vic, and did. "Damn."

He selected a group of folders. "I hope these are important," he said, dragging them to the Trash and emptying it.

A leather edge protruded from a low sliding tray. "Chello," he said. "What's this?" He tugged out her paper grade book, erased and scribbled.

"Vic," yelped Kaylee.

He jumped to his feet and started sharpening a pencil just as Alexis and Schroeder returned. "Wow, I guess it really looked like our poster," Alexis said. The teacher shook her head.

"Oh, my God," Alexis whispered, when they had sat safely. "Did you get it?"

"Yeah," said Vic. He grinned. "We're good on all the community experience and the multiple choice."

Her smile collapsed like Padma at a party. "Vic, we haven't taken the multiple-choice yet. She'll know something's up. You've gotta erase that!"

"Distract her again," he ordered. He snapped his pencil point and rose to sharpen it for the second time.

Alexis looked around desperately. She hurried back to the teacher's desk. "Ms. Schroeder? Don't you think like one of those signs on the gate had inappropriate language on it?"

Schroeder turned slides in her carousel. "I didn't notice anything, no."

"I thought I did," said Alexis. "I think it might be like really offensive to everybody to have it hanging up."

Schroeder seemed caught between the simple contentment of slides and the lure of possible inappropriate language to punish, but the latter proved too much to resist and she followed Alexis from the room.

Vic erased while everyone kept vigil through the door. Wild, giggling joy erupted after he fell back into his seat. A whole lot more happy seniors looked set to graduate.

Evelyn snorted. "Now this class is *totally* useless," she muttered.

SO BEAUTIFUL

At lunch, Charity checked her phone and found a message waiting. Her heart pounded as the electronic voice slowly recited twenty-five-year-old Caleb's number. Maybe he had plans for them tonight, the night before the prom. Maybe he had fallen in love.

"Hey," said the recording, "look, some stuff came up and my band's not letting me go to your dance thing tomorrow, sorry about that. I'm sure you're cool with it, but I just wanted to give you the heads-up so you don't like wait for me or whatever."

Charity leaned against a wall for support. As soon as she could think again she slammed in the number for the Westside Pavilion store and misdialed twice.

They had finished her dress that morning and charged her card five hundred and seventy-five dollars.

"You can come pick it up anytime!" burbled the woman. "It's beautiful."

"Can I return it?" said Charity.

The woman paused, shocked. "No," she said, "it's custom-made just for you. Why would you want to? It's beautiful."

Charity shoved her way through the crowds of people in the food court and central quad but couldn't find Sara. As she pushed she started to cry. "Alexis Newton," she sobbed, "fucking Alexis Newton."

The pack of freshman girls saw her and laughed.

She called her mom on the phone. "I hate school," she said. "I have one friend and that's Sara."

She dried her tears in front of the cracked aluminum mirror in a smelly bathroom with paper towels strewn across the floor. She walked to the junior steps and listened to all the girls talk about their prom groups.

SELFISH

Thea came back from the theater along the tennis courts and saw Wil and a few other people gathered by the chain-link fence. Sara slid her hands into his back pockets and the two of them laughed.

Evelyn stood at the salad bar, sprinkling vinegar over the organic chickpeas she had brought from home. Thea collapsed onto the plastic shield next to her.

"Oh, my God," she gasped. "I just saw this annoying cheerleader in my bio class throwing herself all over Wil in her slut makeup. How can he possibly like her? She's so superficial. Wil doesn't even know *me* at all."

She took a breath and blinked fast. "He doesn't know what I'm like. It's like with everybody, like I don't have any close friends at this school. People know who I am and they're like, 'Oh, that girl, she's in my class' or whatever, but that's it."

Evelyn rounded on her. "You're a selfish baby," she snapped. "It's always the same stuff. I don't have time for it in my life."

She left the salad bar and Thea didn't move. As the striped scarf disappeared into the crowds, Thea began to cry.

LOSING EVERYTHING

Alexis sat on the concrete ring of the senior circle with her watery ice pop. She had just chain-smoked two cigarettes.

One of the staples had fallen off the Dove sign and it jerked wildly in the breeze. Mr. Mulligan held up a hand in greeting as he walked past the circle.

Alexis opened her purse, and then pawed deep through the bag. "Oh, my God," she said, and tense fever quivered in her voice. "Oh, my, God. I don't believe it."

"What?" said Brian.

"I don't believe it," said Alexis. "I lost another cell phone. What the fuck is wrong with me?"

Brian rolled his eyes. "This always happens with Alexis," he told Steve.

She stared helplessly at the tree. Lilac-blue jacaranda blossoms had opened across the campus and now drifted in the warm wind.

"So what's the deal?" said Kaylee. "Are you going to stay with us or are you going to Europe?"

Ten people looked at her.

"I don't know," pleaded Alexis. "It's driving me crazy. I have like five hours to decide the next four years of my life. You don't understand, it's like such a weird school. It's not like anything here. It doesn't have any sororities or any sports. I'd lose all my family and friends and everything, and I wouldn't see them again like ever, and I miss you all and everyone already so much just thinking about it. But if I like stay in Emerald Valley, live at home, go to community college, I don't know. I mean, I should probably stay. . . ."

She trailed off, and her eyes watered. "Like whatever I do in my life, I'm always losing everything."

OUT

Charity's pale and haggard face towered above the office receptionist.

"Can I see like whatever papers you need for transferring?" she asked.

EMERGENCY

Thea hurried toward the auditorium with her prize.

She had stood in the Save Our School ice cream line behind that beautiful blond senior Alexis Newton. Everybody in the line pushed and shoved and Thea pressed up against Alexis's back. Their skin contacted, and Thea couldn't really understand what separated their two existences, besides everything, of course.

Skin to skin, although an alien electricity moved in Alexis that kept her unfathomably remote from an ordinary creature like Thea. Only Derrick Littlefield seemed more unreal. Like a celebrity or the president, he existed as pure image and not as a human being.

Thea couldn't understand the secret of Alexis, how to make a life so beautiful, perfect, and distant, but she knew how to deal with objects. She had noticed that Alexis had a cell phone sticking out of her little purse, and she had taken it almost automatically.

So now she had this cell phone. It looked pretty cheesy, and it didn't even have any numbers in it. Wasn't Alexis supposed to be like the most popular girl in the school? Hah. *Hah.*

She crossed the lunch court past a thousand people who didn't look at her. She saw her brother patiently lugging his shiny garbage bag.

She stepped in the side door of the auditorium, walked through the abandoned creaking world of backstage, and pressed herself behind a dusty curtain.

Thea knew how to be tricky and pulled her long-sleeve T-shirt down over her hands so she wouldn't leave fingerprints. She wiped the cell phone clean. Then action seized her, almost as if she watched herself behind a wall of glass.

She dialed a few numbers and pressed Talk. The line rang only once.

"Verizon 911," said a woman's voice. "Emergency operator."

"There's a bomb in the sciences quad at Mirador High School in Emerald Valley," said Thea. "Every student is going to die."

The voice hesitated only a fraction of a second. "When's the bomb scheduled to explode?"

"Now," said Thea.

"Where exactly is the bomb locat—" the voice began, but Thea hit End.

She tossed the cell phone into an open locker in the languages quad and resumed her role, walking beneath the light purple blossoms as someone who didn't matter and whom nobody noticed.

But her heart pounded, because now she only played a role. She knew that she had turned the world upside down, and that right now she mattered more than Derrick Littlefield himself.

The sirens screamed less than three minutes later.

UNTIL THE CEREMONY

Mirador executed its classroom earthquake drills with the precision of science and the grace of art. White-gloved proctors, student volunteers, and neatly directed battalions of evacuees all marched along in a rousing Victorian parade.

During a real emergency, however, nobody had the slightest idea what to do.

The two penetrating alarm notes oscillated, and an oracular command rang from the immense array of speakers. "Mirador, this is Dr.

Chao, and this is a level one evacuation. Please proceed immediately to your rendezvous points." *Click.*

Two thousand students and a hundred and fifty faculty and staff members promptly froze up.

Why had Dr. Chao taken over herself?

"What's going on? Why isn't it Pooper?"

What was a Level One evacuation?

"Is it a drill? Wait, is this a drill? It's a drill, right?"

Who would direct people, and to where?

Everyone looked around but nobody seemed to step up and take charge. The proctors jogged around as confused as everybody else.

"What are we supposed to do?" everybody asked them, but they had no idea.

What rendezvous point corresponded to people who ate lunch by the lockers in the language arts quad?

Enterprising faculty searched the walls. Some quads had Level One evacuation maps encased behind plastic, other quads didn't. The majority of evacuation maps assumed the modular buildings and the assembly hall didn't exist. They called for a heroic charge through several walls' worth of concrete and plywood.

The thousands swarmed, ambled. They found consensus. "It's a fire drill. It's a new kind of fire drill."

Then people heard police sirens and panic thrilled through the crowds.

"Bomb," said somebody. "It's a bomb, fool."

Official rendezvous point or not, over two thousand bodies soon found themselves huddled out in the parking lots as far from the concrete starfish as possible.

"Everyone's giving me strange looks," said Darius the Persian guy.

Charity wandered through the tense and babbling assembly gathered on the asphalt. Sirens warbled and lights flashed as police and staff teams combed through trash cans and classrooms. Blue-jacketed bodies appeared on roofs.

She drank evenly from a chilly plastic bottle of Diet Coke. She didn't care what happened to Mirador or any of them. Let them all blow up. She hated the school in general, and one person in specific.

"I'm going to kick her ass," she mumbled. Her hands felt clammy, but she knew if she could do one thing, it was fight. Everything had to end now.

She spotted Alexis's long blond hair easily among the seniors. The homecoming queen seemed quiet and withdrawn, huddled in on herself.

Charity took a quick breath, walked up behind her, and pretended to stumble over Padma's foot. "Oh," she said, "whoops," and emptied the bottle of Diet Coke all over Alexis.

Alexis just froze for a moment, sticky and dripping. She shook liquid from her hand, pushed back her wet hair. "Ohhhhhhh," chorused a bunch of people.

She turned slowly and saw Charity.

"Bitch," snarled Alexis. "Fuck you." Her hand whirled up and slapped Charity in the face.

Charity screamed and lashed at her, Alexis grabbed for Charity's neck, and they sagged first to grappling on knees, and then fell backward onto the rough blacktop in a scratching, punching pile.

"Fight!" yelled the person who always yelled it.

Alexis knocked Charity's head on the ground and Charity yanked a strand of hair from Alexis's head. The long blond wisp hit the asphalt.

Padma gasped. "Oh, my God." She jumped into the fight and kicked Charity. Kaylee joined her. Sara pushed through the crowd and punched Padma.

Cody threw them all back. "Everyone clear away," he screamed. "One-on-one." His face had flushed and his eyes gleamed. "This is a clean fight. This is one-on-one."

The crowds stumbled away and juniors, seniors, everybody formed a growing circle around the two girls fighting in the center of an empty patch of ground.

Klaxons and sirens howled and lights flashed and Charity and Alexis rolled in a churning free-for-fall, clawing at each other's faces, grunting, shrieking, bleeding, and crying.

"This is like so much worse than a guy fight," mumbled a junior.

People pulled out their cell phones and trained the ring of plastic lenses in and downward. Everybody wanted to capture the action with photos and full-motion video.

"I'm gonna stab you," gasped Charity. "I have a knife. I'm gonna cut you."

She pulled a penknife from the elastic band around her tiny skirt, but she couldn't even get it open before Alexis knocked it from her hand and it spun away across the asphalt.

And then it seemed like the fight flipped, and Alexis kneeled on top of Charity, held her down, and punched her in the throat. Charity seemed to stop fighting back, just tried to move away from Alexis's blows and shield herself.

The crowd cheered when Alexis stood unsteadily and Charity didn't.

"Hah!" said someone. "Nobody liked her."

A dozen people surrounded Alexis. "Are you okay?" they asked. She had some bruises and a bleeding lip.

She laughed weakly and rubbed her head. "Yeah. I just kicked my way out."

Padma hugged her. "Yeah, girl."

Brian held up her arm. "Alexis fucking kicked ass!"

"I've got to clean up for prom." She giggled.

Shawn hugged her. "You're hot anyway."

Distant parts of the parking lot began to laugh as action shots of Charity getting socked in the face passed from phone to phone. Somebody made it his background image.

Charity hauled herself painfully to her feet and stumbled away in silence, head down.

After an hour the police pronounced the sciences quad clean, and everybody went to sixth period as usual. Mr. Popper took the PA to inform the school that "the bomb threat was a learning experience."

Detectives had quickly identified that the phone used to make the call belonged to one Alexis Newton, but she had forty witnesses to both her whereabouts in the circle at the end of lunch and her inability to hang on to a phone. The cops recovered and returned it to her with a warning to keep closer watch on her property. She promised she would.

When last bell rang, everybody talked about the big party that night at Nicole's house, and the girls agreed to meet beforehand and drink.

Padma drove her home, and Alexis smoked a cigarette under the palms and bright sun before she entered. She walked through the living room past the portrait of her mother on the old piano and climbed the creaky stairs to her neat color-coordinated room. She saw the Monaco papers lying in a pile on her desk and barely hesitated.

She picked them up and filled them out and dropped them into the corner mailbox, legally and contractually binding herself to a completely new life on the far side of a much wider planet.

Thea's housekeeper Conchi hit the button on the remote attached to the sun visor and the iron gates to the Danielian house swung open. She parked and Thea and Aram climbed from the Jaguar XJ sedan.

The mahogany reception table by the indoor fountain lay empty.

"No mail today, huh?" Thea said.

"*Ay,*" said Conchi, "I just go and take it." She handed Thea a packet from the Getty.

Inside lay a letter. "You are a brilliant young visual artist," it said. It contained details about the award ceremony live on television where she would claim second place in the photography division and speak about her art to all of Southern California. It contained her admission to a selective art camp over the summer and her five-thousand-dollar prize check.

"Oh, my God," said Thea, and started to cry for the second time that day.

In the administration building at Mirador, a hundred faculty members gathered before a group of policemen.

One officer took out a digital voice recorder. He pressed a button and a girl's trembling tones rose from the tiny speaker. "There's a bomb in the sciences quad at Mirador High School in Emerald Valley. Every student is going to die."

"Is this a student in any of your classes?" he asked. "Does anybody recognize this voice?"

Ms. Horn looked up. "Yes," she said. "I do."

An hour later, the gate buzzed, and the sonorous bell tolled throughout the Danielian house.

Conchi opened the door to find two squad cars parked around the fountain with an arrest warrant for Thea. They handcuffed and Mirandized her and put her in the back of a cruiser. They booked her into Orange County Juvenile Hall, where she would wait until her felony court trial.

Like everything in this world, the event contained an admixture of good and bad. On the plus side, it meant that everyone knew who she was, and she could sound more badass on future standardized surveys.

BACK TO A BEGINNING

Thus spun the wheel of life.

For me prom time held a different kind of trauma.

When the shimmering concourses of our great formal dance glittered in the distance, I called my cousin and begged for a stunning classmate. I actually knew women in their midtwenties who wanted to go, but I realized I couldn't just trot out a derivatives analyst and expect her to transform into a plausible seventeen-year-old. I needed the real deal.

One twist—since we had to preserve secrecy, my cousin couldn't describe the project until we had sworn the chosen girl to silence. He could only plead with various possibilities to go "as friends" on a blind date to a random prom.

One brave soul agreed. Her name turned out to be Heather—the same appellation I had given my imaginary girlfriend.

"Dude." He laughed. "That's the girl I wanted to get. She's the best-looking girl at my school."

O miraculum miraculorum.

Terrorist attacks abroad meant Heather came back from her program in Barcelona just in time for prom. After the dance she vanished again. Perhaps she couldn't get away on the weekends. Maybe she went to her aunt's alfalfa farm in Fresno. It never came up.

The great thing about life is that everyone is so wrapped up in themselves that they don't care about stuff like that.

But now Heather is very much here, to bring us to the point we left off long ago, and we are dancing in the ancient sandstone shell under bright stars.

Suddenly the music halts. Voices whisper and stomachs clench. Has the moment arrived for Derrick to crown a prom king and queen?

The microphone clunks. Everyone turns, expecting magic. They get a retina-full of livid Mr. Popper standing in front of the DJ, bright red face and bloodshot eyes.

"Stop," he commands. "We're stopping this dance. I want everyone to take out their list of prom guidelines."

Muttering and whispering.

He starts to point to people. "You, why aren't you taking out your guidelines? Where's your sheet?"

We all got a scrap of paper when we arrived at the dance and promptly forgot it. Soon most of us dig it from our tuxedo pockets and squint at the tiny print.

"Read with me," he says. "Item number six. 'Mirador Senior High School prohibits sexually explicit dancing, including freaking, bumping, grinding, juking, lap dancing, go-go, innuendo, prone positions, straddling, fondling, crotch-to-crotch dancing, inappropriate hand placement, floor dancing, booty dancing, and sandwich dancing.' Right there. Maintain your distances."

Popper turns slowly to glare at the silent throng of tuxedos and sparkling gowns. His voice rings off the primeval stone. "This school isn't MTV. You aren't dancing like you see on TV. Your behavior is unacceptable, and now we're enforcing the rules."

PART FOUR

ACCREDITATION

However, grown-up games are known as "business," and even though the games of youth are much the same, they are punished for them by their elders.

—Saint Augustine of Hippo,
Confessions

THE SEASON BEFORE WASC

"Good morning, Mirador Senior High School," trilled the announcements girl.

Her words rang from cinder block walls hastily plastered with computer-printed posters. Did they announce a club meeting, a sports event, a dance or play? Oh, no.

One green poster read: ESLR #5C—STUDENTS WILL BE HIGHER-ORDER INFORMATION-SEEKING CRITICAL THINKERS WHO ACCESS MEDIA RESOURCES AND MULTIPLE LEARNING STRATEGIES IN THE FORMULATION OF PERSUASIVE INDUCTIVE AND DEDUCTIVE ARGUMENTS.

"Please join me in the pledge of allegiance!"

As the school recited the pledge and the girl read the daily bulletin, dozens of pages flapped from the metal gates across the six empty quads. A large pink sign caught the breeze: ESLR #4A—STUDENTS WILL EMBRACE AND ANALYZE A DIVERSITY OF AESTHETIC, HISTORICAL, AND SOCIOCULTURAL PERSPECTIVES AND PARADIGMS.

The girl finished her announcements and wished everyone a great day. "The Word of the Day," said Derrick Littlefield's voice, "is *metemptosis.* Noun. The suppression of the bissextile day once every one hundred and thirty-four years in a lunar calendar. *Metemptosis.*"

A bright blue poster fluttered on the flagpole in the center of campus: ESLR #6D—STUDENTS WILL BE DEMOCRATIC AND PLURALISTIC CITI-

ZENS OF, AND CONTRIBUTORS TO, THE LOCAL, NATIONAL, AND GLOBAL
COMMUNITY WHO LINK THE STANDARDS-BASED CURRICULUM TO THEIR
PERSONAL GOALS.

The unmistakably accented voice of the principal clicked on. "Good
morning, Mirador High School, this is Dr. Chao. I want you all to remember that the standards are like the rain, and the ESLRs are like the
umbrella. Pitter, patter, pitter, patter, Mirador.

"My ESLR Challenge for you all today is to look around your rooms
and find any class work that meets Result 4C and tell your teacher to
write 'Result 4C' on it."

Several people tentatively scanned the walls of Mr. Lamarque's rigidly
ordered classroom.

"Don't you dare," he snapped.

He leaned on his labeled podium and spoke in quiet and carefully
modulated tones. "As you know, many teachers are panicking about our
six-year accreditation. They're worried about meeting the standards."

A long pause. He blinked. "I don't panic. I am always in complete
control of all situations. In this room . . . nothing changes. We're doing
everything perfectly already."

He adjusted his glasses. "To reconcile my strong disagreement with
using Class Time for this madness, we are dealing with these weeks as
quickly and efficiently as possible."

He pulled out the 890-page textbook. "Everybody take out a pencil
and open your copy of *Algebra and Trigonometry*. We're going to go
through every section of every chapter, and we're going to find and list
all of the standards we've met on every page."

Next period, Ms. Horn clapped her hands together above the din.
"Shhhhh, you guys, shhhhh. Come on, guys, shhhhh. We have to do the
standards."

The room quieted marginally. "My friend Ms. Dunbar, please read
me a standard for our class."

"Uh," said Sara, "okay." She picked up the sheet everyone had received.
Like almost everybody at Mirador raised on California's discarded
Whole Language program, she read in a halting monotone, and Ms.
Horn helped her on some words.[1]

"Standard 9H," read Sara. "As a result of the coordinated structures and functions of organ systems, the internal environment of the human body remains relatively homeostatic despite changes in the outside environment. As a basis for understanding this concept, students know the cellular and molecular basis of muscle contraction, including the roles of actin, myosin, Ca^{+2}, and ATP."

Ms. Horn sipped from her #1 TEACHER mug. "Uh, okay. How do we meet that standard?"

Even the usual conversations fell silent.

After a while Forrest spoke. "Is our school going to fail this?"

Ms. Horn smiled weakly.

Vic pushed his headphones onto his neck. "I can't believe this stupid shit. Why do we have to do this?"

"This is the way schools operate, my friends," said Ms. Horn. "I'll tell you the secrets of what we've all been doing here for the past few weeks."

"We don't want to know," mumbled Charity.

The teacher swiveled back and forth on her stool. "We have two things to deal with. One is ESLRs, which are our, uh, Expected Schoolwide Learning Results that everybody has to know. The other is our standards, which are different for every class." She pronounced "ESLRs" as "ehs-luhrs" like the rest of the school.

"When our friends on the WASC accreditation committee come next week, they're going to be inspecting everything and interviewing us at random to make sure we're a good school, and they judge us based on the ESLRs and the standards."

Jasmine drew on the lab bench. "What is WASC anyway?" she asked. Everybody pronounced it "wais."

"I believe it's the Western Association of Schools and Colleges. The basic idea is they accredit us for either six years, or three years, or no years. Six is the best, three means we have problems but pass, and zero is really bad."

Vic laughed. "Go for three!"

"Go for three," said Sara.

Ms. Horn snipped a new Lakers article from the paper. "It may be more likely than you think."

*   *   *

Mr. Mulligan scratched his frazzled white head as he looked at the standards sheet in his hand during third period.

"This stuff is driving me crazy," said one guy.

"I tend to agree with you," said Mulligan. "*Je suis d'accord.*"

"Everyone wants to ditch," said Alexis. "We're going to have senior ditch day then."

Mr. Mulligan laughed. "I'm tempted to ditch myself. I'm old as dirt, and I can just say I need to go *au médecin*. They don't even let us teachers ditch, we have to give a good reason and sign out with these forms." He held up a blue sheet.

"This WASC stuff is like the most boring and horrible thing we've ever done here," said a girl.

Mr. Mulligan coughed. "Listen, I'm not arguing. I'd rather just conduct my class as I usually do than focus on so-called standards."

One junior closed his sheet in his binder. "Let's not do it."

"Sack up and deal," said another guy. "It looks good when you apply to college to say the school has like a six-year rating."

"The seniors don't care about that," said Alexis. "They're already going to college."

Mr. Mulligan sighed and waggled the sheet. "*Venez.* We've got to go through these. '3F. We value and appreciate imagination and creativity.'"

Thirty-four voices chorused after him. "'We value and appreciate imagination and creativity.'"

Ms. Schroeder intertwined her fingers and stared at her standards sheet.

She had conspicuously taped a huge banner decorated with shooting stars and rainbows above the center of her whiteboard. I LOVE THE ESLRs! it read. THEY HELP ME PLAN MY FUTURE AND MAKE ME A BETTER PERSON!—A MIRADOR STUDENT.

Since everyone—students and teachers alike—loathed and despised the ESLRs with blazing and uniform passion, the puzzle existed as to whether it was a) painfully ironic and Schroeder hadn't caught on, b) made by Schroeder herself as an exceptionally cynical ploy, or c) understood by Schroeder to be ironic and hung up as a passive-aggressive statement of defiance.

All evidence pointed to c.

"These standards are very important for all of us," she said at last, with all the conviction of a Three Mile Island spokesperson.

Cody snorted. "If they're so important, why do we only like concentrate on them when WASC is here?"

Schroeder paused and shifted within her clothing. "Well," she said. "Imagine they're guests in our house. Don't you like to clean your house when guests come?"

"No," said Brice. "I leave it a mess."

"It's so fake," said Cody. "It's misrepresenting to pretend we've been doing this stuff forever."

Schroeder forged on. "I like to make a nice dinner and clean up when guests come, even though I don't do that every day. But that isn't misrepresenting."

Kaylee chewed on her pen cap. "Yeah, it kinda is."

"Okay," said Schroeder. "This is what we're going to do now. I'm going to pretend I'm someone from the accreditation team, okay?"

She walked out the door.

"Shut it," mumbled someone.

Schroeder reappeared in the doorway with the same burnt expression on her face. She stalked over to Cody.

"Hello," she said. "I'm here visiting to accredit your government class. Where's your ESLR poster?"

He didn't even look at her, just pointed an arm at the wall.

"Very good," she said. "Now tell me, what standards are you fulfilling in this class?"

Cody smirked. "All of them."

"No," she said. "What's the evidence? What specific standards are you fulfilling?"

He pointed to 12.1.1 on the list of wildly unfulfilled standards. STUDENTS WILL ANALYZE THE INFLUENCE OF ANCIENT GREEK, ROMAN, ENGLISH, AND LEADING EUROPEAN POLITICAL THINKERS SUCH AS JOHN LOCKE, CHARLES-LOUIS MONTESQUIEU, NICCOLÒ MACHIAVELLI, AND WILLIAM BLACKSTONE ON THE DEVELOPMENT OF AMERICAN GOVERNMENT.

"That one," he said.

Ms. Schroeder hovered right over him. "Where's the evidence?"

He held up his hands.

"I need to see evidence," cried Schroeder. "I'm on the committee and I need to see evidence." She grabbed his jersey and tugged it.

He shied away and shot her a sidelong glance. "This is so gay."

At lunchtime the senior circle gained a few extra bodies. Everybody watched two gardeners plant a bed of tulips into the wood-chipped soil around the tree, onto which three ESLRs had been plastered.

"What's happening to our school?" said Ross. "This is hilarious."

Vic and Shawn got into a brief shoving match, and Shawn spilled some soda as he pushed back. Vic slapped him on the side of the head. "You're messing up our campus cleanness for WASC, fool!"

"The administration is like freaking out," said Alexis. "They know if the standards stuff doesn't go through they're all getting fired."

"Good," said Padma. "I hope so. Nobody likes them."

"They don't care about us at all," said Ross. "They like only care about WASC and the school looking good to the public."

Brian broke out in a huge grin. "Dude, you know what we need? We've already got senior ditch day, but we need to get some pranks going too."

A dozen people laughed.

"We should like graffiti up, 'WASC sucks Popper's cock' on the day they arrive," said Steve.

Shawn unwrapped his burrito. "Krazy Glue the locks on the quads at like 4:00 A.M. The janitors wouldn't be able to open the school and they'd all just be standing outside."

"Put up a huge balloon over the administration building that says 'WASC' with a line though it," suggested someone.

"Smash all the windows," offered another.

"No," laughed Kaylee. "You know what the best one is? We get three pigs like down in Saddleback Valley, and we put a big number 'one,' 'two,' and 'four' on them, and we let them go here. They'd like go totally insane looking for pig number three."

Eyes widened as people contemplated the devious wisdom encapsulated therein.

The next morning, after Derrick read the Word of the Day, an increasingly familiar voice filled every room.

"Good morning, Mirador High School! This is Dr. Chao, and I have a new ESLR Challenge for you today. The first ten people who write down at least one standard from their classes on a piece of paper and bring it to central quad will win free In-N-Out gift certificates! Now let's all give our teachers a round of applause for posting the standards in their classrooms."

"Don't," said Mr. Lamarque, before a single set of palms could impact.

At lunch, Derrick stood in center quad with a stack of ten coupons for free hamburgers at In-N-Out. He waited for the contest entries to pour in.

Other ASB people had received crates of ESLR pencils and T-shirts for distribution to all the students and teachers. Ross brought a load of standards merchandise by the senior circle.

Cody stared at his green pencil, engraved with the Mirador Marlin and an acronym composed of the first letters of the ESLR headings. "I can't believe we're spending money on this shit."

Shawn held up his bounty. "This is my new shirt, fool. It'll be good for washing cars."

Vic pulled his on backward. "Now I can look cool in front of my cool friends."

"Burn that shirt," said Alexis.

Cody shook his head. "It comes out of your taxes."

Kaylee looked down at the pencil and the shirt in her hands, the posters on the tree and everywhere. "Aaaaaah," she cried. "Is this driving anyone else crazy? I hate WASC and I hate ESLRs and I hate standards, and they're like taking over our lives."

"Seriously," said Vic. "We've heard it so much before, we know the freaking standards. It's like, 'Sweet Jesus, don't tattoo them to my skull.'"

"We don't know the standards," said Shawn. "Who the fuck knows the standards?"

"I do," said Vic.

Shawn laughed. "Bullshit, you do not."

"Sure," said Vic. "They're easy."

Aram came by with his trash bag and stepped on some of the new flowers. Alexis picked a fresh one and put it in her hair.

In the center of the quad, Derrick waited. Sweat warped the gift certificates in his hand.

After a while freshman Leo puffed up with a piece of loose-leaf paper.

"I did the ESLR Challenge," he said, and presented the page proudly.

Derrick looked down at it. "Uh," he said, "you're supposed to have a standard from like each class, not just one standard from any class."

Leo's shoulders slumped. "Oh." He pulled his roller bag away.

Much later the tiny Asian sophomore who had danced with him at Brian's party handed over a piece of paper.

"Cool," he said, and smiled, but she kept her head down and wouldn't make eye contact. He looked at her page.

"Uh," he said, "you're like supposed to have one standard from each of your classes, not just one standard from like any of your classes."

She hurried off.

Soon the bell rang and lunch ended.

Derrick followed all the corridors to the corner of the administration building and knocked on the door to Dr. Chao's wood-paneled office. She looked up from her big desk and smiled hopefully. "How did it go?"

"Uh," said Derrick. "Like not that great."

The executive council of the Associated Student Body of Mirador Senior High School received a visitor that day.

Dr. Chao stood at the front of the room in her crisp blue suit with a handkerchief tucked into the pocket. "Listen," she said, "I have to admit something to you. We've done a few mock visits, and the early results from this process aren't looking very strong for our school."

She looked at the narrow walls of the little room.

"We've never had anything but a six-year accreditation, but there's an incredible amount to be done if we want to get one this year. We may be in some trouble.

"I know this process isn't easy on you. It's not easy on any of us, but it's extremely important to everyone in our community. It makes your diploma more valuable. It makes the house you live in more valuable. It makes all of Emerald Valley more valuable. It matters enormously to our alumni and our students who want to attend selective colleges. We need to do whatever it takes to get there. We're going to have to, as the saying goes, put lipstick on a pig."

A bizarre mental circus of Chao, pigs, and lipsticks pitched its tent on everyone's internal screens.

"You're the student leadership and everyone is looking to you to be our leaders in this process," she said. "I'm relying on you guys to get the word out and make sure that the process runs smoothly. Right now I need to teach the school the standards."

El Presidente twitched his eyebrows. "Why don't you rap them or something?"

The table giggled.

Beeeeeeeep.

"Good morning, Mirador Senior High School!"

Two thousand students and faculty pledged, sat, heard the bulletin, learned and promptly forgot the Word of the Day.

Beeeeeeeep.

"Good morning, Mirador. This is Dr. Chao." The principal paused.

In his math room, Mr. Lamarque rolled his eyes. "'The ESLR Challenge for today is . . . ,'" he mimicked, and held out his hand.

"But," the principal's voice continued, "today is ESLR Wednesday, so it's not time for Dr. Chao, it's time for M. C. Chao. Drop a beat."

A tinny rhythm rolled across the newly landscaped quads strewn with heaps of standards posters. It filled a hundred classrooms packed to the district limit with motionless faces staring at the beige box on the wall.

And Dr. Chao let loose, tortured rhymes garbling up in the static:

Standard number four,
Can I say any more?
You teach Mirador
How to be a superstar!

Standard number four,
Tells us to be,
Critical thinkers just like me,
Dr. Chao your emcee!

Standard number four,
Now I speak of part (e)

Says we practice decision-making strategies,
And so we are, so we are, so we are happy!

Standard number four,
Part (e) that is,
Subdivides into analysis and synthesis,
and application for your own situation!

Word.

The music cut out. "Okay, back to Dr. Chao again. Remember, Mirador, the standards are like the rain, and the ESLRs are like the umbrella. Pitter, patter, pitter, patter."

The PA clicked off.

Mr. Lamarque looked like he had just woken up in the Incan Empire. He opened his mouth but he couldn't say a word. He sat down on the side of his desk. The world had found a situation beyond even his powers of control.

Ms. Schroeder didn't even bother playing the lecture tape of the day.

"I'll tell you what I'm doing," she said quietly. "Gosh, it might be bugged. There might be speakers around. I'm actually in the process of writing my own textbook. If that's successful, no one here will see me again in one or two years."

A secretary from the administration office walked into the classroom with a package for Ms. Schroeder.

Vic blinked at the stranger. "The standards are over there!" he screamed, and pointed at the wall. Everyone laughed.

"Sweet Jesus," he whispered at lunchtime.

Thousands of students mobbed central quad, wandering among popcorn machines and cotton candy machines and ball-throwing contests. A DJ spun 50 Cent, and the special ed people linked arms to dance as Aram got down and funky with his wildest moves.

A huge overhead banner proclaimed the pandemonium an ESLR CARNIVAL.

Alexis ate her ice pop in a daze. "I'm so embarrassed for our school."

"If I didn't hate coming here before WASC, I really do now," said Brian. "Let's just take a senior ditch week."

Ross manned the cotton candy machine. He raised a wispy cloud of spun sugar. "Okay," he said to the dozens around him. "How much do I hear for this one?"

"Ten cents," said somebody.

"A quarter?" offered another person.

"How about a buck?" said a third.

"Okay," said Ross. "A dollar. Do I have anything better than a dollar? Going, going . . . sold!" He pocketed the bill.

"Uh," said Derrick, "we're like not really supposed to charge anybody." Ross shrugged.

Toward the end of lunch, Mr. Popper called Derrick into his office and shut the door.

"How's everything going?" he asked.

Derrick looked at the brass letter opener. "Okay."

"I know ASB can sometimes be a little, uh, unorganized," said Popper. "But I know you're someone I can count on. We've been working for two years to put together our self-study material for this process, and it's all coming down to one week.

"I trust that you're going to be a leader and do the right thing for our school. We need openness and full communication with the students here, and I'm counting on you to bridge the gap by keeping me informed about what's going on."

Mr. Popper's voice roared onto the PA during fifth period. It rang out across the athletic fields where hundreds gathered for gym class.

"Mirador. I am extremely upset."

Hot sun blazed from a bright blue sky as everyone stopped midfield in their gym clothes.

"Some of you, especially our seniors, who should be our school leaders, are planning pranks and 'senior ditch days' during the accreditation visit. Anyone who is absent from any class at any point at all during the visit without a signed doctor's note with a valid medical reason and excuse will be subject to extreme disciplinary action. The accreditation is important to us, to our alumni, and to those who will come after us, and you will respect that."

He clicked off.

Nobody kicked the soccer ball. They started to grumble in a field surrounded by ESLR posters.

"The administration's turned this school into a WASC-induced prison," fumed Evelyn.

Travis Newton laughed quietly to himself.

After a while the gym teacher called all the sections to the field house. "Okay," he said, "I need everyone to write an essay about an ESLR."

Hundreds of people fell into a mixture of stunned giggles and blinking. "You're joking, right?" said Charity.

A big gelled-hair guy in his early thirties, he jumped on the defensive. "It's not my idea. Mirador High School says you have to, do you want to see the paper? I have it right here." He waved a form.

"Now," he said, "you have to start with a sentence that is good, and then the body and the conclusion, okay?"

Momentary silence. "Like what are we supposed to write it about exactly?" asked one girl.

He pronounced every word carefully, as if he had just come from a staff meeting on it. "Use an ESLR as a writing prompt. Maybe you want to write about composition, which is interesting. Like there's a law of threes, like God created you, or your God created you, my God created me, in threes. This is the classical composition."

Travis Newton muttered, "Does this make any sense at all? What's he talking about?"

The gym teacher looked sharply at everyone. "I have to grade it in accordance with this ERB rubric." He pulled out a laminated sheet that contained phrases like "organizational devices are subordinate to meaning," and wrote "Rubicks" on the chalkboard.

A few people got into a scribbling-on-one-another's-sheets-of-paper war. Sara had been drinking. "I'm so fucked up," she said. She sat down with her pencil and wrote her essay: "Basically if your nice to you body, your body will be nice to you. Composition is also cool and very important!"

During passing period, everyone shot even more baleful glares toward the administration building.

"Fuck them," said Cody. "What is this 'doctor's notes' bullshit?"

"We're not going to get the damn six years, give up already, guys," said Kaylee.

"Dude," said Brian, "we've got to do so many pranks. This is going to be hilarium!"

Derrick sat on the concrete ring, bouncing his knee and looking up at the tree drooping flowering branches around them. He felt emptiness and tension hovering close, and he fought to hold them back.

Beeeeeeeep.

"Good morning, Mirador. It's M. C. Chao here to 'rap' about the standards with you. Where's my beat?"

Mr. Lamarque paced the cinder block walls of his classroom like a frantic hamster the next morning as the principal processed yet another Expected Schoolwide Learning Result into phatty rhymes.

"Thank you all for being such a wonderful school, Mirador," she concluded, and signed off.

Then Mr. Popper came onto the system. He sounded totally unhinged. All his p's exploded and s's hissed and the speakers squealed.

"It has come to my attention," he barked, "that some seniors are continuing to plan to disrupt the accreditation process by ditching or acts of vandalism. If anybody is absent from a single class during accreditation week, they aren't graduating from this school and we're putting them up for immediate expulsion.

"We will have police and proctors on duty at all hours and anybody planning to sabotage and derail this process by committing pranks will be subject to arrest and jail time, and will be prosecuted in court to the fullest extent of the law." *Click.*

Mr. Lamarque actually laughed. "Wow," he said.

Ms. Schroeder examined the back of her hand under the giant I LOVE THE ESLRs! banner.

"So," she said, "what do you all think of today's announcement?"

Cody leaned forward in his chair. "It pisses me off."

"Me too," said Alexis. "They can't treat us like that."

"Yeah, they can't do this to us," said Kaylee. "I feel like such an object."

Doug the Canadian sneered. "It's so obvious Chao had him say it. She was just trying to avoid saying it herself to look good."

"Well," said Ms. Schroeder, "them over there"—she nodded in the direction of the administration building—"are totally paranoid right now. They've got a lot on the line, and I think they're going a little crazy."

"Screw this school," said Errol, "screw them all."

Evelyn sniffed. "I hope some committee picks me so I can tell them all the corrupt and repressive things that go on here."

"Yeah," said Vic, "it's so dumb. They're just making everybody hate them."

Ms. Schroeder sighed. "Okay. Today I need everyone to take out a piece of paper, choose one of the standards, and start a composition with the sentence, 'We meet this standard by . . . , '"

Shawn slapped his binder shut. "Screw the standards," he announced.

A few people laughed.

"Screw the standards," he said again.

The ultimate thought crime touched off a wild and singing chord. "Screw the standards," called Kaylee tentatively.

"Screw the standards," bellowed Errol, with conviction.

And then half the room started chanting it—"Screw the standards! Screw the standards!"—chanting it and laughing while Ms. Schroeder shut her eyes tightly.

Toward the end of lunch, Derrick followed the long corridors to Dr. Chao's office. She and Mr. Popper waited for him behind the big desk piled with WASC materials, pallid and eager.

She bit her lip. "Well?"

"It's like pretty bad," he said. "I don't think people responded really well to the announcement. Everyone's gonna have like a revolt."

Chao and Popper exchanged glances. The vice-principal looked down at the desk and then back up at him.

"Derrick," he said, and paused. "Derrick, do you think you could explain to everybody how important this process is for our community?"

During fifth period, Derrick sat in the tiny hot PA room on the folding metal chair, while Popper stood behind him with arms crossed.

Beeeeeeeep.

"This is Derrick Littlefield," he said, "and I'd like to talk a little bit about everything that's going on here."

The gym coach blew the whistle out on the blazing fields, but everyone had already stopped to listen.

"A lot of people are angry about the announcement this morning, and they should be angry. I don't agree with it, because I don't think we need threats and policemen to have pride in ourselves and our school during the visit."

Derrick grasped the microphone with both hands. "We have a trust and a legacy. If our school has the good reputation it does, and we're proud of it and ourselves, it's because of the sacrifices one anonymous class of seniors made six years before us. They knew things would be tough and that they themselves wouldn't get an easy payoff, but *they weren't doing it for themselves.* They did it for us, for you and me, as classes before did it for them, and have always made a sacrifice here, every six years.

"We received a gift from them. They passed us a torch, seniors. You have the chance now to guard that trust and pass it down. Children in elementary school right now will go to better colleges because of you and the way you inspire pride in the next week. Anything you do to hurt accreditation hurts those children, and the underclassmen, and your younger brothers and sisters, and them alone.

"We have always had six years and our class will honor itself and Mirador by holding up our legacy.

"I will not ditch or pull pranks because I have too much pride—in myself, in this school, in this city, and in those who came before us and will come after us, in their sacrifices and dreams for us and Mirador. Please join me."

He turned off the microphone.

"Uh," he said. "Is that okay?"

Well, hello.

"That was a really good speech," he heard over and over again during passing period.

Nobody rushed out to get a sleeve tattoo of ESLR #5C, but he had managed to damp down the hottest flames of rebellion.

That night, he went to SpiriTeen.

The leaders divided everyone into four groups for a game called Bigger and Better. They presented each group with a plastic fork and the great commission to go unto the nations and trade the fork for a bigger and better item. The resultant item needed trading for something yet bigger and better still, and so on, with only an hour and the carrying capacity of fifteen people forming the theoretical limit of size and goodness.

Chanting "junior-senior guys," Derrick's group returned with a sofa, a huge porcelain lamp with two shades, a giant dog cage, a cheese presser, and an industrial double-oven on a dolly.

The junior-senior girls brought their own sofa, not to mention a dresser, a massive freestanding mirror, and a lamp.

Ross indicated that the guys' sofa was in fact a sofa bed, and therefore better than the girls' sofa.

The judges deliberated and finally gave it to the girls. Everyone proclaimed the match close, and really only the host family lost, because everything ended up on their lawn.

Derrick spent the weekend sitting in his room and trying to stay functional. The television repeated stories about wildfire conditions.

THE FIRST DAY OF WASC,
ALSO CALLED THE DAY OF EXPECTATION

Beeeeeeeep.

"Good morning Mirador High School," said Dr. Chao over the PA on Monday.

Her words carried across immaculate grounds. All the ESLR signs had disappeared. Maintenance had touched up the paint on the bright green gates.

"Today I would like to welcome the visiting committee from the Western Association of Schools and Colleges to our campus. Please help make them feel at home here at Mirador for the next four days. They will be with us today and tomorrow, at the district office on Wednesday, and back on our campus on Thursday."

Mr. Lamarque fixed everyone with a steady gray gaze. "Nothing changes," he said. "Should a committee member come into our class, you have all the evidence you need."

Pages and pages of section-by-section demonstration of standards fulfillment jammed everyone's notebook. The Angel of WASC would pass over this room.

The door clicked open and the entire class, including Mr. Lamarque, jumped.

Ross entered and held up some papers. "I have slips from the office."

"Put them on the desk," said Mr. Lamarque quietly.

Ross advanced through the silent room and began to put the slips on his podium.

"On the desk!" screamed Mr. Lamarque. He ran to a table in the corner and began pounding it with his fist. "The desk is over *here*."

Ross dropped the slips on the desk and fled for his life.

Mr. Lamarque picked up the chalk and walked back to the board. "I restrained myself," he said calmly. "I am a volatile mixture of Italian and Russian blood, and when things get out of hand, I get"—he threw back his head and swung up his arms—"WHEEEEE!"

Ms. Horn had made herself a "WASC Box," and it sat proudly in the center of her second-period lab desk, covered in drawings of smiley faces and confetti dancing around the word "Evidence!"

"Isn't it pretty, my friends?" she asked. "If the committee comes in, I'm just going to point them to that box. I put reports in there that show we're meeting the standards, and that should be all we need."

She sat behind her desk typing on her computer, and pretty soon everyone wandered around the room like usual. She seemed distracted, so Sara took a metallic blue boa and wrapped it around Horn's neck, and a few people took pictures of her with their cell phones.

"Hee hee," said Ms. Horn, engrossed with the computer. "Look at all the ratings we've gotten on RateMyTeachers.com. 'Mr. Lamarque is pure evil.' I bet I know who wrote that one. I have a student who always says people are 'pure evil.'"

Charity picked up one of the teacher's SUPERSTAR STUDENT! stamps and began stamping a booklet of hall passes. Then she looked over Horn's shoulder.

"You're a nosy bitch," said Vic.

"Viiiiiiic," Charity whined.

Vic took the stamp away from her.

"Give it back, asshole," she said, and started to hit his arm, but not very hard. At this point, interacting with her constituted an act of mercy. "I bet you can't be nice to me for like one full week."

"Oh, yeah?" he said.

"Yeah," she said. "I bet you can't."

He held out his hand, and they shook. "I totally can. Watch. Sweet Jesus, this is gonna be so hard."

The door clicked open, and Horn in her sparkly boa and everybody else whipped around.

Mario the proctor walked in with a pink slip. "Vic Reyes? You've got ISS."

Vic dropped the stamp. "What did I do? I didn't do anything."

"I don't know," said Mario. He waved the slip. "I just know you have ISS this week."

He took Vic away on his electric golf cart.

At fourth period, Ms. Schroeder opened her classroom and turned on the lights and everyone followed her in.

"Holy fuck," said Cody.

Several dozen condoms lay scattered around the room. Wrapped in their brightly colored packets, they rested on desktops and seats and the carpet.

Everybody started to laugh. They began to throw condoms at one another. Cody tossed one and it landed in the pen tray on the whiteboard.

Ms. Schroeder looked suspiciously around the room. "Hmmm," she said, "are we missing some people here today?"

Everyone exchanged puzzled looks. Some seats were in fact empty, but attendance didn't seem to constitute the immediate concern.

"Uh, I think they sent like all the 'bad' people to ISS," said Ross.

"Oh," said Ms. Schroeder, and bent over her attendance book.

After a while no one could stand it anymore. "Look at your whiteboard," said Kaylee.

Ms. Schroeder scanned the area under her I LOVE THE ESLRs! banner.

"Look at the tray," said Alexis.

Ms. Schroeder eventually worked her way to the Durex and gasped. Everybody laughed.

"There's condoms all over your room," Cody remarked.

Classmates helpfully indicated them. Schroeder covered her mouth. "Oh, God. Oh, God. I hope the people I have to put on my little dog-and-pony show for don't walk in now."

Everyone picked up the nearby packets, and Schroeder took her enormous arm-scoop of condoms and dumped them into the trash. The sight of Schroeder bearing condoms likely helped further the cause of abstinence education for many students.

The class fell into a stunned silence. Kaylee looked down at one of the innumerable standards, ESLR, and rubrics sheets. "What does 'first-person' mean?" she asked.

"Oh," said Ms. Schroeder. "It's like this."

She drew a grid on the board, and filled it in:

I	Our	
You	Your	
He/she	Their	

"That's first, second, and third person, okay?"

The door opened, and an elderly black man in a tweed jacket with a beard and glasses stepped in.

Schroeder grinned as though her case had gotten bumped to the top of the liver transplant list. The board contained something totally inane, but it looked educational, and everybody sat quietly in their seats.

"Just continue on," said the bearded man.

Ms. Schroeder blinked. "So," she said, "what happened today in current events?"

Everyone worked through a two-minute discussion of the latest carnage in Iraq, raising hands and not advocating genocide, and then the bearded man slipped away.

At lunch everyone in the senior circle talked about their run-ins with WASC.

"Did you see them?"

"This woman stood in the door and no one noticed her for like five minutes and like everyone was talking in the back."

"This guy started asking Mr. Mannis all these questions."

"I think one of them talked to Alikah from ASB."

"Oh, my God, they're like everywhere."

That night the nervous families of Emerald Valley pressed for news of accreditation and wondered about the value of their properties in an uncertain real-estate market. They ate dinner and watched wildfires tear through the hills on television.

THE SECOND DAY OF WASC, ALSO CALLED THE FEAST OF FOOLS

The next day Vic reported straight to ISS. A lot of good company packed the modular room, including Shawn, the redneck, the skin, and a number of other internees who might potentially prove disloyal to the cause should it come down to war with WASC.

He sighed and took his seat. The mean attendance counselor seemed to realize that the majority of them didn't really have a firm reason for incarceration, and that containment mattered more than punishment. Vic put on his headphones and kept his cell phone under the desk, texting away.

"The Word of the Day," said Derrick, "is *keraunoscopia*. Noun. Fortune-telling by means of thunder. *Keraunoscopia*."

He scraped in the metal chair and nodded to Popper. As he hurried through the lobby of the administration building, he almost ran into an elderly black man with a beard standing by the door.

"Hello," said the man.

"Hi," said Derrick.

The man reached into his suit pocket. "Did you ever see, or preferably read, *Charlie and the Chocolate Factory*?"

"Yeah," said Derrick. "Both."

The man smiled. "I'm giving out five golden tickets to let you miss your fourth-period class and eat free pizza, and you're a lucky winner." He handed a yellow slip of paper to Derrick.

"Huh," said Derrick. "Wow, thanks, but I don't know if I—"

The man winked. "It's mandatory. I promise your teachers will understand."

*   *   *

Evelyn went to the library during passing period to return a dog-eared book called *Shelter* with collapsing binding. In the line, she talked with two people from the Mirador *Mirror*.

"It's amazing," she said. "You just take a giant balloon, inflate it, and like spray it with polyurethane foam, and you've got a house. You can build it in a few days, it's cheap, and it's totally energy efficient. I want to live in a big foam dome home."

"I think one of the UCs has a big dome," said the girl.

The guy sighed. "I just got my PSATs back, and I was like, 'Okay, I'm not going to a UC.'"

Evelyn snorted. "Hah. The colleges totally exaggerate. Like UCSC says you need a 2000, that's so not true, it's more like a 1700. Even at Stanford it's only 2050."[2]

Someone tapped her on the shoulder.

"Hi," said an elderly black man, holding up a yellow ticket.

Samantha stood on the junior girls' steps after second period.

"Oh, my God," she said, "so like Charity's off complaining about the drama again. Don't say it to her, but I think she makes it all herself."

"No, of course she does," said another girl.

"Oh, my God," said Samantha, "so I was at the beach over the weekend, and I got so drunk that I fell down on the sand and was puking all over myself. And the girls were so sweet, they like put me in the backseat of the car with the windows open. Like anybody else would've just abandoned me, you know?"

"Totally," said one of the girls. "They're so sweet."

"I also made a decision that night, like I only go for Mexican guys. I didn't used to, but now I do. Oh!"

An elderly man in a tweed jacket gave her a yellow ticket.

"Oh, my God, you guys, I get to miss fourth period!"

For Leo the freshman it had started out like any other day. He hauled his roller bag across the sciences quad from health class when a man in a tweed jacket intercepted him and offered free food.

Vic raised his hand toward the end of third period.

The stocky counselor nodded at him. "Yes?"

"Can I go to the bathroom?" he asked.

She scrutinized him in silence for a few moments before reaching for the hall passes. "Five minutes," she said. "Everybody take exactly five minutes."

The room got up and stretched.

Vic cocked his cap diagonally and left the modular buildings with a couple of girls.

"I've gotten so fat," said one of the girls.

Vic put his arms around her and lifted her to shrieks. "I still can pick you up!"

"I bet I can pick *you* up," she said, and did. "Help me!" she called to the other girl, and together they ran forward carrying Vic, everybody laughing.

They had gotten halfway to the food court when Mr. Popper drove past in his golf cart.

He saw a laughing Vic borne aloft on the shoulders of shrieking girls and spun the wheel hard left. Vic held up his hall pass but Popper kept bearing down and the girls dropped him.

"Excuse me."

Vic fixed his cap, gasping, and tore his eyes from Popper to see a formal gentleman holding out a yellow slip.

The vice-principal stopped his golf cart and just looked back and forth between Vic and the smiling tweed-jacketed man. All human effort had proved vain. The lock and key to the netherworld gate had joined at last in accordance with the dread prophecy.

"Uh," said Popper. "I, uh—"

The man put his hand on Vic's shoulder. "I'd like to speak with this student."

Popper opened his mouth. "Right," he managed.

So Derrick, Evelyn, Samantha, Leo, and Vic sat around a circular table in the soundproof conference room at the back of the library and ate pizza.

The elderly black man smiled at them. "My name is Dr. Kempner, and I'm the chair of the WASC visiting committee. This is Mr. Cohen and Mrs. Estrada. I don't know how clearly your school explained this process to you, but one of the most important elements for us is being able to talk in complete candor with a diverse group of students away from all the teachers and administrators. That's you guys."

Everybody chewed.

"We want to know everything," said Dr. Kempner. "What do you guys think of Mirador? What do think about your classes and teachers? What do you think about the way this place is run? We want to hear what works"—he looked at Evelyn—"and what the problems are"—he smiled at Vic.

"Tell us everything. It's all private here. No raising hands or anything. Yes?"

"Yeah," said Evelyn. "I have like a really big problem with the way this place is run. We don't like learn anything. This school's so easy, I mean, I haven't done any homework in three months, and everybody just like sits around and talks in class."

The three committee members looked at one another and scribbled on legal pads.

Vic's eyes widened, and he hissed at Evelyn. "Shut the fuck up."

He turned to the committee. "I don't know what she's talking about," he said. "I'm here on Inter-District Transfer from Santa Ana and there's just no comparison. You don't have any idea what Santa Ana is like. Mirador is like really, really good for academics. It's like the second-best school in America. I know so many families who moved here just so their kids could go to Mirador. I swear to God one of my friends' families moved to Emerald Valley from Argentina just because they like wanted him to have the opportunity to go here."

Dr. Kempner blinked, as though all the characters in the scenario he had cast had taken precisely the wrong roles.

Evelyn's face began to flush. "Opportunity! To go to an institution where the administration represses student freedom? They censor like all the voting lists so only the people they want to win things, and it's all rigged, and there's like no way to know how any decisions are made. I'm an editor on the school paper the *Mirror,* and they censor every issue, and we have no freedom of the press."

Derrick looked down at the table.

"Come on," said Vic. "I'm sorry if you didn't like get on homecoming court or whatever, but that makes you just jealous, it doesn't make it rigged. And you people write stuff that embarrasses the administration all the time. What did they ever censor of yours? And we have like a bunch of different papers, too, like that freak girl came into our English class to tell us about her photo art journal or something, I don't know, it's not for me, but it's there for whoever wants it. We have a lot of press freedom. What are you talking about?"

The fire in Evelyn's cheeks deepened to scarlet. She leaned over the table toward her new nemesis. "They spent over a hundred thousand dollars on repressive measures like policemen and dogs, and they can't even afford textbooks or APs. They invade our privacy and make everyone feel like criminals. I know *you* aren't in favor of the police dog."

Derrick folded his pizza plate, breathing deeply.

Vic gave her a look as cold as a Brussels tariff commission. "Why should anybody worry about a drug dog if they don't have drugs at school? How could it possibly be violating anyone's privacy to say they shouldn't bring drugs to school? The administration has the right to say they don't want drugs here, and if people have a problem with it, they shouldn't be bringing drugs to school and then complaining about getting caught. The administration's getting us ready for the real world."

Dr. Kempner turned to Derrick, who had shuddered several times. "You've been very quiet over here," he said. "Usually student leadership has a lot to say. Do you have anything to add?"

"No," said Derrick numbly. "No, thanks."

Evelyn faced the committee, her fists balled and trembling, and blurted out: "The entire place is fake. It's famous for being fake! They even planted fake flowers. They've been trying to shove the ESLRs down our throats for a month now and nobody knows them, I mean, like I've been here for three years and nobody even talked about them until now. They stuck them up on everything, they took down all these huge banners right before you guys got here, and the principal even rapped them. We had a carnival, and they bribed us with ice cream and gift certificates and told us we'd go to jail if we protested. It was a really pathetic charade."

Mrs. Estrada whistled inward. "*Really?*"

The committee's pens flew across their pads.

Vic Reyes glared calm hatred at Evelyn's whales-of-Belize sweatshirt. "Are you sneerious? Maybe *you* don't know the standards." He turned to the committee. "I apologize for Evelyn. She's generally known as a rude person and she tells lies on occasion, and she really isn't representing our school well. The ESLRs are easy, like, hang on a second, I can do them."

He looked at the words "Amor Roma" on the pizza boxes. "Okay, the first one is like, uh, 'Students will develop in an integral and balanced manner the intellectual, physical, social, and moral capacities needed to achieve excellence in the pursuit of successful life outcomes,' right?"

Three graying heads pivoted down to their material packets.

"That's the first part," said Vic, "and then B goes like 'Students will value and demonstrate mastery of the California content-area learning standards with honesty and respect as community partners who balance self- and peer-focus.'"

Dr. Kempner stared at Vic as though he had found the new lama.

Vic had found his rhythm. "Okay," he said, "and 1C is like . . ."

When the lunch bell rang, WASC released the five of them.

Evelyn stormed off behind the library.

Derrick caught up with Vic as he headed through the food court toward the modular buildings.

"Dude . . . ," said Derrick, and then stopped. "Dude, you were like the big defender of the school."

Vic shrugged. "That ESLR shit's easy. Hah, I told Evelyn to 'shut the fuck up,' bro! I like actually said it in front of the WASC people."

"Are you coming to the circle?" asked Derrick.

Vic looked around at the milling hundreds. "I've got ISS."

"Why?" asked Derrick.

Vic hoisted his backpack higher. "I don't know."

A piercing whine cut the crowd noise. "Viiiiiiiiic . . ."

He turned to see skinny Charity tottering on her tremendous platform sandals in her tiny skirt. She stood by a big green Mirador garbage can and ate a banana.

Vic pointed at her and laughed. "Oh, my God," he said, "I'm like so tempted to put you in that garbage can."

"Viiiiiiiic," she said, "you're supposed to be niiiiiiiice to me. You promised for a week."

He cringed. "Ahhh, it's like irresistible."

She tottered back and giggled uncertainly. "Viiiiiiiic," she said. "You *wouuuuldn't*."

With a whoop, he darted forward, scooped her up flailing and gig-gling, and dropped her feetfirst into the garbage can. She stood there, to-tally embarrassed and laughing, and everyone who watched laughed too, laughed at this pale storklike creature with heavy makeup standing in a garbage can holding a banana.

A whistle shrilled, and someone yanked Vic's shoulder back. He twisted his head around and saw Mr. Popper's blazing eyes.

"All right," said the vice-principal. "That's it, Vic. That's strike three."

Vic sat on the concrete bench of the senior circle and cried.

"I'm getting expelled," he choked through the tears. "They're kicking me out. They don't want me here. I disappointed my mother, and I dis-appointed my father. I'm a disappointment to them. Their oldest son didn't graduate from high school."[3]

Brian closed his eyes. "Holy fuck," he said. "They're kicking you out?"

Alexis knelt down next to him. "Can't your mother talk to them?"

Vic shook his head. "My mother already talked to Chao. She already came in about the drinking thing."

"Can't she come in again?" said Alexis.

Vic sniffed deeply. "She's not my bitch."

"You've gotta fight this," said Ross. "There's gotta be like something you can do."

Vic stared at the ground and tears hit cement. "There's nothing I can do. They don't want me here. It's over."

"Listen," said Padma. "Say you want to talk to Dr. Chao. She has to talk to you. They have like all that 'open-door policy' bullshit, so they can look like they care about what we think and they're open to us. If she won't talk to you then that's really bad."

Cody clenched his fists. "Fuck that shit. They can't do that to you, bro. I'd go down fighting. I'd smash all the trophies in that office. There's six-teen fucking school days left. That's bullshit."

"We should sign like a petition or something," said Ross.

Vic dragged a sneaker over the concrete. "Nothing will help, they want me out of here."

Derrick stood right outside the senior circle, watching helplessly.

"They did a petition for Marisa and she got to stay," said Kaylee. "But that happened like sophomore year and then you have choices. Now . . ."

Brian trashed his Doritos bag. "What are you going to do?"

Vic shook his head slowly as he sniffed the words. "I don't know. Maybe like go to Verdugo Adult School. I guess I should try to get a GED maybe, I don't know."

Alexis put her hand on his. "Vic, you know anyone here in this circle would do anything to help you, like go in and talk to them, sign something, whatever it takes."

He looked at forty silent and anxious faces. A wild yell arose from some rehearsal in the auditorium.

He smiled softly. "Can I go over there?"

People chuckled.

"Okay," he said, "that's my last joke."

The PA system clicked on. "Victor Reyes. Please come to Mr. Popper's office immediately."

Vic sat in the wooden chair in Mr. Popper's office and cried. Through tear-filled eyes he looked around the empty room with his stomach clenched.

A door clunked shut outside, and Mr. Popper's footsteps creaked down the corridor. The vice-principal walked into his office holding a white slip in his hand, closed the door, and settled into the leather chair behind the desk.

"Okay, Vic," he said, "I'm going to need you to sign right here." He pushed the page across the glossy wood.

Vic managed to force out a few words. "I want to talk to Dr. Chao."

Mr. Popper shook his head. "She doesn't want to see you, Vic. She doesn't want to see you except to say good-bye."

Vic stood up and Popper rolled back in his chair. "God damn it," sobbed Vic, "I want to talk to Dr. Chao!"

Popper grabbed his phone and hit a button. "It's Stan," he said. "I need a proctor in here."

Vic's hot cheeks stung. He thrust his middle finger, tense and quivering, in the vice-principal's face. "Fuck you, Mr. Popper," he screamed as the tears rolled down his chin. "Fuck you, Mr. Popper."

Popper spoke into the phone. "And I need the officer right now, and call the station, too."

Vic threw open the door to the office and ran, just ran. The whole circle saw him run.

In the parking lot he jumped into his Baja Bug, turned the ignition. The car growled, the tires squealed, and he screeched out of the lot onto Orchard Road, tearing through a red light as he sped into the distance.

Steve sighed as the roar faded. "He's never going to survive at Verdugo. I'm gonna like call Hector and Manny and see if they can get his back."

Cody grabbed the pepper tree and began to shake it. Leaves and flowers cascaded down onto the clean-swept concrete. "This is bullshit," he yelled. "This is bullshit!"

Mario the proctor jogged over with a faint smile on his face. Cody whirled on him. "No," he said. "Don't smile. I'm not joking. I love Vic."

The proctor's grin faded, and he shook his head. "Come on, let's not have a disturbance."

"I love Vic," yelled Cody, and he shook the tree so hard it looked like it would snap.

"I know," said Mario. "I'm sorry."

Cody pointed a finger in his face. "No, you're not sorry, you're kicking him out."

Mario said nothing. He just stood back and waited for Cody to calm down. When the tide of anger seemed to have ebbed, he beckoned Cody a few yards away from the circle.

"Hey, man," he said, "I can tell you're using."

Cody said nothing.

Mario smiled and rippled his beefy arms. "Me too, man. How much you get your gear for? You get a good price? I pay so much, man."

Derrick looked around wildly. Everything everywhere seemed totally wrong.

"Dude," said Ross, "that really sucks, with only like two weeks left. How did the meeting thing go?"

"It was like—" said Derrick. "I . . ."

He noticed Mr. Popper step out of the administration building. He ditched Ross and jogged across the quad.

Popper squinted at the panting public chair. "It's so unfair," said Derrick. "It's so unfair. You work the four years and one small thing . . ."

Popper shook his head. "Choices have consequences. You're young adults and you're responsible for your lives, or you will be soon."

After last bell, forty upset seniors met at the circle.

"We're not just going to let Vic disappear," said Kaylee. "We need to make this like an issue that the whole campus is aware of, that the administration needs to deal with."

"Uh," said Derrick, "there's like the whole WASC thing . . ."

But he said it very softly and only a couple of people looked over at him.

"We should put up flyers like they did," said Shawn.

Alexis nodded. "We should make T-shirts like they did."

"Oooh," said Olivia, "we've got like boxes and boxes of balloons we could use in the ASB office."

Brian nodded. "Let's do it."

About twenty-five people worked nonstop until sundown.

THE THIRD DAY OF WASC, ALSO CALLED JUDGMENT DAY

Always good and bad come conjoined, but rarely in equal measure.

WASC had decided to spend Wednesday reviewing curricula at the district office and thereby give everyone a little break. That news fell under the heading of "positive."

On the bad, or rather cataclysmic, front, a dense mass of icy air had built up in the vast gray wastes of the Great Basin Desert beyond the Sierra Nevada Mountains. Now it seeped through the high rocky passes and rushed downward to the sea.

The air mass compressed, speeded up, dried, and heated thirty degrees for every mile it fell. The Santa Ana winds had become a bone-dry near-gale inferno by the time they tore over a little town named Emerald Valley. The scrub where Evelyn and Thea had shot Airsoft BBs shriveled into kindling. Any spark sufficed.

On Wednesday morning, a wall of roaring orange flame and choking black smoke filled the hills over the city. The California wildfires had come home.

Alexis's father opened the venetian blinds on a second-floor window of his house and beheld a vision of the fire abyss of Tartarus.

"Dear God," he said.

The television in the den announced that sixty-three homes had burned down so far in Emerald Valley.

Alexis yawned and shivered. "We don't have school today, right?"

Her father laughed nervously. "I can't imagine you possibly do. I'm sure we're going to get national disaster funds." One of his two statements turned out correct.

"The levels of ash and particulate in Emerald Valley local air are fully twice the USEPA safe limit," said the newscaster. "Here's the school closure report for district schools." Three of the four high schools appeared on the list.

Alexis stared at the screen. "What?"

Her father smiled. "I'm sure they just haven't put up Mirador yet."

The newscaster looked calmly into the camera. "Despite the fire and ash, one school won't be closing its doors."

Cut to "DR. IRMA CHAO," looking chipper in her blue suit with the livid orange sky behind her and a few specks of what seemed like snow drifting past the lens. "I've held extensive consultations and done a considerable quantity of research, and I've determined that Mirador can be open and productive today. We're going to do everything we can to ensure students' comfort and safety."

"What?" said Alexis. "What? What?"

Travis slotted down his mirrored sunglasses. "Oh, I can tell this is going to be an enlightening day of learning."

As the very first people drifted into school from the parking lot under gray haze and hills filigreed by rivers of flame, they hacked and coughed up black mucus. Proctors stood with giant cardboard boxes of surgical face masks and distributed them to the arrivals.

"Get your face masks," called Mario. "Be safe."

Wil Kormer voiced the obvious question: "If we need face masks to be safe, why are we here at all?"

But Travis almost quivered with manic energy as he tightened the elastic on his white surgical filter. He watched forty seniors in SAVE VIC T-shirts spread out across campus and begin to plaster the quads with SAVE VIC posters and tie up clusters of brightly colored SAVE VIC balloons.

He grabbed Wil and pulled him over to the DJ stand in central quad.

"Can you play a song for me?" he asked. "Can I make like a song request? I think all of life should have a soundtrack, like I always imagine one for myself."

Wil shrugged, and put Bad Religion's "Los Angeles Is Burning" on the huge speakers.

Travis's chest heaved as he surveyed the quads. "Oh, thank you so much."

"You can't deny that living is easy, if you never look behind the scenery. . . ."

His normally expressionless face broke into a huge grin behind the layers of woven polypropylene. "Mirador is falling apart, and I love the world for it!"

He whooped, jumped onto the stage, and raised his arms to the roaring hot wasteland winds. His sunglasses reflected the ash raining from a luminous gray-orange sky.

"We're all getting burned at the stake on this one!"

"It's showtime for dry climes, and Bedlam is dreaming of rain. . . ."

As surely as the ESLR signs had dominated Mirador, SAVE VIC now became the school's unofficial theme. The ash stung, but the circle seniors kept taping and tying, and a growing stream of students arriving for first period looked around the campus, eyes wide over their poly filters.

"Hah," laughed Alexis through her mask. The back of her SAVE VIC shirt featured a giant heart with his name inside. "The whole school is going to know what they did. They're gonna have to respond to this!"

And so they did.

Popper stepped out of the administration building in his face mask, coughed, choked, grabbed his walkie-talkie, and summoned the five proctors.

"Proctors," he wheezed, "get all of this material down by first bell."

Padma yelped as Mario slashed her balloons with a knife. Other proctors ripped down signs and stuffed them in industrial garbage bags. Within six minutes, the entire campus had returned to a swept-concrete status quo ante as though SAVE VIC and all the hours of work had never existed. The acrid breeze raked a few popped-balloon shreds along the ashy ground of empty quads.

The seniors met back at the circle. "Dude." Brian blinked. "They just like totally silenced us completely."

"It was pretty impressive how fast they did it," said Kaylee, dazed.

Cody sat on the concrete ring. "I feel like my freedom of speech was just taken away."

"Save Vic!" Alexis called hopefully but not very effectively at three freshmen rushing for cover in their masks.

Derrick swallowed. "I'm going in to talk to them," he said. "Everything's gone completely insane."

He found Popper in his office.

"Uh," said Derrick, "I was wondering why you guys took down signs that we have like a constitutional right to post."

Mr. Popper stared at his pen point and clicked it in and out again very fast. "The *Tinker* verdict says you only have the right to post in accordance with school guidelines. Our school guideline is that you have to receive clearance from the office to post any sort of material, and I can't tell you how long that clearance might take. Come on, Derrick, I'm counting on you to be a leader here and do what's right for the school."

Derrick looked out the window at the flames against the orange sky. "Yeah."

Popper glanced at his watch. "We've got announcements in three minutes."

A hundred speakers hummed to life.

"Good morning, Mirador Senior High School!" warbled the unflappable ASB girl.

Two thousand students, faculty, and staff hauled themselves to their feet, faced the flag, and slapped hands on their hearts. Some had fled their homes during the night or dawn hours before the advancing walls of fire.

The girl picked up her bulletin sheet. Derrick and Mr. Popper stood behind her in the stifling and closetlike PA booth. "Here are today's announcements!"

Ash-dusted walls echoed the clubs, activities, and end-of-semester sports schedules across desolate quads and tightly shut classroom doors. Flame crackled on the towering hills a few miles from campus.

Derrick furrowed his brow under blond curls and held the dictionary open to a page with his thumb.

"Thank you, Mirador, and have a *great* day!" The announcements girl slid out of the little metal chair.

Mr. Popper nodded curtly, and Derrick sat down as he had almost two hundred times before. He pulled the microphone to his mouth. He carefully opened the dictionary and ran his finger along the tiny print.

"Today," he said, "we are missing Victor Reyes, the latest in an endless list of developments that shows our administration cares very little about its students. Please join us tomorrow as we pass around petitions of no confidence in their leadership and present them to the school district. We're going to bring Victor Reyes back. Thank you."

He said the last part fast because Popper's florid hand slammed down the power switch.

Two thousand people sat dead silent, staring at the beige boxes on the walls of their rooms.

In the social sciences quad, a harsh laugh bubbled out of Ms. Schroeder's lips. "Hah! The administration doesn't care about us either."

Thirty-six heads swiveled from the speaker to her. She looked around.

"Uh," she said. "You never heard me say that."

A long pause. Olivia raised her eyes piously heavenward. "Say what, Ms. Schroeder?"

In the AP calculus room, one girl frowned. "Who's Vic Reyes?"

Evelyn pulled the stripy scarf tighter around her neck. "He had a big mouth. He was kinda obnoxious." She glared. "That's too bad though, with fifteen days. That's like too much."

"Derrick's right," said a guy. "This school doesn't care."

Most classrooms just filled with muttered expressions of "holy shit."

Derrick sat in the chair across Dr. Chao's big desk in the corner room of the administration building. Two proctors flanked the door. Mr. Popper paced somewhere by the miniature palm, his mustache twisting word-lessly.

Dr. Chao folded her hands on the dark green blotter and looked at the white form.

"Effective immediately," she said, "you're dropped from ASB with an F on your transcript. You're on suspension. No ISS, just go straight home, Derrick. We're going to be composing a letter to the University of Virginia to inform them of your actions, and I'm sure they'll withdraw your admissions offer. You have a disciplinary hearing on Monday, and we'll be recommending your expulsion."

Derrick swallowed and nodded. His eyes stung, but no tear had fallen.

Dr. Chao nodded to Mario.

The proctor grabbed Derrick's arm. "Come on."

Ross had office duty first period. He had listened at the door and now watched the ASB public officer getting led away under the wall of pic-tures of himself.

The bell for passing period rang and two thousand students stumbled from their classrooms and tightened their surgical masks.

Derrick rode in the passenger seat of the golf cart. "I'm bringing the student to the front gate," Mario radioed into the system.

The cart streaked past the food court, where gouts of flame streamed upward from the infamous garbage can. Had a burning cinder from the sky ignited it or had someone set it on fire? The flare stack blazed like a primal warning, green paint curling and blackening.

Two proctors ushered him into his 4Runner. They opened the front gate of the school just for him and clanged it shut behind. The radio crackled and they stood sentry to prevent any Napoleonic returns from Elba.

Derrick drove a quick six minutes home. He creaked open the door to the empty and spotless living room, marred only where the closet stood ajar that held his uncle's shotgun. He found his mother in the kitchen, calling her volunteer lists in her I'M A UVA MOM sweatshirt.

She crossed out a name and then looked up to see him standing in the doorway. Surprise hardened to anger.

"What are you doing here?" she snapped. "Why aren't you at school?"

He walked over to her and told her everything. She looked at him trembling for a moment, and then she reached back and slapped him as hard as she could across the face.

"You put your entire future on the line for a loser who's going nowhere," she screamed. "I just spent over six hundred dollars on a digital camera so I could take pictures of your graduation. I can't tell you how furious I am. You wait till I tell your father. Get up to your room and don't you dare come out."

Derrick turned from the kitchen.

Face mask smothering me, I leaned against the cinder block wall of the administration building with a clenched stomach and a racing pulse. Ross had told us all what happened.

At this point I could no longer write myself out of the story.

No matter how much I wanted to preserve a smooth and transparent narrative flow, I wasn't really a disembodied, objective chronicler.

I was a real person and I existed and I couldn't stand pretending otherwise for one flesh-and-blood heartbeat longer. I was just this guy, see.

They had targeted Vic. He deserved a high school diploma. He deserved a chance like anyone else. He needed the option to become something besides a mechanic if he wanted. Getting expelled after a lifetime in school, with only sixteen days until graduation? A nightmare.

And Derrick. My God, the guy had everything going for him, but he had voluntarily thrown it all away, sacrificed his life for what he believed was right in an eighteen-year-old *now,* for the sake of someone else. Another human on such a different path from him. I couldn't imagine somebody from my adult life taking a bullet like that, ever.

His act inspired awe. It demanded reward, not punishment. The highest nobility glimmered within it. I wished I could be that brave.

I knew a few days now could make such a difference for them over decades and decades. What happened now would matter in a distant future long after all the Chaos and Poppers of the world had passed away, and Mirador itself had turned into a branch of the California Department of Agriculture before finally collapsing into a heap of cement and cinder. They couldn't lose their options in life, not now, not so early.

Despite the arid wind, veins of ice webbed my chest. If anyone could raise a magic scepter and make everything all right, bring justice to the world and a fairy-tale ending to this story, I could.

Everybody else moved like pieces in a game around me. They all had strict roles—as administrators, students, teachers, proctors, parents—and each had to play his or her piece as best he or she could, given its particular goals and limitations. But who was I? A guy from midtown Manhattan standing in the middle of the board. A total wild card answerable to no one. Even my two rules were self-imposed. I spent all my days constraining myself to the role of a seventeen-year-old C+ So Cal surfer, but in reality I had options and abilities that no one else did. I had enormous power if I chose to use it.

How many times did I watch passively as special ed students got kicked around or say something moronic as sixteen-year-olds began to shoot up steroids? All in the name of Not Getting Involved? No more. Sorry, objective observer status, those people were my friends. "I've always got your back, homie," Vic had told me. I couldn't just stand by and watch their lives get steamrolled without doing anything.

My idea was completely unthinkable, straight out of a movie, but every day I lived a movie, so that made no difference. Anything could happen because most of it already had.

I would walk right into Dr. Chao's office. To me the dark corridors mattered less than a shadow. I would tell her that if she didn't bring back Vic and Derrick, I would bust her.

Yes, if she didn't revoke her totally arbitrary and senselessly punitive decisions and bring them back, I would announce then and there, first to Dr. Kempner of WASC and continuing on to the national media, that Mirador Senior High School had allowed a random guy in his midtwenties to pretend to be a student. I'd expose them all. It was no sweat off her back to hand out two more diplomas, and I could save and protect two friends and give them another chance in life.

It was an awesome idea, a terrifying idea. I knew it would work. Fuck "consequences." Things like résumés and corporate-tower paper dithering belonged to an unreal and distant universe. Life and meaning here by the lockers under the blazing sun had become so much more—elemental.

Just look what you could do once you jumped all the tracks that bound you.

I, I would make the world the way it should be.

The swordfish on the gym grinned through the rippling heat.

I blinked.

What the hell was I thinking? Under months of the illusion of control, I had plunged straight into my own Stanford Prison Experiment. I had lost any broader perspective. Dr. Chao had let me in, trusted me, and this is how I would repay her kindness and faith? Blackmail? No way. Never.

But Derrick and Vic had trusted me, too, been friends and believed in me. Anyone at the circle would do whatever they could to help them. Shouldn't I?

No. I had obligations to more people than just the circle crowd. Think about it: Careers, thirty-year careers stood on the line, people who had seriously pursued lives in the field of education since before my birth. Vic and Derrick were nice guys, but they had knowingly broken the rules and there were consequences.

But that severe and that permanent? Everyone tripped once in a while, and a guillotine blade didn't need to drop. The law convicts everyone, and power requires accountability. That meant oversight and enforceable sanctions, and I was the only immediate entity capable of applying the two.

So playing drastic hardball with Chao would make me a good and moral person, then? A true friend and a real member of the senior class?

No, I was still lying to all my schoolmates, and it would just compound the problem by making me a backstabbing blackmailer in the adult camp.

Ashes danced in the hot wind, and the critical point finally insisted itself: Where was *my* accountability?

I couldn't take anyone's side. I could watch the situation around me, but messing with it meant pushing everything headlong into a terrible void. I needed to stay an observer—and no more. If a moral path remained anywhere, it consisted of being the best observer I possibly could be.

Never before or since did I feel so alone, the twin worlds of Vic Reyes and Mr. Popper remote as pinprick lights across a cold and limitless fissure.

I closed my eyes and sighed very deeply. I sheathed the fiery sword of justice and hoisted my backpack.

*   *   *

The seniors stood shocked in the circle as the three-minute bell rang. The branches of the pepper tree bent and rustled in the roaring hot wind.

Cody finally spoke. "Let's like boycott graduation. Let's not get our diplomas."

Shuffling and muttering. "Uh . . . ," said Kaylee.

Cody glared at her. "Well, we've gotta do something."

Ross jogged over from the administration building. "I just talked to Popper. He was like, 'What Derrick did was illegal.'"

"It's not illegal," sneered Alexis. "It's freedom of speech."

"Welcome to Cuba, or any other Communist country," said Cody in his filter mask.

Ross leaned on the tree. "He was all like, 'You don't know why those two were expelled. They won't tell you the real reason they were expelled.'"

Olivia clenched her fists. "Ahhh. It's so annoying, they always do that, like 'You wouldn't understand, it's over your head.' And then they roll their eyes and shake their heads at you."

"They don't take us seriously at all," said Padma.

Alexis lifted her slender arms. "Well, they have to. We're like as much a part of this school as they are, and we're here right now, and their little accreditation won't work without us, and we're voting for their bosses in November, and sorry, but they're going to have to pay attention to us. Let's have like a sit-in."

Cody smiled behind his mask. "Just not leave the circle? I'm down."

"We're going to get in so much trouble, fool," said Brian.

"Don't be a pussy," said Cody. "What, are they going to expel everybody? Forty people? Hah!"

"All right," said Padma, "I'm sitting."

She dropped her backpack and settled onto the bench. Slowly, everybody else sat too, although a few kept their backpacks on and stayed poised at the edge of the concrete.

Beeeeeeeep.

The last students disappeared from central quad into their classrooms. The flames undulated and smoke rose on the distant hillsides.

Mario drove up his golf cart under the orange sky.

"Come on," he said, "go to class."

Brian looked at him. "We're having a sit-in for Derrick."

Mario paused. "Are you sure?"

"Yeah," said Alexis. Heads nodded. The people on the edge of their seats settled back. The chance for escape had passed.

Mario looked around the circle. "All of you?"

"Yeah," said Alexis.

He shook his head and drove away. And so they sat as the winds rushed over them. Toward the end of second period, Nicole appeared at edge of the quad, crying.

"Why are all you guys sitting here?" She sniffed.

Alexis explained.

"I just lost my room," Nicole said. "My room and like half my house burned down last night and we're all living at my grandma's house. Everything that I've ever had in my life was in my room, like all my clothes and all my things were there."

Alexis hugged her, and Padma hugged her, and Nicole sat next to them.

Groups of sympathetic people stopped by the circle after second period to chat. El Presidente wheezed in the particulate air and huffed on his inhaler.

Aram wandered the multitudes and pulled people's shirts. "What's happening? What's happening?"

Travis stood toward the back of the crowd. "As much as I like Derrick Littlefield . . ." He smirked and went to third period. When the bell rang, most people but the original seniors went the way of Travis.

Mr. Popper stalked across the desolate quad after the classroom doors shut. "If you don't go to class right now," he said, "you're all going to ISS."

Nobody said anything, didn't even want to look at one another in case someone lost the nerve.

"Okay," said Mr. Popper. He picked up the walkie-talkie. "You're all going to ISS."

Proctors on golf carts emptied the entire senior circle and herded forty more bodies into the airless modular room already packed with "bad" people. The stocky counselor looked as though the helicopters in the hills had just started pouring lava on the flames. Perhaps she realized that even her cherished meanness posed no match for a decent percentage of the school population.

"Oh, my," she said.

*   *   *

At the beginning of fourth period, Schroeder surveyed her room.

"Where is half my class?" she asked.

"They're in ISS," said Evelyn. "Because of Derrick."

Schroeder rubbed her forehead. "Hoo, boy." She marked them present.

The ISS counselor gave up on disciplinary enforcement and everybody talked. When final bell rang, Mr. Popper opened the door to the modular room and looked at the standing-room-only crowd. The throngs fell silent and the unnatural orange light reflected off scores of bright baleful eyes all staring at him.

"And what do you all intend to do tomorrow?" he asked.

Alexis leaned on the back of Shawn's chair. "Sit out."

"You'll get ISS again," Popper warned.

Alexis shrugged.

He grunted and vanished from the doorway. The crowds streamed away behind him.

But of course he couldn't disappear his entire school leadership until graduation, and parents would ask questions, and fire regulations probably meant they weren't all supposed to be in ISS anyway, and he certainly couldn't have sit-ins and proctors dragging dissidents away to forbidden Gothic wings of undesirables for the final day of WASC.

The simple thought of Dr. Kempner turning in slow motion, asking, "What's in here?" and opening the modular building door would probably have sufficed to make him issue everyone in the circle three platinum cards in the name of Stanley Otis Popper.

Senior classes came and senior classes went, sometimes in fifteen days. A six-year accreditation was, well, for six years.

The phone rang in the Littlefield house an hour later.

Derrick looked up from his iMac.

After his mother had slapped him, he had walked into the living room. He didn't even glance at the small door to his uncle's closet. He just strode calmly up the steps, his head raised, his breathing steady and deep. He felt really good for the first time in years.

And now he had a meeting with Dr. Chao.

*   *   *

The Santa Ana winds died by sunset, and few people could ever recall such a spectacular display of colors in the sky. At evening, FEMA and the Red Cross set up an emergency wildfire aid center in Emerald Valley City Hall. The state of California distributed aid checks to victims who had lost their homes to the flames, including Nicole's family. They had fortunately insured their property, so rebuilding mainly required time.

Over the night, firefighters and the consumption of kindling reduced the flames to a much smaller region. Smoke still rose from the hills, but not enough to bring down ash.

THE FINAL DAY OF WASC,
ALSO CALLED THE DAY OF WONDERS

The next morning, the Mirador thousands arrived at school for a cool and beautiful day. Yellow sun shone in a clear blue sky, the janitors had swept the ground ash-free, and Derrick Littlefield sat in the circle ring.

"Hey," he said. "Thank you guys all so much. I can't like thank you guys enough."

"Oh, absolutely," said Alexis.

Brian shrugged. "Yeah, bro, I know you'd do it for us."

Hand-slaps and hugs passed around.

Most people had already heard the news the night before, but he explained for those who hadn't. "The only thing that happened was she dropped me from ASB. I'm not even getting an F, it's just that there's like not going to be any more Word of the Day."

People may have cried inside.

"Actually," he said, "I'm kinda glad I'm not on ASB anymore. It was like a lot of work." Then he looked down at the new flowers. "She said bringing back Vic was out of the question."

Through a moment of silence, everyone bit their lips, kicked at the ground, and remembered. "Well, fuck *her*," Shawn said.

"He was a really good guy," said Alexis.

"Yeah," said Cody. "I loved that guy. Life isn't fair, is it?"

And I thought, "No, it isn't fair, but actions like all of yours can make it better. I didn't need to worry about creating a happy enough ending. You did it yourselves."

*   *   *

After school, the WASC committee entered the assembly hall to present their official report. Six of them sat behind tables on the stage with their hands folded. Dr. Kempner stood at a podium with the school's coat of arms embossed in bronze on the front.

Before him sat an audience of administrators, district and city officials, teachers and staff, local media, and a few dozen students. Dr. Chao sat with her entourage in the front row. Cameras flashed.

Dr. Kempner looked out at the crowd and sucked on a tooth. "Mirador Senior High School," he said. "There's so much to say, it's hard to know where to begin."

He moved the papers on the podium, sucked on his tooth again. The PA system beeped to summon a student to the office and he chuckled. "We all work in this situation." He sipped some water.

"There are so many, many points that I and my colleagues could bring up," he said, and looked at the committee's impassive faces. He turned back to his pages.

"So let me just start by saying that I made a bet with myself that I'd find a phenomenal school here, and I win my bet. Mirador Senior High School is a safe, caring, and well-organized environment. The support you provide your students both inside and outside of classroom walls is outstanding. You have an extraordinary community of purpose, inspiration, and achievement with ambitious plans for further success, a community where every voice is heard and respected.

"Plus we have these wonderful scarves that you were so kind to provide us with." He waved the deep green Mirador scarf that hung around his neck. The other six committee members held theirs up and beamed.

He sipped some water. "There's a minor issue with drugs and alcohol that I'd like to underscore, but overall I wish . . ." He looked up proudly in the direction of the control room as the cameras flashed. "I wish that every child in America had the opportunity to come to a school as wonderful as Mirador."

As the site received a full six-year accreditation with the highest marks possible, one interesting detail may have caught the eyes of the committee.

Several dozen sheets of letter paper hung from the walls. One dangled from the podium where Dr. Kempner spoke, right underneath the seal of Mirador. Each sheet contained a picture printed from the Internet. Cartoon pigs, 4-H prize hogs, Miss Piggy, all pigs, each wearing a streak of bright red lipstick.

THE SEASON AFTER WASC,
ALSO CALLED THE BEGINNING OF LIFE

On Friday morning, one thing alone tempered Mr. Lamarque's smile at announcements without the Word of the Day. He realized he only got thirteen more before the school year ended and a new ASB public officer stepped up to the unabridged dictionary.

Beeeeeeeep.

"Good morning, Mirador. This is Dr. Chao. I want to congratulate everyone on their behavior during the period of accreditation. The visit was positive, and good work to everyone. At lunchtime we'll be distributing free ice pops to thank you for the wonderful WASC work."

"Yay," said the skin. "You can keep your jobs."

IN THE MAGIC KINGDOM

This ain't no song by the Boss, this is reality.
My last shot, all I got, and it means everything.
No more magnet town. Tonight I defy gravity.
              —Army Of Freshmen,
                "Road Less Traveled"

CHIRON AMONG LIGHTS

The Mirador Marlins baseball team made it to the quarterfinals of the CIF playoffs, where an aggressive north San Diego squad called the Chieftains bumped them from the bracket.

As Cody's final season ended and his cleats scraped the stadium dust, he watched the manager reverently fold Dove's green jersey and place it into the cardboard box for the very last time ever.

During lunch three days later his team met in the gymnasium. Several hundred students filled the bleachers.

A very tall ladder, unnaturally high, leaned against the wall. It stretched all the way up, beyond the words of Mirador's alma mater, into a clear space near the rafters.

The team stood on the lacquered floor. They took off their baseball caps. New Marlins would need Strength now for seasons yet unplayed.

They watched the janitor climb slowly, step by step bearing his heavy load upward. In his hands he held a plastic frame encasing the shimmering green jersey alongside Dove's huge senior portrait.

"As the season is now concluded," said Coach Mulligan, "Mirador Senior High School is officially retiring Robert Doveman's jersey. The number seventeen will never again be worn at this school, and this memorial to Dove will hang forever on the wall of our gymnasium."

The janitor reached the apex and pressed the frame onto its hooks.

He descended and collapsed the upward path. Dove remained on high, wreathed in the sweet smell of varnish. The restless green jersey had come to its final home.

Cody fumbled with the cap in his hand.

GOING NOWHERE

Two days later during lunch, everyone messed around at the circle.

"Look at my exit essay for government," said Shawn, passing it to interested parties. The page read: "I went to the city council with some of my friends. After five minutes I was bored out of my mind. These jack-offs just sit around deciding how to spend our money. God damn. You know they just want to blow it on cheap booze and cigarettes. Okay, I'm outtie. . . ."

Brian laughed. "You're not getting points for that."

"It makes a point, fool," Shawn protested. "And like none of the teachers like having to give exit essays anyway, and they all like complain about it and come up with ways we can get around doing it."

Everybody fell silent as Mr. Popper's golf cart closed in on the circle. Mario stopped the cart, and Popper eased out with a stack of white forms.

He looked down at the pages and intoned a list of names. "Alexis Newton, Derrick Littlefield, Cody Reisling, Padma Kalyani, Brian Olvera . . ." People choked and squeezed their eyes shut.

"What?" cried Alexis. "What?"

Mr. Popper smiled. "You guys need to pick up your graduation announcements."

He handed over the white pages, which turned out to be slips from the printing company. Forty people started to breathe again.

"Oh," murmured Padma, "you gave me a shock."

Popper chuckled, mounted his golf cart, and buzzed away.

When she'd recovered enough to speak, Alexis narrowed her eyes. "Let's like not shake hands with him." She extended her palm. "As soon as I get my diploma, I'm going to go like"—she swung her hand back to fix her hair—"'Ohhhh, psych, asshole!' I want everyone to see. I want it to be really obvious."

The girls started to laugh.

Cody smiled softly. "I'm going to walk straight up to him and say, 'Popper, I'm graduating, but you're still in high school.'"

PRACTICE MAKES PAIN

The next morning, the rest of the school took finals, while seniors had graduation rehearsal for the big event a few days later.

Although the silver hands on Cody's watch pointed to eight o'clock, the sun burned bright and hot. Everyone sweated and complained, and the piercing light plunged all partiers into the agonies of splitting headaches.

"Why didn't I wear sunglasses?" moaned Alexis.

Sir Edward Elgar's "Pomp and Circumstance"—popularly known as "that graduation song"—roared on infinite repeat from a dozen massive speaker assemblies around the expansive and immaculately trimmed turf of the school football stadium.

Perhaps in one last burst of spiteful payback, the administration had assigned none other than Mr. Percy Lamarque to manage graduation. He stood backlit in the distance on an elevated stage at the front of the stadium. He saw an elaborate ceremonial scheme in the neatly labeled chambers of his mind, and he now tried to impose it over and over and over again on the waking world in a nightmare panopticon.

"I'm so hung over, bro," muttered Brian Olvera.

Bum bum BUM bum bum BUMMMMM bum . . .

"Steve!" Lamarque's nasal tone bit through the speakers over the swelling strings. "Keep the five yards!"

The helpless guy speeded up somewhere in the middle of field.

Bum bum BUMMMM bum bum BUMMMMMMMMMMM . . .

"On the left in the white!" Lamarque's voice banged a thousand eardrums. "Down the *middle* of the numbers!"

Cody turned back to look at the waiting faces of his lined-up classmates, their ranks stretching away into the parking lot. "Who the hell are all these people?" he said. "God, I thought I knew like everybody."

Here stood the underwater bulk of the Mirador iceberg, the groups of three or four, the segment of the school that did not hang out at the circle, did not get invited to big parties, did not become homecoming queen or win every ASB election.

The sun scorched faces. "Keep the five yards! Come on, people, five yards!" Lamarque bleated at his current victims. "No one here needs to graduate."

Sir Elgar's music swelled and the drums rolled for perhaps the seventy-ninth time. Bodies baked in the hot sun.

A skinny guy with glasses laughed to his friend. "Yeah!" he said. "Go me! I've got two hundred fifty credits and a point-eight GPA."

Padma rolled her eyes and muttered. "Wow. Way too much Dungeons and Dragons for that one."

Kaylee giggled. "'Zelda must have really gotten a hold of you, huh?'"[1]

Shawn shook his head. "What a waste of four years. I got drunk every night and partied and I'm still graduating."

"Square off those corners in the green stripes! Square them off!" Lamarque blustered. "I can see everything from up here."

Padma shivered near the front of the line. "I'm nervous. I'm so nervous. I've got like goose bumps. What if my belt falls off? What if I trip?"

The sun burned hotter. The skinny guy in glasses started to laugh about something with his friend.

Cody wheeled on them. "Are you laughing at me?" he demanded. "I hear you making noises. You don't want to go back to your parents with two black eyes."

Lamarque screamed down at Padma as she walked across the field toward her assigned seat. "Close the gap, you in the red! We're all going to stay here as long as we need to until we have this right."

Apparently everyone needed to stay three hours longer. Then he moved them to the blocks of white folding chairs arranged on the turf. He cut the music and the sun sweltered like it never had before in the deepest Sahara.

"Well," he said into the microphone. "I do want to congratulate your class. This is the first time a majority of students have been dynamic enough to choose to attend this practice event. In past years only a quarter or so have arrived."

Within their living sauna, five hundred bodies froze.

"We didn't have to be here?" Ross mumbled through parched lips.

Shawn spoke everyone's thoughts in a hollow voice. "The gates of hell just opened."

WAKING UP

"Remember, your Grad Nite starts tonight at *10:00 P.M.* at the gates to the Magic Kingdom," Lamarque called, but everyone had already bolted halfway to the fence.

I picked up my C+/B- grades and went to meet Dr. Chao that afternoon at four.[2] She expected a researcher to deliver a full report on his participant observation study.

Until I walked into her wood-paneled office, I didn't realize just how much I identified with my classmates.

I didn't eat lunch with teachers, I didn't hang out with them after school, I didn't go to their houses. I had the role of a student, and teachers seemed like foreign others, a different order of being with unimaginable lives and authority that we simply didn't have. They sent us to detention and confiscated our cell phones.

But even the teachers themselves feared and obeyed a higher power, who stood to them as they did to us: the remote and sovereign figure of Dr. Irma Chao. She was the empress, the source and support of the whole structure, the keeper of all keys, the goddess of necessity, the guardian of grades and fates and futures and reward and discipline. I approached her nervous and guarded, ready to be in trouble for some failing, to have the vast weight of her authority descend on me.

In shorts and a backpack, I had gotten sent to detention for standing outside a classroom when a bell rang and harassed by police for walking on an Emerald Valley sidewalk at 10:03 P.M. But I put on a suit, and suddenly, I met the empress as an equal.

She smiled at me, oval glasses winking. Of course, she never dreamed in a million years that I would have spent months hoping that her proctors didn't catch my friends. She and I were both adults, of course. We were, by default, on the same team, the side of maturity and authority and Proper Pedagogy for Our Children.

Right?

My entire value set of half a year was being flipped within the space of five minutes.

I faced the principal and felt like a teenager pretending to be an adult. No, I was an adult who had just pretended to be a teenager, and now I had reverted to a real self named Jeremy Iversen. Even though that guy's last name sounded so unfamiliar and I saw his far-off memories through the wide end of a telescope. Only this one tiny woman believed that he existed, and all the paperwork and IDs proclaimed otherwise, and right outside her office door, over two thousand people and the entire community beyond thought I was a teenager named Jeremy Hughes. The preponderance of evidence lay with them.

"Teenager?" "Adult?" At different moments in life I had wanted to be one or the other so badly. I searched back through my experience, but I couldn't say what the sounds referred to anymore. The world felt so fragile.

And upon waking, Zhuāngzǐ no longer knew if he was a man who had dreamed he was a butterfly, or whether he was a butterfly dreaming that he was a man.[3]

Vertigo.

But as we talked, I held to the moment, and I remembered something simple. Dr. Chao was my buddy, she was my friend. I liked her. It had been so easy to forget. When you spent months and months around thousands of people who saw her as a distant and menacing demigod, it couldn't help but have an impact. But she was funny and quick and grimaced with me about rapping the standards. I knew her before I knew anybody else at Mirador; in fact, she had effectively introduced us. She had a breathtakingly tough job managing over two thousand employees, so to speak, with everyone ready to scapegoat her for anything at all that went wrong. What wouldn't *I* do if I had to get Mirador accredited?

"I have to admit I forgot about you," she said. "I saw you once in the office, and I thought, 'That kid looks familiar.'"

As the hours passed, her perspective made sense, made growing sense. Of course you can't seize the PA system and broadcast anti-administration messages. Of course you can't throw students into garbage cans. Of course fourteen-year-olds needed to dress to learn, not in nine-inch skirts. Look at the ranks, the scores, the statistics. The faces of everyone I knew blurred together, became aggregate, became "kids," became "children." Her school among twenty-five thousand other schools fulfilled this republic's annual call to pour its thimbleful of five hundred into an ocean of three million new graduates. The tide would renew a summer later with a different set of in-vogue names and ephemeral trends, trends that occasionally offended decency and decorum and must be specifically prohibited in letters home. The vast and functional cycle, far greater than she or any other entity, would repeat without end until the civilization that sustained it ultimately dissolved as all phenomena must.

Popper came to sit in our meeting. She told him about my other identity and got a highly skeptical narrow-eyed look, as though he feared Ms. Horn might pop out from behind a potted palm and start laughing at him.

I tossed around a few words like "aggregate" and "functional," and then he nodded very slowly. "I guess I can see it, with you talking like this." His eyes glazed as he surely and suddenly recalled how he had sent me to detention three times for tardies and I had unloaded the appropriate sullenness in his direction.

"Please," he added, "you can call me Stan." There the mind revolted, and I stuck with "Mr. Popper."

I told them basically everything that I had seen, without naming anybody—neither students nor teachers.

"Well," said Dr. Chao, shaken, "you certainly put your finger on the pulse of this school." Then she looked at me and lowered her voice. "So who *is* dealing drugs? Who *is* using drugs and drinking? You can tell us."

Well, that would basically indict everybody but Littlefield, and she had already tried to expel him. I laughed. "I'm not actually a narc."

Mr. Popper aka Stan picked at his mustache. "Come on. We've given you a pretty nice ride here with your project. We've let you do all your research. You've gotten a very good deal."

"Please?" said Dr. Chao. "I know the drugs and alcohol are a serious problem, and I'd really like to work to eliminate them."

"No," I said. I smiled to diffuse the tension of what was about to happen. "I can't do that."

A moment passed. Then she looked wistful and sad, shrugged and turned back to the papers I had given her, shrugged and turned her face back downward to behold the world below her. We moved onto the lack of critical-thinking assignments.

She only wanted to do the best job she possibly could in her role, and that included the unfortunate task of identifying and punishing rule breakers. But just as I had clung to objectivity during the rain of fire, I sure wouldn't take anybody's side now.

I bet if you really enter enough viewpoints, the whole of creation makes sense. To understand all is to forgive all.

On the wall hung an ink sketch of a stone bridge vanishing into mist.

In one of many ironies, I had never grown up until I went back to high school.

AT THE CIRCULAR FOUNTAIN

The yellow Grad Nite buses waited in the dark Mirador parking lot.

Disneyland opens its doors just to graduating high school seniors for an all-night lock-in a few times toward the end of the year. Nearly every school in Southern California attends.

Four hundred seniors climbed aboard, even though they had spent their lives in the shadow of the Magic Kingdom's fantasyland spires and most of them knew the resort better than the school library. The buses would reclaim them around dawn when the park closed.

They brought yearbooks, senior standout surveys, weed.

As her bus rolled onward in the night, Kaylee pulled out her survey. "Hey, who in our class do you think is most likely to win the Nobel Peace Prize?"

Padma snorted. "I don't think we're going to have any Nobel Prizes here."

"It's going to be Cody Reisling," said Steve.

Cody smiled as everybody laughed.

"Hey," said Padma, "that's what we should do, like fill them all out the opposite way. So Cody's getting the Peace Prize. Who has fugly hair? Who has a unibrow? Who has a really annoying laugh?"

Kaylee looked at her page. "Who's like the best booty shakers? We need a girl and a guy."

Brian laughed. "No doubt, no doubt whatsoever, it's Dr. Chao and Mr. Pooper. Did you hear her rapping?"

"Oh, my God," said Alexis, "can you imagine that? It would be so gross. This is my Dr. Chao booty dance." She jumped into the aisle, gave herself fake glasses, buck teeth, and a truly dorky expression. She shook her thing.

"Bruce Lee," said Shawn, "that's what I call her. From a distance she totally looks like Bruce Lee."

Nicole waved her yearbook. "Who hasn't signed mine yet?"

Pink and blue colored lights swirled across the castle turrets in the distance.

"We don't have time now," said Alexis. "Let's like sign them all at the park."

The buses drew up in a line, and an endless flow of seniors from high schools all over the region swarmed across the lot toward the bright golden spires rising under the onyx vault of a star-dusted sky.

Right inside the gates Steve approached the attendant. "I need a wheelchair," he said. "I tore my ACL."

"Oh," she said, "okay."

Pretty soon he rolled happily amid the swelling throngs. "Check this out," he said, and popped a wheelie.

Then he hunted down a giant Goofy cast member waving to crowds of seniors. He maneuvered himself around behind Goofy's back and carefully plowed into the huge costumed dog.

As Goofy turned, Steve hung his head sideways, let his tongue loll, and curled his arm across his chest. "Buhhh," he mumbled, doing his best impression of the mentally challenged.

Goofy moved away as quickly as politeness allowed. Steve turned, grinned at the crowds, and rammed him again. "Buhhhhh," he said, when the plush dog turned.

After a few more attacks, he wheeled back to the group. "Damn," he said. "I could do that for hours."

Brian pointed at a man in a striped shirt. "Look, it's a mime! Get the mime."

Steve tilted his head and scooted toward him. The mime had a better field of vision than Goofy and fled. Shawn tore after him and chased him past the monorail.

In Pirates of the Caribbean, everybody packed the weed into the bowls during the dark tunnel so they could smoke in the sea-battle scene.

Alexis sparked the pipe as fake cannon bursts exploded red in the water around them. "Security totally can't tell if you smoke in here." Padma giggled.

Shawn nodded at the animatronic pirates lifting beer steins and chasing automated wenches. "This was us back in the day."

Cody had drunk before the bus ride. Now he cupped his hands and yelled, "This is fun. We're having a good time."

Brian laughed and punched his arm. "Dude, shut up."

Cody stood. "Wheee! I'm enjoying myself."

His boat jerked to a halt. A disembodied voice cut over the pirate song. "If you don't sit down, I'm going to have to call security."

"Then call security," Cody yelled into the maritime darkness.

"Dude," said Brian, and pulled him back down onto his plastic seat. Everybody got into a water-splashing fight.

They cut the line to the Haunted Mansion.

"This is such a fucking retarded ride," said Brian. "It's so fucking lame."

"Dude," said Steve, "what the fuck are you talking about?"

They launched into a debate on the merits of the Haunted Mansion.

"You shouldn't be arguing about that shit," said Cody. "That's not important. You should be arguing about fucking politics."

The attendant, a blond woman, glared at them. "Could you stop with the cursing?"

"What the fuck are you going to do about it?" asked Cody. Then their conveyance arrived and whisked them away.

Ghosts appeared and disappeared in the mirrors. "Lame," said Brian, "lame, lame, lame."

Even Ross succumbed to the general mania. He slipped under the safety bar of his conveyance and hid behind a tombstone in one of the scenes. When Brian traveled past he leapt out and yelled.

Brian screamed, and Ross laughed.

"I'm calling security," said the voice in the darkness.

They arrived at the end station to find that a guard had come for Ross. "Wait here," he commanded, and turned to talk to the attendant. Ross just walked away.

At last everybody sat on the stone benches around the great circular fountain and signed yearbooks. They had piled the volumes up and went to the heap to take albums they hadn't gotten yet. Colored illumination floated over the park and thousands of seniors streamed around them.

"Oh, my God," said Alexis. "This is so sad."

Brian shook his head. "Dude, no way. We should've graduated like two years ago."

The special ed chaperone stood nearby with her charges, some really in wheelchairs or using oxygen tanks. Aram wandered over to the pile of yearbooks and picked through it.

"Hey," said Olivia. "Leave those alone."

Cody fell quiet and sat apart on the bench. He looked past the bright spires at pale stars shining behind the phosphorescent glow of the lights of the Southland.

"What's up?" said Alexis after ten minutes. "Why aren't you signing books?"

Cody glanced down. "I remember all the crazy shit me and Dove used to pull here. He was all about like taking advantage of the moment, you know? He always said 'Yesterday is history and tomorrow is a mystery. Today is a gift. That's why they call it the present.'"

Alexis watched the rise and fall of water in the circular fountain. "Wow," she said. "That's really sweet." She took Cody's volume off the pile and put it in his lap. "So don't like be sad. See all the people who signed your book."

He took the album and flipped through it. "Yeah," he said faintly. "Did you see like the whole two-page spread thing they dedicated for Dove?" He searched through the pages, and then he opened to the big picture, the same one that hung on the gym wall, Dove smiling on the filmy background of a placeless sky.

He almost couldn't see the pen because it was so dark. But in the cycling neon lights he realized someone had drawn on the photograph.

Dove had devil horns and the word ASSHOLE scrawled across his chest.

Cody stared at the picture, and the entire world melted downward. From somewhere to the side in the bleeding rush of lights and sound, he heard Olivia's voice. "Eh, this is so annoying. Aram's like been drawing graffiti on the yearbooks."

Aram giggled as he pushed them around the pile. In his hand he held a black Bic pen.

Reality became Aram's dull vacuous eyes, his thick tongue, his greasy little mustache. Cody stood and the volume slid from his hands onto the asphalt. "I'm going to kill him," he said.

PGD had ended, a dream dissolving into the past. The season had ended. The future contained only a blank.

Alexis saw his face and gasped. "Cody. Cody, he's like handicapped. He's retarded. Cody."

The only thing left of Dove now was memory, and he had maintained himself pure in memory. Now his icon had been pulled out of peace and light down into the filthy heap of common life by a giggling, grasping retard, a subhuman midget. He had fouled the image permanently and it could never return to clarity and exaltation. It was buried forever beneath the grime of earth and breath.

"I'm going to kill him," said Cody.

Of course he could kill.

Everything happened in an instant. He turned with snakelike speed, vaulted the concrete ledge behind the bench, and darted toward Aram. Aram saw him coming and ran. He could run very, very fast.

The chaperone didn't move. She had seen Cody's face and couldn't move.

They ran through the crowds of high schools, the two of them. Aram ran and Cody ran after him.

The colored lights flashed, and the giant projected letters that spelled GRAD NITE swirled. Countless faces whipped past, the youth of the land accelerating into a single static blur as Cody closed in on his quarry, charging down a rushing corridor of body heat and strobing neon.

He had failed at everything else, failed to beat H.C., failed to take Mirador to the finals, failed to make Alexis understand how he needed her, failed to stand up for his best friend the only time it really mattered. Now at least he could do one thing for Dove.

Aram veered around the great moat, a tiny point lost beside the hollow stone darkness and lighted golden minarets of the Fantasyland Castle. He didn't even look back, just ran with his arms pumping at his side, until he tripped on a decorative flagstone and fell and hit the ground. Cody stood above him in an instant and Aram looked up with wide eyes and mouth open. He cowered and held his hands over his head.

Behind Cody a Disneyland officer yelled, "You're going to jail for three years if you touch him."

But Cody pulled his elbow back to hurl himself downward and drive it straight into Aram's face, snap his neck, kill him, and Aram stared up with brown eyes and the universe dilated.

One interlocking piece shattered, or snapped into place.

Cody roared and grabbed his own head, fingers raking through his light brown crew cut. Anguish twisted his face, and he screamed.

"Why did you do that? Huh? Why did you *do* that?"

Aram huddled, confused.

"Why did you do that?" Cody repeated. "Why'd you do that? Why?"

He kicked the empty concrete, and the words quivered. "Why'd you do that? Why, Aram, why?" No reply seemed forthcoming.

His voice weakened and trailed off. "Why'd you do that."

The massive outline stood, poised, over the axis that would determine a lifetime.

And slowly, Cody turned away. He saw fifty people watching him. Teachers and students and park officers had all gathered in silence. He looked beyond their gazes and walked stiffly through the crowd, wiping off a tear.

In the morning, he called his mother.

"Hey," he said.

"Hi," she said.

He swallowed. "Can I come back?"

Cody said good-bye to his brother and moved home the next day.

He realized he had gotten a lot of messages. Maybe the time had come for him to answer.

IF YOU INSIST

The evening before graduation, Derrick came home from waiting tables at the Italian restaurant.

His uncle sat by the kitchen counter with a Michelob longneck. "Hey, Derrick," he said. "You know how I always keep my word, right?"

"Yeah," said Derrick. "Yeah. I think that's a really awesome thing about you."

His uncle chuckled and stubbed out his cigarette. "Well, I'm going to give you three thousand dollars as a graduation present."

The slush from the ice machine missed Derrick's cup entirely. "What?" he said. "Are you serious?"

"Oh, yeah," said his uncle. "Only one catch."

"What?" asked Derrick.

His uncle laughed triumphantly. "You've gotta take a girl on a date and kiss her! Heh heh heh!"

Derrick shrugged. "Okay."

His uncle's laughter trailed off. "What?"

"Okay," said Derrick. "Sure. Like I'm going to do it eventually anyway, right?"

"Wait," his uncle said, "are you serious?"

"Oh, yeah," said Derrick. He picked up his cell phone, wandered into the living room, and called Padma. "Hey. Uh, remember how you like wanted to be my first kiss?"

His uncle stammered after him. "Now hang on here a second . . ."

That night Derrick took Padma out for Thai food and kissed her for a very long time in the car outside her house.

When he got home his uncle wrote him a check, but Derrick agreed to accept only a thousand of it because the guy insisted so much.

GRADUATION

Everything you are and do from fifteen to eighteen is what you are
and will do through life.

> —F. Scott Fitzgerald,
> letter to his daughter,
> September 19, 1938

THE FINAL ACT

While I still had the power to create reality, I decided to fix everything
wrong in my life.

My real father was much older than my mother, and he died when I
was little. I had always wanted a normal family with a father, and now I
would focus and have one.

Jeremy Hughes had a dad. We had moved because of his computer
graphics business. An actor friend of my mother's who grew up in Emerald Valley would play him. He would come to my graduation and the
dinner afterward.

In real life, I had a half-sister who was twenty-seven years older than
me. She was fifty-one. Because of the age difference and deep family
drama, to say we were estranged would put it very gently. I saw her
maybe one hour a year at most.

But now I concentrated. Jeremy Hughes had a sister, named Cameron
in tribute, a nineteen-year-old sophomore in college at Cal State North-
ridge. Jeremy and Cameron had grown up together in the same house
with their parents.

Cameron would come to graduation, too. She was played by Dulcie,
who had done me a special favor for the occasion. I barely recognized
her when she showed up at my door. She had put away her beloved
cuffed white jeans and cat-eye glasses, and she wore instead a simple

black dress, like any girl from the first decade of a bold new millennium.

She smiled a little shyly. "Just this one time."

My mother played my mother. Her plane touched down from Manhattan. She had never set foot in Emerald Valley before in her life, and now she had to pretend to live there for an audience of thousands.

"Oh, this is just going to be a disaster," she said. "What if they ask me questions? I'm going to have to have a cold or a sore throat. I'll just say, 'mmm-hmm.'"

But I knew everything would work out perfectly.

It was my final act. I gathered everybody into my apartment and distributed briefing sheets detailing each person's birth date, background, address, phone number, job, hobbies, interests, reasons for and feelings about the move. I had us rehearse them to letter-perfection. Everyone had a past and a present, but no future, of course—they would live for only one day. The last of my mayfly magic would fade for good as the sun went down. Then all illusions would dissolve, and four grown-ups, myself included, would head back to separate apartments. As morning alarm clocks shrilled, we would wake to adult lives: working, paying correct dues, hoping, waiting.

But not yet.

For one day, for that one day, the great and dread powers of time and fate would themselves stand down. Jeremy Hughes, a seventeen-year-old surfer from Hermosa Beach, would graduate from his suburban California public high school at the height of a vast wave of teen culture, surrounded by his loving family.

THE MOMENT

A brilliant noon sun blazed at the height of a cloudless sky. Most of the five hundred graduates wore sunglasses against the glare. They sat silently in the two blocks of folding chairs in the center of the stadium, dressed in gowns and caps of deep Mirador green.

On the seats by the back aisles, one hundred teachers waited quietly in their black academic robes, hands folded across their laps.

Thousands of parents, family members, and friends packed the aluminum bleachers that rose steeply on both sides of the field. They hushed their crying toddlers. Their cameras flashed like a nightclub.

At the front of the stadium, an elevated stage held the administrators and the dignitaries of the city of Emerald Valley. The school board, the superintendent, the mayor, and the city manager sat in state to review the proceedings, framed by a vivid arrangement of flowers.

All eyes focused on Principal Instructor Irma Chao. She stood center stage behind the podium embossed with the brass coat of arms of Mirador Senior High School. She wore her full ceremonial regalia, a sweeping black gown and wide hood trimmed in the light blue velvet of a doctor of education.

She spoke into a microphone, and her voice rang out across the silent stadium through the dozen massive speaker assemblies.

"This has been a challenging year for our Mirador High School family. A year of ups and downs, wins and losses. As a senior class, you have prevailed, and we are truly proud of how you stuck together and cared for each other."

She paused. Her syllables hung, faded.

"On behalf of Mirador Senior High School and the Mirador High School family of students, staff, and administration, and especially the senior class, I'd like to take this moment to remember the exuberant life of Robert 'Dove' Doveman with a special tribute."

She raised her arms in a wide arc, long black sleeves trailing, and lifted a silver cage onto the podium.

"Graduate Cody Reisling, who was Robert's best friend, will now release eighteen white homing doves. One will represent Dove, and seventeen will follow in honor of his baseball jersey number. Please join me in silence."

In his plastic chair at the back of the stadium, Cody looked around, one green-clad body among hundreds. Faces on his row turned to watch him.

He swallowed and stood, and the entire arena noticed him. He had the spotlight. He squeezed his big frame past dozens of feet to get to the center aisle. "Sorry," he mumbled, as he bumped into legs.

The stands hushed, craning down for a look at his tiny green figure. Everyone knew the story of Cody and Dove.

He made it out into the wide avenue of grass that cut between the two blocks of chairs. At the distant end, the dark form of Dr. Chao stood motionless behind the gleam of silver on the podium.

Cody pushed his shoulders back and raised his head. He set his pale eyes forward, and walked. Flashbulbs glittered around him like a net of diamonds.

He passed through the faculty section. Ms. Horn grinned at him and gave a little finger wave. Mr. Lamarque sat rigidly upright. Ms. Schroeder twisted her hands. Coach Mulligan's eyes watered, white hair curling under his black cap.

Cody walked by.

Out in the left stands Adam Hammersmith and a bunch of the alumni stood around making cracks. They always came to graduations but knew fewer people every year. Vic Reyes leaned against the chain-link fence to get a better view, mesh hat resting sideways on his spiky hair. He felt a tug on his belt and Charity Warner passed him the Gatorade bottle of mixed vodka. She sat on the metal bench and looked wearily through the links, digging her palms into her cheeks, resting her elbows on her spindly legs.

And Cody walked past.

In the right bleachers, Wil and Sara watched, pressing on each other. The skin glared at the redneck. Samantha and Jasmine whispered back and forth while Leo the freshman ate a dripping Nestlé Crunch ice cream bar.

A few rows behind them, Travis Newton sat next to his father, expressionless as a soapstone statue in mirrored aviators. He checked the time on his cell phone.

Down in the broad avenue, Cody walked on.

El Presidente pushed up his glasses and breathed heavily. At the special ed section, Aram suddenly grinned, causing the chaperone to glance over.

And Cody walked, the eyes of thousands following him.

Theodora Danielian crouched at the side of the aisle of pristine turf, snapping pictures of him with her silver bracelets jangling. Beside her Evelyn scribbled on a Mirador *Mirror* notepad.

Cody kept his head fixed straight ahead as he left them behind, shiny black dress shoes pressing into the grass blades.

He passed through the front tract where most of the circle seniors sat. Shawn wore sneakers under his gown. Steve sat on the edge of his seat. Brian leaned back in his chair as he watched, arms crossed on his chest. Jeremy the new kid looked spacey like usual, mouth open loosely in a faint smile.

Cody moved beyond them all.

Nicole tilted her head. Padma adjusted her gown, while Kaylee's tassel flopped in her eyes. Alexis Newton watched him, bright sparkles on her cap, kicking her sandaled feet.

And Cody walked onward. The stage now lay close at hand.

Olivia sat primly as befitted this occasion. Ross bounced his knee and watched, a flowered lei around his neck. Derrick Littlefield's forehead furrowed, his gown hung heavy with a range of golden honor cords and embroidered silver shawls and bronze excellence medals.

Cody reached the end of the aisle, the vast ocean of silent flashes winking like the stars of a new firmament. He climbed the carpeted steps to the dais.

The dignitaries studied his face from their high-backed chairs. Mr. Popper, lips pursed and mustache twitching, peered down his sweating red nose as if expecting him to trip.

And Dr. Chao stretched out her robed arms behind the podium, beatifically, and stepped back.

The sun shone at its height in the sky.

Cody stood before the silver cage. He reached out his hand and put a finger on its latch. He tussled briefly with the metal, and the door swung free.

A white head appeared in the opening. The dove fixed him for an instant with its bright red gaze.

Then it took the air with a fluttering of wings.

Cody darted back as seventeen more birds streamed forth from their prison of silver in an explosion of flight.

They banked and swooped and arced above the football field, beating their wings and gaining height. They flew upward in wide, lazy sweeps, snow white against celestial blue, absorbed into the majesty and unity and radiance of the blazing light. Before this sight all utterance was stilled, motion ceased, breath suspended, and self forgotten. All eyes were fixed on the distant shapes in silence as they climbed, caught updrafts, and tumbled and soared farther into the sky.

And this day, in this moment, now everyone is sitting and watching the doves circle higher toward the sun.

IT AIN'T OVER 'TIL . . .

The earth is silent beneath absolute light.

Then Dr. Chao, a mischievous twinkle behind her oval glasses, snatches the mike.

"And now," she says, "I have chosen to paraphrase a song by Elton John that I would like to dedicate to the graduating class."

With a sudden fall from the sublime, the space between heaven and earth explodes back into infinity.

Tears are abruptly sniffed back from shock. Eyes widen and exchange troubled looks. The crowd murmurs, noting her massively amplified voice and the dozen colossal speakers that ring their seats.

Dr. Chao stands on tiptoe, shades her eyes, and surveys the thousands filling the bleachers with curiosity. She's never had an audience this big before.

She grabs a deep breath and begins:

Look out, world, here they come
Brave, intrepid—and then some!

Toes curl back, and mouths twist as if they had bit into accidental limes. Involuntary choking sounds escape into the hot air as she finds her groove.

Where did the time go?
It went so very fast now!
You developed like a precious work of art,
Packed it all in, conquered it—oh, wow!

She's not singing her lyrics. She's rhyming them, with a lilting rhythmic cadence. A casual observer might say the principal is—rapping?

The mayor and school board sit stunned. Five hundred seniors writhe. Her rhythm gets funkier. The doves, unnoticed, flee to a quieter place beyond the horizon.

So charge into this next step,
We wish you all farewell.
'Cause the Marlin swims behind you,
And I know you'll all be swell!

Teeth clench as Chao belts it out across the stadium.

Then she stabs her finger downward with theatrical flair, black academic robes and doctoral trim billowing around her tiny frame. "Drum line—take it away!"

At rigid attention in their silver uniforms and feathered hats, the assembled ranks of the Mirador marching band begin to pound a percussive beat.

Brian Olvera rubs his forehead and shoots the onrushing world an I-told-you-so glance. "Best booty shaker," he says.

NOTES

THIS NIGHT

1. *Fool* means "dude," but depending on how it's said, it can be slightly deprecating at the same time. It's almost exclusively used by males to address or refer to other males.

DIVING IN

1. Fifteen percent of America is ten to nineteen years old. Nine percent of Manhattan is, according to the 2000 Census of New York County. Also, as a note for non-New Yorkers, "midtown" is how Manhattanites refer to the center of their city; the same area is called "downtown" in other American cities.

2. I was born into a demographic dip directly between the targeted masses of Generation X and the Millennial Generation. Wherever our cohort is, buzzwords and marketing aren't, so when I hit my teen years, teenagers temporarily ceased to be a phenomenon across the national board.

Roughly *one-sixth* as many teen films were made between 1990 and 1997 as in the three years immediately before and after. There were only children's movies aimed toward Millennials and angsty slacker dramas aimed toward Gen X.

We had no music of our own, either. Nowadays adults and fifteen-year-olds aren't expected to listen to the same music. In fact, adults don't even know the names of half of the bands that teenagers enjoy. But during the majority of the 1990s—when teens didn't exist—Collective Soul, the Lilith Fair, and Dishwalla were for everyone: Baltimore graphic artists, Seattle code warriors, and, theoretically, high schoolers alike.

3. The annual meeting of the World Economic Forum at Davos, Switzerland, unites several thousand of the Earth's mightiest business, political, and intellectual leaders to compose perhaps the Track's most exalted stratosphere.

4. When gladiators entered the arena in ancient Rome, before they began their final combat, they would turn to the imperial seat and proclaim, *"Ave, Caesar, morituri te salutant."* The words mean "Hail, emperor, those who are about to die salute you."

5. Having just been through the looking glass and back again, so to speak, I have become convinced that words like *kids, children,* and especially the tooth-grinding *our children* of political speech are automatically patronizing when said by adults about anyone over the age of twelve. If you want to take somebody seriously as a fellow human—rather than just a passive object of policy, incapable of making decisions or offering valid opinions—you have to consider him or her a "person," not a "kid." Young people themselves mainly use the term *kid* to refer to one of their number as opposed to adults (e.g., "kids can't stay out late in this town"), and they generally refer to themselves otherwise as *people,* according one another the same personhood the rest of the population gives itself.

From this point onward, I have banned the offending terms throughout the book, almost as an experiment. According to the Sapir-Whorf hypothesis, the use of language structures our thought, and I think this one simple linguistic change helps to effect a fundamental shift in perspective.

6. The CIF is the California Interscholastic Federation, the organizing body of California high school sports.

YOU MAKE IT REAL

1. Fifty percent of Americans live in suburbs, 30.3 percent in cities, and 19.7 percent in rural areas, according to the U.S. Census Bureau's November 2002 special report *Demographic Trends in the 20th Century*. The percentage of suburbanites has steadily climbed over the decades.

2. The 2000 U.S. Census and www.publicschoolreview.com provided these data.

3. A plug is a type of generally metal, thick, cylindrical earring, often affiliated with the various punk-inspired cultures. They come in various gauges, from small to quite wide indeed, that can be employed to gradually (and usually painfully) stretch the earlobe around the metal tube. A number of people at Mirador wore plugs.

POPULAR

1. Yes, he did. For over twenty-four thousand miles, roughly the circumference of the Earth. And his leg was wounded.

2. Southern Californians prefix all highway numbers with the definite article, which often sounds bizarre to the rest of America. Where Easterners say

"take I-95," and Midwesterners say "take 80," you're going to "take *the* 5" from Santa Barbara onward.

3. Over the twenty years before 1970, the population of Orange County exploded a staggering sevenfold, a figure courtesy of the U.S. Census Bureau.

Southland is a colloquial term principally used to refer to Southern California.

4. *Tight* means "cool."

5. The CDC's National Center for Chronic Disease Prevention and Health Promotion reports in its 2003 *Youth Risk Behavior Survey* that under 22 percent of high schoolers get enough fruits and vegetables in a day.

6. Okay, a brief explanation of screamo entails entering a minefield, because two definitions exist. The first is narrow and purist and refers to a specific set of largely obscure bands that mostly flourished and declined in the 1990s. I am going to talk about the word in the *popular* sense, however, in the way it is used and understood by the average high schooler.

Screamo is guitar-driven, melodic, intense, alternative rock with varying measures of punk influence. The singer expresses his usually angsty and tragic emotions very candidly: For example, his girlfriend died and he despairs, stumbling lost and bleeding in an empty world. At the same time, the music is catchy and pretty poppy. And he, uh, screams verses or just howls besides just singing. That's what makes it "screamo" versus "emo," which is the term for the broader genre.

A lot of people like emo and a lot of people hate it. It's very of this minute. Emo's popularity and oversaturation are undoing the supposedly counterculture image it's based on, and the contradiction is giving way to a much more conformist, appearance-oriented, trend-conscious, hard-core-music-inspired lifestyle known largely under the umbrella of "the scene"—or, more derogatorily, as "fashioncore." Enthusiasts adopt an androgynous look of elaborately styled, straightened dyed hair, eyeliner, and tight jeans. Within a little over a year of publication its emo forebearer will become a footnote for real.

I know the Claymores are exploding on all sides, but that's it in a nutshell.

7. *Yu-Gi-Oh!*, in its American incarnation, is a cartoon show with Japanese-style animation. Its characters play a card game where they magically sic monsters and spells on one another. By a stunning coincidence, these cards are available for purchase, so you too can play an imaginary version of the card game against your friends!

Most mainstream high school populations would consider Yu-Gi-Oh! to be something played by nerdier and younger people, perhaps junior high schoolers.

See "Collision," note 3 about "Magic cards."

8. In-N-Out is an extremely popular burger chain in Southern California and the Southwest.

9. *Sick* means "cool."

10. Bros are people who adhere to a certain style prevalent in the Southwest, especially in the inland areas of Southern California. You'll see a lot of lifted and customized trucks, spiked hair, piercings, sideways mesh hats, iron crosses, tattoos, trips to the desert to race and jump motocross and off-road vehicles and party, gothic lettering, bandanas, skate-influenced clothing, and rap and hard-core music. The term *bro* was self-selected—because it's a common form of address among bros—but is not universally used and is often employed pejoratively.

Bros are usually white, occasionally Latino, and virtually never black. There is sometimes a nativistic or racist strain in the culture, which can appear in the use of Confederate symbolism.

No one fits the mold exactly, of course. Vic and Shawn are very close approximations, and Charity is more or less the female version, often derogatively referred to as "bro hos" or just "hos," "ho" being short for "whore."

11. This is the infamous 1971 Stanford Prison Experiment, of course, described by Zimbardo as "a classic demonstration of the power of social situations to distort personal identities." It ended prematurely—after only six days—with once-hippie "guards" blasting their "prisoners" with fire extinguishers, bagging their heads, forcing them to sleep naked on concrete floors, chaining them together, force-feeding hunger strikers, and so on. Meanwhile, the "prisoners" had mental breakdowns, referred to themselves by number, believed there was no way to quit or exit, and waited patiently for the decision of a parole board. Perhaps most distressing, the researchers began to forget they had created an experiment, and they carried out the role of "wardens" with terrifying zeal.

Zimbardo was actually my psych professor. Freshman year, I looked for the bathroom before my first day of his class. I took a wrong turn in the dark basement passageways and I ran into a jail cell.

12. To explore the different dimensions of this phenomenon, it holds equally true were you to find yourself suddenly as a crew member on an eighteenth-century pirate ship or abruptly tapped for succession to the British monarchy. Within a month you'd be "aargh"-ing or golf-clapping with the best of them.

13. Carl's Jr. is a Southwestern-themed chain of fast-food burger restaurants in the Western United States.

14. In the class of 2004–2005, 3.01 million seniors graduated from America's 22,180 public high schools (figure from 2002) and 2,538 private ones

(figure from 2000), according to the National Center for Education Statistics's *Digest of Education Statistics, 2004.*

COLLISION

1. The iron cross is not a Christian or religious symbol. Originally a German military decoration adopted by a number of American subcultures, the type of supremacy it represents can be far right-wing and nativist. This particular twist is usually diluted in the popularized versions, especially where surf and skateboard companies are concerned. You may have seen it featured on the ubiquitous West Coast Choppers motorcycle T-shirts or in the logo of the skate brand Independent. It frequently appears in the Southwest, especially in inland and desert areas, where it's linked to off-roading, racing, and custom-car culture. Racial overtones vary. In Southern California, you will see whites using the iron cross, and you may very well spot a Latino driving a lifted truck with an iron cross, but black people rarely, if ever, associate with the symbol.

See "Popular," note 10 on *bros* for more details.

2. According to the article "More Newly Licensed Teens Score Pricey Wheels" in the November 8, 2004 *Washington Post,* twice as many teens owned cars in 2003 as in 1985, and twice as many parents had paid for them: a sharp rise from roughly 20 percent to 40 percent total in under two decades.

3. A *grip of* means a "bunch of."

Magic cards is shorthand for the collectible card game *Magic: The Gathering,* an old (i.e., introduced in 1993) role-playing game created by a math professor whose participants pretend to be wizards casting spells at one another. Its aficionados are usually considered to be dorky or uncool by the mainstream population.

TWO WEEKS GO DEEP

1. Yes, this is a real book and a real series and my classmate was really reading it.

2. Apparently Evelyn's adherence to the dharma of not-taking-what-is-not-given stopped abruptly at cold-blooded animals.

3. What California calls a "swap meet" is known as a "flea market" in many other parts of the nation.

4. *Meth* is short for the illegal stimulant methamphetamine.

5. In sharp contradistinction to the monotonous "Oh, the cool kids always torment us" stories, out-groups at Mirador often hated and resented the in-groups, but the in-groups rarely bothered with the rest of the campus. This makes sense, of course. You probably know someone who talks endlessly at the

slightest provocation about how abhorrent she finds Donald Trump or Martha Stewart, but how many times have those celebrities come over to her house to make fun of *her*?

6. Because it's a small world, AVID—which is now a national program—was created at the San Diego high school that Cameron Crowe attended undercover, the year after he graduated. I support its aims 100 percent, and data indicate that it can work quite well. I only offer firsthand knowledge, of course, of how Mirador implemented it. There, depending on the teacher, it either meant you got periodic writing assignments checked over or you spent time in a zoolike holding pen talking with your friends and watching movies such as *Ferris Bueller's Day Off*.

7. According to the 2003–2004 California Student Survey, one-quarter of all eleventh-graders have gotten drunk or high *at school*.

8. The Warners are not alone; the number of homeschooled students in America is apparently rising rapidly. According to the National Center for Education Statistics's *The Condition of Education 2005*, the number of homeschooled students increased by 29 percent from just 1999 to 2003.

9. *MILF* stands for "Mom I'd Like to Fuck," that is, an attractive middle-aged mother. The term was popularized by the 1999 teen movie *American Pie*. It's also the name of the Filipino Islamist jihad organization, which, if you're in the right frame of mind, can make otherwise grim news reports amusing.

10. In November 2005, California voters hit the polls to decide the hot-button issue of teacher tenure.

All new teachers in the state go through a two-year "probationary period." During this period, they receive annual evaluations at which time the school can decline to rehire them. It's almost like a normal job. But after those two years, they become tenured and can only be dismissed after an expensive and lengthy process that contains "about a dozen stages," to quote the California Legislative Analyst.

Ballot Proposition 74 intended to hold teachers more accountable for what they do in the classroom by raising the probationary period to five years and allowing cause for the dismissal of a tenured teacher who doesn't improve after two negative evaluations.

Both sides launched the standard propaganda and scare tactics, and California turned down Prop 74 by a 10 percent margin.

Now we have the opportunity to put away the polemics and simply review the evidence.

If you believe that Ms. Horn—and the thousands for whom she proxies—are teachers you would like your children to have, and who should hold their jobs with far less accountability than Starbucks employees until they retire in some forty-odd years, the 2005 vote represents a triumph of public policy.

Teachers do have difficult work, but they also have a number of options in life. It is impossible not to sympathize more with the students who must depend on them.

11. Usually.

12. Okay, we've seen a number of students drinking so far, and odds are we're going to see a lot more. At this point it becomes important to address a critical misconception.

"But," cry the people who have read certain Millennial-themed literature, "but, we *know* about the Millennials. They don't drink! Statistics show that teen alcohol and drug use and pregnancy are down from the early 1990s. This cannot be the state of our children."

Ah, yes. I, too, had heard that same sound bite over and over again before I undertook this project. Based on all the hype, I expected a rising nation of Prohibitionists, and I was shocked by what I saw around me every day.

Everything became clear when I actually looked at the data. First we may wish to ask precisely how far "down" teen alcohol use is, exactly. Well, according to the annual Monitoring the Future Survey funded by the National Institute on Drug Abuse (NIDA), regular teen alcohol use fell 2.1 percentage points from 1994 to 2004. From this sort of deeply precipitous plunge, all the spurious generalizations about a radical shift in youth behavior have arisen. I had no idea everyone had gotten so worked up over *two percentage points*. Neither do most of them, because the numbers are never attached to the sound bite we've all heard.

Well, the drop still might be significant. Did the number of regular drinkers fall from 3 to 1 percent?

Oh, no. NIDA goes on to report that *half* of all high school seniors have drunk alcohol in the past month. *One out of every two*. That is the new "low" number, and it squares precisely with what I saw: that half of my class drank regularly.

There exists a radical inconsistency between the reality of these numbers and the wishful public perception of Millennials as teetotalers.

Now, for those who love numbers, from 1995 to 2004, tranquilizer use among teens has spiked a shocking 49 percent! Are we in the throes of a national crisis? Have "our children" become the Xanax Generation?

No. The figure rose from 7.1 percent to 10.6 percent. But it's still a more significant and accurate statement to make than touting any alcohol drop.

Ah, statistics.

Point being, half of high schoolers drink regularly, and often drink a lot.

13. Cheating at Mirador was rampant, rampant, rampant and the teachers seemed completely oblivious, made a very token effort to be vigilant, or even gave it a nod and a wink. Once again, Mirador was right on statistical average. In a 2001 survey of forty-five hundred high school students nationwide, the Duke University Center for Academic Integrity found that *three-quarters* of high schoolers admitted to "one or more instances of serious test cheating" (74 percent) and "serious cheating on written work" (72 percent).

And one-third admitted to regular, serious cheating. If you're a teacher, that's *at least one out of every three* students in your class cheating regularly, and those are just the ones who admit to it. Based on my Mirador experience, I would say the number who regularly cheat—essentially on every exam or whenever they are able—is closer to one-half.

I agree wholly with the assertion of public policy researcher David Callahan in the 2003 book *The Cheating Culture* that two rationales for cheating exist. The AP students of the world may copy part of an essay off the Internet because of pressure to succeed and to get ahead, while a Vic Reyes will cheat "just to stay even," feeling he cannot pass otherwise.

The simplest answer to the problem, besides real vigilance, is to give critical-thinking exercises rather than drill and recall. It's obvious if your students have copied one another's essays or projects, rather than just a pattern of fill in the blanks. During testing, get rid of the cell phones, make sure *no one* speaks, check the laps, check the backs and palms of hands, look at pages sticking out of backpacks on the floor, look inside desks. Be especially vigilant for little scraps of paper or anyone leaning forward or back or looking down into their laps. Also stagger tests, giving different versions to adjacent students, and for the love of God, don't leave the test or the answer key on your desk. Yes, your students will go through your papers and your folders and your drawers. I saw tests and answer keys stolen three times in that manner during my one semester.

Several teachers at Mirador also told our classes they didn't like to spot cheaters because parents would complain. School and district administrations must support their teachers and their educational mission in these instances rather than caving in to parent pressure.

14. Cypress Hill is a prominent L.A.-based Latino rap group that stridently advocates the legalization of marijuana.

15. Among slightly under half of young Americans—including Californians—the intransitive slang phrase *smoking out* refers to smoking marijuana. Most of the rest of the nation uses the phrase *smoking up*. A generally accepted alternative to either is just the word *smoke,* almost inevitably said with a low-

ered voice tone to distinguish between marijuana and cigarettes. Believe it or not, I actually did a study on the nationwide distribution of these lexical variants—as well as *beer bong* versus *funnel*—in linguistics at Stanford, thus making me perhaps the global expert on this crucial matter.

16. I certainly wish that Shawn and his classmates didn't say things like "Jew on a power trip," too, but the fact of the matter is that they did, and, like almost every word in this book, it is quoted verbatim.

At this point, much as with the drinking question, it might be nice to reconcile—say—Jew comments with the Millennial sound bites about diversity and pluralism.

As we may be realizing, a large part of the Millennial propaganda is hooey. Just because a group is diverse does not necessarily entail that the diversity is well accepted or integrated, and that point has been critically missed in the wishful attempt to paint a broad-stroked portrait of a generation of Boy and Girl Scouts. But there exists less of a problem than may appear at first glance. Ideologically, a number of my classmates held and articulated some pretty shocking prejudices, but I think they mainly repeated their parents and the adults around them in their lives away from school. I don't think those beliefs bore a deep impact on the actual behavior of the majority of them when confronted with concrete cases—like deciding whether to be nice to someone.

The senior circle comprised a multiethnic group. Charity, despite the white-pride rhetoric, considered black Dove her best friend. Students would voice terrifying "bomb them all" opinions in government class and then go and smoke marijuana with a Lebanese student. Aside from the decently well-integrated "popular groups" in each grade, the students more or less self-segregated—but only a few explicitly racial or ethnic fights took place, as far as I saw.

17. A blunt is a cigar emptied of its tobacco and refilled with marijuana.

18. Declarations of omniscience proved a favorite Lamarque theme over the course of the semester. Whenever he got especially worked up over it, an innocent little voice within me wondered: "Uh, how come you don't know that one of your students is TWENTY-FOUR?"

19. As a Mirador twelfth-grader, I never had to write a paper longer than two pages. I never had to find any source beyond the one assigned book.

20. Older generations may react with knee-jerk horror. But is any one symbolic system—images and sounds versus printed words—necessarily better than another? Their purpose is to communicate and, rigorously speaking, their value should be determined solely by their fitness in that respect.

So is a bunch of dense black squiggles really a better way to communicate thoughts, ideas, and emotions than fast cuts and DD-Plus 5.1 surround sound? A better way to create a persuasive argument? Raised in the contemporary

American media environment, a lot of young people don't see the conclusion as a foregone one. Would the scribes of Uruk have hacked up dry clay to get their message across if they had plasma widescreens and Final Cut Pro?

To generalize, my Mirador classmates communicated better in the audiovisual medium and more poorly with the printed word than do members of previous American generations. Despite the fodder this sentence will provide for reviewers, I venture to say that written work at Mirador often became an incoherent and painful calvary for writer and reader alike. (A typical example may help. Ross—an eighteen-year-old, college-bound, white, middle-class ASB senior and school leader—wrote me the following yearbook message: "Jeremy, dude your new but you a good guy. To bad you came prety late. Well have fun in colleges.")

But the average student's average video was far better than any of the programming adults put on public access, not to mention any low-budget, supposedly professional ad for a car dealership or a phone-in product. And some videos were truly exceptional.

However one may feel about the possibility of dawning postliteracy, the video projects failed as an educational practice. Graded almost solely on form and presentation, they did not require or demonstrate comprehensive mastery of the material and they did not include any critical-thinking aspects. Video finals in some math classes (not, needless to say, Mr. Lamarque's) extended the practice beyond the point of absurdity.

According to the University of Michigan's Panel Study of Income Dynamics, the average teen from ages fifteen to seventeen watches fifteen hours of TV a week, and reads for less than one.

21. *Bomb* means "cool."

22. Like almost every high school baseball federation in America, California Interscholastic Federation baseball has seven innings, not nine.

23. *T.J.* is how many young Southern Californians refer to the Mexican border city of Tijuana, a popular party spot owing to its rarely enforced drinking age of eighteen.

24. Orange County as a whole is considered a conservative region—and rightly so, according to poll results. However, not every community in the county is by any means conservative. The site we are calling Emerald Valley, in fact, has if anything a decidedly liberal bent; in the 2004 general election, precinct data indicate that residents voted for Democrat Kerry over Republican Bush by a margin of three to two.

The conservative views of Mirador students, then, must largely be understood as a separate phenomenon, one distinct from the views of their parents or community.

Indeed, high school news station Channel One held a massive nationwide mock presidential election in 2004, with 1.4 million high school students casting their ballots.

Among high schoolers, the conservative Bush *decimated* the liberal Kerry. Bush received 393 electoral votes to Kerry's 145—a whopping 38 percent more votes than the adult population actually awarded him in November (286 to Kerry's 252).

25. A note to any impressionable readers:

Muscle-building anabolic steroids come in several forms. All are more or less hepatotoxic, that is, damaging to the liver.

The oral form taken in pills by the majority of steroid-using Mirador students is highly hepatotoxic and, to put it bluntly, can fill your liver with blood and kill you. Injectable steroids like Cody's seem to damage the liver only negligibly, although some experts differ in opinion on this point.

Obviously all steroids possess a wide set of other serious side effects apart from hepatotoxicity. Frequent problems include face and back acne, baldness, male breast growth, stunting height in teens, violent urges, infertility, and—yes—testicle shrinkage.

26. Combining the population figures from the U.S. Census Bureau's May 2005 report *School Enrollment—Social and Economic Characteristics of Students* with the percentage data from the Centers for Disease Control's 2003 *Youth Risk Behavior Survey,* we find that approximately 1.04 million American high schoolers have used illegal steroids at least once in their lives, either oral or injected. Of course these are only the self-reported numbers.

27. Calling "shotgun" means you get to sit in the desirable front passenger seat in a vehicle.

28. If you're interested, go to the source at www.breakthechain.org/exclusives/rickmathes.html.

29. GPA, or grade point average, traditionally goes no higher than four, which corresponds to an A. However, common practice now is to "weight" honors- and AP-class GPAs by adding an extra number or two respectively to the grade a student receives in the course; so a B in an AP class might become a five, and an A might become a six.

Owing to this practice, GPAs of over four have become reasonably and increasingly common.

30. Ugg boots had reached the tail end of their market saturation when I was at Mirador. They are no longer cool in high school or, if I may presume, anywhere outside their home base of Oceania.

31. Thirty-six percent of seniors who plan to attend four-year colleges volunteer, according to 2003 analysis in the Child Trends DataBank. How sin-

cere is this activity? Well, it's twice the percentage of seniors who don't have four-year-college aspirations—and therefore aren't trying to impress admissions committees.

32. "Old skool" or "old school" refers to something retro or old-fashioned, usually seen as a little hokey, but often recalled with a certain nostalgic fondness.

In this example, an "old-skool high-five" would be a high-five as they appeared in the 1980s, two flat vertical palms smacking against each other high in the air, as opposed to a contemporary hand slap, usually horizontal, around waist-height, looser, and more casual.

This hand slap is commonly used between individuals as a gesture of greeting, parting, or exultation. Occasionally fists are punched after, or in lieu of, the slap itself.

33. *Stepped to you* means "started problems with you" or "talked back to you."

34. There does not currently exist enough concrete evidence for either the effectiveness or long-term safety of GH as either a muscle-building or anti-aging supplement. It appears to increase lean muscle mass and have few side effects, but hopefully future research will provide clearer indications.

Three notes: First, injecting GH—which, despite some snake-oil "supplement claims," is the only effective method—is stunningly expensive, easily several thousand dollars per month. Second, its only legal and clinically proven use remains the treatment of people who have an underproductive pituitary gland. Third, extra GH is likely unnecessary and potentially very dangerous for an adolescent in the midst of the exceedingly complex processes of natural growth.

35. Teens spend an average of ninety-one dollars a week, according to a December 2004 press release from Teenage Research Unlimited.

36. Cranberry juice helps the body to excrete marijuana metabolites faster.

37. The Urban Institute's 2002 round of its National Survey of America's Families reports that almost half (46 percent) of adolescents twelve to seventeen don't live with two biological parents, a figure that my experiences at Mirador and this book reflect.

38. A hookah is a large water pipe of Middle Eastern origin used to smoke a very smooth tobacco often flavored with fruit or molasses. In Western culture, a hookah bar prepares and serves these pipes to customers in a usually trendy atmosphere. One hookah is shared among each group, and alcohol is either downplayed or nonexistent. In the past few years hookah bars have become quite popular and mainstream for young people, especially for college students, and especially on the West Coast.

39. As the New Kid, I was invited to do a scene, but I decided the less Evidence I left behind, the better. I did a voice-over in a fake ASB ad, though.

40. According to *Educator Sexual Misconduct,* a June 2004 report to the U.S. Congress by the federal Department of Education, over 4.5 million young Americans will suffer sexual abuse or misconduct by school employees before graduating from high school.

We live in a big country, so let's put the number 4.5 million in perspective. It is somewhat greater than the entire population of the Irish Republic.

This figure seems to represent a lowball estimate, as it is based on data that are typically quite underreported.

41. A longboard skateboard, quite simply, has a longer deck than the standard freestyle board that one usually sees.

The increased weight and volume of the longboard make a number of even the most basic shortboard tricks hard or impossible to perform. Instead, speed and stability are the longboard's forte, cementing its status as an ideal vehicle for travel versus tricks. When cruising downhill, a rider can easily clock over thirty miles per hour.

42. The 2002–2003 National Study of Youth and Religion took a look at spirituality in America.

A stunning 36 percent of American teens aged thirteen to seventeen attend a religious youth group like SpiriTeen at least once a month.

Seventy-two percent feel close to God.

Only 3 percent are atheists.

43. "The snap" adds another twist on the modern-day hand slap. (See "Two Weeks Go Deep," note 32.)

In the snap, after the palms of both participants strike each other loosely, each person quickly bends his fingers inward and pulls them back against the digits of the other person's hand. When both sets of fingers strike back against their respective palms, a sound akin to a snap is generated.

Participants may then choose to punch fists to complete the gesture, according to preference.

44. Sacramento centralized all school funding chiefly to eliminate differences between how much the districts of, say, Beverly Hills and Compton could afford to spend. Now every district in the state receives about sixty-eight hundred dollars per student per year. It looks great on paper.

So has the problem of inequality gone away? Nope. What happens now is that parents raise extra money privately and give it to the school through "educational foundations."

The foundation in a wealthy district like Beverly Hills may raise a million extra dollars a year.

A middle-class community like Emerald Valley may raise three hundred thousand dollars.

A poor district like Compton usually does not have an educational foundation.

45. The notion that Darwin underwent a deathbed conversion and recanted his theory of evolution is a popular, yet untrue, evangelistic legend.

INTERMEZZO IN D-FORCE MINOR

1. *Sloots, slooties, sloos, slizzuts, sloozies,* and so on may sound like Dutch but refer rather to "sluts."

2. This drinking game is technically known as *beirut,* but it's commonly called *beer pong.* Actual beer pong involves Ping-Pong paddles.

Beirut is played nationwide with many localized varieties. In its purest doctrinal essence, two teams of two players each face each other across a table. Each team arranges a horizontal pyramid of eight cups of beer in front of themselves. The players alternate in attempting to toss a Ping-Pong ball into the cups of the opposing team.

If the ball makes it into a team's cup, a member of that team must drink the beer it contains and remove the cup from the table. A team wins by removing all of its opponent's cups.

Beirut arose amid the Northeast fraternity scene of the mideighties, and it's wildly popular among high school and college students across America, except perhaps in Utah. It can be found at almost any sizable party.

3. A beer bong is, roughly, a funnel attached to a tube. One person kneels and puts the tube in his or her mouth, while another holds up the funnel and pours in a beer, or two, or more. The kneeling person has to drink the onrushing liquid as quickly as possible.

In some areas the practice is referred to as "funneling"; see "Two Weeks Go Deep," note 14.

4. Similar to the "Millennials don't drink" propaganda, which I addressed in "Two Weeks Go Deep," note 11, another sound bite we all hear is that "teen pregnancy is down."

It really is, too, down from 12 percent (!) of all pregnancies happening to girls fifteen to nineteen in 1990 to 8.5 percent in 2000, according to the Child Trends DataBank.

Well, that squares with what I saw, and with all the condoms around Brian's house. Aside from "the pregnant girl" and one or two others, Mirador did not exactly suffer from a pregnancy pandemic. I'm sure most cases were kept in the very strictest secrecy, but pregnancy hardly formed a mainstream issue.

But aside from pregnancy, how about teen sex in general?

The Centers for Disease Control's September 2005 report *Sexual Behavior and Selected Health Measures* has the data. The percentage of seventeen-year-olds who have had either vaginal or oral heterosexual sex is—drum roll . . .

Sixty-one percent of males and 64 percent of females.

Yes, two out of any three seventeen-year-old girls you see have had sex. Think of any seventeen-year-old girl in your family or school, and there is a two-thirds' chance that she has had sex.

Again, a stunning disconnect exists between reality and a public discourse that acts as though these things were not happening.

5. *"Pulling a train"* on a girl means for a number of males to serially have sex with her. Your guess is as good as mine as to how voluntary this event was on the girl's part—probably somewhat but not fully.

6. According to the 2003 *Youth Risk Behavior Survey,* 41 percent of high school males have been in a physical fight in the past year.

7. "Oh my fucking God, hide. The cops are in the house. Are you okay?" To which Kaylee responds, "Yes. Talk to you later."

8. In fact, I actually had to have a city council member sign off to confirm my attendance at a council session for my government project.

I ended up with the mayor himself. "Ah, Mirador High School," he said. He signed my paper and then glared at me suspiciously. "You're not planning on leaving this meeting *early,* are you?"

O GIRLS, TO WAR

1. A MilSim is a military simulation. Here Evelyn is playing situation-based Airsoft, where opposing teams employ real military tactics, gear, and weapons in pursuit of strategic objectives—except the weapons fire little plastic BBs instead of metal bullets.

Airsoft and MilSim paintball are rapidly growing in popularity in the United States.

2. William Mulholland was the cantankerous and somewhat shady Irish engineer whose "octopus" of water-sucking pipes corralled the vast aquatic resources of the West at the start of the twentieth century. His cosmic-scale machinery greened the inhospitable scrub desert of Southern California into the population-supporting Eden we know today.

Tens of millions owe their existences to him, but many counties, states, and ecosystems on the other ends of the pipes are still very angry.

3. According to the University of Michigan's *Panel Study of Income Dynamics,* the average fifteen- to seventeen-year-old only spends about forty minutes a day on homework. Then he or she watches exactly *three times* as much TV—one hundred and twenty minutes.

Which medium is the primary educator?

4. *Vata,* as understood here by Kaylee, basically means "Latina home-girl."

5. Something Corporate is a popular rock band originally hailing from Orange County.

6. *The des* or *dez,* pronounced as the latter, is short for "the desert."

ACCREDITATION

1. English involves combinations of letters that relate to sounds, often not directly phonetically. The traditional way to teach reading is to show children the sounds that belong to different letter clusters. The reverse skill, of course, is spelling, only and needlessly tricky because we choose to write English in nonphonetic code.

In 1987, California totally changed the way it taught reading in school.

Rather than actually teaching children to break down and sound out words, it "immersed" them in reading—Whole Language. The state denied funding to schools that didn't comply.

By 1995, California had the worst reading scores in America, above only Guam, and education officials scuttled the program. Some people say the program was a scapegoat for other factors. Whatever the case, my classmates learned to read and spell under Whole Language, with the results that you can see.

2. These numbers are scores on the new SAT test, introduced by the College Board in March 2005.

SAT used to stand for "Scholastic Aptitude Test" until 1994, when the College Board officially declared that it really didn't stand for anything but "SAT." Regardless, admissions offices across America still use the score as a primary determinant of how a high school student compares academically to over 1.4 million test-taking peers.

The old SAT had two sections called Math and Verbal, each worth 800 points and yielding a total perfect score of 1600. The new SAT made some fiddly changes and added a third musketeer called "Writing," also scored out of 800, to raise the new highest mark to a 2400.

"Writing" demands that one write an essay, and it is strikingly similar to the old SAT II Writing test, which has been mysteriously discontinued.

One excellent and highly non–College Board–approved way to approximate a new SAT score from an old SAT score is to simply take your old SAT score and add your grade on the SAT II Writing. Those who like a walk on the wild side might even try the dangerously risqué act of multiplying their old scores by one and one-third.

The PSAT is essentially an SAT Lite (only 240 points!) that younger students take to practice for the big enchilada and to win scholarships.

3. In the April 2002 revision of his landmark study *High School Gradua-tion Rates in the United States,* education researcher Jay Greene calculated a fig-ure that shall speak for itself.

Using federal data, he demonstrated that roughly one-third—29 percent—of American high schoolers simply don't graduate.

Only 56 percent of African-Americans graduate, and the rate is even lower for Latinos, with only 54 percent graduating.

Merely owing to his ethnicity, statistically speaking, whether Vic would grad-uate from Mirador or not could have been determined by a simple coin toss his freshman year.

IN THE MAGIC KINGDOM

1. "Zelda" is shorthand for the Legend of Zelda, an extremely popular videogame series consisting of more than a dozen games released over the course of two decades. The action takes place in a fantasy kingdom called Hy-rule, where the titular character Zelda is a princess whom the player must often rescue.

2. Mr. Lamarque hammered me for my "excessive tardies" and "inconsis-tent effort." But Ms. Horn and Mr. Mulligan commented that I was "a pleasure to have in class," which really touched me. No less than their students, they felt genuine sympathy for a new person and acted kindly toward him. I really ap-preciated their gestures.

Aside from my planned and predicted grades, I got a B in the sole class where I actually worked to succeed. After I spent two to three hours each evening typ-ing notes on the day's events, I would take out *On Y Va!* and desperately teach myself third-year second-semester French.

3. In an ancient Taoist legend, the sage Zhuāngzǐ fell asleep under a tree and dreamed he became a butterfly. He thought he awoke to become Zhuāngzǐ again, but then realized he didn't know which state was the dream and which was reality. He could find no way to know which was which, or if any distinc-tion actually existed.

The implications center roughly around the idea that whatever names, cate-gories, and labels we cling to as real dissolve under examination and reveal themselves as empty of existence outside our minds. In the end, no lines divide and distinguish anything beyond our stubborn habit of complicating a single, fluid, pure, and perfect reality with differences, definitions, and thorough end-notes.